1989

# AmericanMix

# AmericanMix
## The Minority Experience in America

**Edited by**

## Morris Freedman
University of Maryland

## Carolyn Banks
University of Maryland

## J. B. LIPPINCOTT COMPANY

Philadelphia          New York          Toronto

ISBN: 0-397-472U1-3

Library of Congress Catalogue Card Number: 73-170857

Printed in the United States of America

# Acknowledgements

We thank the following persons for helping us try out ideas for this collection and for various suggestions; as usual, of course, we ourselves are responsible for all shortcomings: Norman Antokol, Jack C. Barnes, Carl Bode, Paul B. Davis, Robert A. Ellis, Molly G. Emler, Paul Freedman, Gladys-Marie Fry, Joseph Glazer, Nathan Glazer, Harry L. Jones, Norma Maness, Cynthia Milkman, Lawrence Mintz, Paul Piazza, John Raaf, Susan Robinson, Ann Schofed, Alvin L. Schorr, Kathleen Walton, and Aubrey W. Williams, Jr.

Carolyn Banks: "GROWING UP POLISH IN PITTSBURGH"
Reprinted by permission of the author.
Gino Baroni: "THE ETHNIC BAG"
Reprinted by permission of the publisher and Stephen Clapp from the *Washingtonian,* Volume 5, Number 10, July 1970.
"The Black Panther Party PLATFORM AND PROGRAM"
From *The Black Panthers Speak,* Edited by Philip S. Foner:
Copyright © 1970, by Philip S. Foner. Reprinted by permission of J.B. Lippincott Company.
Arna Bontemps: "A SUMMER TRAGEDY"
From *The Best Short Stories by Negro Writers* published by Little, Brown and Company. Copyright © 1933 by Arna Bontemps. Reprinted by permission of Harold Ober Associates Incorporated.
El Malcriado: "INTERVIEW WITH CESAR CHAVEZ"
From *The Catholic Worker,* February 1971. Reprinted by permission of *The Catholic Worker.*
Robert Coles: "THE LIVES OF MIGRANT FARMERS"
Paper presented at the 121st Annual Meeting of the American Psychiatric Association, May 3-7, 1965. Reprinted by permission of the author.
Eleanor Flexner: "EARLY STEPS TOWARD EQUAL EDUCATION"
From *Century of Struggle: The Woman's Rights Movement in the United States.* Copyright © 1959 by Eleanor Flexner. Reprinted by permission of the publisher, The Belknap Press of Harvard University Press.
Craig Fisher: "THE ICE PEOPLE"
A television documentary originally presented by NBC News in cooperation with The National Academy of Sciences. Reprinted by permission of the author.

# Contents

# III. White on Black, Black on Black

# IV. Immigration and Assimilation: The Others

# V. The Isolatoes:
## The Expatriates Among Us

# VI. The American Ideal:
## Documents, Assessments

# General Introduction

Stereotype is a word that's used a lot these days. It's a word that will come up many times throughout this book. A stereotype is an easy way of classifying a group of people, because it doesn't take into account particular traits of individuals. It just lumps everyone together. Whether you know it or not, you are familiar with many stereotypes.

Take the phrase, "typical American family." What do you think of? Most likely you see white people. Probably a tall man in a business suit. His wife is blonde and she wears an apron over a crisp house-dress. They never have too many kids, but usually they have more than one. The little boy wears a crew-cut, the little girl has ribbons in her hair (she's blonde too). If the kids get dirty it's "nice" dirt, picked up in the backyard or on the baseball diamond, and they say things like "Oh gosh, Pop," or "Gee whiz, Mom."

We don't necessarily learn about stereotypes in school. They are everywhere—on TV, in the movies, in magazines and comic books. Get on any bus and look around. How many people look like the people who are held up to us as models? We catch sight of ourselves in plate glass windows and, perhaps un-knowingly, we measure ourselves against the various models which have been presented to us throughout our lives.

1

And then there are the stereotypes that weren't used as models or ideals, but as warnings. These tell us women, or blacks, or Italians are stupid, or lazy, or inferior. They "save us the trouble" of finding out for ourselves and in the process cut us off from whole groups of people. These are the ones about which the essays in this book seek to change your mind.

The slogan, "Black is Beautiful," is a commonplace now. But even today, in the popular culture, the area that touches most people in our society, black faces are uncommon. There was a time when magazines which appealed mostly to black readers, *Ebony*, for example, chose models whose features differed little from those in "white" magazines. Has there ever been a black Miss America? An Eskimo Miss America? An Indian Miss America? Santa Claus was a white man. Superman, Batman, Robin, the Green Hornet, Plasticman, white men all. When you saw a black man in a movie he was either a slave or a handyman, depending on when the story took place. There were a few other acceptable roles. He could be an athlete. He could be a tap dancer or a musician. Black women were maids. The movie, "Guess Who's Coming to Dinner," was an outrage to many blacks. It's true that Sidney Poitier was a doctor, but in order to make his marriage to a white girl acceptable to many Americans, he had to be, in the words of one black student, "super nigger." America's view of the black, especially as it has been expressed in popular culture, has been rigorously stereotyped.

And what do you know about Indians? You may have cheered them in the movies, but the "good guys" were the cowboys, and they always won. And if the Indians weren't represented on the screen as out and out bad guys, as savages waiting to attack settlers' women and children, you were led to believe they were stupid. You know the story—it's been told a thousand times and is *still* being shown on TV: The Indians are okay enough, but the "bad" white man gives them "fire water" and then the scalping and plunder begins. The "bad" white man got his in the end, but not until the Indians were rubbed out along with him. Just as the intelligence of blacks was insulted by the popular culture, so was the intelligence of the red man. What do Indians say in movies? "White man speak with forked tongue."

These stereotypes weren't undone by what we learned in school. They may not have been as blatant, but they were there. Even if our own teachers had realized that they were there, they were hardly in a position to correct them. And so we went on reading biased textbooks which ignored the contributions of blacks and reds and browns, of immigrants, of women. We heard about "The Melting Pot" and how all men were created equal, and nobody ever stopped to think about whether or not a melting pot was a good image—whether differences should be treasured and respected rather than obliterated. And no one ever questioned whether the events outside the schoolroom matched the words we had to memorize, "with liberty and justice for all."

Perhaps this sounds very cynical. As good Americans we have been taught to "look at the bright side," to "count our blessings." The people you will meet in this book *are* the bright side. They *are* our blessings. There is a new awareness in this country. It's Black Awareness. It's belonging to La Raza. It's being a woman. Or a Jew. And when you finish this book, perhaps you'll agree that it's about time!

*The Declaration of Independence* □ KING *I Have a Dream* □ KENNEDY *Civil Rights Speech, 1963* □

# The American Ideal:
### hopes and dreams

*"Joe, these people say they want flesh-colored Band-Aids."*

# Introduction

Given the fact that we're all "just everyday people," can we ever achieve any ideal, let alone something as ambitious as "The American Ideal"? Have we indeed made any real progress toward it? It isn't enough to put words on paper. Everyone knows the old saw, "Actions speak louder than words." The words that express America's ideals are words we've grown up with, so familiar that you could probably recite many of them from memory. It's hard to think of hopeful words, words embodying dreams, being spoken aloud in classrooms where whites are favored, where most of the teachers are white, where some children may be ignored, or have been neglected, because their eyes slant, or their skin never freckles. Many of us pretend we don't know that "The American Ideal" is still just an empty slogan for too many Americans.

The Declaration of Independence is reprinted in junior high and high school textbooks. Even so, it is unlikely that you were ever asked to think about it. More likely, like the Constitution and its amendments, it was something to be memorized or studied. If this isn't the case, you're lucky! If it *is* the case, it will be hard for you to put aside all the barriers "education" has put up between you and the document. Only the part that is directly related to the other essays in this book is reprinted here. Instead of memorizing or studying it, try *understanding* it. What are the words

7

trying to say, and why?

The Declaration of Independence clearly states that all men are created equal. Not some men. *All* men. Some of the men who wrote and signed these words owned slaves. Slaves could not vote. Nor could Indians vote. Nor could women. You may well ask what is meant by "all men." Did anyone then see the contradiction between what was said and what was done? How can Martin Luther King, in 1963, dream about something that should have been guaranteed by the words written in 1776? Why does the fact that the actions haven't lived up to the words seem so apparent to us today?

Have a look at the cartoon in this section. The first time around it's funny. The next time around it's too real to be just funny. A lot of people have taken a good hard look at those flesh-colored bandaids—the color of whose flesh?—and decided that their color was being ignored. Somehow, the American ideal had overlooked them. They decided that the time had come to make sure everyone heard about and knew about the American ideal in its fullest, richest, best sense. The hope, the dream, the ideal was that maybe when people really listened and tried to live it, all the people would care enough to make it the American *reality*.

# The Declaration of Independence
## We Hold These Truths to be Self-Evident

We hold these truths to be self-evident: that all men are created equal, that they are endowed by their Creator with certain unalienable rights, that among these are life, liberty, and the pursuit of happiness. That to secure these rights, governments are instituted among men, deriving their just powers from the consent of the governed; that whenever any form of government becomes destructive of these ends, it is the right of the people to alter or to abolish it, and to institute new government, laying its foundation on such principles and organizing its powers in such form, as to them shall seem most likely to effect their safety and happiness.

# Martin Luther King, Jr.
## I Have a Dream

Five score years ago, a great American, in whose symbolic shadow we stand, signed the Emancipation Proclamation. This momentous decree came as a great beacon light of hope to millions of Negro slaves who had been seared in the flames of withering injustice. It came as a joyous daybreak to end the long night of captivity.

But one hundred years later, we must face the tragic fact that the Negro is still not free. One hundred years later, the life of the Negro is still sadly crippled by the manacles of segregation and the chains of discrimination. One hundred years later, the Negro lives on a lonely island of poverty in the midst of a vast ocean of material prosperity. One hundred years later, 10 the Negro is still languishing in the corners of American society and finds himself an exile in his own land. So we have come here today to dramatize an appalling condition.

In a sense we have come to our nation's Capitol to cash a check. When the architects of our republic wrote the magnificent words of the Constitution and the Declaration of Independence, they were signing a promissory note to which every American was to fall heir. This note was a promise that all men would be guaranteed the unalienable rights of life, liberty, and the pursuit of happiness.

It is obvious today that America has defaulted on this promissory note 20 insofar as her citizens of color are concerned. Instead of honoring this sacred obligation, America has given the Negro people a bad check; a check which has come back marked "insufficient funds." But we refuse to believe that the bank of justice is bankrupt. We refuse to believe that there are insufficient funds in the great vaults of opportunity of this nation. So we have come to cash this check—a check that will give us upon demand the riches of freedom and the security of justice. We have also come to this hallowed spot to remind America of the fierce urgency of *now*. This is no time to engage in the luxury of cooling off or to take the tranquilizing drug of gradualism. *Now* is the time to make real the promises of Democracy. *Now* is the time to rise from the dark and desolate valley of segregation to the sunlit path of racial justice. *Now* is the time to open the doors of opportunity to all of God's children. *Now* is the time to lift our nation from the quicksands of racial injustice to the solid rock of brotherhood.

It would be fatal for the nation to overlook the urgency of the moment and to underestimate the determination of the Negro. This sweltering summer of the Negro's legitimate discontent will not pass until there is an invigorating autumn of freedom and equality. 1963 is not an end, but a beginning. Those who hope that the Negro needed to blow off steam and will now be content will have a rude awakening if the nation returns to business as usual. There will be neither rest nor tranquillity in America until the Negro is granted his citizenship rights. The whirlwinds of revolt will continue to shake the foundations of our nation until the bright day of justice emerges.

But there is something I must say to my people who stand on the warm threshold which leads into the palace of justice. In the process of gaining our rightful place we must not be guilty of wrongful deeds. Let us not seek to satisfy our thirst for freedom by drinking from the cup of bitterness and hatred. We must forever conduct our struggle on the high plane of dignity and discipline. We must not allow our creative protest to degenerate into physical violence. Again and again we must rise to the majestic heights of meeting physical force with soul force. The marvelous new militancy which has engulfed the Negro community must not lead us to a distrust of all white people, for many of our white brothers, as evidenced by their presence here today, have come to realize that their destiny is tied up with our destiny and their freedom is inextricably bound to our freedom. We cannot walk alone.

And as we walk, we must make the pledge that we shall march ahead. We cannot turn back. There are those who are asking the devotees of civil rights, "When will you be satisfied?" We can never be satisfied as long as the Negro is the victim of the unspeakable horrors of police brutality. We can never be satisfied as long as our bodies, heavy with the fatigue of travel, cannot gain lodging in the motels of the highways and the hotels of the cities. We cannot be satisfied as long as the Negro's basic mobility is from a smaller ghetto to a larger one. We can never be satisfied as long as a Negro in Mississippi cannot vote and a Negro in New York believes he has nothing for which to vote. No, no, we are not satisfied, and we will not be satisfied until justice rolls down like waters and righteousness like a mighty stream.

I am not unmindful that some of you have come here out of great trials and tribulations. Some of you have come fresh from narrow jail cells. Some of you have come from areas where your quest for freedom left you battered by the storms of persecution and staggered by the winds of police brutality. You have been the veterans of creative suffering. Continue to work with the faith that unearned suffering is redemptive.

Go back to Mississippi, go back to Alabama, go back to South Carolina, to back to Georgia, go back to Louisiana, go back to the slums and ghettoes of our northern cities, knowing that somehow this situation can and will be changed. Let us not wallow in the valley of despair.

I say to you today, my friends, that in spite of the difficulties and frus- 10 trations of the moment I still have a dream. It is a dream deeply rooted in the American dream.

I have a dream that one day this nation will rise up and live out the true meaning of its creed: "We hold these truths to be self-evident; that all men are created equal."

I have a dream that one day on the red hills of Georgia the sons of former slaves and the sons of former slaveowners will be able to sit down together at the table of brotherhood.

I have a dream that the state of Mississippi, a desert state sweltering with the heat of injustice and oppression, will be transformed into an 20 oasis of freedom and justice.

I have a dream that my four little children will one day live in a nation where they will not be judged by the color of their skin but by the content of their character.

I have a dream today.

I have a dream that the state of Alabama, whose governor's lips are presently dripping with the words of interposition and nullification, will be transformed into a situation where little black boys and black girls will be able to join hands with little white boys and white girls and walk together as sisters and brothers. 30

I have a dream today.

I have a dream that one day every valley shall be exalted, every hill and mountain shall be made low, the rough places will be made plain, and the crooked places will be made straight, and the glory of the Lord shall be revealed, and all flesh shall see it together.

This is our hope. This is the faith with which I return to the South. With this faith we will be able to hew out of the mountain of despair a stone of hope. With this faith we will be able to transform the jangling discords of our nation into a beautiful symphony of brotherhood. With this faith we will be able to work together, to pray together, to struggle together, to go to 40 jail together, to stand up for freedom together, knowing that we will be free one day.

This will be the day when all of God's children will be able to sing with new meaning

> My country, tis of thee
> Sweet land of liberty,
>   Of thee I sing:
> Land where my fathers died,
> Land of the pilgrims' pride,
> From every mountain-side
>   Let freedom ring.

And if America is to be a great nation this must become true. So let freedom ring from the prodigious hilltops of New Hampshire. Let freedom ring from the mighty mountains of New York. Let freedom ring from the heightening Alleghenies of Pennsylvania!

Let freedom ring from the snowcapped Rockies of Colorado!

Let freedom ring from the curvacious peaks of California!

But not only that; let freedom ring from Stone Mountain of Georgia!

Let freedom ring from Lookout Mountain of Tennessee!

Let freedom ring from every hill and molehill of Mississippi. From every mountainside, let freedom ring.

When we let freedom ring, when we let it ring from every village and every hamlet, from every state and every city, we will be able to speed up that day when all of God's children, black men and white men, Jews and Gentiles, Protestants and Catholics, will be able to join hands and sing in the words of the old Negro spiritual, "Free at last! free at last! thank God almighty, we are free at last!"

# John F. Kennedy
## Civil Rights Speech, 1963

Good evening, my fellow citizens.

This afternoon, following a series of threats and defiant statements, the presence of Alabama National Guardsmen was required on the University of Alabama campus to carry out the final and unequivocal order of the United States District Court of the Northern District of Alabama.

That order called for the admission of two clearly qualified young Alabama residents who happened to have been born Negro.

That they were admitted peacefully on the campus is due in good measure to the conduct of the students of the University of Alabama who    10 met their responsibilities in a constructive way.

I hope that every American, regardless of where he lives, will stop and examine his conscience about this and other related incidents.

This nation was founded by men of many nations and backgrounds. It was founded on the principle that all men are created equal, and that the rights of every man are diminished when the rights of one man are threatened.

Today we are committed to a worldwide struggle to promote and protect the rights of all who wish to be free. And when Americans are sent to Vietnam or West Berlin we do not ask for whites only.    20

It ought to be possible, therefore, for American students of any color to attend any public institution they select without having to be backed up by troops. It ought to be possible for American consumers of any color to receive equal service in places of public accommodation, such as hotels

14

and restaurants, and theaters and retail stores without being forced to resort to demonstrations in the street.

And it ought to be possible for American citizens of any color to register and to vote in a free election without interference or fear of reprisal.

It ought to be possible, in short, for every American to enjoy the privileges of being American without regard to his race or his color.

In short, every American ought to have the right to be treated as he would wish to be treated, as one would wish his children to be treated. But this is not the case.

The Negro baby born in America today, regardless of the section or the state in which he is born, has about one-half as much chance of completing high school as a white baby, born in the same place, on the same day; one-third as much chance of completing college; one-third as much chance of becoming a professional man; twice as much chance of becoming unemployed; about one-seventh as much chance of earning $10,000 a year; a life expectancy which is seven years shorter and the prospects of earning only half as much.

This is not a sectional issue. Difficulties over segregation and discrimination exist in every city, in every state of the Union, producing in many cities a rising tide of discontent that threatens the public safety.

Nor is this a partisan issue. In a time of domestic crisis, men of goodwill and generosity should be able to unite regardless of party or politics.

This is not even a legal or legislative issue alone. It is better to settle these matters in the courts than on the streets, and new laws are needed at every level. But law alone cannot make men see right.

We are confronted primarily with a moral issue. It is as old as the Scriptures and is as clear as the American Constitution. The heart of the question is whether all Americans are to be afforded equal rights and equal opportunities; whether we are going to treat our fellow Americans as we want to be treated.

If an American, because his skin is dark, cannot eat lunch in a restaurant open to the public; if he cannot send his children to the best public school available; if he cannot vote for the public officials who represent him; if, in short, he cannot enjoy the full and free life which all of us want, then who among us would be content to have the color of his skin changed and stand in his place?

Who among us would then be content with the counsels of patience and delay? One hundred years of delay have passed since President Lincoln freed the slaves, yet their heirs, their grandsons, are not fully free. They are not yet freed from the bonds of injustice; they are not yet freed from social and economic oppression.

And this nation, for all its hopes and all its boasts, will not be fully free until all its citizens are free.

We preach freedom around the world, and we mean it. And we cherish our freedom here at home. But are we to say to the world—and much more importantly to each other—that this is the land of the free, except for the Negroes; that we have no second-class citizens, except Negroes; that we have no class or caste system, no ghettos, no master race, except with respect to Negroes?

Now the time has come for this nation to fulfill its promise. The events in Birmingham and elsewhere have so increased the cries for equality that no city or state or legislative body can prudently choose to ignore them.

The fires of frustration and discord are burning in every city, North and South. Where legal remedies are not at hand, redress is sought in the streets in demonstrations, parades and protests, which create tensions    10
and threaten violence—and threaten lives.

We face, therefore, a moral crisis as a country and a people. It cannot be met by repressive police action. It cannot be left to increased demonstrations in the streets. It cannot be quieted by token moves or talk. It is a time to act in the Congress, in your state and local legislative body, and, above all, in all of our daily lives.

It is not enough to pin the blame on others, to say this is a problem of one section of the country or another, or deplore the facts that we face. A great change is at hand, and our task, our obligation is to make that revolution, that change peaceful and constructive for all.    20

Those who do nothing are inviting shame as well as violence. Those who act boldly are recognizing right as well as reality.

Next week I shall ask the Congress of the United States to act, to make a commitment it has not fully made in this country to the proposition that race has no place in American life or law.

The Federal judiciary has upheld that proposition in a series of forthright cases. The Executive Branch has adopted that proposition in the conduct of its affairs, including the employment of Federal personnel, and the use of Federal facilities, and the sale of Federally financed housing.

But there are other necessary measures which only the Congress can    30
provide, and they must be provided at this session.

The old code of equity law under which we live commands for every wrong a remedy. But in too many communities, in too many parts of the country wrongs are inflicted on Negro citizens and there are no remedies in law.

Unless the Congress acts their only remedy is the street.

I am, therefore, asking the Congress to enact legislation giving all Americans the right to be served in facilities which are open to the public —hotels, restaurants and theaters, retail stores and similar establishments. This seems to me to be an elementary right.    40

Its denial is an arbitrary indignity that no American in 1963 should have to endure, but many do.

I have recently met with scores of business leaders, urging them to take voluntary action to end this discrimination. And I've been encouranged by their response. And in the last two weeks over 75 cities have seen progress made in desegregating these kinds of facilities.

But many are unwilling to act alone. And for this reason nationwide legislation is needed, if we are to move this problem from the streets to the courts.

I'm also asking Congress to authorize the Federal Government to participate more fully in lawsuits designed to end segregation in public education. We have succeeded in persuading many districts to desegregate voluntarily. Dozens have admitted Negroes without violence.

Today a Negro is attending a state-supported institution in every one of our 50 states. But the pace is very slow.                                  10

Too many Negro children entering segregated grade schools at the time of the Supreme Court's decision nine years ago will enter segregated high schools this fall, having suffered a loss which can never be restored.

The lack of an adequate education denies the Negro a chance to get a decent job. The orderly implementation of the Supreme Court decision therefore, cannot be left solely to those who may not have the economic resources to carry their legal action or who may be subject to harassment.

Other features will be also requested, including greater protection for the right to vote.

But legislation, I repeat, cannot solve this problem alone. It must be    20
solved in the homes of every American in every community across our country.

In this respect, I want to pay tribute to those citizens, North and South, who've been working in their communities to make life better for all.

They are acting not out of a sense of legal duty but out of a sense of human decency. Like our soldiers and sailors in all parts of the world, they are meeting freedom's challenge on the firing line and I salute them for their honor—their courage.

My fellow Americans, this is a problem which faces us all, in every city of the North as well as the South.                                        30

Today there are Negroes unemployed—two or three times as many compared to whites—inadequate education; moving into the large cities, unable to find work; young people particularly out of work, without hope, denied equal rights, denied the opportunity to eat at a restaurant or a lunch counter, or go to a movie theater; denied the right to a decent education; denied, almost today, the right to attend a state university even though qualified.

It seems to me that these are matters which concern us all—not merely Presidents, or Congressmen, or Governors, but every citizen of the United States.                                                                40

This is one country. It has become one country because all of us and all the people who came here had an equal chance to develop their talents.

We cannot say to 10 per cent of the population that "you can't have that right. Your children can't have the chance to develop whatever talents they have, that the only way that they're going to get their rights is to go in the street and demonstrate."

I think we owe them and we owe ourselves a better country than that.

Therefore, I'm asking for your help in making it easier for us to move ahead and provide the kind of equality of treatment which we would want ourselves—to give a chance for every child to be educated to the limit of his talent.

As I've said before, not every child has an equal talent or an equal ability or equal motivation. But they should have the equal right to develop their talent and their ability and their motivation to make something of themselves.

10

We have a right to expect that the Negro community will be responsible, will uphold the law. But they have a right to expect the law will be fair, that the Constitution will be color blind, as Justice Harlan said at the turn of the century.

This is what we're talking about. This is a matter which concerns this country and what it stands for, and in meeting it I ask the support of all of our citizens.

Thank you very much.

# Red and Brown

*"Let me do the palavering. My tongue is more forked than yours."*

•    •

# Introduction

Many of us are frightened by anger. We've been taught not to raise our voices; we've been told to settle our differences politely. With the exception of the piece by Thomas Jefferson, all of the selections in this section are angry. Their authors resent the superiority which the white man has assumed for so long, and they try to point out the injustice of this assumption. Each piece masks its anger in a different way, but it's always there.

Why is Jefferson an exception to this anger? In his Second Inaugural Address his attitude is paternal, fatherly. He feels sorry for the Indians and cannot understand why the red man rejects the ways of the white. "I have regarded them," he tells us, "with the commiseration their history inspires." The Indian Declaration of Independence included in this section is a sarcastic response to men like Jefferson, men who, however well-meaning, still consider themselves superior. The Indians turn the tables, offering to raise "their white brothers up from their savage and unhappy state." These are the voices of our own generation shouting back at over two hundred years of injustice.

Mari Sandoz has written many books about Indians. The selection we've chosen is an historical account from *Cheyenne Autumn*. In these few pages she tells us again and again of the white man's treachery, "one more promise that was like the wind on the grass."

21

Scott Momaday writes in a wholly different way about the same theme. While Miss Sandoz chooses an objective documentary style, Mr. Momaday writes lyrically, poetically, and in the first person. He invests the daily lives of the people with sunlit beauty and against this background shows us "the grim, unrelenting advance of the U.S. Cavalry." The short story by Oliver LaFarge describes the gap between the two worlds today, the wounds that cannot be healed, the values that cannot be reconciled.

*Ramona* has frequently been compared to *Uncle Tom's Cabin*. Both were very early attempts to call attention to unjust situations. In a later section we have reprinted a selection from *Uncle Tom's Cabin*.

We present a sociological account of Mexican-Americans in Ozzie Simmons' essay, followed by a more appealing piece by Stan Steiner. Notice that Mr. Steiner is able to engage your sympathies so much more easily than Mr. Simmons by beginning with the story of one girl. He knows well that facts and statistics alone cannot do the job. Ozzie Simmons writes a formidable prose which almost scares us away, while Stan Steiner draws us closer with language we can readily understand. Even the title of Ozzie Simmons' selection stands out against the others, "The Mutual Images and Expectations of Anglo-Americans and Mexican-Americans." Cesar Chavez is someone you've probably heard about. He's a twentieth-century hero and this interview will give you a chance to know him better.

We said earlier that most of these pieces are angry. The Young Lords selection is perhaps most clearly so. It is militant in tone, a far cry from the happy Puerto Ricans that Hollywood portrayed, dancing and singing on the rooftops in *West Side Story*. The demands that the Young Lords make will tell you what's been missing from their lives.

In each of these selections demands are being made. All are not as obvious as those of the Young Lords. In some of the selections, for example, the demand might be in the form of a request, a request that we take a few moments to look at lives other than our own in ways which, perhaps, we've never done before. For some of us it's an old story; for too many others, a startling revelation.

# Thomas Jefferson
## From The Second
## Inaugural Address

The aboriginal inhabitants of these countries I have regarded with the commiseration their history inspires. Endowed with the faculties and the rights of men, breathing an ardent love of liberty and independence, and occupying a country which left them no desire but to be undisturbed, the stream of overflowing population from other regions directed itself on these shores; without power to divert, or habits to contend against, they have been overwhelmed by the current, or driven before it; now reduced within limits too narrow for the hunter's state, humanity enjoins us to teach them agriculture and the domestic arts: to encourage them to that industry which alone can enable them to maintain their place in existence,    10
and to prepare them in time for that state of society, which to bodily comforts adds the improvement of the mind and morals. We have therefore liberally furnished them with the implements of husbandry and household use; we have placed among them instructors in the arts of first necessity; and they are covered with the aegis of the law against aggressors from among ourselves.

But the endeavors to enlighten them on the fate which awaits their present course of life, to induce them to exercise their reason, follow its dictates, and change their pursuits with the change of circumstances, have powerful obstacles to encounter; they are combated by the habits of their bodies,    20
prejudice of their minds, ignorance, pride, and the influence of interested and crafty individuals among them, who feel themselves something in the present order of things, and fear to become nothing in any other. These persons inculcate a sanctimonious reverence for the customs of their an-

cestors; that whatsoever they did, must be done through all time; that reason is a false guide, and to advance under its counsel, in their physical, moral or political condition, is perilous innovation: that their duty is to remain as their Creator made them, ignorance being safety, and knowledge full of danger; in short my friends, among them is seen the action and counteraction of good sense and bigotry; they, too, have their anti-philosophers, who find an interest in keeping things in their present state, who dread reformation, and exert all their faculties to maintain the ascendency of habit over the duty of improving our reason, and obeying its mandates. . . .

# Mari Sandoz
## The People and the Time

### THE INDIANS

*Little Wolf,* one of the Old Man Chiefs of the tribe, was bearer of the
Sacred Chief's Bundle of the Northern Cheyennes, carrying with it the
highest responsibility for the preservation of the people. He was also
the tribe's fastest runner at fifty-seven, and soft-spoken but like a wounded
grizzly in anger. His reputation as a bold warrior started back around
the 1830s, in the intertribal conflicts of the time, given up temporarily in
1851 when the Cheyennes signed away their rights to the Overland Trail
and to the joys of the warpath for annuities and an Indian agency to
administer their tribal business with the government.

Although the agency was never established and the goods seldom came,   10
the Cheyennes tried hard to remain at peace with the encroaching whites.
Little Wolf did almost no warring against the troops, except during the
one year of 1865—to avenge the unprovoked attack on the Cheyennes at
Sand Creek the fall before. Since then, he had asked many times for the
promised agency and the goods that were their due. He had even gone to
Washington and received a big peace medal from President Grant. And
next there was an order that they must all stay at Red Cloud, the Sioux
agency in northwest Nebraska, where even the Sioux were hungry and the
Cheyennes unwelcome interlopers.

In 1876 Little Wolf took his starving followers out on the regular treaty-   20
sanctioned summer hunt. He was too late for the Custer fight, but in time
for the Army's pursuit of the Indians afterward, and their destruction of
Dull Knife's village on the Powder, where the Wolf helped the women
and children escape and received seven bullets before it was done. They
fled on through the hungry winter snows of the Yellowstone country until

*132,727*

25

they finally had to listen to the promises of good treatment and an agency
in their north country from the emissaries of both General Miles on the
Yellowstone and General Crook down in Nebraska. Little Wolf and Dull
Knife surrendered at Red Cloud, where the promises that Crook had made
to them in good faith were all broken, although the Wolf had enlisted as a
scout for Crook's troops immediately. The Indians were told they could
not have the promised agency and that there would be no more food for
their families until they started to the hated Indian Territory far to the
south. When they still refused to go, they were told that, if they did not
like it, they could return—one more promise that was like the wind on        10
the grass.

Little Wolf had two warrior sons along: Pawnee and the Woodenthigh
who was named for the strong legs that were characteristic of the family.
The daughter was called Pretty Walker, as also seemed fitting. The Wolf's
two wives were Quiet One and Feather on Head, with a guest following
them, an uninvited guest—the Thin Elk that Little Wolf had warned
away from his wives twenty years ago. Now once more the Elk sat at his
fire, but as an Old Man Chief and the bearer of the Sacred Bundle, he
must think only of the good of the people and not see a man there with
his women.                                                                    20

*Dull Knife,* also an Old Man Chief, had been a famous Dog soldier in
his youth, but as early as 1846 he had talked for peace to preserve the
tribe. Although his band was closely tied to the Red Cloud Sioux by
marriage, Dull Knife did little fighting against the whites except in 1865.
He went to Washington with Little Wolf and Hog and the rest to ask for
an agency, and when nothing came, he took his people north to the buffalo herds of the Crazy Horse Sioux. Then in November the troops
destroyed his village, killing many Cheyennes, including his son and
son-in-law, two of the family that the troops had called the Beautiful
People.                                                                       30

Now they were all here in Indian Territory, his northern tribesmen dying
of malaria with no quinine, and of dysentery and starvation. But to this
old-time Cheyenne the promise of the officers in the north was like iron,
and so he was going home. With him were his two wives, Pawnee Woman
and Short One, and two sons. The elder, Bull Hump, was a prominent
Dog soldier, and his wife Leaf was one of the bravest, boldest young
women of the tribe. The younger son was nicknamed Little Hump because
he followed the elder brother in everything. The five handsome young
daughters were called the Princesses by the troops, two of them probably
nieces, but beautiful too.                                                    40

Wild Hog, one of the headmen under the two chiefs, was a big broad
man with a broad humorous face. He had his sickened Sioux wife along,
a young son nicknamed Little or Young Hog, and a daughter, a quiet girl,
beautiful in the reserved Cheyenne way, who was called Hog's Daughter.

The camp finder was, as usual, old Black Crane. He was a patient, judicious man who knew the vast country between them and the Yellowstone: Indian Territory, Kansas, Nebraska, Dakota Territory, Wyoming, and southern Montana. He could soothe the weary querulous women at the end of a hard day of travel and perhaps preserve peace and good humor among the hotheaded, frustrated young warriors. No one had given him real trouble except the young subchief Black Coyote, a very prominent fighter whose wife was Buffalo Calf Road, the Cheyenne warrior woman who had charged her horse into the thick of the battle in the Rosebud fight, to save her brother who was set afoot among Crook's firing troops. Of all the angry agency-hating Cheyennes, Black Coyote *10* was the worst, and while old Crane sympathized with such fine hot anger, he realized that violence now would only bring destruction upon them all.

There were many younger people along too—the future of the tribe. One of the finest was the warrior Little Finger Nail, the artist and sweet singer of the Cheyennes. Then there was a light-haired boy called Yellow Swallow, the Cheyenne son of General Custer.

The *warrior societies,* sometimes called soldier societies, were the organized military and police force of the Cheyennes, and carried out the orders of the council chiefs. The society chiefs, without a place in the council as such, led the members in their duties and in any social and reli- *20* gious activities centered about the warrior lodge. The societies cut across the Cheyenne bands and beyond; there were strong Dog soldier lodges among the Sioux. A general war party, a concerted hunt, or a village camped or moving was always in charge of a designated warrior society. But the Dog soldiers had a permanent duty. They could never move until all the village was safely started. Because they were the perpetual rear guard of the people, their reputation for bravery and desperate last-ditch stands grew tremendously during the years of pursuit by the troops, and their membership vastly reduced.

The Elks, Little Wolf's society, took great pride in their war strategy *30* and their scouting. Even in Dull Knife's village on the Powder, they had reported the coming attack and were caught only because some Fox society men came in with scalps and insisted on making a scalp dance instead of letting the people flee.

The warrior societies included most but not all of the able-bodied ambitious men of the tribe. When a prominent old chief explained to General Miles that he had never joined one, the general laughed. "I'm not a West Point man myself."

## THE INDIAN AGENT

*John A. Miles,* of the Cheyenne and Arapahoe Agency, Indian Territory, *40* was one of the Quakers appointed as Indian agents after years of scandal and graft in the Indian service, particularly under Secretary of War Belknap in the Grant administration. But honesty was not the sole requirement for dealing with the proud, independent element of a nomadic hunting people, suddenly pushed upon an agency, with nothing to do or eat.

## THE MILITARY DEPARTMENTS

The path of the Cheyennes fleeing from Indian Territory to the Yellowstone crossed two military departments, the Missouri and the Platte, and entered the Department of Dakota. Troops pursuing the Indians out of their own command were dependent upon the host department for supplies and support, both often unavailable or not graciously given. No department commander welcomed the capture of Indians in his area by troops from the outside.

## THE MILITARY MEN

*Gen. George Crook* commanded the Department of the Platte, which 10 included Fort Robinson, in northwest Nebraska. He had taken the field against the Sioux and the Northern Cheyennes in the spring of 1876, with a notable encounter on the Rosebud in Montana, on the seventeenth of June. That fall and winter he and General Miles, who operated on the Yellowstone, each maneuvered to get as many Sioux and Cheyenne Indians to surrender within his department as possible. Some of the Northern Cheyennes went in to Miles, but Little Wolf and Dull Knife were among the chiefs who listened to the bidding of Crook's emissaries and went down to Fort Robinson, where their few goods had come in the past.

*Gen. Nelson A. Miles* was at Fort Keogh on the Yellowstone, keeping 20 Sitting Bull's Sioux from coming down out of Canada, and in charge of the Cheyennes not yet transferred to Indian Territory. His relentless pursuit of the Sioux and the Cheyennes the winter of 1876-1877 had helped to reduce them so near to nakedness and starvation that they had to surrender.

*Col. Caleb H. Carlton,* Third Cavalry, was ordered to Fort Robinson, Nebraska, and through the sandhills to intercept the fleeing Cheyennes when it was plain they were eluding the troops through Kansas.

*Gen. George Armstrong Custer* was given command of the Seventh Cavalry when it was created in 1866, to provide positions, it was said, 30 for some of the surplus officers of the Civil War—Custer, in particular, because he campaigned with President Johnson in the off-year election. The fall of 1867 Custer was suspended on charges that included desertion of his post. When restored to his command in the fall of 1868, he was determined to make a showing and fell upon the Cheyennes camped on the Washita where the military agent had told the Indians, just the day before, their families would be safe. Among the captive women and children was a young girl, Monahsetah, whom he kept with him all winter and spring and who bore him a son in the fall—the Yellow Swallow along in the flight north.

In 1874 Custer was sent into the Black Hills where no white man had 40 the treaty right to go. He was to locate gold and thereby stimulate financing for the stalled railroad illegally coming up the Yellowstone. In 1876 he attacked the great Indian camp on the Little Big Horn and died there.

The first Indians to open fire on his column were four Cheyennes, one of them now with Little Wolf. Some of the Custer guns were still hidden among them; a carbine, taken down, hung under the buckskin dress of one of the women.

## THE TIME

After the Civil War and through the depression years of the 1870s, there was a great push of white men into the Indian country, the land hunger augmented by the gold rushes, the buffalo-hide bonanza, the expanding railroads, and the cattle business. The demand to clear the Indians out grew louder: tear up the treaties, bribe and drive the treach-   10
erous redskins to small restricted reservations that were set up on land no white man would ever want, at least not until oil and uranium were discovered. There they would be supervised by an Indian agent, a political appointee with absolute power. Often he had the help and connivance of some government-elevated nonentity made the agency chief. Normally the Indian Bureau was under the Department of the Interior, but whenever there was serious trouble with the Indians, the civilian agents were replaced by army officers, perhaps the whole Bureau moved to the War Department, and then back when it was argued that the military was really not equipped to make good citizens of the aborigines. "The bureau   20
on wheels" the newspapers called it.

During the Grant administration the grafting in the Indian appropriations was at its height, first in contract letting (pants that went to pieces like blotting paper in water, sugar that was half sand) and then through actual thievery by both the contractors and the agency employees. The resultant starvation fell with particular weight upon the Northern Cheyennes, always stepchildren on the hungry Sioux agency. Now they were thrust upon the most shaming dependence of all—upon the hospitality of their relatives, the Southern Cheyennes, with a cut below the appropriations that those people had last year just for themselves. But they were   30
all helpless, as all the western tribes were helpless. Congress knew this and took the occasion to grow economical, cutting appropriations far below treaty stipulations, and with much encouragement from army contractors, who made millions out of all the starvation flights of 1877 and 1878.

But Little Wolf and Dull Knife knew only that there was not a lodge free of sickness and the keening for death. So the chiefs decided they must take the people home. When they were told they would be whipped back by the troops, they started anyway, and some of them made it through.

# N. Scott Momaday
## From The Way to Rainy Mountain

A single knoll rises out of the plain in Oklahoma, north and west of the
Wichita Range. For my people, the Kiowas, it is an old landmark, and
they gave it the name Rainy Mountain. The hardest weather in the world
is there. Winter brings blizzards, hot tornadic winds arise in the spring,
and in summer the prairie is an anvil's edge. The grass turns brittle and
brown, and it cracks beneath your feet. There are green belts along the
rivers and creeks, linear groves of hickory and pecan, willow and witch
hazel. At a distance in July or August the steaming foliage seems almost
to writhe in fire. Great green and yellow grasshoppers are everywhere in
the tall grass, popping up like corn to sting the flesh, and tortoises crawl
about on the red earth, going nowhere in the plenty of time. Loneliness is    10
an aspect of the land. All things in the plain are isolate; there is no confusion of objects in the eye, but *one* hill or *one* tree or *one* man. To look
upon that landscape in the early morning, with the sun at your back, is
to lose the sense of proportion. Your imagination comes to life, and this,
you think, is where Creation was begun.

I returned to Rainy Mountain in July. My grandmother had died in the
spring, and I wanted to be at her grave. She had lived to be very old and
at last infirm. Her only living daughter was with her when she died, and
I was told that in death her face was that of a child.

I like to think of her as a child. When she was born, the Kiowas were    20
living the last great moment of their history. For more than a hundred
years they had controlled the open range from the Smoky Hill River to
the Red, from the headwaters of the Canadian to the fork of the Arkansas
and Cimarron. In alliance with the Comanches, they had ruled the whole of
the southern Plains. War was their sacred business, and they were among

the finest horsemen the world has ever known. But warfare for the Kiowas was preeminently a matter of disposition rather than of survival, and they never understood the grim, unrelenting advance of the U.S. Cavalry. When at last, divided and ill-provisioned, they were driven onto the Staked Plains in the cold rains of autumn, they fell into panic. In Palo Duro Canyon they abandoned their crucial stores to pillage and had nothing then but their lives. In order to save themselves, they surrendered to the soldiers at Fort Sill and were imprisoned in the old stone corral that now stands as a military museum. My grandmother was spared the humiliation of those high gray walls by eight or ten years, but she must have known from birth the affliction of defeat, the dark brooding of old warriors.

Her name was Aho, and she belonged to the last culture to evolve in North America. Her forebears came down from the high country in western Montana nearly three centuries ago. They were a mountain people, a mysterious tribe of hunters whose language has never been positively classified in any major group. In the late seventeenth century they began a long migration to the south and east. It was a journey toward the dawn, and it led to a golden age. Along the way the Kiowas were befriended by the Crows, who gave them the culture and religion of the Plains. They acquired horses, and their ancient nomadic spirit was suddenly free of the ground. They acquired Tai-me, the sacred Sun Dance doll, from that moment the object and symbol of their worship, and so shared in the divinity of the sun. Not least, they acquired the sense of destiny, therefore courage and pride. When they entered upon the southern Plains they had been transformed. No longer were they slaves to the simple necessity of survival; they were a lordly and dangerous society of fighters and thieves, hunters and priests of the sun. According to their origin myth, they entered the world through a hollow log. From one point of view, their migration was the fruit of an old prophecy, for indeed they emerged from a sunless world.

Although my grandmother lived out her long life in the shadow of Rainy Mountain, the immense landscape of the continental interior lay like memory in her blood. She could tell of the Crows, whom she had never seen, and of the Black Hills, where she had never been. I wanted to see in reality what she had seen more perfectly in the mind's eye, and traveled fifteen hundred miles to begin my pilgrimage.

Yellowstone, it seemed to me, was the top of the world, a region of deep lakes and dark timber, canyons and waterfalls. But, beautiful as it is, one might have the sense of confinement there. The skyline in all directions is close at hand, the high wall of the woods and deep cleavages of shade. There is a perfect freedom in the mountains, but it belongs to the eagle and the elk, the badger and the bear. The Kiowas reckoned their stature by the distance they could see, and they were bent and blind in the wilderness.

Descending eastward, the highland meadows are a stairway to the plain. In July the inland slope of the Rockies is luxuriant with flax and buckwheat, stonecrop and larkspur. The earth unfolds and the limit of the land recedes. Clusters of trees, and animals grazing far in the distance, cause the vision to reach away and wonder to build upon the mind. The sun follows a longer course in the day, and the sky is immense beyond all comparison. The great billowing clouds that sail upon it are shadows that move upon the grain like water, dividing light. Farther down, in the land of the Crows and Blackfeet, the plain is yellow. Sweet clover takes hold of the hills and bends upon itself to cover and seal the soil. There 10 the Kiowas paused on their way; they had come to the place where they must change their lives. The sun is at home on the plains. Precisely there does it have the certain character of a god. When the Kiowas came to the land of the Crows, they could see the dark lees of the hills at dawn across the Bighorn River, the profusion of light on the grain shelves, the oldest deity ranging after the solstices. Not yet would they veer southward to the caldron of the land that lay below; they must wean their blood from the northern winter and hold the mountains a while longer in their view. They bore Tai-me in procession to the east.

A dark mist lay over the Black Hills, and the land was like iron. At the top of a ridge I caught sight of Devil's Tower upthrust against the gray 20 sky as if in the birth of time the core of the earth had broken through its crust and the motion of the world was begun. There are things in nature that engender an awful quiet in the heart of man; Devil's Tower is one of them. Two centuries ago, because they could not do otherwise, the Kiowas made a legend at the base of the rock. My grandmother said:

*Eight children were there at play, seven sisters and their brother. Suddenly the boy was struck dumb; he trembled and began to run upon his hands and feet. His fingers became claws, and his body,* 30 *was covered with fur. Directly there was a bear where the boy had been. The sisters were terrified; they ran, and the bear after them. They came to the stump of a great tree, and the tree spoke to them. It bade them climb upon it, and as they did so it began to rise into the air. The bear came to kill them, but they were just beyond its reach. It reared against the tree and scored the bark all around with its claws. The seven sisters were borne into the sky, and they became the stars of the Big Dipper.*

From that moment, and so long as the legend lives, the Kiowas have 40 kinsmen in the night sky. Whatever they were in the mountains, they could be no more. However tenuous their well-being, however much they had suffered and would suffer again, they had found a way out of the wilderness.

My grandmother had a reverence for the sun, a holy regard that now is all but gone out of mankind. There was a wariness in her, and an ancient awe. She was a Christian in her later years, but she had come a long way

about, and she never forgot her birthright. As a child she had been to the
Sun Dances: she had taken part in those annual rites, and by them she
had learned the restoration of her people in the presence of Tai-me. She
was about seven when the last Kiowa Sun Dance was held in 1887 on the
Washita River above Rainy Mountain Creek. The buffalo were gone. In
order to consummate the ancient sacrifice—to impale the head of a buffalo
bull upon the medicine tree—a delegation of old men journeyed into Texas,
there to beg and barter an animal from the Goodnight herd. She was ten
when the Kiowas came together for the last time as a living Sun Dance
culture. They could find no buffalo; they had to hang an old hide from the    10
sacred tree. Before the dance could begin, a company of soldiers rode out
from Fort Sill under orders to disperse the tribe. Forbidden without cause
the essential act of their faith, having seen the wild herds slaughtered
and left to rot upon the ground, the Kiowas backed away forever from the
medicine tree. That was July 20, 1890, at the great bend of the Washita.
My grandmother was there. Without bitterness, and for as long as she
lived, she bore a vision of deicide.

Now that I can have her only in memory, I see my grandmother in the
several postures that were peculiar to her: standing at the wood stove on
a winter morning and turning meat in a great iron skillet; sitting at the    20
south window, bent above her beadwork, and afterwards, when her vision
failed, looking down for a long time into the folds of her hands; going
out upon a cane, very slowly as she did when the weight of age came upon
her; praying. I remember her most often at prayer. She made long rambling
prayers out of suffering and hope, having seen many things. I was never
sure that I had the right to hear, so exclusive were they of all mere custom
and company. The last time I saw her she prayed standing by the side of
her bed at night, naked to the waist, the light of a kerosene lamp moving
upon her dark skin. Her long, black hair, always drawn and braided in
the day, lay upon her shoulders and against her breasts like a shawl. I do    30
not speak Kiowa, and I never understood her prayers, but there was something inherently sad in the sound, some merest hesitation upon the
syllables of sorrow. She began in a high and descending pitch, exhausting
her breath to silence; then again and again—and always the same intensity
of effort, of something that is, and is not, like urgency in the human voice.
Transported so in the dancing light among the shadows of her room,
she seemed beyond the reach of time. But that was illusion; I think I knew
then that I should not see her again.

Houses are like sentinels in the plain, old keepers of the weather watch.
There, in a very little while, wood takes on the appearance of great age.    40
All colors wear soon away in the wind and rain, and then the wood is
burned gray and the grain appears and the nails turn red with rust. The
windowpanes are black and opaque; you imagine there is nothing within,
and indeed there are many ghosts, bones given up to the land. They stand
here and there against the sky, and you approach them for a longer time
than you expect. They belong in the distance; it is their domain.

Once there was a lot of sound in my grandmother's house, a lot of coming and going, feasting and talk. The summers there were full of excitement and reunion. The Kiowas are a summer people; they abide the cold and keep to themselves, but when the season turns and the land becomes warm and vital they cannot hold still; an old love of going returns upon them. The aged visitors who came to grandmother's house when I was a child were made of lean and leather, and they bore themselves upright. They wore great black hats and bright ample shirts that shook in the wind. They rubbed fat upon their hair and wound their braids with strips of colored cloth. Some of them painted their faces and carried scars of   10 old and cherished enmities. They were an old council of warlords, come to remind and be reminded of who they were. Their wives and daughters served them well. The women might indulge themselves; gossip was at once the mark and compensation of their servitude. They made loud and elaborate talk among themselves, full of jest and gesture, fright and false alarm. They went abroad in fringed and flowered shawls, bright beadwork and German silver. They were at home in the kitchen, and they prepared meals that were banquets.

There were frequent prayer meetings, and great nocturnal feasts. When I was a child I played with my cousins outside, where the lamplight fell   20 upon the ground and the singing of the old people rose up around us and carried away into the darkness. There were a lot of good things to eat, a lot of laughter and surprise: And afterwards, when the quiet returned, I lay down with my grandmother and could hear the frogs away by the river and feel the motion of the air.

Now there is a funeral silence in the rooms, the endless wake of some final word. The walls have closed in upon my grandmother's house. When I returned to it in mourning, I saw for the first time in my life how small it was. It was late at night, and there was a white moon, nearly full. I sat for a long time on the stone steps by the kitchen door. From there I could   30 see out across the land; I could see the long row of trees by the creek, the low light upon the rolling plains, and the stars of the Big Dipper. Once I looked at the moon and caught sight of a strange thing. A cricket had perched upon the handrail, only a few inches away from me. My line of vision was such that the creature filled the moon like a fossil. It had gone there, I thought, to live and die, for there, of all places, was its small definition made whole and eternal. A warm wind rose up and purled like the longing within me.

The next morning I awoke at dawn and went out on the dirt road to Rainy Mountain. It was already hot, and the grasshoppers began to fill   40 the air. Still, it was early in the morning, and the birds sang out of the shadows. The long yellow grass on the mountain shone in the bright light, and a scissortail hied above the land. There, where it ought to be, at the end of a long and legendary way, was my grandmother's grave. Here and there on the dark stones were ancestral names. Looking back once, I saw the mountain and came away.

# Oliver La Farge
## The Happy Indian Laughter

Three men sat, each on one of three wooden steps. The one on the top step was young. His hair was cut short. He wore a fairly large, neat, light gray Stetson, a blue Air Force officer's shirt, a blue silk scarf at his throat, neatly pressed Levis, and cowboy boots. He was waiting for something. He sat as quietly as the others, but you could tell that he was waiting.

The two others were past middle age. Their large black felt hats were battered. One had a beadwork hatband, the other a hatband made of dimes. From under the hatbrims, just behind their ears, their braided hair hung down wrapped in two colors of tape, crisscrossing. These two were not waiting for anything, they were just relaxing. 10

When a big blue convertible with the top up came around the corner at the end of the dusty street, all three looked up. The car seemed to hesitate, then came toward them slowly.

The man on the middle step said, "Tourists." He looked at the one below him, who was thin, and older than he. "Show your moccasins, brother; perhaps they'll pay to take your picture."

"Run tell your wife to weave a basket."

They both laughed. The young man's face had become blank.

The old man said, "Just one tourist—a woman, young. Perhaps we can be Apaches and frighten her." 20

The two laughed again—the pleasant, light laughter of Indians. The young man said, using a title of respect, "Grandfather, I know this woman. She was a friend when I was in the Air Force."

The old man said, "Good. Let her walk in peace."

The girl had put up the top of her convertible when she encountered the penetrating dust of the road that led from the sad little town of Arenosa

35

to the Indian Agency. The road appalled her. The dirt was hard, cut by ruts, and washboarded, and, for all its hardness, produced fine, clayey dust in quantity. She came to a cattle guard, a strong barbed-wire fence, and a sign reading, "Department of the Interior—U.S. Indian Service— Gohlquain Apache Indian Reservation—No Trespassing." She stopped the car and studied the sign, half minded to turn back. Then, with a jerk, she started forward again. She had overcome too much opposition, in herself and from others, to turn back now.

The Agency was five miles inside the boundary, Ralph had written, and the high country of grass and trees not far beyond. She could see the high country ahead of her, blue and inscrutable. She'd find out soon enough what it was really like. She'd find out a lot, and above all the difference between a handsome—you could almost say beautiful—Air Force pilot with a bronze skin and an Apache cattleman. As she had pointed out to friends and relatives, he was a college man as well as a pilot, and she would be the same in any setting, with the same nice manners and the same humor. She wished now that she were sure of that.

The Agency was a village, strung out along a wide, straight section of road. There were white wooden houses, some adobe ones, and a couple of dreary brick buildings. Ralph had written that he would be waiting for her in front of the Agency proper, which she could recognize by the sign over its door and the clock in the little tower on top. She came almost to a stop, looked about, then proceeded slowly.

She passed two women walking in the opposite direction, on her side of the road. Their hair hung, rich and black, over their shoulders. They wore calico blouses and full calico skirts. As she passed them, they did not glance but looked at her for a measurable time, their faces impenetrable, their eyes dismissing. So those were Apache women; even their manner of walking was alien.

She identified the Agency, which was one of the smaller structures— she had expected it to be large—and saw the three men sitting. That was surely Ralph on the top step, and by now he must have seen her Ohio license plates and recognized the car, but he did not get up. She felt a sudden anger.

The Agency building stood on the left-hand side of the street. She came to a stop opposite it, on the right. As she did so, the young man rose, came down the steps, and walked to the car, not hurrying. The two older men sat gazing at her. All three faces showed nothing but blankness it was difficult not to read hostility into.

Ralph stopped with his hand on the door. "You got here." The remark was neutral.

She said, "Did I?"

A trace of smile showed about his mouth. "Hard to tell in all this dust. You'd better let me drive; I know these roads, and I can take your car over them with less of a beating than you can."

She was within a hairbreadth of saying "Thanks, I'm going back now," but she didn't, for the same reason that she hadn't turned back at the boundary, and because she remembered how guarded and withdrawn he had been, for all his wings and ribbons, the first time she took him to the country club. She said, "All right," and moved over.

He drove without speaking for nearly five minutes, handling the car carefully and well. Shortly beyond the Agency grounds, the road began to climb. Instead of the hard, dust-yielding baked mud, its surface was of a coarser, reddish earth, less dusty and less dramatically rutted. Scattered cactus and sagebrush on either hand were replaced by occasional piñons and junipers. The land seemed greener; she could not decide whether there was actually more vegetation or whether it was merely that the grass and small plants were not dust-coated and showed up more strongly against the warmer-colored earth.

The cowboy outfit was becoming to him. He was tanned, darker than when she had known him at the base. His nose was high and straight, his lips sculptured, his chin strong. There was the intriguing extra height of his cheekbones, and above them the dark eyes, slightly Oriental. They were not slanted, but at the outer corners of the upper lids there was a fascinating curve. All this was familiar, but the expressionless face remained strange.

They passed a single tall white pine by the side of the road. As if reaching that point released him, he looked at her and said, "You know, I didn't really believe you'd come until I saw the car." His face had come alive. This was Ralph, after all.

She was astonished to feel so much relief. "I wouldn't have missed it for anything. It isn't everyone who gets formally invited to spend a weekend with Indians."

"My dad was tickled with the whole idea. Mother said I was nuts; she said it would be too strange for you. Still, she's kind of looking forward to it. I think you'll find it interesting."

Of course he had not mentioned the real purpose of her visit, any more than they were able to speak of it between themselves; it mattered so much and seemed so beyond reason. She wondered what that dark Apache mother was thinking, and the sisters—especially the one who had served in the Waves.

He slowed to a stop alongside a pickup truck parked by the road. The driver of the truck wore his hair in braids, heavy ones, the hair black and shiny where it was not wrapped. Ralph had told her once that long-haired Indians were mostly over forty. This one looked middle-aged. He had a blobby big nose in a broad, heavy face. As the two men talked, she thought he seemed a cheerful type.

The language sounded slurred, soft, with a good many "sh" and "l" sounds, punctuated by harsh, throaty consonants. There was a rise and fall of tone. The speech was milder than she had expected, faintly musical, and yet virile. She did not think she could ever hope to understand it.

Presently the man in the truck laughed. Ralph turned to her. "This is my uncle, Juan Grijalva. He and Dad and I run our cattle together."

She smiled at the Indian, who studied her gravely. "You got a gun with you?" he asked.

She saw that his intent was humorous. "No. Do I need one?"

He shook his head. "These Inyans are mighty rough people. And these Inyan veterans, you gotta watch them all the time. You need help, you let out a whoop and I'll come. I gotta keep my nephew in line."

He and Ralph laughed. She didn't think it particularly funny, but she    10
liked the friendliness. She said, "Thanks, I'll remember that."

Ralph said to his uncle, in English, "All right. You'll bring up the salt then?"

"Yeh. Your friend ride?"

Ralph looked at her. She said, "Pretty well—that is, I've been on dude ranches."

Uncle Juan told Ralph, "You pick her out an easy horse, and we can take her along while we set out the salt, and let her view the configuration of the landscape."

As he said the last words, he was watching her closely and his eyes    20
were dancing. Her mouth twitched.

Abruptly, he said, "Well, so long. *Ta'njoh.*"

Ralph said, *"Ta'njoh."*

Both men started their cars and moved along.

"He took two years at Colorado A. & M.," Ralph told her. "He's really a fine cattleman; I'm learning from him right along. He's my dad's brother, so we kid each other all the time."

"Do uncles and nephews usually kid each other?"

"Only on your father's side. On your mother's side, you use respect. It's the custom."                                                                30

"Oh." It sounded surprisingly complicated and artificial.

Pines were appearing among the smaller evergreens, and the grass was definitely richer. Presently Ralph said, "Anthropologists call it 'the joking relationship'—I mean relations who kid, like Juan and me. When I marry, he'll kid my wife the same way. It's fun if you're used to it."

For a moment she stiffened, feeling the remark probe toward the central, unmentioned thing, the thing that had seemed possible at the officers' club, at the country club, in the city, and so totally impossible when the young man came down from the steps. She let it pass before speaking the thought that came to her, lest the connection be apparent. "You aren't    40
going back into the Air Force?"

"Not unless they call me back. I belong here. These people are coming up, in the cattle business and a lot of other ways. There are only four of us in the tribe who've been all the way through college, besides maybe half a dozen like Juan, who went part way and then came back. Besides, it's good here. Look at it."

They had never ceased climbing. The air was fresher, the country greener and more rugged. At some distance to their right, a handsome bank of red cliffs paralleled the road, contrasting nicely with the pine and spruce at its base. They came into a long, wide, open meadow on which a score or more of beef cattle were grazing. It was good country.

He asked, "Did you bring a tent, and all?"

"Yes, one of those little green tents, and a cot."

"Good. It's not so long since we lived in tepees, and we're used to being kind of crowded together. There's five of us in the two rooms in Dad's house. You'll be more comfortable in a tent of your own." 10

When they had driven a little farther, he said, "I'll show you where I'm laying out my house. After the cattle sales this fall, I'll have enough cash to go ahead and build it. I'm going to put in butane gas for the kitchen, and there's a spring above it, so I can bring water in on straight gravity. I figure on three rooms and a bath to start with, and then build on later. Maybe you can give me some advice. There's good stone handy, as well as lots of timber; I don't know which to build in."

He could not possibly have sounded more casual, nor could she as she answered, "I'd like to see it."

Even so, she was relieved when he started reading brands on the cattle 20 near the road and explaining to her which were good Herefords, which off-color or poorly made. As she already knew, he had delicacy; his capacity for perception and tact had surprised her friends.

Ralph's father's name was Pedro Tanitsin; she must find out, she thought, why Juan had a different surname. Tanitsin had put his house in a fairly narrow, craggy-sided valley with an outlook to the south. It was a simple, small frame house, slightly overdue to be repainted. There were no grounds—that is no fenced area, smooth grass, or planting of any kind. At the east end of the house was a large, flat-topped shelter, its roof thickly covered with evergreen branches. Beyond that was the bare 30 pole skeleton of a tepee. A heavy truck with a tarpaulin over the hood stood by the house. A hundred feet or so behind it, she made out the horizontal bars of a corral crossing the lines of the ruddy stems of the pines around it and she saw a horse move. Ralph parked the car beside the truck. Two dogs came skulking, but no human being came to meet them.

At the east end of the shelter was a wide opening. When they came to it, Ralph stopped, so she did, too, beside him and a step behind him. Inside were the people—Ralph's father, sitting on a bench, and his mother and his two sisters, standing. There was an interval of silence; she felt 40 awkward, and saw before her the same blank, guarded faces that had repulsed her at the Agency. She was aware of a camp stove, a fire pit in the middle of the floor, some cooking utensils, and a large barrel, in addition to the bench.

Pedro Tanitsin's hair was braided, and he wore a brilliant beadwork vest over a bright flannel shirt, and levis and moccasins. Ralph's mother wore the native dress; so did the older of his sisters, but instead of wearing her hair loose over her shoulders, she had it clubbed at the back of her neck. That must be Juanita, who had been in the Waves. The other, then, was Mary Ellen. Her hair was bobbed and curled, and she wore one of those gaudy silk blouses servicemen bring back from Japan, and slacks that had never been intended for outdoor life.

The mother spoke a single word, in Apache, and followed it with "Come een." Ralph moved forward, and the girl followed. She felt that she was moving against a wall of rejection. Ralph said something in his own 10 tongue; then, gesturing, "This is my father."

She turned toward him. He nodded once, slowly.

Ralph said, "And this is my mother."

The older woman put out her hand, so the girl took it. The clasp was limp, there was no response to her motion of shaking, and the hand was quickly withdrawn. Then the mother spoke, ending with a laugh.

Ralph said, "She says — Well, you see, a while back one of the government women, some kind of social worker, came here, and she came in talking her head off before anybody had time to get used to her. You came in quietly, like an Indian. So she says, 'This one has good manners.'" 20

The woman laughed again. "Yess, not walk in talking."

The girl felt pleased and relieved. Then she saw that all of them were smiling except Mary Ellen.

Juanita gave her a somewhat firmer handclasp and said, "We were wondering whether you would really come here, to an Indian camp. I hope you like it." Mary Ellen's touch was limp and even more fleeting than her mother's; she kept her eyes down and did not speak.

It seemed that in summer they lived in the shelter, using the house only for sleeping and storage. Their housekeeping was easy and relaxed, rather like a well-organized picnic. She thought it better not to offer to 30 help with getting supper; instead, she watched and took it easy. Hold back and go slow, she had decided, were essential elements of Apache etiquette. Cooking was well advanced when Pedro addressed some commonplace questions to her in heavily accented English. It was a little as if one of the pines had decided to speak, and the product, she thought, should have been less banal.

They all settled on the ground to eat, in a half circle. Ralph's mother insisted on giving her an angora skin, dyed deep blue, to sit on. The food was good, the utensils clean. In the middle of eating, to which the Indians devoted themselves with very little talk, Mary Ellen said something that 40 made the others laugh. Juanita interpreted. "She says Ralph said that you were the kind who would wear Levis and sit on the earth, and you are."

She began to see that what she had taken for hostility in Mary Ellen was defensiveness, just as the inappropriate, pseudo-elegant costume was. The younger girl had not been out into the world, like her older brother and sister; nor had she the self-assurance, the satisfaction with plainly

being Apache, of her parents. Her English was limited and unsteady.
The presence of a strange white woman made her uneasy, and in an
Indian, the visitor was beginning to see, uneasiness takes on the face of
guarded enmity.

She herself was beginning to feel at home here. She looked around her.
The incoming night air from beyond the shelter was chill. A generous fire
burned in the central pit. About her were dark, friendly faces. In the air
she breathed were the smells of smoke, food, coffee, pine needles, and the
near-perfume of juniper boughs that had been brought up from lower
country to make the walls of the shelter thicker and more fragrant. It was    10
incredible that she should be here at this moment, stirring the sugar in a
fresh cup of coffee, listening to the musical rise and fall of a woman's
voice saying something in that mysterious tongue. She looked sidelong at
Ralph. In the shifting, reddened firelight, he was darker, at once familiar,
loved, and alien, primitive. Could it be possible, after all? Was it anything
more than a remnant of a madness that had seized her when she went
visiting a friend who had married a fly-boy major?

By the end of the third day she had to remind herself that all this was as
strange as it was. Ralph planned to build a modern house, but the family's
half-camping mode of life was agreeable; come winter, though, the inside    20
of that little house would be on the grim side. The family were friendly,
easy to be with, especially once Mary Ellen, feeling secure, had returned
to native costume.

They had a radio, which they listened to chiefly for news, weather, and
cattle price reports, Ralph or Juanita translating for their parents. Mary
Ellen read movie magazines. Juanita dipped into textbooks that would
help her in college (the University of New Mexico had accepted her for
next fall) and, for the same purpose, was struggling through *Vanity Fair*.
The white woman was able to help her there, realizing as she did so what
a staggeringly broad context an educated white person moved and thought    30
in, learned without effort, all of which an Indian had to grasp item by
item. To speak English, read, and write was only the beginning.

Ralph and Uncle Juan, who visited daily, went in for bulletins from the
extension service and agricultural colleges, reading them and then ex-
pounding their contents to Pedro. She was amused by the automatic gesture with which Uncle Juan would brush a braid back when it fell on the
page. She had thought she had learned a little of the cattle business on a
dude ranch near Tucson, where they made a big thing of running beef
stock; not until now had she imagined it could be a bookish vocation with
a highly technical vocabulary. Ralph and Juan turned to her to verify the    40
meaning of "it is a far cry from," and in the same sentence were two words
they had to explain to her. This amused Pedro greatly; he didn't know
much English, but he had learned those.

Reading was occasional and in the daytime. After dinner, in the firelit
dark, they told stories. Pedro, it turned out, was a noted storyteller in his
own language. He talked and Ralph translated and explained. The stories

had quality, and through them she saw that the Apaches, too, had a considerable context to be learned.

In her cot that night, with the sweet, cold air on her cheek, hearing the shushing rise and fall of a soft breeze in the high pines, she thought that it was possible, it could happen. It was just possible. Ralph in the saddle was magnificent. Uncle Juan sat his horse like a rock that had become one with the animal, but Ralph was fine-waisted live whalebone. They were fun to ride with—considerate, instructive, humorous.

As they went about the range, there was nothing that moved, nothing out of place, that they did not see, at the farthest distance to which good eyes could reach. They made no apparent effort, she was not conscious that they were scouting, but they saw everything and were not content until it was explained. A pinto horse, an over-age steer with long horns— whose? A truck, two mounted men—to her, when she finally made them out, no more than dots on a distant road—who were they? Where were they going?

It made her think of bygone days and Apaches on the warpath. Some of those warriors had still been alive when Ralph was a boy. The warpath training had not been dropped. It made her think, as well, of Ralph high in the air alongside the Yalu, and his record of kills. There was a closer link between a deadly grandfather with a painted face and the skilled pilot than one would have thought.

Nothing was quite what she had expected, and least expected of all was the constant thread of laughter—the happy Indian laughter running through everything, so light and so easily provoked. And it was possible, just barely possible—that is, if *they* accepted *her.* Before she came here, she had not thought of that. What was definite was that she was in love with Ralph. When she had fully faced that, tired as she was, she was long in falling asleep.

The following afternoon, Ralph told her, "There's a neighbor of ours had a curing ceremony a while back. What he had was a virus and a touch of pneumonia, and they cured that at the hospital, but he had a sing, too. They do that a lot. There's something to it; the doctor takes care of the physical end, and the medicine man takes care of the psychosomatic. Anyway, now he has to 'pick up' the ceremony, as they say. It's a kind of thanksgiving. He puts up a tepee, and they make *tulapai*—that's a kind of beer made from corn. The neighbors come in, and there's a little singing and a feast, and we drink *tulapai* and talk, then at the end everybody gets blessed."

She said, "It sounds interesting. Do they get drunk?"

"You'd have to work hard to get drunk on *tulapai*. It just makes every-body happy. While you're seeing the Apaches, you ought to see this, only—Well, it's kind of unsanitary. They fill a lard pail and pass it around. Of course, you're not an Indian, so it will be all right if you want to use a cup."

"I don't think that's necessary."

Ralph was pleased. "All right. Anyway, it will be just us and Uncle

Juan's family, and this man's—his name is Pablo Horses. They're all healthy, and they're clean."

Near sundown, they drove the mile to Pablo's place in her car and the truck. That was her first sight of a real-life tepee; she was struck by its symmetry, the way in which the curved canvas caught the light, and the effect of the long, sloping white line against a green background. Inside, the tepee seemed even roomier than it had looked from the outside.

The door faced east. In the middle, there was a small, fragrant fire, and a kerosene lantern hung near the host's place at the back. The men sat on the south, the women on the north. All of them were wearing elements of   10
Indian costume—items of buckskin, beadwork, Navajo silver, and Pueblo turquoise and shell. Pedro had his beaded vest on again; she knew now that his donning it that first day had been in honor of her. Ralph had put a wide band of beadwork around his hat, and at his throat, instead of his cowboy's scarf, he wore a broad choker of elk bone and beads. It was becoming.

All of them had blankets. Juanita had insisted that she take one, and had given her a handsome, soft, expensive Pendleton. The idea of wearing it had embarrassed her, but now she felt that it helped her to blend in. She'd turn into an Apache yet, she thought.                                          20

Their host, a craggy man with definitely gray hair, was older than Pedro Tanitsin. Because this was a ceremony, he had an eagle feather tied to the top of his head.

All of them, and especially the women, were amused that a white woman should come to drink *tulapai.* There were comments and laughter. Juanita, sitting next to her, said, "You mustn't mind. It's good. You are giving people a good feeling, so that helps what we are doing."

Pablo Horses took up a rattle and began a chant, in which the older men joined. The time was slow and monotonous, the music narrow in range, and heavy. It was dull, and yet, as the girl listened, the monotonous   30
rhythm and droning voices took hold of her. There was a curious power there.

After four songs, Pablo's daughter brought in a pail of *tulapai,* which was passed around solemnly, clockwise. Unsanitary, certainly; the girl wished she had asked for a cup, but they did seem a healthy lot. The drink itself was good, like beer but with a fresh quality that suggested hard cider. There were four more sets of four songs each, with a circuit of the pail after each set, and then the business of sprinkling a yellow powder and brushing the air with feathers. Everyone had sat still during the chant; the refreshment period was a break, when people changed   40
positions. Pablo's women brought in food. The girl felt no noticeable lift from the small amount of beer she had taken, but it did seem to have sharpened her appetite.

When they had eaten, Pablo said, "Young lady, where you come from?"
She said, "Ohio—Cleveland."
A young man, Uncle Juan's son, said, "I was there one time when I was

in the Army. They got a good U.S.O." That took care of Cleveland.

An elderly man—Pablo's brother, she believed—asked, "How you like it here?"

"I like it. This is beautiful country."

Ralph took the trouble to translate that. Pablo said, "Yess. This is our country, Apache country." Then he went on at some length in Apache.

Juanita explained, "He's taken what you said as a kind of text, and he's telling how this is our country, and we must keep it, and we must live up to our Apache traditions."

More *tulapai* was brought in. The women were speaking up more than usual. There was an atmosphere of geniality and relaxation, but no ugliness, nothing one could call drunkenness.

The man she believed to be Pablo's brother, after a good draught of beer, launched upon a long story. Soon someone laughed. A little later, they all laughed. There were interruptions of laughter all through the latter part of the narration.

When he had finished, Ralph translated. "This is Tomás Horses speaking. He lives about five miles from here, and in between Pablo's place and his there is a place called Yellow Spring, where people camp. That's important.

"He says there is a Pueblo Indian called Malaquias he knows pretty well, a smart trader. Three or four times, when Tomás has visited that Pueblo, Malaquias has given him wine, then traded with him when he was high, and outsmarted him. So he's been waiting for a chance to get even."

They were all listening eagerly. Hearing the story a second time, knowing the point, made it all the more delightful.

"Well, about a week ago Malaquias came trading jewelry, and he camped at Yellow Spring. Tomás had some whiskey, so he made his plan. He came and borrowed Pablo's buckskin; that's a fast, strong horse and hard to hold once he gets going."

There were giggles.

"Then he drove to Yellow Spring in his wagon and told this man, 'My friend, put your goods in my wagon and come to my house. I'll give you a drink, and you can have supper with me, and perhaps we can do a little business.'"

This, it seemed, was hilarious.

"So he went along, and Tomás poured whiskey for him." More laughter. "Tomás went light. All the same, they traded, and the Pueblo traded him out of that buckskin for that string of turquoise he's wearing. The poor Apache had been gypped again." Ralph's own voice shook as he said this.

"So he gave the man some more whiskey, and kept him there for supper. Meantime, his two boys—this one here and another one, who's away now— went down the road about a mile and strung wire across between two trees."

The punctuations of laughter were almost continuous.

"So Tomás gave Malaquias a hackamore for the buckskin, and Mala-

quias started for his camp after dark, and good and tight. The buckskin was
headed toward home, you understand, and Malaquias could not stop him
when he started running. So they came to that wire, and it took him just
right, under the chin, and threw him right off the horse. The horse came
on back to Pablo's."

The telling had to stop for seconds of laughter.

"Then Tomás and the boys went and got the wire, and he sent this boy
to the ranger station to tell how there was this foreign Indian lying in the
road with his neck all torn and they'd better pick him up. By and by, they
picked him up and took him to the hospital. He's still there." 10

Ralph looked about him, chuckling over the humor of it, feeling the
successful narrator's glow. His audience was given over to laughter—all
but the girl he loved, who seemed somehow alien, remote, so that he was
unusually conscious of her paleness. He caught Juanita's eye, and she
threw back her head to laugh again. Then he looked at the girl once more.
She was so still, her eyes fixed on the ground. Wanting her to share in this
as she had in so much else these last days, he forgot his satisfaction with
his performance and studied her with concern, trying to reach what was
in her mind, what was the matter. At that moment, she raised her eyes
and looked directly at him. The last traces of pleasure left his face, 20
because, as he read her now, her thoughts all laid open, he knew that
this had ended it, and that she would start home the first thing tomorrow.

# Indian Declaration
## of Independence
## from Alcatraz Island

### PROCLAMATION

*To The Great White Father and All His People*

We, the native Americans, re-claim the land known as Alcatraz Island
in the name of all American Indians by right of discovery.

We wish to be fair and honorable in our dealings with the Caucasian
inhabitants of this land, and hereby offer the following treaty:

We will purchase said Alcatraz Island for twenty-four dollars ($24)
in glass beads and red cloth, a precedent set by the white man's purchase
of a similar island about 300 years ago. We know that $24 in trade goods
for these 16 acres is more than was paid when Manhattan Island was
sold, but we know that land values have risen over the years. Our offer
of $1.24 per acre is greater than the 47¢ per acre the white men are now    10
paying the California Indians for their land.

We will give to the inhabitants of this island a portion of that land for
their own, to hold in perpetuity—for as long as the sun shall rise and the
rivers go down to the sea. We will further guide the inhabitants in the
proper way of living. We will offer them our religion, our education, our
life-ways, in order to help them achieve our level of civilization and thus
raise them and all their white brothers up from their savage and unhappy
state. We offer this treaty in good faith and wish to be fair and honorable
in our dealings with all white men.

We feel that this so-called Alcatraz Island is more than suitable for an    20
Indian Reservation, as determined by the white man's own standards.
By this we mean that this place resembles most Indian reservations,

46

in that:

1. It is isolated from modern facilities, and without adequate means of transportation.
2. It has no fresh running water.
3. It has inadequate sanitation facilities.
4. There are no oil or mineral rights.
5. There is no industry and so unemployment is very great.
6. There are no health care facilities.
7. The soil is rocky and non-productive; and the land does not support game.
8. There are no educational facilities.
9. The population has always exceeded the land base.
10. The population has always been held as prisoners and kept dependent upon others.

Further, it would be fitting and symbolic that ships from all over the world, entering the Golden Gate, would first see Indian land, and thus be reminded of the true history of this nation. This tiny island would be a symbol of the great lands once ruled by free and noble Indians.

### Proposal for Utilization of Alcatraz Island in Behalf of All Indian Tribes

Since the San Francisco Indian Center burned down, there is no place for Indians to assemble and carry on our tribal life here in the white man's city. Therefore, we plan to develop on Alcatraz several Indian institutes:

1. A Center for Native American Studies will be developed which will train our young people in the best of our native cultural arts and sciences, as well as educate them to the skills and knowledge relevant to improve the lives and spirits of all Indian peoples. Attached to this center will be traveling universities, managed by Indians, which will go to the Indian Reservations in order to learn the traditional values from the people, which are now absent in the Caucasian higher educational system.

2. An American Indian Spiritual and Medical Center will be developed which will practice our ancient tribal ceremonies and arts of healing. Our religious and cultural arts will be revitalized and our young people trained in medicine, in spiritual music, and dance.

3. An Indian Center of Ecology will be built which will train and support our young people in scientific research and practice in order to restore our lands and waters to their pure and natural state. We will seek to depollute the air and the water of the Bay Area. We will seek to restore fish and animal life, and to revitalize sea life which has been threatened by the white man's way. Facilities will be developed to desalt sea water for human use.

4. A Great Indian Training School will be developed to teach our peoples how to make a living in the world, improve our standards of living and end hunger and unemployment among all our peoples. This training school will include a center for Indian arts and crafts and an

Indian Restaurant serving native foods and training Indians in culinary arts. This center will display Indian arts and offer the Indian foods of all tribes to the public, so that all may know of the beauty and spirit of the traditional Indian ways.

5. Some of the present buildings will be taken over to develop an American Indian Museum, which will depict our native foods and other cultural contributions we have given to all the world. Another part of the Museum will present some of the things the white man has given to the Indians, in return for the land and life he took: disease, alcohol, poverty and cultural decimation (as symbolized by old tin cans, barbed wire,  10 rubber tires, plastic containers, etc.). Part of the Museum will remain a dungeon, to symbolize both those Indian captives who were incarcerated for challenging white authority, and those who were imprisoned on reservations. The Museum will show the noble and the tragic events of Indian history, including the broken treaties, the documentary of the Trail of Tears, the Massacre of Wounded Knee, as well as the victory over Yellow-Hair Custer and his army.

In the name of all Indians, therefore, we re-claim this island for our Indian nations, for all these reasons. We feel this claim is just and proper and that this land should rightfully be granted to us for as long as the  20 rivers shall run and the sun shall shine.

*Signed*

INDIANS OF ALL TRIBES
November 1969
San Francisco, California

# Helen Hunt Jackson
## From Ramona

The Señora Moreno's house was one of the best specimens to be found
in California of the representative house of the half barbaric, half elegant,
wholly generous and free-handed life led there by Mexican men and women
of degree in the early part of this century, under the rule of the Spanish
and Mexican viceroys, when the laws of the Indies were still the law of
the land, and its old name, "New Spain," was an ever-present link and
stimulus to the warmest memories and deepest patriotisms of its people.

It was a picturesque life, with more of sentiment and gayety in it, more
also that was truly dramatic, more romance, than will ever be seen again
on those sunny shores. The aroma of it all lingers there still; industries    10
and inventions have not yet slain it; it will last out its century,—in fact,
it can never be quite lost, so long as there is left standing one such house
as the Señora Moreno's.

When the house was built, General Moreno owned all the land within
a radius of forty miles,—forty miles westward, down the valley to the
sea; forty miles eastward, into the San Fernando Mountains; and good
forty miles more or less along the coast. The boundaries were not very
strictly defined; there was no occasion, in those happy days, to reckon
land by inches. It might be asked, perhaps, just how General Moreno
owned all this land and the question might not be easy to answer. It was    20
not and could not be answered to the satisfaction of the United States
Land Commission, which, after the surrender of California, undertook to
sift and adjust Mexican land titles; and that was the way it had come
about that the Señora Moreno now called herself a poor woman. Tract
after tract, her lands had been taken away from her; it looked for a time
as if nothing would be left. Every one of the claims based on deeds of

gift from Governor Pio Pico, her husband's most intimate friend, was
disallowed. They all went by the board in one batch, and took away from
the Señora in a day the greater part of her best pasture-lands. They were
lands which had belonged to the Bonaventura Mission, and lay along
the coast at the mouth of the valley down which the little stream which
ran past her house went to the sea; and it had been a great pride and
delight to the Señora, when she was young, to ride that forty miles by her
husband's side, all the way on their own lands, straight from their house
to their own strip of shore. No wonder she believed the Americans thieves,
and spoke of them always as hounds. The people of the United States       10
have never in the least realized that the taking possession of California
was not only a conquering of Mexico, but a conquering of California as
well; that the real bitterness of the surrender was not so much to the
empire which gave up the country, as to the country itself which was
given up. Provinces passed back and forth in that way, helpless in the
hands of great powers, have all the ignominy and humiliation of defeat,
with none of the dignities or compensations of the transaction.

Mexico saved much by her treaty, in spite of having to acknowledge
herself beaten; but California lost all. Words cannot tell the sting of such
a transfer. It is a marvel that a Mexican remained in the country; probably   20
none did, except those who were absolutely forced to it.

Luckily for the Señora Moreno, her title to the lands midway in the
valley was better than to those lying to the east and the west, which had
once belonged to the missions of San Fernando and Bonaventura; and
after all the claims, counter-claims, petitions, appeals, and adjudications
were ended, she still was left in undisputed possession of what would
have been thought by any new-comer into the country to be a handsome
estate, but which seemed to the despoiled and indignant Señora a pitiful
fragment of one. Moreover, she declared that she should never feel secure
of a foot of even this. Any day, she said, the United States Government   30
might send out a new Land Commission to examine the decrees of the
first, and revoke such as they saw fit. Once a thief, always a thief. Nobody
need feel himself safe under American rule. There was no knowing what
might happen any day; and year by year the lines of sadness, resentment,
anxiety, and antagonism deepened on the Señora's fast aging face.

It gave her unspeakable satisfaction, when the Commissioners, laying
out a road down the valley, ran it at the back of her house instead of past
the front. "It is well," she said. "Let their travel be where it belongs, behind
our kitchens; and no one have sight of the front doors of our houses,
except friends who have come to visit us." Her enjoyment of this never   40
flagged. Whenever she saw, passing the place, wagons or carriages belonging to the hated Americans, it gave her a distant thrill of pleasure to
think that the house turned its back on them. She would like always to
be able to do the same herself; but whatever she, by policy or in business,
might be forced to do, the old house, at any rate, would always keep the
attitude of contempt, —its face turned away.

One other pleasure she provided herself with, soon after this road was opened,—a pleasure in which religious devotion and race antagonism were so closely blended that it would have puzzled the subtlest of priests to decide whether her act were a sin or a virtue. She caused to be set up, upon every one of the soft rounded hills which made the beautiful rolling sides of that part of the valley, a large wooden cross; not a hill in sight of her house left without the sacred emblem of her faith. "That the heretics may know, when they go by, that they are on the estate of a good Catholic," she said, "and that the faithful may be reminded to pray. There have been miracles of conversion wrought on the most hardened by a sudden sight of the Blessed Cross."

There they stood, summer and winter, rain and shine, the silent, solemn, outstretched arms, and became landmarks to many a guideless traveller who had been told that his way would be by the first turn to the left or the right, after passing the last one of the Señora Moreno's crosses, which he couldn't miss seeing. And who shall say that it did not often happen that the crosses bore a sudden message to some idle heart journeying by, and thus justified the pious half of the Señora's impulse? Certain it is, that many a good Catholic halted and crossed himself when he first beheld them, in the lonely places, standing out in sudden relief against the blue sky; and if he said a swift short prayer at the sight, was he not so much the better?

The house was of adobe, low, with a wide veranda on the three sides of the inner court, and a still broader one across the entire front, which looked to the south. These verandas, especially those on the inner court, were supplementary rooms to the house. The greater part of the family life went on in them. Nobody stayed inside the walls, except when it was necessary. All the kitchen work, except the actual cooking, was done here, in front of the kitchen doors and windows. Babies slept, were washed, sat in the dirt, and played, on the veranda. The women said their prayers, took their naps, and wove their lace there. Old Juanita shelled her beans there, and threw the pods down on the tile floor, till towards night they were sometimes piled up high around her, like cornhusks at a husking. The herdsmen and shepherds smoked there, lounged there, trained their dogs there; there the young made love, and the old dozed; the benches, which ran the entire length of the walls, were worn into hollows, and shone like satin; the tiled floors also were broken and sunk in places, making little wells, which filled up in times of hard rains, and were then an invaluable addition to the children's resources for amusement, and also to the comfort of the dogs, cats, and fowls, who picked about among them, taking sips from each.

The arched veranda along the front was a delightsome place. It must have been eighty feet long, at least, for the doors of five large rooms opened on it. The two westernmost rooms had been added on, and made four steps higher than the others; which gave to that end of the veranda the look of a balcony, or loggia. Here the Señora kept her flowers; great red water-

jars, hand-made by the Indians of Săn Luis Obispo Mission, stood in close
rows against the walls, and in them were always growing fine geraniums,
carnations, and yellow-flowered musk. The Señora's passion for musk she
had inherited from her mother. It was so strong that she sometimes
wondered at it; and one day, as she sat with Father Salvierderra in the
veranda, she picked a handful of the blossoms, and giving them to him,
said, "I do not know why it is, but it seems to me if I were dead I could
be brought to life by the smell of musk."

"It is in your blood, Señora," the old monk replied. "When I was last
in your father's house in Seville, your mother sent for me to her room,   10
and under her window was a stone balcony full of growing musk, which
so filled the room with its odor that I was like to faint. But she said it
cured her of diseases, and without it she fell ill. You were a baby then."

"Yes," cried the Señora, "but I recollect that balcony. I recollect being
lifted up to a window, and looking down into a bed of blooming yellow
flowers; but I did not know what they were. How strange!"

"No. Not strange, daughter," replied Father Salvierderra. "It would
have been stranger if you had not acquired the taste, thus drawing it in
with the mother's milk. It would behoove mothers to remember this far
more than they do."                                                        20

Besides the geraniums and carnations and musk in the red jars, there
were many sorts of climbing vines,—some coming from the ground, and
twining around the pillars of the veranda; some growing in great bowls,
swung by cords from the roof of the veranda, or set on shelves against
the walls. These bowls were of gray stone, hollowed and polished, shining
smooth inside and out. They also had been made by the Indians, nobody
knew how many ages ago, scooped and polished by the patient creatures,
with only stones for tools.

Among these vines, singing from morning till night, hung the Señora's
canaries and finches, half a dozen of each, all of different generations,   30
raised by the Señora. She was never without a young bird-family on
hand; and all the way from Bonaventura to Monterey, it was thought a
piece of good luck to come into possession of a canary or finch of Señora
Moreno's raising.

Between the veranda and the river meadows, out on which it looked,
all was garden, orange grove, and almond orchard; the orange grove
always green, never without snowy bloom or golden fruit; the garden
never without flowers, summer or winter; and the almond orchard, in
early spring, a fluttering canopy of pink and white petals, which, seen from
the hills on the opposite side of the river, looked as if rosy sunrise clouds   40
had fallen, and become tangled in the tree-tops. On either hand stretched
away other orchards,—peach, apricot, pear, apple, pomegranate; and
beyond these, vineyards. Nothing was to be seen but verdure or bloom
or fruit, at whatever time of year you sat on the Señora's south veranda.

A wide straight walk shaded by a trellis so knotted and twisted with
grapevines that little was to be seen of the trellis wood-work, led straight

down from the veranda steps, through the middle of the garden, to a little
brook at the foot of it. Across this brook, in the shade of a dozen gnarled
old willow-trees, were set the broad flat stone washboards on which was
done all the family washing. No long dawdling, and no running away
from work on the part of the maids, thus close to the eye of the Señora
at the upper end of the garden; and if they had known how picturesque
they looked there, kneeling on the grass, lifting the dripping linen out of
the water, rubbing it back and forth on the stones, sousing it, wringing
it, splashing the clear water in each other's faces, they would have been
content to stay at the washing day in and day out, for there was always   10
somebody to look on from above. Hardly a day passed that the Señora had
not visitors. She was still a person of note; her house the natural resting
place for all who journeyed through the valley; and whoever came, spent
all of his time, when not eating, sleeping, or walking over the place, sitting
with the Señora on the sunny veranda. Few days in winter were cold
enough, and in summer the day must be hot indeed to drive the Señora
and her friends indoors. There stood on the veranda three carved oaken
chairs, and a carved bench, also of oak, which had been brought to the
Señora for safe keeping by the faithful old sacristan of San Luis Rey, at
the time of the occupation of that Mission by the United States troops,   20
soon after the conquest of California. Aghast at the sacrilegious acts of the
soldiers, who were quartered in the very church itself, and amused themselves by making targets of the eyes and noses of the saints' statues, the
sacristan, stealthily, day by day and night after night, bore out of the
church all that he dared to remove, burying some articles in cottonwood
copses, hiding others in his own poor little hovel, until he had wagonloads
of sacred treasures. Then, still more stealthily, he carried them, a few at
a time, concealed in the bottom of a cart, under a load of hay or of brush,
to the house of the Señora, who felt herself deeply honored by his confidence, and received everything as a sacred trust, to be given back into the   30
hands of the Church again, whenever the Missions should be restored, of
which at that time all Catholics had good hope. And so it had come about
that no bedroom in the Señora's house was without a picture or a statue
of a saint or of the Madonna; and some had two; and in the little chapel
in the garden the altar was surrounded by a really imposing row of holy
and apostolic figures, which had looked down on the splendid ceremonies
of the San Luis Rey Mission, in Father Peyri's time, no more benignly
than they now did on the humbler worship of the Señora's family in its
diminished estate. That one had lost an eye, another an arm, that the
once brilliant colors of the drapery were now faded and shabby, only   40
enhanced the tender reverence with which the Señora knelt before them,
her eyes filling with indignant tears at thought of the heretic hands which
had wrought such defilement. Even the crumbling wreaths which had been
placed on some of these statues' heads at the time of the last ceremonial
at which they had figured in the Mission, had been brought away with
them by the devout sacristan, and the Señora had replaced each one, hold-

ing it only a degree less sacred than the statue itself.

This chapel was dearer to the Señora than her house. It had been built by the General in the second year of their married life. In it her four children had been christened, and from it all but one, her handsome Felipe, had been buried while they were yet infants. In the General's time, while the estate was at its best, and hundreds of Indians living within its borders, there was many a Sunday when the scene to be witnessed there was like the scenes at the Missions, — the chapel full of kneeling men and women; those who could not find room inside kneeling on the garden walks outside; Father Salvierderra, in gorgeous vestments, coming, at         10
close of the services, slowly down the aisle, the close-packed rows of worshippers parting to right and left to let him through, all looking up eagerly for his blessing, women giving him offerings of fruit or flowers, and holding up their babies that he might lay his hands on their heads. No one but Father Salvierderra had ever officiated in the Moreno chapel, or heard the confession of a Moreno. He was a Franciscan, one of the few now left in the country; so revered and beloved by all who had come under his influence, that they would wait long months without the offices of the church, rather than confess their sins or confide their perplexities to any one else. From this deep-seated attachment on the part of the          20
Indians and the older Mexican families in the country to the Franciscan Order, there had grown up, not unnaturally, some jealousy of them in the minds of the later-come secular priests, and the position of the few monks left was not wholly a pleasant one. It had even been rumored that they were to be forbidden to continue longer their practice of going up and down the country, ministering everywhere; were to be compelled to restrict their labors to their own colleges at Santa Barbara and Santa Inez. When something to this effect was one day said in the Señora Moreno s presence, two scarlet spots sprang on her cheeks, and before she bethought herself, she exclaimed, "That day, I burn down my chapel!"                  30

Luckily, nobody but Felipe heard the rash threat, and his exclamation of unbounded astonishment recalled the Señora to herself.

"I spoke rashly, my son," she said. "The Church is to be obeyed always; but the Franciscan Fathers are responsible to no one but the Superior of their own order; and there is no one in this land who has the authority to forbid their journeying and ministering to whoever desires their offices. As for these Catalan priests who are coming in here, I cannot abide them. No Catalan but has bad blood in his veins!"

There was every reason in the world why the Señora should be thus warmly attached to the Franciscan Order. From her earliest recollections         40
the gray gown and cowl had been familiar to her eyes, and had represented the things which she was taught to hold most sacred and dear. Father Salvierderra himself had come from Mexico to Monterey in the same ship which had brought her father to be the commandante of the Santa Barbara Presidio; and her best-beloved uncle, her father's eldest brother, was at that time the Superior of the Santa Barbara Mission. The sentiment and

romance of her youth were almost equally divided between the gayeties, excitements, adornments of the life at the Presidio, and the ceremonies and devotions of the life at the Mission. She was famed as the most beautiful girl in the country. Men of the army, men of the navy, and men of the Church, alike adored her. Her name was a toast from Monterey to San Diego. When at last she was wooed and won by Felipe Moreno, one of the most distinguished of the Mexican generals, her wedding cere-monies were the most splendid ever seen in the country. The right tower of the Mission church at Santa Barbara had been just completed, and it was arranged that the consecration of this tower should take place at the       10 time of her wedding, and that her wedding feast should be spread in the long outside corridor of the Mission building. The whole country, far and near, was bid. The feast lasted three days; open tables to everybody; singing, dancing, eating, drinking, and making merry. At that time there were long streets of Indian houses stretching eastward from the Mission; before each of these houses was built a booth of green boughs. The In-dians, as well as the Fathers from all the other Missions, were invited to come. The Indians came in bands, singing songs and bringing gifts. As they appeared, the Santa Barbara Indians went out to meet them, also singing, bearing gifts, and strewing seeds on the ground, in token of       20 welcome. The young Señora and her bridegroom, splendidly clothed, were seen of all, and greeted, whenever they appeared, by showers of seeds and grains and blossoms. On the third day, still in their wedding attire, and bearing lighted candles in their hands, they walked with the monks in a procession, round and round the new tower, the monks chant-ing, and sprinkling incense and holy water on its walls, the ceremony seeming to all devout beholders to give a blessed consecration to the union of the young pair as well as to the newly completed tower. After this they journeyed in state, accompanied by several of the General's aids and officers, and by two Franciscan Fathers, up to Monterey, stop-       30 ping on their way at all the Missions, and being warmly welcomed and entertained at each.

General Moreno was much beloved by both army and Church. In many of the frequent clashings between the military and the ecclesiastical powers he, being as devout and enthusiastic a Catholic as he was zealous and enthusiastic a soldier, had had the good fortune to be of material assistance to each party. The Indians also knew his name well, having heard it many times mentioned with public thanksgivings in the Mission churches, after some signal service he had rendered to the Fathers either in Mexico or Monterey. And now, by taking as his bride the daughter of a       40 distinguished officer, and the niece of the Santa Barbara Superior, he had linked himself anew to the two dominant powers and interests of the country.

When they reached San Luis Obispo, the whole Indian population turned out to meet them, the Padre walking at the head. As they ap-proached the Mission doors the Indians swarmed closer and closer and still closer, took the General's horse by the head, and finally almost by actual force compelled him to allow himself to be lifted into a blanket, held high up by twenty strong men; and thus he was borne up the steps across the corridor, and into the Padre's room. It was a position ludicrously undignified in itself, but the General submitted to it good-naturedly.

"Oh, let them do it, if they like," he cried, laughingly, to Padre Martinez, who was endeavoring to quiet the Indians and hold them back; "Let them do it. It pleases the poor creatures."

On the morning of their departure, the good Padre, having exhausted all his resources for entertaining his distinguished guests, caused to be driven past the corridors, for their inspection, all the poultry belonging to the Mission. The procession took an hour to pass. For music, there was the squeaking, cackling, hissing, gobbling, crowing, quacking of the excited Indian marshals of the lines. First came the turkeys, then the roosters, then the white hens, then the black and then the yellow; next the ducks, and at the tail of the spectacle long files of geese, some strutting, some half flying and hissing in resentment and terror at the unwonted coercions to which they were subjected. The Indians had been hard at work all night capturing, sorting, assorting, and guarding the rank and file of their novel pageant. It would be safe to say that a droller sight never was seen, and never will be, on the Pacific coast or any other. Before it was done with, the General and his bride had nearly died with laughter; and the General could never allude to it without laughing almost as heartily again.

At Monterey they were more magnificently feted; at the Presidio, at the Mission, on board Spanish, Mexican, and Russian ships lying in harbor, balls, dances, bull-fights, dinners, all that the country knew of festivity, was lavished on the beautiful and winning young bride. The belles of the coast, from San Diego up, had all gathered at Monterey for these gayeties; but not one of them could be for a moment compared to her. This was the beginning of the Señora's life as a married woman. She was then just twenty. A close observer would have seen even then, underneath the joyous smile, the laughing eye, the merry voice, a look thoughtful, tender, earnest, at times enthusiastic. This look was the reflection of those qualities in her, then hardly aroused, which made her, as years developed her character and stormy fates thickened around her life, the unflinching comrade of her soldier husband, the passionate adherent of the Church. Through wars, insurrections, revolutions, downfalls, Spanish, Mexican, civil, ecclesiastical, her standpoint, her poise, remained the same. She simply grew more and more proudly, passionately, a Spaniard and a Moreno; more and more stanchly and fierily a Catholic, and a lover of the Franciscans.

During the height of the despoiling and plundering of the Missions, under the Secularization Act, she was for a few years almost beside herself. More than once she journeyed alone, when the journey was by no means without danger, to Monterey, to stir up the Prefect of the Missions

to more energetic action, to implore the governmental authorities to interfere, and protect the Church's property. It was largely in consequence
of her eloquent entreaties that Governor Micheltorena issued his bootless
order, restoring to the Church all the Missions south of San Luis Obispo.
But this order cost Micheltorena his political head, and General Moreno
was severely wounded in one of the skirmishes of the insurrection which
drove Micheltorena out of the country.

In silence and bitter humiliation the Señora nursed her husband back
to health again, and resolved to meddle no more in the affairs of her unhappy country and still more unhappy Church. As year by year she saw     10
the ruin of the Missions steadily going on, their vast properties melting
away, like dew before the sun, in the hands of dishonest administrators
and politicians, the Church powerless to contend with the unprincipled
greed in high places, her beloved Franciscan Fathers driven from the
country or dying of starvation at their posts, she submitted herself to
what, she was forced to admit, seemed to be the inscrutable will of God
for the discipline and humiliation of the Church. In a sort of bewildered
resignation she waited to see what farther sufferings were to come, to
fill up the measure of the punishment which, for some mysterious purpose, the faithful must endure. But when close upon all this discomfiture   20
and humiliation of her Church followed the discomfiture and humiliation
of her country in war, and the near and evident danger of an English-
speaking people's possessing the land, all the smothered fire of the Señora's nature broke out afresh. With unfaltering hands she buckled on her
husband's sword, and with dry eyes saw him go forth to fight. She had
but one regret, that she was not the mother of sons to fight also.

"Would thou wert a man, Felipe," she exclaimed again and again in
tones the child never forgot. "Would thou wert a man, that thou might
go also to fight these foreigners!"

Any race under the sun would have been to the Señora less hateful than   30
the American. She had scorned them in her girlhood, when they came
trading to post after post. She scorned them still. The idea of being forced
to wage a war with peddlers was to her too monstrous to be believed. In
the outset she had no doubt that the Mexicans would win in the contest.

"What!" she cried, "shall we who won independence from Spain, be
beaten by these traders? It is impossible!"

When her husband was brought home to her dead, killed in the last
fight the Mexican forces made, she said icily, "He would have chosen to
die rather than to have been forced to see his country in the hands of the
enemy." And she was almost frightened at herself to see how this thought,   40
as it dwelt in her mind, slew the grief in her heart. She had believed she
could not live if her husband were to be taken away from her; but she
found herself often glad that he was dead, — glad that he was spared the
sight and the knowledge of the things which happened; and even the
yearning tenderness with which her imagination pictured him among the
saints, was often turned into a fierce wondering whether indignation did

not fill his soul, even in heaven, at the way things were going in the land for whose sake he had died.

Out of such throes as these had been born the second nature which made Señora Moreno the silent, reserved, stern, implacable woman they knew, who knew her first when she was sixty. Of the gay tender, sentimental girl, who danced and laughed with the officers, and prayed and confessed with the Fathers, forty years before, there was small trace left now, in the low-voiced, white-haired, aged woman, silent, unsmiling, placid-faced, who manoeuvred with her son and her head shepherd alike, to bring it about that a handful of Indians might once more confess their   10 sins to a Franciscan monk in the Moreno chapel.

# Ozzie G. Simmons
## The Mutual Images and Expectations of Anglo-Americans and Mexican-Americans

A number of psychological and sociological studies have treated ethnic and racial stereotypes as they appear publicly in the mass media and also as held privately by individuals. The present paper is based on data collected for a study of a number of aspects of the relations between Anglo-Americans and Mexican-Americans in a South Texas community, and is concerned with the principal assumptions and expectations that Anglo- and Mexican-Americans hold of one another; how they see each other; the extent to which these pictures are realistic; and the implications of their intergroup relations and cultural differences for the fulfillment of their mutual expectations.                                      *10*

## THE COMMUNITY

The community studied (here called "Border City") is in South Texas, about 250 miles south of San Antonio. Driving south from San Antonio, one passes over vast expanses of brushland and grazing country, then suddenly comes upon acres of citrus groves, farmlands rich with vegetables and cotton, and long rows of palm trees. This is the "Magic Valley", an oasis in the semidesert region of South Texas. The Missouri Pacific Railroad (paralleled by Highway 83, locally called "The longest street in the world") bisects twelve major towns and cities of the Lower Rio    *20* Grande Valley between Brownsville, near the Gulf of Mexico, and Rio Grande City, 103 miles to the west.

Border City is neither the largest nor the smallest of these cities, and is physically and culturally much like the rest. Its first building was constructed in 1905. By 1920 it had 5,331 inhabitants, and at the time of our study these had increased to an estimated 17,500. The completion of

the St. Louis, Brownsville, and Mexico Railroad in 1904 considerably
facilitated Anglo-American immigration to the Valley. Before this the valley had been inhabited largely by Mexican ranchers, who maintained large
haciendas in the traditional Mexican style based on peonage. Most of these
haciendas are now divided into large or small tracts that are owned by
Anglo-Americans, who obtained them through purchase or less legitimate
means. The position of the old Mexican-American landowning families
has steadily deteriorated, and today these families, with a few exceptions,
are completely overshadowed by the Anglo-Americans, who have taken
over their social and economic position in the community.                        10

The Anglo-American immigration into the Valley was paralleled by that
of the Mexicans from across the border, who were attracted by the seemingly greater opportunities for farm labor created by the introduction of
irrigation and the subsequent agricultural expansion. Actually, there had
been a small but steady flow of Mexican immigration into South Texas
that long antedated the Anglo-American immigration. At present, Mexican-
Americans probably constitute about two-fifths of the total population
of the Valley.

In Border City, Mexican-Americans comprise about 56 percent of the
population. The southwestern part of the city, adjoining and sometimes        20
infiltrating the business and industrial areas, is variously referred to as
"Mexiquita," "Mexican-town" and "Little Mexico" by the city's Anglo-
Americans, and as the *colonia* by the Mexican-Americans. With few
exceptions, the *colonia* is inhabited only by Mexican-Americans, most of
whom live in close proximity to one another in indifferently constructed
houses on tiny lots. The north side of the city, which lies across the railroad tracks, is inhabited almost completely by Anglo-Americans. Its
appearance is in sharp contrast to that of the *colonia* in that it is strictly
residential and displays much better housing.

In the occupational hierarchy of Border City, the top level (the growers,   30
packers, canners, businessmen, and professionals) is overwhelmingly
Anglo-American. In the middle group (the white-collar occupations)
Mexicans are prominent only where their bilingualism makes them
useful, for example, as clerks and salesmen. The bottom level (farm
laborers, shed and cannery workers, and domestic servants) is overwhelmingly Mexican-American.

These conditions result from a number of factors, some quite distinct
from the reception accorded Mexican-Americans by Anglo-Americans.
Many Mexican-Americans are still recent immigrants and are thus relatively unfamiliar with Anglo-American culture and urban living, or else   40
persist in their tendency to live apart and maintain their own institutions
whenever possible. Among their disadvantages, however, the negative
attitudes and discriminatory practices of the Anglo-American group must
be counted. It is only fair to say, with the late Ruth Tuck, that much of
what Mexican-Americans have suffered at Anglo-American hands has
not been perpetrated deliberately but through indifference, that it has

been done not with the fist but with the elbow. The average social and economic status of the Mexican-American group has been improving, and many are moving upward. This is partly owing to increasing acceptance by the Anglo-American group, but chiefly to the efforts of the Mexican-Americans themselves.

### ANGLO-AMERICAN ASSUMPTIONS AND EXPECTATIONS

Robert Lynd writes of the dualism in the principal assumptions that guide Americans in conducting their everyday life and identifies the attempt to "live by contrasting rules of the game" as a characteristic  10
aspect of our culture. This pattern of moral compromise, symptomatic of what is likely to be only vaguely a conscious moral conflict, is evident in Anglo-American assumptions and expectations with regard to Mexican-Americans, which appear both in the moral principles that define what intergroup relations ought to be, and in the popular notions held by Anglo-Americans as to what Mexican-Americans are "really" like. In the first case there is a response to the "American creed," which embodies ideals of the essential dignity of the individual and of certain inalienable rights to freedom, justice, and equal opportunity. Accordingly, Anglo-Americans believe that Mexican-Americans must be accorded full acceptance and  20
equal status in the larger society. When their orientation to these ideals is uppermost, Anglo-Americans believe that the assimilation of Mexican-Americans is only a matter of time, contingent solely on the full incorporation of Anglo-American values and ways of life.

These expectations regarding the assimilation of the Mexican are most clearly expressed in the notion of the "high type" of Mexican. It is based on three criteria: occupational achievement and wealth (the Anglo-American's own principal criteria of status) and command of Anglo-American ways. Mexican-Americans who can so qualify are acceptable for membership in the service clubs and a few other Anglo-American  30
organizations and for limited social intercourse. They may even intermarry without being penalized or ostracized. Both in their achievements in business and agriculture and in wealth, they compare favorably with middle-class Anglo-Americans, and they manifest a high command of the latter's ways. This view of the "high type" of Mexican reflects the Anglo-American assumption that Mexicans are assimilable; it does not necessarily insure a full acceptance of even the "high type" of Mexican or that his acceptance will be consistent.

The assumption that Mexican-Americans will be ultimately assimilated was not uniformly shared by all the Anglo-Americans who were our  40
informants in Border City. Regardless of whether they expressed adherence to this ideal, however, most Anglo-Americans expressed the contrasting assumption that Mexican-Americans are essentially inferior. Thus the same people may hold assumptions and expectations that are contradictory, although expressed at different times and in different situations. As in the case of their adherence to the ideal of assimilability,

not all Anglo-Americans hold the same assumptions and expectations with respect to the inferiority of Mexican-Americans; and even those who agree vary in the intensity of their beliefs. Some do not believe in the Mexican's inferiority at all; some are relatively moderate or sceptical, while others express extreme views with considerable emotional intensity.

Despite this variation, the Anglo-Americans' principal assumptions and expectations emphasize the Mexicans' presumed inferiority. In its most characteristic pattern, such inferiority is held to be self-evident. As one Anglo-American woman put it, "Mexicans are inferior because they are so typically and naturally Mexican." Since they are so obviously inferior, their present subordinate status is appropriate and is really their own fault. There is a ready identification between Mexicans and menial labor, buttressed by an image of the Mexican worker as improvident, undependable, irresponsible, childlike, and indolent. If Mexicans are fit for only the humblest labor, there is nothing abnormal about the fact that most Mexican workers are at the bottom of the occupational pyramid, and the fact that most Mexicans are unskilled workers is sufficient proof that they belong in that category.

Associated with the assumption of Mexican inferiority is that of the homogeneity of this group—that is, all Mexicans are alike. Anglo-Americans may classify Mexicans as being of "high type" and "low type" and at the same time maintain that "a Mexican is a Mexican." Both notions serve a purpose, depending on the situation. The assumption that all Mexicans are alike buttresses the assumption of inferiority by making it convenient to ignore the fact of the existence of a substantial number of Mexican-Americans who represent all levels of business and professional achievement. Such people are considered exceptions to the rule.

## ANGLO-AMERICAN IMAGES OF MEXICAN-AMERICANS

To employ Gordon Allport's definition, a stereotype is an exaggerated belief associated with a category, and its function is to justify conduct in relation to that category. Some of the Anglo-American images of the Mexican have no ascertainable basis in fact, while others have at least a kernel of truth. Although some components of these images derive from behavior patterns that are characteristic of some Mexican-Americans in some situations, few if any of the popular generalizations about them are valid as stated, and none is demonstrably true of all. Some of the images of Mexican-Americans are specific to a particular area of intergroup relations, such as the image of the Mexican-American's attributes as a worker. Another is specific to politics and describes Mexicans as ready to give their votes to whoever will pay for them or provide free barbecues and beer. Let us consider a few of the stereotypical beliefs that are widely used on general principles to justify Anglo-American practices of exclusion and subordination.

One such general belief accuses Mexican-Americans of being unclean. The examples given of this supposed characteristic most frequently refer to a lack of personal cleanliness and environmental hygiene and to a high incidence of skin ailments ascribed to a lack of hygienic practices. Indeed, there are few immigrant groups, regardless of their ethnic background, to whom this defect has not been attributed by the host society, as well as others prominent in stereotypes of the Mexican. It has often been observed that for middle-class Americans cleanliness is not simply a matter of keeping clean but is also an index to the morals and virtues of the individual. It is largely true that Mexicans tend to be much more casual in hygienic practices than Anglo-Americans. Moreover, their labor in the field, the packing sheds, and the towns is rarely clean work, and it is possible that many Anglo-Americans base their conclusions on what they observe in such situations. There is no evidence of a higher incidence of skin ailments among Mexicans than among Anglo-Americans. The belief that Mexicans are unclean is useful for rationalizing the Anglo-American practice of excluding Mexicans from any situation that involves close or allegedly close contact with Anglo-Americans, as in residence, and the common use of swimming pools and other recreational facilities.

Drunkenness and criminality are a pair of traits that have appeared regularly in the stereotypes applied to immigrant groups. They have a prominent place in Anglo-American images of Mexicans. If Mexicans are inveterate drunkards and have criminal tendencies, a justification is provided for excluding them from full participation in the life of the community. It is true that drinking is a popular activity among Mexican-Americans and that total abstinence is rare, except among some Protestant Mexican-Americans. Drinking varies, however, from the occasional consumption of a bottle of beer to the heavy drinking of more potent beverages, so that the frequency of drinking and drunkenness is far from being evenly distributed among Mexican-Americans. Actually, this pattern is equally applicable to the Anglo-American group. The ample patronage of bars in the Anglo-American part of Border City, and the drinking behavior exhibited by Anglo-Americans when they cross the river to Mexico indicate that Mexicans have no monopoly on drinking or drunkenness. It is true that the number of arrests for drunkenness in Border City is greater among Mexicans, but this is probably because Mexicans are more vulnerable to arrest. The court records in Border City show little difference in the contributions made to delinquency and crime by Anglo- and Mexican-Americans.

Another type of image in the Anglo-American stereotype portrays Mexican-Americans as deceitful and of a "low" morality, as mysterious, unpredictable, and hostile to Anglo-Americans. It is quite possible that Mexicans resort to a number of devices in their relations with Anglo-Americans, particularly in relations with employers, to compensate for their disadvantages, which may be construed by Anglo-Americans as evidence of deceitfulness. The whole nature of the dominant-subordinate relationship does not make for frankness on the part of Mexicans or encourage them to face up directly to Anglo-Americans in most intergroup contacts. As to the charge of immorality, one need only recognize the strong sense of loyalty and obligation that Mexicans feel in their familial and interpersonal relations to know that the charge is baseless. The claim that Mexicans are mysterious and deceitful may in part reflect Anglo-American reactions to actual differences in culture and personality, but like the other beliefs considered here, is highly exaggerated. The imputation of hostility to Mexicans, which is manifested in a reluctance to enter the *colonia,* particularly at night, may have its kernel of truth, but appears to be largely a projection of the Anglo-American's own feelings.

All three of these images can serve to justify exclusion and discrimination:          10
if Mexicans are deceitful and immoral, they do not have to be accorded equal status and justice; if they are mysterious and unpredictable, there is no point in treating them as one would a fellow Anglo-American; and if they are hostile and dangerous, it is best that they live apart in colonies of their own.

Not all Anglo-American images of the Mexican are unfavorable. Among those usually meant to be complimentary are the beliefs that all Mexicans are musical and always ready for a fiesta, that they are very "romantic" rather than "realistic" (which may have unfavorable overtones as well), and that they love flowers and can grow them under the most adverse          20
conditions. Although each of these beliefs may have a modicum of truth, it may be noted that they tend to reinforce Anglo-American images of Mexicans as childlike and irresponsible, and thus they support the notion that Mexicans are capable only of subordinate status.

## MEXICAN-AMERICAN ASSUMPTIONS, EXPECTATIONS, AND IMAGES

Mexican-Americans are likely to hold contradictory assumptions and distorted images as are Anglo-Americans. Their principal assumptions, however, must reflect those of Anglo-Americans—that is, Mexicans must          30
take into account the Anglo-Americans' conflict as to their potential equality and present inferiority, since they are the object of such imputations. Similarly, their images of Anglo-Americans are not derived wholly independently, but to some extent must reflect their own subordinate status. Consequently, their stereotypes of Anglo-Americans are much less elaborate, in part because Mexicans feel no need of justifying the present intergroup relation, in part because the very nature of their dependent position forces them to view the relation more realistically than Anglo-Americans do. For the same reasons, they need not hold to their beliefs about Anglo-Americans with the rigidity and intensity so often char-          40
acteristic of the latter.

Any discussion of these assumptions and expectations requires some mention of the class distinctions within the Mexican-American group. Its middle class, though small as compared with the lower class, is powerful within the group and performs the critical role of intermediary in negotiations with the Anglo-American group. Middle-class status is based on education and occupation, family background, readiness to serve the interests of the group, on wealth, and the degree of acculturation, or command of Anglo-American ways. Anglo-Americans recognize Mexican class distinctions (although not very accurately) in their notions of the "high type" and "low type" of Mexicans.

In general, lower-class Mexicans do not regard the disabilities of their status as being nearly as severe as do middle-class Mexican-Americans. This is primarily a reflection of the insulation between the Anglo-American world and that of the Mexican lower class. Most Mexicans, regardless of class, are keenly aware of Anglo-American attitudes and practices with regard to their group, but lower-class Mexicans do not conceive of participation in the larger city society as necessary nor do they regard Anglo-American practices of exclusion as affecting them directly. Their principal reaction has been to maintain their isolation, and thus they have not been particularly concerned with improving their status by acquiring Anglo-American ways, a course more characteristic of the middle-class Mexican.

Mexican-American assumptions and expectations regarding Anglo-Americans must be qualified, then, as being more characteristic of middle- than of lower-class Mexican-Americans. Mexicans, like Anglo-Americans, are subject to conflicts in their ideals, not only because of irrational thinking on their part but also because of Anglo-American inconsistencies between ideal and practice. As for ideals expressing democratic values, Mexican expectations are for obvious reasons the counterpart of the Anglo-Americans—that Mexican-Americans should be accorded full acceptance and equal opportunity. They feel a considerable ambivalence, however, as to the Anglo-American expectation that the only way to achieve this goal is by a full incorporation of Anglo-American values and ways of life, for this implies the ultimate loss of their cultural identity as Mexicans. On the one hand, they favor the acquisition of Anglo-American culture and the eventual remaking of the Mexican in the Anglo-American image; but on the other hand, they are not so sure that Anglo-American acceptance is worth such a price. When they are concerned with this dilemma, Mexicans advocate a fusion with Anglo-American culture in which the "best" of the Mexican ways, as they view it, would be retained along with the incorporation of the "best" of the Anglo-American ways, rather than a one-sided exchange in which all that is distinctively Mexican would be lost.

A few examples will illustrate the point of view expressed in the phrase, "the best of both ways." A premium is placed on speaking good, unaccented English, but the retention of good Spanish is valued just as highly as "a mark of culture that should not be abandoned." Similarly, there is an emphasis on the incorporation of behavior patterns that are considered characteristically Anglo-American and that will promote "getting ahead," but not to the point at which the drive for power and wealth would become completely dominant, as is believed to be the case with Anglo-Americans.

Mexican ambivalence about becoming Anglo-American or achieving a fusion of the "best" of both cultures is compounded by their ambivalence about another issue, that of equality versus inferiority. That Anglo-Americans are dominant in the society and seem to monopolize its accomplishments and rewards leads Mexicans at times to draw the same conclusion that Anglo-Americans do, namely, that Mexicans are inferior. This questioning of their own sense of worth exists in all classes of the Mexican-American group, although with varying intensity, and plays a substantial part in every adjustment to intergroup relations. There is a pronounced tendency to concede the superiority of Anglo-American ways and consequently to define Mexican ways as undesirable, inferior, and disreputable. The tendency to believe in his own inferiority is counterbalanced, however, by the Mexican's fierce racial pride, which sets the tone of Mexican demands and strivings for equal status, even though these may slip into feelings of inferiority.

The images Mexicans have of Anglo-Americans may not be so elaborate or so emotionally charged as the images that Anglo-Americans have of Mexicans, but they are nevertheless stereotypes, overgeneralized, and exaggerated, although used primarily for defensive rather than justificatory purposes. Mexican images of Anglo-Americans are sometimes favorable, particularly when they identify such traits as initiative, ambition, and industriousness as being peculiarly Anglo-American. Unfavorable images are prominent, however, and, although they may be hostile, they never impute inferiority to Anglo-Americans. Most of the Mexican stereotypes evaluate Anglo-Americans on the basis of their attitudes towards Mexican-Americans. For example, one such classification provides a two-fold typology. The first type, the "majority," includes those who are cold, unkind, mercenary, and exploitative. The second type, the "minority," consists of those who are friendly, warm, just, and unprejudiced. For the most part, Mexican images of Anglo-Americans reflect the latter's patterns of exclusion and assumptions of superiority, as experienced by Mexican-Americans. Thus Anglo-Americans are pictured as stolid, phlegmatic, cold-hearted, and distant. They are also said to be braggarts, conceited, inconstant, and insincere.

## INTERGROUP RELATIONS, MUTUAL EXPECTATIONS, AND CULTURAL DIFFERENCES

A number of students of intergroup relations assert that research in this area has yet to demonstrate any relation between stereotypical beliefs and intergroup behavior; indeed, some insist that under certain conditions ethnic attitudes and discrimination can vary independently. Arnold M. Rose, for example, concludes that "from a heuristic standpoint it may be desirable to assume that patterns of intergroup relations, on one hand, and attitudes of prejudice and stereotyping, on the other hand, are fairly unrelated phenomena although they have reciprocal influences on each other . . . " In the present study, no systematic attempt was made to investigate the relation between the stereotypical beliefs of particular individuals and their actual intergroup behavior; but the study did yield much evidence that both images which justify group separatism and separateness itself are characteristic aspects of intergroup relations in Border City. One of the principal findings is that in those situations in which contact between Anglo-Americans and Mexicans is voluntary (such as residence, education, recreation, religious worship, and social intercourse) the characteristic pattern is separateness rather than common participation. Wherever intergroup contact is necessary, as in occupational activites and the performance of commercial and professional services, it is held to the minimum sufficient to acccmplish the purpose of the contact. The extent of this separateness is not constant for all members of the two groups, since it tends to be less severe between Anglo-Americans and those Mexicans they define as of a "high type." Nevertheless, the evidence reveals a high degree of compatibility between beliefs and practices in Border City's intergroup relations, although the data have nothing to offer for the identification of direct relationships.

In any case, the separateness that characterizes intergroup relations cannot be attributed solely to the exclusion practices of the Anglo-American group. Mexicans have tended to remain separate by choice as well as by necessity. Like many other ethnic groups, they have often found this the easier course, since they need not strain to learn another language or to change their ways and manners. The isolation practices of the Mexican group are as relevant to an understanding of intergroup relations as are the practices of the Anglo-Americans.

This should not, however, obscure the fact that to a wide extent the majority of Mexican-Americans share the patterns of living of Anglo-American society; many of their ways are already identical. Regardless of the degree of their insulation from the larger society, the demands of life in the United States have required basic modifications of the Mexicans' cultural tradition. In material culture, Mexicans are hardly to be distinguished from Anglo-Americans, and there have been basic changes in medical beliefs and practices and in the customs regarding godparenthood. Mexicans have acquired English in varying degrees, and their Spanish has become noticeably Anglicized. Although the original organization of the family has persisted, major changes have occured in patterns of traditional authority, as well as in child training and courtship practices. Still, it is the exceedingly rare Mexican-American, no matter how acculturated he may be to the dominant society, who does not in some degree retain the more subtle characteristics of his Mexican heritage, particularly in his conception of time and in other fundamental value orientations, as well as in his modes of participation in interpersonal relations. Many of the most acculturated Mexican-Americans have attempted to exemplify what they regard as "the best of both ways." They have become largely Anglo-American in their way of living, but they still retain fluent Spanish and a knowledge of their traditional culture, and they maintain an identification with their own heritage while participating in Anglo-American culture. Nevertheless, this sort of achievement still seems a long way off for many Mexican-Americans who regard it as desirable.

A predominant Anglo-American expectation is that the Mexicans will be eventually assimilated into the larger society; but this is contingent upon Mexicans becoming just like Anglo-Americans. The Mexican counterpart to this expectation is only partially complementary. Mexicans want to be full members of the larger society, but they do not want to give up their cultural heritage. There is even less complementarity of expectation with regard to the present conduct of intergroup relations. Anglo-Americans believe they are justified in withholding equal access to the     10
rewards of full acceptance as long as Mexicans remain "different," particularly since they interpret the differences (both those which have some basis in reality and those which have none) as evidence of inferiority. Mexicans, on the other hand, while not always certain that they are inferior, clearly want equal opportunity and full acceptance now, not in some dim future, and they do not believe that their differences (either presumed or real) from Anglo-Americans offer any justification for the denial of opportunity and acceptance. Moreover, they do not find that acculturation is rewarded in any clear and regular way by progressive acceptance.     20

It is probable that both Anglo-Americans and Mexicans will have to modify their beliefs and practices if they are to realize more nearly their expectations of each other. Mutual stereotyping, as well as the exclusion practices of Anglo-Americans and the isolation practices of Mexicans, maintains the separateness of the two groups, and separateness is a massive barrier to the realization of their expectations. The process of acculturation is presently going on among Mexican-Americans and will continue, regardless of whether changes in Anglo-Mexican relations occur. Unless Mexican-Americans can validate their increasing command of Anglo-American ways by a free participation in the larger society, how-     30
ever, such acculturation is not likely to accelerate its present leisurely pace, nor will it lead to eventual assimilation. The *colonia* is a relatively safe place in which new cultural acquisitions may be tried out, and thus it has its positive functions; but by the same token it is only in intergroup contacts with Anglo-Americans that acculturation is validated, that the Mexican's level of acculturation is tested, and that the distance he must yet travel to assimilation is measured.

## CONCLUSIONS

There are major inconsistencies in the assumptions that Anglo-Americans     40
and Mexican-Americans hold about one another. Anglo-Americans assume that Mexican-Americans are their potential, if not actual, peers, but at the same time assume they are their inferiors. The beliefs that presumably demonstrate the Mexican-Americans' inferiority tend to place them outside the accepted moral order and framework of Anglo-American society by attributing to them undesirable characteristics that make it

"reasonable" to treat them differently from their fellow Anglo-Americans. Thus the negative images provide not only a rationalized definition of the intergroup relation that makes it palatable for Anglo-Americans, but also a substantial support for maintaining the relation as it is. The assumptions of Mexican-Americans about Anglo-Americans are similarly inconsistent, and their images of Anglo-Americans are predominantly negative, although these are primarily defensive rather than justificatory. The mutual expectations of the two groups contrast sharply with the ideal of a complemmentarity of expectations, in that Anglo-Americans expect Mexicans to become just like themselves, if they are to to accorded equal status in the larger society, whereas Mexican-Americans want full acceptance, regardless of the extent to which they give up their own ways and acquire those of the dominant group.

Anglo-Americans and Mexicans may decide to stay apart because they are different, but cultural differences provide no moral justification for one group to deny to the other equal opportunity and the rewards of the larger society. If the full acceptance of Mexicans by Anglo-Americans is contingent upon the disappearance of cultural differences, it will not be accorded in the foreseeable future. In our American society, we have often seriously underestimated the strength and tenacity of early cultural conditioning. We have expected newcomers to change their customs and values to conform to American ways as quickly as possible, without an adequate appreciation of the strains imposed by this process. An understanding of the nature of culture and of its interrelations with personality can make us more realistic about the rate at which cultural change can proceed and about the gains and costs for the individual who is subject to the experiences of acculturation. In viewing cultural differences primarily as disabilities, we neglect their positive aspects. Mexican-American culture represents the most constructive and effective means Mexican-Americans have yet been able to develop for coping with their changed natural and social environment. They will further exchange old ways for new only if these appear to be more meaningful and rewarding than the old, and then only if they are given full opportunity to acquire the new ways and to use them.

# Stan Steiner
## The Chicanos

The girl was thirteen when she tried to kill herself. She was "tired of working." But she was too inexperienced with death to die, and she lived through her death. To escape her loneliness she married, at fifteen. Her child was born that year, but her husband was sent to prison. "I got a car. The car broke down. I couldn't pay for it. They wanted to sue me. So I forged a check." In the barrios of Denver to be left with a baby, without a husband, at fifteen, was to be lonelier than death. She became a prostitute.

"I worked the town. They call it hustling. I wouldn't go for less than thirty dollars. Because I needed the money. I got it too. All you have to do is be nice," the young girl said. "But to go out and hustle I had to be under    10
the influence of narcotics."

Diana Perea told her own life story to the National Conference on Poverty in the Southwest, held in January, 1965, to launch the War on Poverty. In the winter sun of Tucson, Arizona, the nearly two hundred delegates who had gathered under the auspices of the Choate Foundation, to hear Vice President Hubert Humphrey, were as overwhelmed by the frail and frightened girl as she was by the presidential emissary. "Go back and tell them [your people] that the war against unemployment, discrimination, disease, and ignorance has begun. Tell them to get out and fight!" the Vice President said. "The wonderful thing about the War on    20
Poverty is that we have the means to win it. We cannot fail." He reminded his listeners, "Fifteen minutes from where we sit tonight there is abject poverty."

In the audience was Diana Perea. A few weeks later she succeeded in killing herself.

Her death was due to an overdose of narcotics, the autopsy report declared. There were some nonmedical causes. On the frontispiece of

70

the Summary Report of the National Conference on Poverty in the Southwest there was a black border of mourning around these simple words:

DIANA PEREA
1946-1965
VICTIM OF POVERTY

Death is an ordinary thing. No one would have heard of the young girl
from the streets of Denver's barrio if she had not happened to share a
microphone with the Vice President of the United States. 10
In the streets misery is said to be so common no one notices. Life in the
barrios is cruel—to outsiders, for the sons and daughters of the poor, it is
said, are too hardened and brutalized to be able to do anything but fight
to survive.
A young girl cries of a brown child dying of hunger in the barrios of
San Antonio:

In the land of the free
and the home of the brave,
He is dying of hunger, 20
he cannot be saved;
Come brothers and sisters
and weep by his grave.
This is our child—

The ordeal of these youths is bemoaned by sympathetic writers. Not
by the youth. Diana Perea did not weep. The Chicana was matter of fact:
this is the way it is. Life in the barrio streets is just a way of life—happy,
unhappy, ordinary, exciting, boring, deadly. The streets are not dangerous,
they are only treacherous. It doesn't frighten youth. Seldom do they curse 30
the barrio. They curse themselves for their inability to survive. It is not
the barrio that the Chicano fears, but the lonely and hostile world outside.
Loneliness, the coldness of urban life, is what depresses the Chicano.
In his family there is a warmth and gregarious love voiced with passion,
uninhibited honesty, and gusto. The city frustrates and mutes this love.
Faced with a society that he feels is hostile, the barrio youth becomes
lost. He tries to defend himself by forming a gang, not just to fight for his
manhood, his *macho,* but for his right to be a Chicano.
"The most brutal method of birth control is the one we practice on ourselves," a young man writes in *La Raza.* 40
To *La Raza Chicano,* a young girl writes a bitter note: "I wish to compli-
ment brother Perfecto Vallego and his friends for doing with Caterino B.
Heredia. Keep up the good work, Baby, you and the cops [can] get together on the Chicano Annual Shoot. Your game is as bad as the racist
cop who goes after Chicanos who fail to halt. You dudes don't have to
kill your brothers; Uncle Sam is doing that for you in Viet Nam. You are

shooting the wrong guy. *No sean tan pendejos.* If you have enough *huevos* [testicles] to shoot your brother you should be able to take on a racist cop."

The street gangs of the barrios are different from those in most ghettos. In a sense they are born not solely of poverty, but also of cultural pride. Like street-corner chambers of commerce the gangs of barrio youth defend the spirit of La Raza with bravado and youthful boisterousness.

Of the many barrio gangs the oldest and best known is that of the legendary Pachucos, who have become a heroic myth. They were born in blood that was real enough, and they not only are remembered but are imitated with awe. They began on a day in August, 1942. In the tensions of World War II, the racial hatreds of Los Angeles were about to erupt in what was to be known as the "Zoot Suit Riots." Two groups of Chicanos had a boyish fight over a pretty girl and hurt pride, in a gravel pit on the outskirts of the city. In the morning the body of young Jose Diaz was found on a dirt road nearby, dead. Bored newspapermen, seeking local color, dubbed the gravel pit the "Sleepy Lagoon" (it had a mud puddle in it), and an orgy of sensational headlines celebrated the boy's death.

Not one but twenty-four Mexican boys were arrested; nine were convicted of second-degree murder. All were freed later, two years later, when the Court of Appeals reversed the sentences unanimously for "lack of evidence."

The "Sleepy Lagoon" case is still remembered bitterly in the barrios, much as the Dreyfus case in France, or that of the Scottsboro Boys in the Deep South.

Amid headlines of hysteria—"Zoot Suit Hoodlums" and "Pachuco Gangsters"—the Los Angeles police raided the barrios, blockaded the main streets, searched every passing car and passer-by. Six hundred Chicanos were taken into custody in a two-day sweep that Police Captain Joseph Reed called "a drive on Mexican gangs." The Los Angeles sheriff's "Bureau of *Foreign* Relations" justified the dragnet by officially philosophizing that the Chicanos' "desire to kill, or at least let blood" was an "inborn characteristic."

The next summer the tensions exploded. When a fist fight broke out on a downtown street between a gang of Chicano boys and U.S. Navy men in June, 1943, fourteen off-duty policemen led by a lieutenant of the Detective Squad set up an impromptu group of vigilantes they named the "Vengeance Squad" and set out "to clean up" the Mexicans.

Night after night hundreds of restless and beached sailors of the U.S. Navy, bored and frustrated by their inaction in the war against Japan, seized upon the nearest available dark-skinned enemies—the young Chicanos—and beat them up. The white rioters toured the barrios in convoys of taxi cabs, attacking every brown boy they found on the streets, in bars and restaurants and movie houses, by the dozens, by the hundreds, while Los Angeles police looked the other way. No sailor was arrested. Inspired by the inflammatory news stories about "zoot suit roughnecks," the white rioters sought out these most of all—zoot suits were an early

Humphrey Bogart style Mexicanized by Chicano boys and lately revived
in its classic form by *Bonnie and Clyde*.

It was a long, hot summer week. When the white rioters exhausted
their racial fervor, the riots—known not as the "U.S. Navy Riots" but
oddly as the "Zoot Suit Riots"—had left hundreds of injured and a residue
of race hatred in Los Angeles.

The zoot-suit boys were Pachucos. Where the name came from is vague,
but it may have been taken from the city of Pachuco in Mexico, known
for its brilliantly hued costumes. In the riots, these gangs of Pachucos
were not the aggressors but the defenders of the barrios. They were an    10
early self-defense group. Youths who never knew the Pachucos remember
them not as victims but as resistance fighters of the streets, the Minutemen
of *machismo,* who fought to defend the reputation of La Raza. Wherever
the barrio youth organize, the spirit of the Pachucos is evoked and revived.

"I hope you tell the story of the Pachucos," a Brown Beret says to me.
"We have to learn about our heroes."

One of many Pachuco-type gangs is the Vatos. It is a fictitious name of
a small gang in the San Fernando Valley of Los Angeles whose "territory"
ranges from Laurel Canyon Boulevard to O'Melveny Street. The Vatos
hang out mostly in the dark alleys near Acala Avenue, a poorly lit    20
thoroughfare.

A member of the Vatos talks of his gang:

"This is the story of life in a Mexican barrio. The barrio is called 'San
Fer.' The kids, so-called Pachucos, run this barrio. Life in this barrio is
rough, harsh. The boys learned early to carry can openers and knives.
As soon as they got a little older they graduated to switch-blades, lengths
of chain, and guns, if they could get hold of them.

"Boys joined together to form street gangs, and some of them sported
the Pachuco brand between the thumb and forefinger of their left hand,"
the Vato says. "This gang is the stuff of life, as the Pachuco knows it."    30

The gang member has to prove his manhood and his ability to survive.
"He will undertake the most fantastic stunts to prove a great deal. He
will risk his life and his freedom to maintain his growing reputation as a
tough fighter, a rugged guy." These rituals are not merely rites of initia-
tion, or idle bravado. The gang youth has to demonstrate not only that he
can fight in the streets, but that he has the strength to withstand the
hostility of society, to stand up to the *placa,* the police, and if he is cou-
rageous enough, to become visible to the outsider, by wearing a Brown
Beret. "That is real *macho,*" a Los Angeles community leader says.

It is a new kind of political and urban *pachuquismo.* The society outside    40
the barrio is defied by the gang. Consciously the rituals of brotherhood
enforce the laws and culture of the barrio. Inside the gang the Chicano is
insulated from his own conflicts. The Chicanos "find conflicts so per-
plexing and so full of both cultures—that of their parents and that of
America—that [they] create their own world of *pachuquismo,*" says the
Vato.

The Vato goes on: "The Vatos have created their own language, Pachucano, their own style of dress, their own folklore, and their own behavior patterns. The Vatos have developed a barrio group spirit. The Vatos in this area are better organized and a little tighter, due to the fact that it is a smaller group; and therefore all the Vatos participate in the activities planned by them.

"They formed a closely knit group that regarded the Anglos as their natural enemies."

In every barrio the social clubs and folk religious societies have always existed in semisecrecy, with their own rules and symbols, hidden from the world outside. Chicano gangs are the progeny of that invisible heritage—to outsiders—by which the barrio has protected itself. They recreate in their own youthful way, the society and culture of their forefathers; yet they are urban.

Eliezer Risco, the editor of La Raza, describes these methods of barrio organizations as "our own survival techniques. It is difficult for the culture of a minority to survive in the larger society. If we can utilize them for social action, now that we are stronger, we will surprise the country," he says. "The country won't know where our strength is coming from or how we organize."

In the dark alleyways and gregarious streets, the Brown Berets began. They have developed a political pachuquismo. A generation ago they would have been a street gang, nothing more. Less obvious are the barrio origins of the youthful leaders of the La Raza movements that have gained national prominence and importance. Cesar Chavez, Rodolfo "Corky" Gonzales, Reies Tijerina: these men learned their organizing techniques on the back streets of the barrio.

"They say the La Raza movements come from the universities. I disagree," says "Jose," the "Field Marshal" of the Brown Berets. "I say they come from the streets."

So few youths in the barrios graduated from high school in the past, or entered college, that those who achieved that miraculous feat feared to look down from their pinnacle of anxiety. If they did, the barrios beneath them seemed a bottomless arroyo. And yet, in the wholly anglicized realms of higher education they were also strangers.

"You see a Chicano [ university] student is alienated from his language; he is de-culturized and finally dehumanized so as to be able to function in white, middle class, protestant bag," the Chicano Student News reports. "It is damn obvious to the Chicano in college that education means one of two things: either accept the system—study, receive a diploma, accept the cubicle and the IBM machine in some lousy bank or factory, and move out of the barrio—or reject the system. . . . "

Youths who made it to the university clung to their privileged and precarious achievements: non-Mexican name and anglicized accent, an Ivy League suit, a blond wife, and a disdain for the "dumb Mexicans" left behind. "THE PURPLE TIO TOMÁS" (Uncle Tom), El Gallo has dubbed these high achievers. "This is the middle class Tomás. He isn't a Tomás because he lives on the other side of town, but because the Purple Tomás believes he is better than other Chicanos. Purple is the Royal Color!" The would-be intellectual *patrons* — "the new conservatives," Corky Gonzales calls them.

Now the university students have begun the climb down from their lonely success to the streets of the barrios and the fields of the campesinos. They come as on a pilgrimage, seeking an identity. Los Angeles community leader Eduardo Perez says, "I find that many Mexicans-turned-Spanish are coming back into the fold and are being identified for what they are: Mexicans." They have a "pride in being Mexican."

In the vineyards of Delano, when the striking grape pickers gathered their banners and walked north on the highway in their 250-mile pilgrimage to Sacramento to see the Governor, the university Chicanos who walked with the *huelguistas* were wide-eyed with wonder. Not only were these young people from the universities, but they were the children of the barrios who had at last escaped, had "made it." Some even had blond hair.

Here were "farm workers with dark faces, aged prematurely by the California sun, marching side by side with students with youthful faces," wrote Daniel de los Reyes in the union newspaper *El Malcriado,* the "farm workers with black hair and a determined look, by the side of blond and red-haired students with brilliant, sparkling eyes." It was a spectacle to see, these thousands and thousands of young people" who had come "because the Farm Workers Organizing Committee had agreed to join side by side with their brothers, the students." There was a tone of wonder in the union newspaper story. It seemed unbelievable, this "brotherhood against ignorance and poverty." These were "the same students we have seen so many times on the picketlines at the vineyards of DiGiorgio, the same youths working so tirelessly on the boycotts," declared *El Malcriado.*

Still it was not to be believed. The university students respected, listened to, and obeyed the campesinos of the fields; that was what was so strange. It was as though they who were illiterate were the teachers of the university students.

The experience of the *huelga* was a strange and exhilarating one for the students as well, for it profoundly affected the lives of many who had come. Luis Valdez, who went on to found El Centro Cultural Campesino, and Eliezer Risco, who became editor of *La Raza,* were but two of dozens of student leaders whose lives were changed by their pilgrimage to the vineyards of Delano.

"I was writing my thesis," Risco recalls. "I came thinking, well, it's a way of doing my research. But it was my Graduate School."

Venustiano Olguin was a brilliant student in a graduate school of the University of California at Los Angeles and was studying for his Ph.D. The son of a bracero who had grown up in the migrant barrios of the Coachella Valley, he had worked his way to first place in his high school class and graduated with honors from the University of Redlands.

"I'd been very successful with the system." But he had begun to have the uneasy feeling he was becoming a "Tio Tomás," an Uncle Tom. "At UCLA I knew that somewhere along the line I had been betraying something." He did not know what.

One summer the young man and some of his fellow students in the United Mexican American Students (UMAS) had a meeting with Cesar Chavez. Olguin went to Delano—not to stay, just to look around and help the farm workers if he could. He decided to join *La Huelga*. He has abandoned the honors of higher education that he says were anglicizing him, indoctrinating him with materialistic values, and forcing him to reject his Mexican heritage. He lives on $5 a week strike pay. "Some people think I am crazy. But I think my life is very rich." In the campesinos he feels he has found "a special kind of courage," of manhood. "I've learned more than in all the time I was in graduate school."

University communities of Chicanos were affected as strongly. In San Antonio, Texas, a leader of the Mexican American Youth Organization recalls how the campesinos of the Rio Grande Valley became godfathers of his group. "The strike of the farm workers got everyone excited. St. Mary's University students got together to see what they could do," says William Vazquez. "And that is how we began."

Luis Valdez, whose life was changed by Delano, feels it is a necessary school for students. "In advance of their people, the Chicano leader in the cities and universities must go through the whole bourgeois scene, find it distasteful, and then strike out in new directions. This is what happened with Corky Gonzales and Cesar Chavez. Divorcing themselves from the petty aims of success, they see the middle class for what it is. Then they can see the lower class plain."

"In short, they discover there is a world out there," Valdez says.

Out of the upheaval have come dozens of new barrio and university clubs. In the last few years there has been more youth organizing than in the entire history of the Chicanos. University students have been especially outspoken and active. The United Mexican American Students (UMAS) in California and the National Organization of Mexican American Students (NOMAS, literally "No More") in Texas are but two of more than thirty groups on the campuses alone.

The university and barrio youth are talking and walking together. David Sanchez, the prime minister of the Brown Berets, talks to students at UCLA, while the students of UMAS walk not only on the picket lines of the campesinos of Delano but also beside the Brown Berets protesting school conditions in East Los Angeles. The *Chicano Student News* reports: "UMAS is an organization of Chicano college students which is bringing the business of education back into the Chicano community;" and the a headline says. "UMAS COMES HOME!"

"Old hatreds and quarrels are being put aside," *La Raza* writes, for *"Todos son Chicanos"*—"We are all Chicanos."

Several dozen Chicanos gathered at a dude ranch near Santa Barbara on the California seacoast for one of the many conferences of students and barrio youths. Eduardo Perez, who helped run the conference, describes the occasion;

"Nowadays the young lions and lionesses have their own cars, buy their own clothes, work their way through college, and are very much on their own. Their whole thinking and outlook on life is as different from ours as night is from day.

"These Mexican American 'world leaders of tomorrow' are an exceptional breed. They can put on a *charro* [the real cowboy Mexican] costume and be proud of it. They can even put on American clothes and feel at ease. They can eat enchiladas and hamburgers on the same plate, tacos and pizza in one sitting, and possibly drink tequila with beer as a chaser and feel right at home. They have become anglicized, but only to the point that there is no excuse for them not being accepted. They take pride in being of Mexican ancestry and do not deny being what they are. These kids don't change their names just to become Spanish or European heirs . . . "

In spite of the ease with which they seemed to go from one culture to another, the young Chicanos suffered an inner paralysis. They doubted not their emotions or their thoughts, but to create one culture out of two so different. Perez had written of another youth conference, "The Mexican Americans attending (most of them) did not really understand themselves . . . and how they happened to be in the mess they're in."

The university and barrio youth had this in common too.

"I stand naked in the world, lost in angry solitude," the Chicano poet Benjamin Luna writes in *La Raza*. The loneliness of the urban society — impersonal, cold, efficient, foreign to his heart — evokes the feeling of a hostile world. The futility the Chicano feels is not fatalism, but a rage of frustration.

> *Soy Indio con alma hambrienta,*
> *traigo en la sangre coraje,*
> *rojo coraje en la sangre.*
>
> I am Indian with a hungry soul,
>    tragic in the passionate blood,
>    red passion in the blood.
>
> I stand naked in the world,
>    hungry
>    homeless
>    despised. . . .

In the barrios, brotherhood is in the blood, the blood of La Raza. "One boy will bring beer, while other will bring *rifa;* still others bring money for the use of activities, or gas in a member's car. This is a thing that goes on every night with something different every night that can be called a 'dead kick.'" At best, their inner brotherhood is limited by the outer world of their "natural enemy," and at worst is defined by it.

A Brown Beret laments, "We are not what we were when we started out. All those TV cameras and news reporters took over our image and changed us into their image of us."

"Who am I?" asks a young woman in a suburban church of Los Angeles. "I have been afraid to speak up for my rights. Rights? What rights do we have? So many of our youth plead guilty in court when they know they are not guilty of anything. Anything but being a Mexican."

> I am Joaquin,
> Lost in a world of confusion,
> Caught up in the whirl of an
>     Anglo society,
> Confused by the rules,
> Scorned by attitudes,
> Suppressed by manipulations,
> And destroyed by modern society.
> My fathers
>     have lost the economic battle,
> and won
>     the fight for cultural survival.

The litany "Who am I?" is echoed in the poem of Rodolfo Gonzales, the leader of La Raza community of Denver. "I am Joaquin" is at once a defiance and a requiem for the history of self-mutilation of those whom the Chicano poet calls "strangers in *their* land":

> In a country that has wiped out
> all my history,
>     stifled all my pride.
> In a country that has placed
> a different indignity
>     upon my ancient burdens.
>     Inferiority
> is the new load. . . .

In time the act of denial becomes a self-denial:

> I look at myself
> and see part of me
> who rejects my father and my mother
> and dissolves into the melting pot
>     to evaporate in shame. . . .

"Soul searching," Dr. Ernesto Galarza calls it. The scholar, a sparse man of wiry thoughts and whitening hair, who talks with hard, dry words, is recognized by many of the Chicano youth leaders as the dean of the La Raza movement; perhaps the dean emeritus. "There is an incredible amount of soul searching going on among this generation. Of questioning. Of seeking," he says one midnight over coffee in a motel in Santa Barbara, where he has gone to teach a youth workshop.

"Many of these youth have been propelled into crises of considerable tension. There have been tragic losses, where some of them have been torn asunder by the conflicts, internal and external, within themselves. There has been a loss of much potential. The youth are resilient, however.

"I believe there are few phoneys in this generation. Anyone who believes this is a time for the promotion of Uncle Toms, of acquiescence, among the younger generation of Mexicans, is mistaken. Unquestionably this generation is confronted with some crippling problems. But *that* is not one of them," says the scholar.

Dr. Galarza's weary eyes light up when he talks of these youths. "I am delighted by the happenstance of the last ten years. There has been the growth of quite a small army of young men, a phalanx of potential leaders who are searching for a breakthrough. The younger generation holds much promise.

"It is too early to foresee where these movements will lead. There is little unity of thought. There is precious little cohesion. Every movement is its own little stirring of activity. In five or ten years, there may be a reckoning; a culmination.

"We will wait," the scholar says, "and we will see."

Of course, the youth will not wait. They want action now, ideology later. Having had a small glimpse of their cultural identity, they want the rest; and having had a foretaste of Chicano power, they yearn for more: "Mañana is here!" says Maclovio Barraza, leader of the Arizona miners.

"Who the hell are we? What are we? Where do we belong? Study it! Announce it to the world!" Joe Benitos, a Chicano leader in Arizona, exclaims impatiently. "Let's end this hangup about identity. We know who we are. In order to survive we have learned survival skills. Sure, but let's not confuse our survival skills in Anglo society with our culture. We have a parallel culture. We have to keep it. I say we can do it. We don't have to be one of *them!*"

His impatience with the talk of the "identity crisis" is typical of the young Chicano. Benitos feels the problem of identity is perpetuated by university study projects, "so that they will have something to study"; he has worked with several of these projects. "I've been there," he says. "And that's not where it's at.

"Yes, having two cultures creates problems. Why emphasize the problems? Why not emphasize the opportunities it gives the Chicano in the new world scene?"

"There is a Chicano wave coming in," says Benitos. "I see it as part of the world-wide scene. As the world shrinks everyone will have to learn more than one language, one culture. Everyone will have to be bilingual and trilingual. It will put us in a fantastic position, if we can keep our languages and cultures.

"Our experience will be a lesson for the whole world," he says.

"Chicano" is a new word, not yet in the dictionary. La Raza writers cannot yet define it except by what it is not; the Chicano is not, they say, half-Mexican, half-American, who blends two cultures in his being. He is not just one more second-and third-generation city-bred descendant of a rural villager who has learned to drive a car like a wild horse and pay for it on the installment plan. La Raza is a new people with a new culture and the Chicano is its youngest offspring. He has inherited many things from Mexico and the United States, but he imitates neither. The Chicano is a new man.

In the La Raza newspapers there appears a "Definition of the Word Chicano" by Benito Rodriguez. He is a member of MANO (Hand), a group of Chicano ex-convicts in San Antonio, Texas. Rodriguez's words, even more than his ideas, the way he writes, the style, the language he uses, give some of the feeling of being a Chicano in the barrio of a modern city. Even in the pale English translation the strong flavor of that life comes through, although it is stronger in the Spanish. He writes:

"Many designations have been used to refer to us, the descendants of Mexicans. Every ten or fifteen years, or so, we feel like searching for a new image of ourselves. First, in the time of the 'Wild West' we were 'Mexican bandits,' then 'greasers,' then 'mescins,' and we are 'Spanish Americans,' 'Mexican Americans,' 'Americans,' etc.

"The migrant Mexicans, workers in the field, call themselves Chicapatas (short legs), or Raza (race, as in Raza del Sol, People of the Sun). City workers use the term Chicano a little more. The phrase Mexican-American is really used by the middle-class Mexicans. What is truly Mexican is covered by a layer, Chicano, to satisfy all the conditions in which we find ourselves. How shall we describe ourselves tomorrow, or the day after?

"Now they want to make us half Mexicans and half Americans, as if they were talking about geography. Well, we already know who we are. Why do we come on like a chicken with its head cut off? Why do we let them make fakes, if we are Chicanos down to the phlegm in our mouths? If you don't like the taste you'll swallow it anyway.

"Just because we've seen their marvelous technology doesn't mean we believe that those who exploit us are gods."

Benito Rodriguez concludes with a curse that is pure Chicano: "A poor man who thinks he lives in heaven is gonna get fucked, coming and going."

# El Malcriado
## Interview With Cesar Chavez

The morning following his release, Cesar was interviewed at his home by *El Malcriado*. The following are Cesar's recollections of his 20 day stay in jail.

EL MALCRIADO—How do you feel after going to jail for civil disobedience?

CESAR—Well, it was partially civil disobedience. It wasn't a real classic case of civil disobedience. I was sentenced to an indefinite period. So I couldn't look forward to a year or two; I didn't know what was going to happen. Really what the judge was saying is that it is up to me to get out of jail if I called off the boycott. That put the responsibility on me to    10
say: No, I'll never call it off. It wasn't the classic civil disobedience case but it was a very good case. It was hard but now that it's over, I feel elated.

EL MALCRIADO—What was your relationship with the other inmates?

CESAR—I made a lot of friends, inside with the inmates, did a little organizing and spread the word around quite a bit. I wasn't too successful in convincing anybody about non-violence inside, but they are all with us. This includes blacks, whites and chicanos. The saddest thing is that the people who are in jail by and large are poor people. Only poor people go to jail and stay there. Also men who don't have anyone on the outside who really cares for them. Or who have someone on the outside who cannot    20
really help them. It's very, very sad. Mostly young people. The routine . . . they put them in jail, they book them. Then they bring them into court and have the hearing and bring them back. It's like a completely different world. I couldn't help feeling sorry for them. At least I had something on the outside going for me and I had the conviction of the cause. But they don't have any of those things. I learned that there is a very

**81**

serious problem on the whole question of parole. Parole, I think is a damaging, unconstitutional and damning thing for people. It gets a guy, puts him on parole, and they'll never let him go.

EL MALCRIADO—Did those on the vigil keep you company?

CESAR—Yeah, I never felt alone. For one thing at night I could hear their singing. I heard the mananitas. Oh great! I was asleep you know. They started singing and the jailer opened the front door. I heard this rapping on the bulkhead "Wake up . . . They're singing!" Then I heard the chicanos in the jail gritando (yelling) you know. "Eran las mananitas," about the second verse and ooi, you know how they feel really good.    10
So I just opened my pillow and blanket. It's the first time they gave me mananitas, you know. Well, they were for the Virgin and the chicanos were all over the jail. Four-thirty in the morning gritando, you know, gritos de la raza, all over. It was really great. The poor guys on the vigil sacrificed more than I did. See the determination? The growers said they were going to do the same thing. They lasted a day. But the people were really beautiful. The visitors were a tremendous support. I talked to about 150 the 1st Saturday and about 300 the 2nd Saturday. I talked to a lot of women, really very sincere. It gives you a tremendous feeling. I was very happy that Coretta King, Ethel Kennedy and Bishop Flores    20
came. They did a lot of good for me spiritually and an awful lot of good to the people.

EL MALCRIADO—What did you think of our opposition's violence during Ethel Kennedy's visit?

CESAR—It's a clear example exactly how violence, whoever does it, really hurts their cause. Those guys really lost points. The day after it was on TV, how bad the guys were. A lady came to the vigil in a Cadillac and gave $25. They wanted to take her name and address and she said no, I trust you: I'm giving you $25 because I think I understand one thing —I want to become an American again. I can't give you my name because    30
my son is a grower." You see, that kind of spirit, that kind of discipline, nobody can reject. You can't beat it.

EL MALCRIADO—During the confinement, how did you feel physically and mentally?

CESAR—Physically very well. Psychologically I was prepared. Spiritually, I knew I was going to jail. So I just made up my mind that I was going to go and not be suppressed. I said that they could have my body here but my spirit's going to be free. It took me a couple of days to get used to the routine. You see, all of a sudden I'm in jail—I'm confronted with just an upside down of my life schedule. On the outside I'm going    40
16 hours a day every day. I had to schedule my time inside so I would use it wisely and make the best out of my stay. I just settled down and said I got to work myself out of it, and I did. In fact the almost three weeks in jail did not seem like a long time. I lost about 15 pounds, eating about a quarter of what I would usually eat outside.

EL MALCRIODO—What are your thoughts about possibly going back to jail?

CESAR—I don't want to go back, but if I have to I will. To commit civil disobedience I wouldn't have had a hearing. I would just tell the judge I'm guilty, give me the maximum time. Although I wanted to do that, I had to consider the union. If it had been me personally I think that I would have pleaded guilty and asked for the maximum time.

EL MALCRIADO—What is in store for our future?

CESAR—Back to the grind.

# The Young Lords Party
## 13-Point Program and Platform

1. *We want self-determination for Puerto Ricans—liberation on the island and inside the united states.*

For 500 years, first spain and then the united states have colonized our country. Billions of dollars in profits leave our country for the united states every year. In every way we are slaves of the gringo. We want liberation and the Power in the hands of the People, not Puerto Rican exploiters.

QUE VIVA PUERTO RICO LIBRE!

2. *We want self-determination for all Latinos.*

Our Latin Brothers and Sisters, inside and outside the united states, are oppressed by amerikkkan business. The Chicano people built the Southwest, and we support their right to control their lives and their land. The people of Santo Domingo continue to fight against gringo domination and its puppet generals. The armed liberation struggles in Latin America are part of the war of Latinos against imperialism.

QUE VIVA LA RAZA!

3. *We want liberation of all third world people.*

Just as Latins first slaved under spain and the yanquis, Black people, Indians, and Asians slaved to build the wealth of this country. For 400 years they have fought for freedom and dignity against racist Babylon (decadent empire). Third World people have led the fight for freedom. All the colored and oppressed peoples of the world are one nation under oppression.

NO PUERTO RICAN IS FREE UNTIL ALL PEOPLE ARE FREE!

4. *We are revolutionary nationalists and oppose racism.*

The Latin, Black, Indian and Asian people inside the u.s. are colonies fighting for liberation. We know that washington, wall street, and city hall will try to make our nationalism into racism; but Puerto Ricans are of all colors and we resist racism. Millions of people are rising up to demand freedom and we support them. These are the ones in the u.s. that are stepped on by the rulers of government. We each organize our people, but our fights are the same against oppression and we will defeat it. POWER TO ALL OPPRESSED PEOPLE!

5. *We want community control of our institutions and land.*   10

We want control of our communities by our people and programs to guarantee that all institutions serve the needs of our people. People's control of police, health services, churches, schools, housing, transportation and welfare are needed. We want an end to attacks on our land by urban removal, highway destruction, universities and corporations. LAND BELONGS TO ALL THE PEOPLE!

6. *We want a true education of our creole culture and Spanish language.*

We must learn our history of fighting against cultural, as well as economic genocide by the yanqui. Revolutionary culture, culture of our people, is the only true teaching.   20

7. *We oppose capitalists and alliances with traitors.*

Puerto Rican rulers, or puppets of the oppressor, do not help our people. They are paid by the system to lead our people down blind alleys, just like the thousands of poverty pimps who keep our communities peaceful for business, or the street workers who keep gangs divided and blowing each other away. We want a society where the people socialistically control their labor. VENCEREMOS!

8. *We oppose the amerikkan military.*

We demand immediate withdrawal of u.s. military forces and bases   30 from Puerto Rico, Vietnam, and all oppressed communities inside and outside the u.s. No Puerto Rican should serve in the u.s. army against his Brothers and Sisters, for the only true army of oppressed people is the people's army to fight all rulers. U.S. OUT OF VIETNAM, FREE PUERTO RICO!

9. *We want freedom for all political prisoners.*

We want all Puerto Ricans freed because they have been tried by the racist courts of the colonizers, and not by their own people and peers. We want all freedom fighters released from jail. FREE ALL POLITICAL PRISONERS!   40

10. *We want equality for women, machismo must be revolutionary . . . not oppressive.*

Under capitalism, our women have been oppressed by both the society and our own men. The doctrine of machismo has been used by our men to take out their frustrations against their wives, sisters, mothers, and children. Our men must support their women in their fight for economic and social equality, and must recognize that our women are equals in every way within the revolutionary ranks.

FORWARD, SISTERS, IN THE STRUGGLE!

11. *We fight anti-communism with international unity.*

Anyone who resists injustice is called a communist by "the man" and condemned. Our people are brainwashed by television, radio, newspapers, schools, and books to oppose people in other countries fighting for their freedom. No longer will our people believe attacks and slanders, because they have learned who the real enemy is and who their real friends are. We will defend our Brothers and Sisters around the world who fight for         10 justice against the rich rulers of this country.

VIVA CHE!

12. *We believe armed self-defense and armed struggle are the only means to liberation.*

We are opposed to violence—the violence of hungry children, illiterate adults, diseased old people, and the violence of poverty and profit. We have asked, petitioned, gone to courts, demonstrated peacefully, and voted for politicians full of empty promises. But we still ain't free. The time has come to defend the lives of our people against repression and for revolutionary war against the businessman, politician, and police. When         20 a government oppresses our people, we have the right to abolish it and create a new one.

BORICUA IS AWAKE! ALL PIGS BEWARE!

13. *We want a socialist society.*

We want liberation, clothing, free food, education, health care, transportation, utilities, and employment for all. We want a society where the needs of our people come first, and where we give solidarity and aid to the peoples of the world, not oppression and racism.

HASTA LA VICTORIA SIEMPRE!

# Oscar Lewis
## I Love My Mama

I speak God's truth. I am just a little girl, nine years old, and don't know much but I do know that I love Arturo, Grandma, Crucita and *mami* very much. *Mami* is good and gives me love. She says all the time, "I have my children. I am not alone. I don't abandon my children." That's why, when I grow up, I want to be a doctor or a chambermaid. So when I work and earn money, I'll put it in the bank and give *mami* the bank book so she can take out what she wants. Then I'll send for Arturo and Quique and I'll buy *mami* furniture and everything. This furniture we have is no good.

I'd like to be happy like other girls and have a *papá* so that when *mami*    10
gets sick she can run and tell him. I love my *mamá* and will never leave her alone. And neither will she leave me.

I am a good girl. I am clean, I sweep, I do everything, and I behave myself. I mind others, obey my *teacher* and all that. I don't ask my *mamá* to buy me things. I say to *mami* in a nice way, *"Mami,* are you going to buy me that dress?" If she can't, then she doesn't buy it. The nuns say that's how you have to be to be good.

The boys say I am pretty, that I have pretty hair, but I think I am ugly. What I would like now is to get this leg of mine cured.

Benedicto said to me, "Don't you worry. One of these days we're going    20
to take you to the hospital and have you fixed up." *Mami* says so, too. But I am afraid of the doctor and I don't want to miss school. So, what I do is go to church a lot so I'll be cured.

The thing is, I am a coward. I'm afraid of the hospital. I'd rather stay home. I'm afraid they will stick a needle in me and open me with a knife. The only way they will ever be able to catch me and give me an injection

is if they get me when I am asleep. They told me they were going to take
X-rays and I got so nervous you could hear my teeth chattering. Toya
came over right away and said, "Did they cut your leg?" I was afraid I
was going to die and then they would pull out all my guts. That's what
they do in the hospital. They cover you with a sheet and put you in a coffin
and bury you. Nobody ever sees you again after you are buried.

I cry when *mami* gets an attack and goes to the hospital, because I have
to stay with the children. That Toya doesn't obey me and begins pestering
me. *Mami* tells her to do something and she doesn't do it. When she behaves
badly I smack her in the face. *Mami* doesn't want me to hit her, but I do it    10
so she won't be calling me nasty names. I'm tired of taking care of the children and it makes me mad.

If my cousin Gabriel stays over it's even worse. If *mami* leaves a sausage,
Gabi and Toya eat the whole thing. They eat all the bread, and when
*mami* comes home I am the one who gets all the blame. That's why I
smack Gabi in the face, too. That child is a big rascal. When I go to his
house he doesn't want me to touch anything. Auntie Flora says to him,
"Whatever is here is for everybody, not just for you."

That boy! One day I dreamed that Auntie died and Uncle wanted the
things in the house for himself and he brought his girl friend Leila there.    20
But I told Leila no, she couldn't have the things. Then, right away Gabi
came and said, "Flora told me that nobody was going to get those things."

And so I said to him, "Look, Gabi, you get out of here! Those things are
not yours. Auntie told me away back to take care of them." That child is
always butting in.

What I would like is to go back to Puerto Rico. I am going to tell *mami*
that when school is over we should leave. They don't cure her here and the
doctors are making her nervous. In Puerto Rico they will cure her. Then
she could go back to work. She can't do that here because she is in the
hospital so much. She says that when I am a big girl and she is working,    30
she is going to buy us real pretty clothes.

My own mother is bad. She has about a hundred children. She gives
some away and the others she neglects. She dresses herself up real pretty
but the children go around the house with shit in their pants.

They say that a man who lived with my *mamá* was my *papá* and that he
gave her a beating for mistreating me and so she threw me against the
drainpipe and broke my leg. That's why *mami* asked her for me. *Mami*
wanted me and asked her for my clothes and took me to a hospital. She
says that she alone is my *mamá* and Arturo is my *papá*.

I remember that we were living in the country with Arturo. *Mami* and    40
Arturo used to fight there. He would hit her hard because she didn't
listen to him. That was why we left and went to La Esmeralda. Arturo
was paying for the room but only one day *mami* began to fight with him
and she picked up a knife and went after him. We took it away from her.
Arturo left but he came back a few days later.

Then *mami* went to work in *don* Camacho's *bar*. She worked selling, collecting the money and serving tables. She sold rum. She worked and paid the rent and Arturo took care of us. He would get up at one to go to the store and brought us *lunch*. Then he would go for Quique and let him play in the street. *Mami* continued in the life and she would leave us with Arturo.

I remember *mami's* dead husband, Tavio. He was very good to me. He gave me a pretty dress. He was very strong, taller than *mami*, and he could jump the fence without hurting himself or anything. But one day he went out with his friend to get some things for *mami* . . . a lot of things all of gold . . . Then when he was coming out, they were waiting for him and they shot him. I think he used to go out to steal, because that's what *mami* said.

That's when *mami's* attacks first began. She loved him very much, just like Arturo. The funeral was real pretty. We still have some pictures of the funeral.

Afterward *don* Camacho used to come to La Esmeralda, but I didn't know him well because he would be in the living room in Grandma's house. What I know is that *don* Camacho was an old man with a house and a wife. But he was real rich and had *bars* on every street.

Simplicio began to work for *don* Camacho, too, because he got married to Flora. I knew Flora when she lived with Fontánez. I used to go there, but Fontánez didn't like me because I would come to tell Flora that Uncle wanted to talk to her.

I remember once I saw Simplicio giving Alvaro's wife some beer and I went and told Grandma. Fernanda and Flora went over there and started a big fight! Alvaro's wife hid because Auntie was going to kill her. Then Uncle took a bat and was going to beat me, but *mami* came and started to fight with him.

After that *don* Camacho paid the fares for all of us to go to New Jersey— Simplicio, too. We went to live with Felícita, who was with Edmundo then. Edmundo made a lot of faces over that. He always had a long face. Simplicio, Flora, Felícita and all the children were living there, except Felícita's twins, Angelito and Gabi, who stayed with Grandma in Puerto Rico.

One day in Fela's house I went through the bedroom and Fela was naked and so was Edmundo. Fela began laughing and I said to her, "You shameless thing," and I went out. I told *mami* but she didn't say anything. And then Felícita made fun of *mami*. So we did it back at her and Quique said, "I have to defend her, she is our mamá."

*Mami* took a room and we began living in that other house. It was a real big one and *mami* worked there. She kept on working and began to live with Eddy. He was all right. But I hate all the husbands *mami* takes and I don't call them *"papá"* or anything. Once he started to fight with *mami* and she went and burned him.

On my birthday they made a *party*. That was when *mami* went crazy. The day of my *party* there was such a fight that *mami* was screaming.

She gets very nervous. She was very pretty that day and they knocked her earrings off. There was a nice glass door there and they smashed it and everything else. *Mami* was biting the man, so he hit her and Cruz grabbed a knife. *Mami* got nervous and began screaming, "Get out of here or I'll kill you!" And she nearly did. Well, he left.

They took my *mami* to the hospital in a car and left her there. The thing is she can't stand it if she gets hit in the head very many times and she was in the crazy house for two months. They took everything away from her in the crazy house, her watch and all.

Eddy used to go see her, and Crucita, too. We used to peek in and see her through the *window*. The *window* was all barred up, because she threw out everything they gave her.

We stayed with Crucita, who was good to us. At lunchtime she fried us eggs and gave us potatoes with sweet sauce, and for dinner she made soups and everything. Crucita wasn't working outside, as there was a man by the name of Jorge Luis who was in love with her and bought her everything.

Crucita wanted to go back to Puerto Rico and abandon us. She had her ticket and money. Then they got a ticket for *mami*, too, while she was in the hospital, and Crucita got tickets for us and we all went to Puerto Rico.

Grandma was glad to see us. She was living with Héctor when this happened. Grandma made a special vow and that was why *mami* got cured. So then *mami* began working for *don* Camacho again. He gave her money and *mami* rented a room.

Arturo used to take care of us. He is really nice and I love him and he loves me. I had a lovely photo of him, and Emilio, Crucita's husband, tore it up. He thought it was some sweetheart of Crucita's.

Then, I don't know, but when *mami* came here to New York she left me behind. She said she didn't have the fare for me but only for Sarita and Toya and I had to stay but that she would come for me later. Quique didn't go either, because he didn't want to.

Well, so I stayed. In the daytime I was at Nanda's house. It was good there because Héctor was nice to me. He worked and bought the food and she would cook a great big potful for everybody. She would give some to Arturo and to Eufemia, the next-door neighbor. I ate a lot, but Grandma always gave me plenty. One day she took one of those short sticks and beat me with it because a neighbor had hit me and I scratched her. I wasn't going to let that woman get away with it. I hit right back. So they came and told Grandma. I got sick with a fever. I would get asthma and I was always catching cold. That's why I am so skinny.

Fernanda didn't pay any attention to me at that time because she was in love with Junior. That is why I hate Junior. I don't like him; I love Héctor. When Héctor went to work, Fernanda would open the *window* and begin whistling. "Who are you whistling to?" I would say to her.

"Junior," she answered.

On *Thanksgiving*, Héctor bought Nanda a roast turkey, and he gave it to her and said, "For you, *negra.*" And would you believe it, but that afternoon when he came back from work he found Junior and Fernanda kissing. So Junior left and I went to his house and said to him, "Why don't you go away?"

Crucita went and said to him, "Junior, why don't you go away? Can't you see she loves Héctor more? Because when she's broke Héctor gives her money."

I slept with Arturo and Quique. I didn't stay at Fernanda's because when she got drunk there was no living with her. She would put on pants and begin dancing and carrying on and Crucita pulling at her to try to make her stop. There was no living with her when she was like that.

Arturo lived alone. He says he doesn't marry because *mami* is his wife. He didn't dare bring many women around because of Quique and me. I would knock on the door real loud and say, "Arturo, let me in. It's nighttime." When he didn't open, I would go looking for Quique and he would come back with me and say *"Papi,* open up, it's me and Catin. It's raining." It wasn't really but he said it just so he would let me in. If he didn't open, Quique would climb over the house and go in through a *window.*

One time I had to throw that drunk Pucha out of there. I said to her, "You get out of this house. You don't live here and can't give orders." I got her out but she gave me a slap, a real hard one. Crucita heard and came right over. I was crying and she spoke real nasty to Pucha. Pucha is a fresh one and that is why Crucita insulted her and bawled her out.

Finally Nanda left Héctor. It happened on a day when we were eating at Crucita's house. Arturo was very warm and Quique was sweating, so we moved to the bench outside to eat. Héctor came and caught Nanda and Junior kissing and said, "What a fine thing this is!" So right then and there Nanda pulled out a *Gem* she had, broke it into pieces and cut Héctor. Arturo jumped in and held her to stop the fight. They were going to send Nanda to jail but Héctor didn't want that. I kept quiet because there were a lot of people around.

Arturo left for the country and we went to live in Crucita's house. *Bendito,* but Crucita didn't have money. She had so many things to pay for and the sick baby to take care of. The little house was so small.

Then Crucita lived with Alejandro. He was good. He bought Crucita a bed and I slept in it with her. When he came off the ship he would give everything to Crucita and tell her to go and pay the grocery bill and buy whatever she wanted. It was fine, except that Emilio still loved her and always kept spying on her. He came to Crucita's at night to fight. "Why do you open the door for him?" I asked her. "He threatens you with a gun but that's nothing to you. If I were you I wouldn't open the door."

Crucita is lame. They are going to send her to New York to see if she can't be cured, but she doesn't want to leave the children with anybody. I feel sorry for her and would like to see her again. She was really nice and would play with us and everything. I would call Angelito and Quique and tell them to get together a gang because Crucita was waiting to play

with us. So we would go there and she would tell us all to line up to play
hide-and-seek or whoever-touches-this-wins. I'd run and run and win.

Once a fight started because Quique called me cripple, even though he
doesn't like it when they say that to Crucita. A kid was saying it to her
and Quique punched him in the mouth. Angelito held the boy and Quique
punched him. Crucita said, "If he calls me cripple again he better get
away because my nephew will beat him up."

But Quique teased me by calling me cripple. He likes cats and has a lot
of them. So I told him that if he called me cripple again I would throw out
his cats and he said, "O.K., I won't call you cripple any more."                    10

Crucita was the one who bought things for me. *Mami* sent Fernanda
money but I never saw any of it. Fernanda wanted it for Junior. Crucita
put me in school and I liked it very much. I was going into the second
grade, and Felícita was still saying I didn't know how to write, that Gabi
was the one who knew. But I was good in school. The *teachers* hit me
only once. Crucita would fix up my clothes to go to school and so did my
Grandma. Nanda would buy me my uniforms. Once she said to me, "Catin,
go and pawn this chain for me. You have to go to school tomorrow and
you have no shoes."

It was Saturday and Arturo had not come for me that day. Arturo came       20
for me on Saturdays and brought me back on Sunday. When I was going
to pawn the chain, Emilio went to Crucita's house to beat Grandma.
Emilio owned a gun and he had traded it with Héctor for a knife. "You're
a no-good *bum*," Nanda said to Emilio and he hit her. I put down the
money I got for the chain and went for Auntie. I knocked and knocked,
and in a minute the police were there and they caught Emilio with that
long knife he had. Arturo and nearly everybody came to see. Crucita did,
too.

What happened was that Héctor gave Emilio the knife to kill Junior.
Héctor didn't want to get into *trouble,* so he sent Emilio. And Emilio       30
said, "All right, if I get into *trouble,* you will too. I know you're a good
man, Héctor. You treat my children good." So Emilio was looking for
Junior. But Junior went running home and Héctor said, "I'll get even for
this sliced-up face of mine. That's how she is, my *negra!*"

Look how nice Héctor is. He told Nanda about the job at *doña* Ofelia's.
Otherwise Nanda wouldn't have gotten it. Sometimes I used to go over
there to help Nanda serve the tables, and wash the dishes and scrub.
After Nanda served all the people and everything, we would shut the door
tight and sit down to eat ourselves. Then we would clean off the tables
and all that.                                                                  40

I can say that Crucita never beat me. But Fernanda did. When I got
home from school, Crucita would send me to wash Chuito's diapers. I
liked doing it. And she would fix my clothes for me and all so I would be
neat and clean. Crucita loves children, but just imagine, Emilio nearly
took her little girl away from her!

Once there was a real big fight in Papo's place. What happened was

that Gladys came to Cruz's house once and Alejandro fell in love with
her, but Gladys is a coward and doesn't fight fair. Luckily, Fela and a
friend mixed in and defended Cruz. You see, Gladys was carrying on
with Alejandro.

"I knew Alejandro before you did," Crucita told her. "We knew him
before anybody here. If you think you're going to get him, you better beat
it right now."

The next day Auntie Fela went out on the street singing, and when she
passed by on the side where Gladys' house is, they tried to hit her with a
bottle. Auntie Fela fought back, though. They took a punch at her but she     10
ducked, and it hit a friend of Auntie Fela's, but he grabbed her and held
her back. Then Crucita got in it and said, "Drop that bottle! I know my
husband is in there. You can have him!"

And that is how life went along there.

Felicita spent all her time picking up men, and she would say to me,
"Put the children to bed for me and I'll give you money." She didn't pay
Crucita anything for taking care of the children at night and that was why
Crucita got angry. Because she can't work much on account of being lame.
She was always fighting with her sister because Fela neglected the children. Cruz spoke real rough to her. "Great whore, why don't you attend to     20
your children," she would say. Taking care of those children of Felícita's
was killing me. I was so skinny that I hardly had any strength to do anything. And I was so nervous I couldn't even pick up Chuito because I was
afraid I would drop him. Then one day when I was coming out of church
with a lot of people around, Felícita got hold of me and slapped me. She
always does things like that so people will talk about us.

Arturo and his son once wanted to take me to the country. Chiripa is
Arturo's son and he has a little girl who looks like Sarita, and a very
pretty wife. I said yes, yes, I wanted to go. Because there is a rowboat
there that belongs to him and a long bridge. I ride in the boat and jump     30
in the river. Arturo made a little playhouse for us and we used to climb
up on top of it. At this hour he would be having us ride horseback or
be bathing us in the river or playing with us. He is very good. I would
like *mami* and Arturo to get together again, but she doesn't want to.

So that is how things were when I was sleeping one day in Crucita's
house. At about one in the morning there was a knock on the door and it
was *mami*. She hugged me right away. I didn't see Sarita but I heard her
talking English: *"Mami, come over here,"* and *"Mami, your friend."* Mami
didn't know any English, though.

*Mami* stayed at Crucita's house. She went to visit Héctor and when she     40
saw his cut-up face, she got furious. "How did that happen?" she wanted
to know.

"Your *mamá.* But that's nothing, she's my *negra,*" he told her. Then
Leonor, the wife he has now came out and gave him a shove. So Héctor
kicked her and she hit Gabi. *Mami* said to her, "Leonor, if you beat that
child, you are going to get into *trouble,* because he is my nephew. If you

touch him, you are going to have to settle with me."

The next day *mami* asked me what Cruz said about her. "Nothing," I told her. "Cruz said you got attacks of hot pants."

"Oh, that's nothing. Don't pay any attention."

I told *mami* I wanted to go back with her, that I was tired of Puerto Rico and didn't want to live there. I said I was dying because Grandma hit me all the time, and I couldn't hold out much longer. *Mami* told me it was a good thing she came to see me. So then I told Cruz and she said, "Don't go. You're in school. Soledad will come again next year and you can leave with her then."                                                                10

I said to her, "No, I'm leaving. I have to learn English. I must learn!"

"Write me," Crucita said. I would but I don't know her address.

The trip was all a blank. I got airsick. When I came to, they were saying, "Fasten your seat belts. We are about to land." I asked *mami* where we were going, but she didn't say anything.

When we came out Benedicto was there, but I didn't recognize him. I kept looking him over because Toya called him papi.

"Toya, don't be calling him *papi*. That's not your *papi*." I told her. Toya's real *papá* is Tavio.                                                                       20

"Yes, he is my *papá*," she said.

When we got to the house I asked *mami*, "*Mami*, who is he?"

"That's my husband," she said.

"Husband? Oh. I'm going out, *mami*. I can't take that," I told her. So I went outside and ate a piece of cake.

I cried all the time when I first came to New York. It was the beginning of the cold weather and I didn't like it. I missed Arturo and kept calling for him. At night I couldn't sleep. I missed Chuito, too.

Benedicto never did anything to me. But it's that I hate all the husbands *mami* ever had. And he beats *mami*. He stays out all night and they fight over that a lot. *Mami* gets furious and beats him. One time he was going   30 to punch *mami*, and she ducked and he hit his fist on a drawer. Then he said to her, "*Ay*, Soledad, fix up my hand for me."

"Drop dead!" she told him.

I loved that. *Mami* had got the better of him. I hate Benedicto because he says that if I keep on hanging out in the street he is going to send me back to Puerto Rico. That is why, when he is around, I lock myself in the bathroom and don't come out. The thing is, he beats *mami* and drives her crazy. He punches her so hard he knocks her against the wall.

I keep saying to *mami*, "Let's go to Puerto Rico to Arturo. Leave Benedicto, because one of these days he's going to hit you and kill you." But   40 she doesn't listen to me. So let her stay with him!

When I am big, I am going to say to Benedicto, "How much money do you want to leave my *mami?*" Then I'll send for Arturo and Quique. If Arturo is around when Benedicto tries to take advantage of *mami* or if he grabs us and smashes us against the floor, he won't get away with it.

I don't know why, but once there was *trouble* and *mami* sent me over to

Uncle Simplicio's house. I slept on the *caucho* there and Flora took me to
Delancy Street. I put on shorts and washed the bathroom and scrubbed
and washed dishes for her. Then, when Flora began to work, I came
back home. But now, since Gabriel is there, they don't want me. I say to
him, "Uncle, can I go for the *weekend?*" But he won't let me. When Gabriel
isn't here, though, he does want me. That's the thing. Now when he wants
to take me home, I tell him I won't go with him. "You want Gabriel?" I
say to him. "Then stick with your Gabriel."

I beat Gabriel because he hits me. If he hits me, I am not just going to
take it. He is a very nice-looking boy and thinks he is *Superman.* The   10
only difference is, everybody loves *Superman* and I hate Gabriel. Uncle is
always buying him a *coat* and everything, and telling me what a good boy
he is. He never stops talking about it. He took him to Pennsylvania twice
already but he wouldn't take me. It doesn't matter though, because *mami*
is going to take me any day now.

Uncle is no saint. He doesn't gamble because he knows they might
arrest him. He drinks, though, and has girls. He is in love with the girl
from across the street. "Let's you and me kiss," he says to her. "Catin,
cover your eyes. Cover your eyes." And he goes chasing her around the   20
table. I know he tries to make love to that little girl. Then she gets mad
and says, "If *papá* knew you were trying to kiss me . . . I am going to tell
my *papá.*" Simplicio is no saint, even though he tries to make people think
he is.

I don't like to play with anybody, just *mami.* We jump rope, but *mami*
comes home late from work. I don't have many girl friends. Those friends
of mine just give a person *trouble.*

One day they said that *mami* is a whore. I answered right back, "Isn't
your *mamá* one, too? She picks up men and takes money from them."

Right away, Aida says to me, "No, she never does that."

"Oh no, never!" I said to her. "Wait till she sends you outside with the   30
*baby* so she can get the money from the men. But don't worry, I'm going
to tell *mami* now."

So I went and told her, "*Mami,* Aida says you're a whore and pick up
men." *Mami* went to Aida's *mamá* and said to her, "Say, tell Aida I'm not
a whore." Then she went and locked herself in the house and right away
she got an attack. She can't have bad things happen to her because she
gets that way and can't speak or breathe. She throws herself on the floor
and bites her tongue. She wants to bite it off.

They say that *mami* goes to men's houses but *mami* says, "Nobody can
say anything about me because I do it so my children can eat."   40

I feel sorry for *mami.* I wish she wasn't in *trouble* with anybody. Let her
not talk to Rosalia because that old woman has a longer tongue than I.
Rosalia is the one to blame for everything that happens because she intro-
duces men to my *mami* and then gets her into *trouble.* I think she told
Benedicto that *mami* was in love with Elfredo.

One day I went looking for *mami* and they told me, "Your *mamá* is at

Elfredo's house."

I acted innocent and said, "Who is Elfredo? I don't know him." I was afraid on account of Benedicto because they fell in love in his house behind his back. Elfredo says he doesn't beat women and I like men like that. Elfredo brought us records and played them. Benedicto came and saw them so I took and gave them back to Elfredo. "Here, Elfredo," I said, "take them so *mami* won't have *trouble.*"

Right now we have to take advantage because Benedicto has a lot of money. He came back from the ship with it. I am going to tell *mami* to ask him to get the *television* out of the *punchoff* so that when I come home from school I can sit on the couch and take a rest watching *television.* 10

Yesterday I told *mami* that Benedicto was talking English to Rosalia. They just said a few words but I went and told *mami* because she gets mad when he speaks English. My *mamá* hates English. So she said, "Listen, go tell Benedicto to come here."

When Benedicto came he said about me, "That child should have her tongue cut off. One of these days she's going to get us all put in jail."

Elfredo and *mami* kept seeing each other, but *mami* wanted him to give her money and buy her things whether he wanted to or not. He would say to her, "Wait a moment! Take it easy, daughter, I haven't collected yet." 20

One time *mami* slapped Elfredo because she saw him with a woman. Then she got very nervous and had an attack. Elfredo stopped coming around to the house and I said, "Elfredo got married." *Mami* told me he was not married and to stop coming around with gossip.

The thing is that Elfredo knew that *mami* was in love with the Colombian and I think Benedicto did, too. It's Rosalia's fault, because she told *mami* that this Colombian was nice and so he gave *mami* the eye and invited us to the movies.

I gave *mami* a dirty look and later I said to her, *"Mami,* is that man going to the movies with me? I won't go. You know I don't like Colombians." 30

When *mami* is in love she acts different. She stays out in the street. I think she is going to stop going with men because she has these attacks. If she is going to have bad times with men, she better leave them. Oh, my Lord! I want her to leave them.

Imagine, that Colombian left *mami* in the lurch. Every few minutes *mami* would tell me to go see if he is coming. And I would answer, *"Oh, mami!* I'm not your servant. I'm not going to be on the lookout for him. I wish all Colombians would drop dead." So she grabbed me and hit me. She gave me two slaps in the face in front of Uncle.

*Mami* was even going to poison herself on account of him. She was 40 lying back on the couch when she called me and said, "Catin, bring me a glass of water. I am going to take these pills to poison myself."

I gave her the water and ran out yelling and crying. When I came back she didn't open her eyes any more or answer, or anything. They called the ambulance and took her away. We stayed with the lady next door but they brought *mami* back right away and she was well.

I am afraid that if Benedicto comes back there is going to be *trouble* here. Rosalia might tell him about *mami* and the Colombian. The thing is that they lie down in *mami*'s bed and we get into the bed in the other room. I have seen them kissing. Yes, that's the truth. If Benedicto goes after *mami* and hits her, I am not going to talk to any of them again.

What I would like to see is Uncle beat up Benedicto. If the police came he could say, "This man began beating my sister and I just defended her." And he could bring *mami* as a witness and nothing would happen.

*Mami* put me in school now, and it's better there. I can learn English. I love to talk English. After I know how, I can talk in English and she won't know what I am saying.

I have been here for a long time already and so I am forgetting Spanish. English is what comes into my head. In school, I want to say *"Ven aca"* and what comes out is "Come on." *Mami* says that if I learn to talk English she'll beat me. But I tell her I would love to learn English. I start talking to Sarita and *mami* says to me, "Listen, you shut that mouth. You are not going to talk English around here." She gets very mad.

So I tell her, "But, *mami,* I have to learn to talk English, because if I don't I'll get left back in school."

*Mami* says, "I hate the Americans but not the ones who speak Spanish."

*Mami* didn't want to buy me a notebook I needed for school. I began to cry but then I stopped. She just left and didn't even listen to me. That's why they give me F. And at home the kids throw my things around and I can't find anything. Now I can't find my pencil case.

The schools are better here. They mistreat you in the schools in Puerto Rico. Mrs. Guerra, my teacher in Puerto Rico, was a bully and made me kneel down and all. If you come late here they leave you alone, but in Puerto Rico you have to go to the stupid *principal.* They grab the children by the hair there and they don't let you play. They tell you to go to the bathroom and come right back. Not here. Here they let you play a lot and the *lunches* are better. They give fresh milk and all kinds of fruit. That's why I like school better here.

But the children here are worse than the ones in Puerto Rico. They bully me. They muss my hair and one girl scratched me and Sarita and didn't let us eat. But that doesn't matter. If that girl hits me, I hit her back. I have two good hands and I can hit back. But believe me, I used to be afraid When I got home I told my mother and she said not to be such a dummy. . . that whoever hit me, I should hit back. Since that time I don't let anybody hit me any more.

When I grow up I am going to get even with all of them. I want to go back to Puerto Rico, but only after I know English so as not to talk Spanish to anybody. Not even to *mami.* I will talk to her in English. I'll call her *"Mother."* As I won't know much Spanish, I will take somebody with me and I will pay their fare just for them to speak Spanish for me. And so, I'll tell this friend of mine who speaks Spanish, "Tell my grandma to leave Junior because Junior won't do her any good."

Then I'll go to Héctor's and tell him, "Don't worry, Héctor," Héctor knows English. He is a *merchant marine* and the *merchant marine* know a lot of English. So I will be able to talk to Héctor and he will understand. I will say to him, "Don't you worry, Héctor. One of these days, Grandma is going to leave Junior and go back to you. *Mami* is coming over here to fix it up."

I am going to tell Junior's *mamá*, too. "Now look, *dona* Celestina, tell your son to go look for somebody else, and that Nanda is not young. So let Junior leave her, because I can't keep on spending money to be coming here." Maybe Celestina will tell him, because she used to hate Nanda.                10

Oh, how Grandma will cry when I get hold of her and say, "When we were little, you didn't want to take care of us. Now you can't be with Simplicio because he is with me in New York."

And if Simplicio is there, I'll say to him, "Listen, Simplicio, tell your *mamá* to forget about me. I didn't come to see her. I just came to see Crucita."

And if Simplicio is there, I'll say to him, "Listen, Simplicio, tell your how it used to be? Sure you remember. You don't know English, Crucita, but come to New York and I will help you take care of the children. Come on. You'll live with *mami*. You know, I'll give you a room for yourself       20 and for Anita and Chuito."

Benedicto has to fix up this house and not keep it like a dump. We have money in the bank. This is a good house. When *mami* fixes it up it is as pretty as it can be. The bad thing is that the neighbors don't let you sleep and those children turn the place upside down. That Toya has her bed all rotted out with pee and that makes *mami* mad.

One day *mami* was going out and Benedicto had to go somewhere too. So gets the attacks more and more on account of Benedicto than anything else. It's because he wants to use her like she was a servant. "Soledad, put my shoes on for me. Soledad, my shirt. Soledad, go buy me this." He        30 orders her and orders her and *mami* can't walk much. And how they fight! One day *mami* was going out and Benedicto had to go somewhere too. So *mami* told him, "I'll be back when you are, because I'm not going to be shut in the house here by myself."

So he said to her, "Who gives the orders? You or me?"

"Me," *mami* said to him, "because you are not my husband any more."

So he grabbed her and punched her and *mami* pulled a knife and was going to stick him with it but he held her off. *Mami* nearly killed me because he grabbed me and shoved me in between the two of them. He tried to cover himself with Sarita, too. He hates us both. *Mami* would have killed     40 him if he hadn't covered himself with us. Then Benedicto tried to get the knife away from her and tried to bend her hand until finally the knife stuck in his finger. "I cut my own self," he said.

I called him a liar and Toya called him a fairy, a son of a whore, and all kinds of bad things. I felt like taking that cover off the knife and sticking it through his head. It is a strong thing and if you stick it into somebody he dies. I wanted to stick it into him, but I got into bed all nervous and shaking.

This is the last time he is going to hit her, because if he does it again, I am going to stick a knife into him so he can't take advantage of *mami* any more. Men are bad, all of them. There isn't a single good one. That's why, when I grow up, I am not going to get married. I am going to be a nun. That way you can be alone and work and earn a lot of money.

Nearly every week we go to the Pee House. That's what they call the movie theater, because everybody pees on the floor. It's down Eagle Avenue and it's cheap. All it costs is a quarter. We go in at one o'clock and don't 10 get back sometimes until ten when the pictures are good.

Oh, how I like to go to the movies with *mami!* Because *mami* likes the funny pictures and enjoys herself. She laughs the most at Cuquita. He is a man who dresses up like a woman. He puts on a dress and a wig and ribbons and he looks like a fat woman and he dances real nice.

I liked the one we saw about Zorro. It was real good. Antonio Aguilar was in it and Antonio Aguilar's brother. He played Zorro. He had daughters and when they grew up they could ride horses and everything. So they grabbed the bad men, the rich ones, and took their money away and gave it to the good ones, you know, the poor people. . . the ones who 20 send their children to school dirty and all that. I feel sorry for them. Then after that the father, Zorro, got old and they shot him with an arrow, but the daughters saved him.

When I grow up I would like to be one of the Zorros so when I go back to Puerto Rico I can put on the Zorro clothes and get a horse and begin helping the poor people and kill the rich ones. They have to get what's coming to them, and I will kill the crooks too.

# White on Black, Black on Black

"Oh, I _beg_ your pardon! I thought you were extinct."

• •

# Introduction

There are people who look at the Black Revolution and ask, "What's all the fuss about?" They'll tell you that blacks have been free since Lincoln's Emancipation Proclamation of 1863. Free? We know better. Even within the Proclamation itself is a hint of what waited ahead for the black man: Lincoln hopes that blacks "in all cases where allowed" will "labor faithfully for reasonable wages." This is a small example of what rankles blacks today. It isn't comfortable or easy to take lightly words like "in all cases where allowed."

The Constitutional amendments which follow the Lincoln selection offer more evidence of the kind of shuckin' and jivin' whitey was doing to push the black man back. Why would the 1870 amendment have been necessary if the 1868 amendment had been taken seriously? More recently, why would the boycotts and freedom marches have been necessary if anyone had taken the Constitution or the Declaration of Independence seriously? There are many questions which can't be answered in any satisfactory way. But these same questions can help us to understand what all the fuss today is about.

*Uncle Tom's Cabin* was an honest attempt to stir up anger about a moral wrong. But *Uncle Tom's Cabin*, by a well-intentioned white woman, remains a source of irritation to the black man. It's no com-

pliment for a black to be called an "Uncle Tom," and
still another of Harriet Beecher Stowe's "good niggers," Jim Crow, has got to go.

Booker T. Washington was a "good nigger" and
so everyone, black and white, has heard about him
in school. He made it in the white man's world and
no one can say that it wasn't hard, or that it didn't
take a lot of guts, or even that it isn't a big deal. But
look at what Booker T. Washington is saying! He
promises that, "in our humble way, we shall stand
by you with a devotion that no foreigner can approach, ready to lay down our lives, if need be, in
defense of yours." It gets worse. "In all things that are
.purely social we can be as separate as the fingers. . . ."
Like Harriet Beecher Stowe, Booker T. Washington
had good intentions, had courage. But neither demanded anything. Each begged, pleaded. A demand
implies strength, a plea implies weakness. Both of
these writers, one a white Southern lady, the other
a black man, assumed without question the superiority of the white race.

It's not surprising that blacks are fed up; what
amazes one is their extraordinary patience. We jump
from Booker T. Washington to the present day with
Coretta King's selection. The black man had "tommed"
long enough. Rosa Parks had "tommed" long enough.
Rosa Parks wasn't a militant, wasn't a trouble-maker.
She hadn't spent any part of her life giving speeches
or in any way fighting back. But one day she'd had
it, and the fight was on. Does it come as any surprise that *all* the people who'd had it would rejoice
that someone had looked the white man in the eye
and said *no*! Things were hell for the blacks in Montgomery but they were fighting for their lives, for
their human-ness. That's a long way from Jim Crow
and Uncle Tom, but not far enough.

"Black at the Gridiron Dinner," a very recent selection, will give you some idea of how much lies
ahead. The injustices described by Roger Wilkins and
Dick Gregory don't really begin to cover all of the
things that fire black anger.

Compare the tone of some of the angrier selections
here to Sam Levenson's reminiscence or to Carolyn
Banks' short story, both in the next section. All of
the writers are looking back at growing up, but growing up for a black was like nothing Banks or Levenson

or maybe you yourself could ever dream of. Growing up is something of a miracle when the odds of your making it are stacked against you. And too many black communities, rich, poor and middle class, face those same odds today.

When you read the Black Panther documents you'll undoubtedly be surprised. TV and the newspapers give us a different image of the Panthers from the one presented here. We thought it best to let them speak for themselves.

Harry Jones presents a change of pace. Black writers have had little time to display the humor that has enabled them to deal with their world, the humor that has helped to preserve their sanity. Jones lets the reader look at a side of black culture often hidden from the white man. And "Vining," by Leon Williams, completes the cycle, supplying the very humor that Jones finds lacking in black literature. Leon Williams was a college student himself when he wrote this.

The Black Revolution isn't over, nor are all the revolutions that it inspired. A long time coming, black identity is here to stay.

# Abraham Lincoln
## The Emancipation Proclamation

Whereas on the twenty-second day of September, in the year of our Lord one thousand eight hundred and sixty-two, a proclamation was issued by the President of the United States, containing, among other things, the following, to wit:

That on the first day of January, in the year of our Lord one thousand eight hundred and sixty-three, all persons held as slaves within any State, or designated part of a State, the people whereof shall then be in rebellion against the United States, shall be then, thenceforward, and forever free; and the Executive Government of the United States, including the military and naval authority thereof, will recognize and 10 maintain the freedom of such persons, and will do no act or acts to repress such persons, or any of them, in any efforts they may make for their actual freedom.

That the Executive will, on the first day of January aforesaid, by proclamation, designate the States and parts of States, if any, in which the people thereof respectively shall then be in rebellion against the United States; and the fact that any State, or the people thereof, shall on that day be in good faith represented in the Congress of the United States by members chosen thereto at elections wherein a majority of the qualified voters of such State shall have participated, shall in the ab- 20 sence of strong countervailing testimony be deemed conclusive evidence that such State and the people thereof are not then in rebellion against the United States.

Now, therefore, I, Abraham Lincoln, President of the United States, by virtue of the power in me vested as Commander-in-Chief of the Army and

Navy of the United States, in time of actual armed rebellion against the authority and government of the United States, and as a fit and necessary war measure for suppressing said rebellion, do, on this first day of January, in the year of our Lord one thousand eight hundred and sixty-three, and in accordance with my purpose so to do, publicly proclaimed for the full period of 100 days from the day first above mentioned, order and designate as the States and parts of States wherein the people thereof, respectively, are this day in rebellion against the United States, the following, to wit:

Arkansas, Texas, Louisiana (except the parishes of St. Bernard, Plaquemines, Jefferson, St. John, St. Charles, St. James, Ascension, Assumption, Terre Bonne, Lafourche, St. Mary, St. Martin, and Orleans, including the city of New Orleans), Mississippi, Alabama, Florida, Georgia, South Carolina, North Carolina, and Virginia (except the forty-eight counties designated as West Virginia, and also the counties of Berkeley, Accomac, Northampton, Elizabeth City, York, Princess Anne, and Norfolk, including the cities of Norfolk and Portsmouth), and which excepted parts are for the present left precisely as if this proclamation were not issued.

And by virtue of the power and for the purpose aforesaid, I do order and declare that all persons held as slaves within said designated States and parts of States are, and henceforward shall be, free; and that the Executive Government of the United States, including the military and naval authorities thereof, shall recognize and maintain the freedom of said persons.

And I hereby enjoin upon the people so declared to be free to abstain from all violence, unless in necessary self-defense; and I recommend to them that, in all cases where allowed, they labor faithfully for reasonable wages.

And I further declare and make known that such persons of suitable condition will be received into the armed service of the United States to garrison forts, positions, stations, and other places, and to man vessels of all sorts in said service.

And upon this act, sincerely believed to be an act of justice, warranted by the Constitution upon military necessity, I invoke the considerate judgment of mankind and the gracious favor of Almighty God.

In witness whereof, I have hereunto set my hand and caused the seal of the United States to be affixed.

*Done at the city of Washington, the first day of January, in the year of our Lord one thousand eight hundred and sixty-three, and of the independence of the United States of America the eighty-seventh.*

ABRAHAM   LINCOLN

# The U.S. Constitution

### ARTICLE XIV (1868)

Sec. 1. All persons born or naturalized in the United States, and subject to the jurisdiction thereof, are citizens of the United States and of the State wherein they reside. No State shall make or enforce any law which shall abridge the privileges or immunities of citizens of the United States; nor shall any State deprive any person of life, liberty, or property, without due process of law; nor deny to any person within its jurisdiction the equal protection of the laws.

Sec. 2. Representatives shall be appointed among the several States according to their respective numbers, counting the whole number of persons in each State, excluding Indians not taxed. But when the right to vote 10 at any election for the choice of electors for President and Vice-President of the United States, Representatives in Congress, the executive and judicial officer of any State, to support the Constitution of the United States, is denied to any of the male inhabitants of such State, being twenty-one years of age, and citizens of the United States, or in any way abridged, except for participation in rebellion, or other crime, the basis of representation therein shall be reduced in the proportion which the number of such male citizens shall bear to the whole number of male citizens twenty-one years of age in such State.

### ARTICLE XV (1870)

20

Sec. 1. The right of citizens of the United States to vote shall not be denied or abridged by the United States or by any State on account of race, color, or previous condition of servitude.

Sec. 2. The Congress shall have power to enforce this article by appropriate legislation.

# Harriet Beecher Stowe
## From Uncle Tom's Cabin

### PREFACE

The scenes of this story, as its title indicates, lie among a race hitherto ignored by the associations of polite and refined society; an exotic race, whose ancestors, born beneath a tropic sun, brought with them, and perpetuated to their descendants, a character so essentially unlike the hard and dominant Anglo-Saxon race, as for many years to have won from it only misunderstanding and contempt.

But, another and better day is dawning; every influence of literature, of poetry, and of art, in our times, is becoming more and more in unison with the great master chord of Christianity, "good-will-to man."

The poet, the painter, and the artist now seek out and embellish the  10
common and gentler humanities of life, and, under the allurements of fiction, breathe a humanizing and subduing influence, favorable to the development of the great principles of Christian brotherhood.

The hand of benevolence is everywhere stretched out, searching into abuses, righting wrongs, alleviating distresses, and bringing to the knowledge and sympathies of the world the lowly, the oppressed, and the forgotten.

In this general movement, unhappy Africa at last is remembered; Africa, who began the race of civilization and human progress in the dim, gray dawn of early time, but who, for centuries, has lain bound and bleeding  20
at the foot of civilized and Christianized humanity, imploring compassion in vain.

But the heart of the dominant race, who have been her conquerors, her hard masters, has at length been turned towards her in mercy; and it has been seen how far nobler it is in nations to protect the feeble than to oppress them. Thanks be to God, the world has at last outlived the slave-trade!

The object of these sketches is to awaken sympathy and feeling for the African race, as they exist among us; to show their wrongs and sorrows, under a system so necessarily cruel and unjust as to defeat and do away the good effects of all that can be attempted for them, by their best friends, under it.

In doing this, the author can sincerely disclaim any invidious feeling towards those individuals who, often without any fault of their own, are involved in the trials and embarrassments of the legal relations of slavery.

Experience has shown her that some of the noblest of minds and hearts are often thus involved; and no one knows better than they do, that what                    10 may be gathered of the evils of slavery from sketches like these, is not the half that could be told, of the unspeakable whole.

In the Northern States, these representations may, perhaps, be thought caricatures; in the Southern States are witnesses who know their fidelity. What personal knowledge the author has had, of the truth of incidents such as here are related, will appear in its time.

It is a comfort to hope, as so many of the world's sorrows and wrongs have, from age to age, been lived down, so a time shall come when sketches similar to these shall be valuable only as memorials of what has long ceased to be.                    20

When an enlightened and Christianized community shall have, on the shores of Africa, laws, language, and literature, drawn from among us, may then the scenes of the house of bondage be to them like the remembrance of Egypt to the Israelite,—a motive of thankfulness to Him who hath redeemed them!

For, while politicians contend, and men are swerved this way and that by conflicting tides of interest and passion, the great cause of human liberty is in the hands of One, of whom it is said:—

> "He shall not fail nor be discouraged                    30
>   Till he have set judgment in the earth."
> "He shall deliver the needy when he crieth,
>   The poor, and him that hath no helper."
> "He shall redeem their soul from deceit and violence,
>   And precious shall their blood be in his sight."

## CHAPTER I

*In Which the Reader is Introduced to a Man of Humanity*

Late in the afternoon of a chilly day in February, two gentlemen were sitting alone over their wine, in a well-furnished dining parlor, in the                    40 town of P——, in Kentucky. There were no servants present, and the gentlemen, with chairs closely approaching, seemed to be discussing some subject with great earnestness.

For convenience' sake, we have said, hitherto, two *gentlemen*. One of the parties, however, when critically examined, did not seem, strictly speaking, to come under the species. He was a short thick-set man, with coarse commonplace features, and that swaggering air of pretension which marks a low man who is trying to elbow his way upward in the world. He was much overdressed, in a gaudy vest of many colors, a blue neckerchief, bedropped gayly with yellow spots, and arranged with a flaunting tie, quite in keeping with the general air of the man. His hands, large and coarse, were plentifully bedecked with rings; and he wore a heavy gold watch-chain, with a bundle of seals of portentous size, and a great variety of colors, attached to it,—which, in the ardor of conversation, he was in the habit of flourishing and jingling with evident satisfaction. His conversation was in free and easy defiance of Murray's Grammar, and was garnished at convenient intervals with various profane expressions, which not even the desire to be graphic in our account shall induce us to transcribe.

His companion, Mr. Shelby, had the appearance of a gentleman; and the arrangements of the house, and the general air of the housekeeping, indicated easy, and even opulent, circumstances. As we before stated, the two were in the midst of an earnest conversation.

"That is the way I should arrange the matter," said Mr. Shelby.

"I can't make trade that way,—I positively can't, Mr. Shelby," said the other, holding up a glass of wine between his eye and the light.

"Why, the fact is, Haley, Tom is an uncommon fellow; he is certainly worth that sum anywhere,—steady, honest, capable, manages my whole farm like a clock."

"You mean honest, as niggers go," said Haley, helping himself to a glass of brandy.

"No; I mean, really, Tom is a good, steady, sensible, pious fellow. He got religion at a camp-meeting, four years ago; and I believe he really *did* get it. I've trusted him, since then, with everything I have,—money, house, horses,—and let him come and go round the country; and I always found him true and square in everything."

"Some folks don't believe there is pious niggers, Shelby," said Haley, with a candid flourish of his hand, "but *I do*. I had a fellow, now, in this yer last lot I took to Orleans,—'t was as good as a meetin', now, really, to hear that critter pray; and he was quite gentle and quiet like. He fetched me a good sum, too, for I bought him cheap of a man that was 'bliged to sell out; so I realized six hundred on him. Yes, I consider religion a valeyable thing in a nigger, when it's the genuine article, and no mistake."

"Well, Tom's got the real article, if ever a fellow had," rejoined the other. "Why, last fall, I let him go to Cincinnati alone, to do business for me, and bring home five hundred dollars. 'Tom,' says I to him, 'I trust you, because I think you're a Christian,—I know you wouldn't cheat.' Tom comes back, sure enough; I knew he would. Some low fellows, they say, said to him, 'Tom, why don't you make tracks for Canada?' 'Ah, master trusted me, and I couldn't,'—they told me about it. I am sorry to part with Tom, I must say. You ought to let him cover the whole balance of the debt; and you would, Haley, if you had any conscience."

"Well, I've got just as much conscience as any man in business can afford to keep,—just a little, you know, to swear by as 't were," said the trader, jocularly; "and, then, I'm ready to do anything in reason to 'blige friends; but this yer, you see, is a leetle too hard on a fellow,—a leetle too hard." The trader sighed contemplatively, and poured out some more brandy.

"Well then, Haley, how will you trade?" said Mr. Shelby, after an uneasy interval of silence.

"Well, haven't you a boy or gal that you could throw in with Tom?"

"Hum!—none that I could well spare; to tell the truth, it's only hard     10
necessity makes me willing to sell at all. I don't like parting with any of my hands, that's a fact."

Here the door opened, and a small quadroon boy, between four and five years of age, entered the room. There was something in his appearance remarkably beautiful and engaging. His black hair, fine as floss silk, hung in glossy curls about his round dimpled face, while a pair of large dark eyes, full of fire and softness, looked out from beneath the rich, long lashes, as he peered curiously into the apartment. A gay robe of scarlet and yellow plaid, carefully made and neatly fitted, set off to ad-     20
vantage the dark and rich style of his beauty; and a certain comic air of assurance, blended with bashfulness, showed that he had been not unused to being petted and noticed by his master.

"Hulloa, Jim Crow!" said Mr. Shelby, whistling, and snapping a bunch of raisins towards him, "pick that up, now!"

The child scampered, with all his little strength, after the prize, while his master laughed.

"Come here, Jim Crow," said he. The child came up, and the master patted the curly head, and chucked him under the chin.

"Now, Jim, show this gentleman how you can dance and sing." The boy commenced one of those wild, grotesque songs common among the     30
negroes, in a rich clear voice, accompanying his singing with many evolutions of the hands, feet, and whole body, all in perfect time to the music.

"Bravo!" said Haley, throwing him a quarter of an orange.

"Now, Jim, walk like old Uncle Cudjoe when he has the rheumatism," said his master.

Instantly the flexible limbs of the child assumed the appearance of deformity and distortion, as, with his back humped up and his master's stick in his hand, he hobbled about the room, his childish face drawn into a doleful pucker, and spitting from right to left, in imitation of an old man.

Both gentlemen laughed uproariously.     40

"Now, Jim," said his master, "show us how old Elder Robbins leads the psalm." The boy drew his chubby face down to a formidable length, and commenced toning a psalm tune through his nose with imperturbable gravity.

"Hurrah! bravo! what a young un!" said Haley; "that chap's a case, I'll promise. Tell you what," said he, suddenly clapping his hand on Mr.

Shelby's shoulder, "fling in that chap and I'll settle the business,—I will. Come, now, if that an't doing the thing up about the rightest!"

At this moment, the door was pushed gently open, and a young quadroon woman, apparently about twenty-five, entered the room.

There needed only a glance from the child to her, to identify her as its mother. There was the same rich, full, dark eye, with its long lashes; the same ripples of silky black hair. The brown of her complexion gave way on the cheek to a perceptible flush, which deepened as she saw the gaze of the strange man fixed upon her in bold and undisguised admiration. Her dress was of the neatest possible fit, and set off to advantage her finely moulded shape; a delicately formed hand and a trim foot and ankle were items of appearance that did not escape the quick eye of the trader, well used to run up at a glance the points of a fine female article.

"Well, Eliza?" said her master, as she stopped and looked hesitatingly at him.

"I was looking for Harry, please sir;" and the boy bounded toward her, showing his spoils, which he had gathered in the skirt of his robe.

"Well, take him away, then," said Mr. Shelby; and hastily she withdrew, carrying the child on her arm.

"By Jupiter," said the trader, turning to him in admiration, "there's an article, now! You might make your fortune on that ar gal in Orleans, any day. I've seen over a thousand, in my day, paid down for gals not a bit handsomer."

"I don't want to make my fortune on her," said Mr. Shelby, dryly; and, seeking to turn the conversation, he uncorked a bottle of fresh wine, and asked his companion's opinion of it.

"Capitol, sir,—first chop!" said the trader; then turning, and slapping his hand familiarly on Shelby's shoulder, he added,—

"Come, how will you trade about the gal?—what shall I say for her,—what'll you take?"

"Mr. Haley, she is not to be sold," said Shelby. "My wife would not part with her for her weight in gold."

"Ay, ay! women always say such things, cause they han't no sort of calculation. Just show 'em how many watches, feathers, and trinkets one's weight in gold would buy, and that alters the case, I reckon."

"I tell you, Haley, this must not be spoken of; I say no, and I mean no," said Shelby, decidedly.

"Well, you'll let me have the boy, though," said the trader; "you must own I've come down pretty handsomely for him."

"What on earth can you want with the child?" said Shelby.

"Why, I've got a friend that's going into this yer branch of the business,—wants to buy up handsome boys to raise for the market. Fancy articles entirely,—sell for waiters, and so on, to rich 'uns, that can pay for handsome 'uns. It sets off one of yer great places,—a real handsome boy to open door, wait, and tend. They fetch a good sum; and this little devil is such a comical, musical concern, he's just the article."

"I would rather not sell him," said Mr. Shelby, thoughtfully; "the fact is, sir, I'm a humane man, and I hate to take the boy from his mother, sir."

"Oh, you do?—La! yes,—something of that ar natur. I understand, perfectly. It is mighty onpleasant getting on with women sometimes. I allays hates these yer screechin' screamin' times. They are *mighty* on-pleasant; but, as I manages business, I generally avoids 'em, sir. Now, what if you get the girl off for a day, or a week, or so; then the thing's done quietly,—all over before she comes home. Your wife might get her some ear-rings, or a new gown, or some such truck, to make up with her."

"I'm afraid not."

"Lor bless ye, yes! These critters an't like white folks, you know; they gets over things, only manage right. Now, they say," said Haley, assuming a candid and confidential air, "that this kind o' trade is hardening to the feelings; but I never found it so. Fact is, I never could do things up the way some fellers manage the business. I've seen 'em as would pull a woman's child out of her arms, and set him up to sell, and she screechin' like mad all the time;—very bad policy,—damages the article,—makes 'em quite unfit for service sometimes. I knew a real handsom gal once, in Orleans, as was entirely ruined by this sort o' handling. The fellow that was trading for her didn't want her baby; and she was one of your real high sort, when her blood was up. I tell you, she squeezed up her child in her arms, and talked, and went on real awful. It kinder makes my blood run cold to think on 't; and when they carried off the child, and locked her up, she jest went ravin' mad, and died in a week. Clear waste, sir, of a thousand dollars, jest for want of management,—there's where 't is. It's always best to do the humane thing, sir; that's been *my* experi-ence." And the trader leaned back in his chair, and folded his arms, with an air of virtuous decision, apparently considering himself a second Wilberforce.

The subject appeared to interest the gentleman deeply; for while Mr. Shelby was thoughtfully peeling an orange, Haley broke out afresh, with becoming diffidence, but as if actually driven by the force of truth to say a few words more.

"It don't look well, now, for a feller to be praisin' himself; but I say it jest because it's the truth. I believe I'm reckoned to bring in about the finest droves of niggers that is brought in,—at least, I've been told so; if I have once, I reckon I have a hundred times, all in good case,—fat and skely, and I lose as few as any man in the business. And I lays it all to my management, sir; and humanity, sir, I may say, is the great pillar of *my* management."

Mr. Shelby did not know what to say, and so he said, "Indeed!"

"Now, I've been laughed at for my notions, sir, and I've been talked to. They an't pop'lar, and they an't common; but I stuck to 'em, sir; I've stuck to 'em, and realized well on 'em; yes, sir, they have paid their pas-sage, I may say," and the trader laughed at his joke.

There was something so piquant and original in these elucidations of humanity, that Mr. Shelby could not help laughing in company. Perhaps you laugh too, dear reader; but you know humanity comes out in a variety of strange forms nowadays, and there is no end to the odd things that humane people will say and do.

Mr. Shelby's laugh encouraged the trader to proceed.

"It's strange now, but I never could beat this into people's heads. Now, there was Tom Loker, my old partner, down in Natchez; he was a clever fellow, Tom was, only the very devil with niggers,—on principle 't was, you see, for a better-hearted feller never broke bread; 't was his *system,* sir. I used to talk to Tom. 'Why, Tom,' I used to say, 'when your gals takes on and cry, what's the use o' crackin' on 'em over the head, and knockin' on 'em round? It's ridiculous,' says I, and don't do no sort o' good. Why, I don't see no harm in their cryin',' says I; 'it's natur,' says I, 'and if natur can't blow off one way, it will another. Besides Tom,' says I, 'it jest spiles your gals; they get sickly and down in the mouth; and sometimes they gets ugly,—particular yellow gals do,—and it's the devil and all gettin' on 'em broke in. Now,' says I, 'why can't you kinder coax 'em up, and speak 'em fair? Depend on it, Tom, a little humanity, thrown in along, goes a heap further than all your jawin' and crackin'; and it pays better, says I, 'depend on 't.' But Tom couldn't get the hang on 't; and he spiled so many for me, that I had to break off with him, though he was a good-hearted fellow, and as fair a business hand as is goin'."

"And do you find your ways of managing do the business better than Tom's?" said Mr. Shelby.

"Why, yes, sir, I may say so. You see, when I any ways can, I takes a leetle care about the onpleasant parts, like selling young uns and that,—get the gals out of the way,—out of sight, out of mind, you know,—and when it's clean done, and can't be helped, they naturally gets used to it. 'Tan't, you know, as if it was the white folks, that's brought up in the way of 'spectin' to keep their children and wives, and all that. Niggers, you know, that's fetched up properly han't no kind of 'spectations of no kind; so all these things comes easier."

"I'm afraid mine are not properly brought up, then," said Mr. Shelby.

"S'pose not; you Kentucky folks spile your niggers. You mean well by 'em, but 'tan't no real kindness, arter all. Now a nigger, you see, what's got to be hacked and tumbled round the world, and sold to Tom, and Dick, and the Lord knows who, tan't no kindness to be givin' on him notions and expectations, and bringin' on him up too well, for the rough and tumble comes all the harder on him arter. Now, I venture to say, your niggers would be quite chop-fallen in a place where some of your planta- tion niggers would be singing and whooping like all possessed. Every man, you know, Mr. Shelby, naturally thinks well of his own ways; and I think I treat niggers just about as well as it's ever worth while to treat 'em."

"It's a happy thing to be satisfied," said Mr. Shelby, with a slight shrug, and some perceptible feelings of a disagreeable nature.

"Well," said Haley, after they had both silently picked their nuts for a season, "what do you say?"

"I'll think the matter over, and talk with my wife," said Mr. Shelby. "Meantime, Haley, if you want the matter carried on in the quiet way you speak of, you'd best not let your business in this neighborhood be known. It will get out among my boys, and it will not be a particularly quiet business getting away any of my fellows, if they know it, I'll promise you."

"Oh, certainly, by all means, mum! of course. But I'll tell you, I'm in a devil of a hurry, and shall want to know, as soon as possible, what I may depend on," said he, rising and putting on his overcoat.                             10

"Well, call up this evening,between six and seven, and you shall have my answer," said Mr. Shelby, and the trader bowed himself out of the apartment.

"I'd like to have been able to kick the fellow down the steps," said he to himself, as he saw the door fairly closed, "with his impudent assurance; but he knows how much he has me at advantage. If anybody had ever said to me that I should sell Tom down south to one of those rascally traders, I should have said, 'Is thy servant a dog, that he should do this thing?' And now it must come, for aught I see. And Eliza's child, too! I     20 know that I shall have some fuss with wife about that; and, for that matter, about Tom, too. So much for being in debt, — heigh-ho! The fellow sees his advantage, and means to push it."

Perhaps the mildest form of the system of slavery is to be seen in the State of Kentucky. The general prevalence of agricultural pursuits of a quiet and gradual nature, not requiring those periodic seasons of hurry and pressure that are called for in the business of more southern districts, makes the task of the negro a more healthful and reasonable one; while the master, content with a more gradual style of acquisition, has not those temptations to hard-heartedness which always overcome frail human     30 nature when the prospect of sudden and rapid gain is weighed in the balance, with no heavier counterpoise than the interests of the helpless and unprotected.

Whoever visits some estates there, and witnesses the good-humored indulgence of some masters and mistresses, and the affectionate loyalty of some slaves, might be tempted to dream the oft-fabled poetic legend of a patriarchal institution, and all that; but over and above the scene there broods a portentous shadow, — the shadow of *law*. So long as the law considers all these human beings, with beating hearts and living affections, only as so many *things* belonging to a master, — so long as the     40 failure, or misfortune, or imprudence, or death of the kindest owner may cause them any day to exchange a life of kind protection and indulgence for one of hopeless misery and toil, — so long it is impossible to make anything beautiful or desirable in the best-regulated administration of slavery.

Mr. Shelby was a fair average kind of man, good natured and kindly, and disposed to easy indulgence of those around him, and there had never been a lack of anything which might contribute to the physical comfort of the negroes on his estate. He had, however, speculated largely and quite loosely; had involved himself deeply, and his notes to a large amount had come into the hands of Haley; and this small piece of information is the key to the preceding conversation.

Now, it had so happened that, in approaching the door, Eliza had caught enough of the conversation to know that a trader was making offers to her master for somebody.

She would gladly have stopped at the door to listen, as she came out; but her mistress just then calling, she was obliged to hasten away.

Still she thought she heard the trader make an offer for her boy;—could she be mistaken? Her heart swelled and throbbed, and she involuntarily strained him so tight that the little fellow looked up into her face in astonishment.

"Eliza, girl, what ails you to-day?" said her mistress, when Eliza had upset the wash-pitcher, knocked down the work-stand, and finally was abstractedly offering her mistress a long nightgown in place of the silk dress she had ordered her to bring from the wardrobe.

Eliza started. "Oh, missis!" she said, raising her eyes; then, bursting into tears, she sat down in a chair, and began sobbing.

"Why, Eliza, child! what ails you?" said her mistress.

"Oh, missis," said Eliza, "there's been a trader talking with master in the parlor! I heard him."

"Well, silly child, suppose there has."

"Oh, missis, *do* you suppose mas'r would sell my Harry?" And the poor creature threw herself into a chair, and sobbed convulsively.

"Sell him! No, you foolish girl! You know your master never deals with those southern traders, and never means to sell any of his servants, as long as they behave well. Why, you silly child, who do you think would want to buy your Harry? Do you think all the world are set on him as you are, you goosie? Come, cheer up, and hook my dress. There now, put my back hair up in that pretty braid you learnt the other day, and don't go listening at doors any more."

"Well, but, missis, *you* never would give your consent—to—to"—

"Nonsense, child! to be sure I shouldn't. What do you talk so for? I would as soon have one of my own children sold. But really, Eliza, you are getting altogether too proud of that little fellow. A man can't put his nose into the door, but you think he must be coming to buy him."

Reassured by her mistress's confident tone, Eliza proceeded nimbly and adroitly with her toilet, laughing at her own fears, as she proceeded.

Mrs. Shelby was a woman of a high class, both intellectually and morally. To that natural magnanimity and generosity of mind which one often marks as characteristic of the women of Kentucky, she added high moral and religious sensibility and principle, carried out with great energy and ability into practical results. Her husband, who made no professions

to any particular religious character, nevertheless reverenced and respected the consistency of hers, and stood, perhaps, a little in awe of her
opinion. Certain it was that he gave her unlimited scope in all her benevolent efforts for the comfort, instruction, and improvement of her servants, though he never took any decided part in them himself. In fact, if
not exactly a believer in the doctrine of the efficacy of the extra good
works of saints, he really seemed somehow or other to fancy that his wife
had piety and benevolence enough for two, — to indulge a shadowy expectation of getting into heaven through her superabundance of qualities
to which he made no particular pretension.                              *10*

The heaviest load on his mind, after his conversation with the trader,
lay in the foreseen necessity of breaking to his wife the arrangement
contemplated, — meeting the importunities and opposition which he knew
he should have reason to encounter.

Mrs. Shelby, being entirely ignorant of her husband's embarrassments,
and knowing only the general kindliness of his temper, had been quite
sincere in the entire incredulity with which she had met Eliza's suspicions.
In fact, she dismissed the matter from her mind, without a second thought;
and being occupied in preparations for an evening visit, it passed out of
her thoughts entirely.                                                  *20*

# Booker T. Washington
## Atlanta Exposition Address

One third of the population of the south is of the Negro race. No enterprise seeking the material, civil, or moral welfare of this section can disregard this element of our population and reach the highest success. I but convey to you, Mr. President and Directors, the sentiment of the masses of my race when I say that in no way have the value and manhood of the American Negro been more fittingly and generously recognized than by the managers of this magnificent Exposition at every stage of its progress. It is a recognition that will do more to cement the friendship of the two races than any occurrence since the dawn of our freedom.

Not only this, but the opportunity here afforded will awaken among  10
us a new era of industrial progress. Ignorant and inexperienced, it is not strange that in the first years of our new life we began at the top instead of at the bottom; that a seat in Congress or the state legislature was more sought than real estate or industrial skill; that the political convention or stump-speaking had more attraction than starting a dairy farm or truck garden.

A ship lost at sea for many days suddenly sighted a friendly vessel. From the mast of the unfortunate vessel was seen a signal: "Water, water; we die of thirst!" The answer from the friendly vessel at once came back: "Cast down your bucket where you are." A second time the signal,  20
"Water, water; send us water!" ran up from the distressed vessel, and was answered: "Cast down your bucket where you are." And a third and fourth signal for water was answered, "Cast down your bucket where you are." The captain of the distressed vessel, at last heeding the injunction, cast down his bucket, and it came up full of fresh, sparkling water from the mouth of the Amazon River. To those of my race who depend

upon bettering their condition in a foreign land, or who underestimate the importance of cultivating friendly relations with the Southern white man who is their next-door neighbor, I would say: "Cast down your bucket where you are"—cast it down in making friends, in every manly way, of the people of all races by whom we are surrounded.

Cast it down in agriculture, mechanics, in commerce, in domestic service, and in the professions. And in this connection it is well to bear in mind that whatever other sins the South may be called to bear, when it comes to business, pure and simple, it is in the South that the Negro is given a man's chance in the commercial world, and in nothing is this 10 Exposition more eloquent than in emphasizing this chance. Our greatest danger is that in the great leap from slavery to freedom we may overlook the fact that the masses of us are to live by the productions of our hands, and fail to keep in mind that we shall prosper in proportion as we learn to dignify and glorify common labor, and put brains and skill into the common occupations of life; shall prosper in proportion as we learn to draw the line between the superficial and the substantial, the ornamental gewgaws of life and the useful. No race can prosper till it learns that there is as much dignity in tilling a field as in writing a poem. It is at the bottom of life we must begin, and not at the top. Nor should we permit 20 our grievances to overshadow our opportunities.

To those of the white race who look to the incoming of those of foreign birth and strange tongue and habits for the prosperity of the South, were I permitted I would repeat what I say to my own race, "Cast down your bucket where you are." Cast it down among the eight million Negroes whose habits you know, whose fidelity and love you have tested in days when to have proved treacherous meant the ruin of your firesides. Cast down your bucket among these people who have, without strikes and labor wars, tilled your fields, cleared your forests, builded your railroads and cities, brought forth treasures from the bowels of the earth, and 30 helped make possible this magnificent representation of the progress of the South. Casting down your bucket among my people, helping and encouraging them as you are doing on these grounds, and to education of head, hand, and heart, you will find that they will buy your surplus land, make blossom the waste places in your fields, and run your factories. While doing this, you can be sure in the future, as in the past, that you and your families will be surrounded by the most patient, faithful, law-abiding, and unresentful people that the world has seen. As we have proved our loyalty to you in the past, in nursing your children, watching by the sick-bed of your mothers and fathers, and often following them 40 with tear-dimmed eyes to their graves, so in the future, in our humble way, we shall stand by you with a devotion that no foreigner can approach, ready to lay down our lives, if need be, in defense of yours, interlacing our industrial, commercial, civil, and religious life with yours in a way that shall make the interests of both races one. In all things that are purely social we can be as separate as the fingers, yet one as the hand in all things essential to mutual progress.

There is no defense or security for any of us except in the highest intelligence and development of all. If anywhere there are efforts tending to curtail the fullest growth of the Negro, let these efforts be turned into stimulating, encouraging, and making him the most useful and intelligent citizen. Efforts or means so invested will pay a thousand per cent interest. These efforts will be twice blessed — "blessing him that gives and him that takes."

There is no escape through law of man or God from the inevitable:

> The laws of changeless justice bind          10
> Oppressor with oppressed;
> And close as sin and suffering joined
> We march to fate abreast.

Nearly sixteen millions of hands will aid you in pulling the load upward, or they will pull against you the load downward. We shall constitute one-third and more of the ignorance and crime of the South, or one-third its intelligence and progess; we shall contribute one-third to the business and industrial prosperity of the South, or we shall prove a veritable body   20 of death, stagnating, depressing, retarding every effort to advance the body politic.

Gentlemen of the Exposition, as we present to you our humble effort at an exhibition of our progess, you must not expect overmuch. Starting thirty years ago with ownership here and there in a few quilts and pumpkins and chickens (gathered from miscellaneous sources), remember the path that has led from these to the inventions and production of agricultural implements, buggies, steam engines, newspapers, books, statuary carving, paintings, the management of drug-stores and banks, has not been trodden without contact with thorns and thistles. While we take   30 pride in what we exhibit as a result of our independent efforts, we do not for a moment forget that our part in this exhibition would fall far short of your expectations but for the constant help that has come to our educational life, not only from the Southern states, but especially from Northern philanthropists, who have made their gifts a constant stream of blessing and encouragement.

The wisest among my race understand that the agitation of questions of social equality is the extremest folly, and that progress in the enjoyment of all the privileges that will come to us must be the result of severe and constant struggle rather than of artificial forcing. No race that has any-   40 thing to contribute to the markets of the world is long in any degree ostracized. It is important and right that all privileges of the law be ours, but it is vastly more important that we be prepared for the exercise of these privileges. The opportunity to earn a dollar in a factory just now is worth infinitely more than the opportunity to spend a dollar in an opera-house.

In conclusion, may I repeat that nothing in thirty years has given us more hope and encouragement, and drawn us so near to you of the white race, as the opportunity offered by the Exposition; and here bending, as it were, over the altar that represents the results of the struggles of your race and mine, both starting practically empty-handed three decades ago, I pledge that, in your effort to work out the great and intricate problem which God has laid at the doors of the South, you shall have at all times the patient, sympathetic help of my race; only let this be constantly in mind, that, while from representations in these buildings of the product of field, of forest, of mine, of factory, letters, and art, much good will *10* come, yet far above and beyond material benefits will be that higher good, that, let us pray God, will come, in a blotting out of sectional differences and racial animosities and suspicions, in a determination to administer absolute justice, in a willing obedience among all classes to the mandates of law. This, this, coupled with our material prosperity, will bring into our beloved South a new earth.

# Coretta Scott King
## From My Life with
## Martin Luther King, Jr.

. . . Of all the facets of segregation in Montgomery, the most degrading were the rules of the Montgomery City Bus Lines. This northern-owned corporation outdid the South itself. Although seventy percent of its passengers were black, it treated them like cattle — worse than that, for nobody insults a cow. The first seats on all buses were reserved for whites. Even if they were unoccupied and the rear seats crowded, Negroes would have to stand at the back in case some whites might get aboard; and if the front seats happened to be occupied and more white people boarded the bus, black people seated in the rear were forced to get up and give them their seats. Furthermore — and I don't think northerners ever realized    10
this — Negroes had to pay their fares at the front of the bus, get off, and walk to the rear door to board again. Sometimes the bus would drive off without them after they had paid their fare. This would happen to elderly people or pregnant women, in bad weather or good, and was considered a great joke by the drivers. Frequently the white bus drivers abused their passengers, called them niggers, black cows, or black apes. Imagine what it was like, for example, for a black man to get on a bus with his son and be subjected to such treatment.

There had been one incident in March, 1955, when fifteen-year-old Claudette Colvin refused to give up her seat to a white passenger. The    20
high school girl was handcuffed and carted off to the police station. At that time Martin served on a committee to protest to the city and bus-company officials. The committee was received politely — and nothing was done.

The fuel that finally made the slow-burning fire blaze up was an almost routine incident. On December 1, 1955, Mrs. Rosa Parks, a forty-two-year-old seamstress whom my husband aptly described as "a charming

123

person with a radiant personality," boarded a bus to go home after a long day working and shopping. The bus was crowded, and Mrs. Parks found a seat at the beginning of the Negro section. At the next stop more whites got on. The driver ordered Mrs. Parks to give her seat to a white man who boarded; this meant that she would have to stand all the way home. Rosa Parks was not in a revolutionary frame of mind. She had not planned to do what she did. Her cup had run over. As she said later, "I was just plain tired, and my feet hurt." So she sat there, refusing to get up. The driver called a policeman, who arrested her and took her to the court-house. From there Mrs. Parks called E.D. Nixon, who came down and    10
signed a bail bond for her.

Mr. Nixon was a fiery Alabamian. He was a Pullman porter who had been active in A. Philip Randolph's Brotherhood of Sleeping Car Porters, and in civil-rights activities. Suddenly he also had had enough; suddenly, it seemed, almost every Negro in Montgomery had had enough. It was spontaneous combustion. Phones began ringing all over the Negro section of the city. The Women's Political Council suggested a one-day boycott of the buses as a protest. E.D. Nixon courageously agreed to organize it.

The first we knew about it was when Mr. Nixon called my husband early in the morning of Friday, December 2. He had already talked to    20
Ralph Abernathy. After describing the incident, Mr. Nixon said, "We have taken this type of thing too long. I feel the time has come to boycott the buses. It's the only way to make the white folks see that we will not take this sort of thing any longer."

Martin agreed with him and offered the Dexter Avenue Church as a meeting place. After much telephoning, a meeting of black ministers and civic leaders was arranged for that evening. Martin said later that as he approached his church Friday evening, he was nervously wondering how many leaders would really turn up. To his delight, Martin found over forty people, representing every segment of Negro life, crowded into the    30
large meeting room at Dexter. There were doctors, lawyers, businessmen, federal-government employees, union leaders, and a great many ministers. The latter were particularly welcome, not only because of their influence, but because it meant that they were beginning to accept Martin's view that "Religion deals with both heaven and earth. . . . Any religion that professes to be concerned with the souls of men and is not concerned with the slums that doom them, the economic conditions that strangle them, and the social conditions that cripple them, is a dry-as-dust religion."

From that very first step, the Christian ministry provided the leadership of our struggle, as Christian ideals were its source.                        40

The meeting opened with brief devotions. Then, because E.D. Nixon was away at work, the Reverend L. Roy Bennett, president of the Inter-denominational Ministerial Alliance, was made chairman. After describing what had happened to Mrs. Parks, Reverend Bennett said, "Now is the time to move. This is no time to talk; it is time to act."

Martin told me after he got home that the meeting was almost wrecked because questions or suggestions from the floor were cut off. However, after a stormy session, one thing was clear: however much they differed on details, everyone was unanimously for a boycott. It was set for Monday, December 5. Committees were organized; all the ministers present promised to urge their congregations to take part. Several thousand leaflets were printed on the church mimeograph machine, describing the reasons for the boycott and urging all Negroes not to ride buses "to work, to town, to school, or anyplace on Monday, December 5." Everyone was asked to come to a mass meeting at the Holt Street Baptist Church on    10 Monday evening for further instructions. The Reverend A.W. Wilson had offered his church because it was larger than Dexter and more convenient, being in the center of Negro district.

Saturday was a busy day for Martin and the other members of the committee. They hustled around town talking with other leaders, arranging with the Negro-owned taxi companies for special bulk fares and with the owners of private automobiles to get the people to and from work. I could do little to help because Yoki was only two weeks old, and my physician, Dr. W.D. Pettus, who was very careful, advised me to stay in for a month. However, I was kept busy answering the telephone, which    20 rang continuously, and coordinating from that central point the many messages and arrangements.

Our greatest concern was how we were going to reach the fifty thousand black people of Montgomery, no matter how hard we worked. The white press, in an outraged exposé, spread the word for us in a way that would have been impossible with only our own resources.

As it happened, a white woman found one of our leaflets, which her Negro maid had left in the kitchen. The irate woman immediately telephoned the newspaper to let the white community know what the blacks were up to. We laughed a lot about this, and Martin later said that we owed    30 them a great debt.

On Sunday morning, from their pulpits, almost every Negro minister in town urged people to honor the boycott.

Martin came home late Sunday night and began to read the morning paper. The long articles about the proposed boycott accused the NAACP of planting Mrs. Parks on the bus — she had been a volunteer secretary for the Montgomery Chapter — and likened the boycott to the tactics of the White Citizens Councils. This upset Martin. That awesome conscience of his began to gnaw at him, and he wondered if he were doing the right thing. Alone in his study, he struggled with the question of whether the    40 boycott method was basically unchristian. Certainly it could be used for unethical ends. But, as he said, "We were using it to give birth to freedom . . . and to urge men to comply with the law of the land. Our concern was not to put the bus company out of business, but to put justice in business." He recalled Thoreau's words, "We can no longer lend our cooperation to an evil system," and he thought, "He who accepts evil without protesting against it is really cooperating with it." Later Martin wrote, "From this moment on I conceived of our movement as an act of massive noncooperation. From then on I rarely used the word 'boycott.'"

Serene after his inner struggle, Martin joined me in our sitting room. We wanted to go to bed early, but Yoki began crying and the telephone kept ringing. Between interruptions we sat together talking about the prospects for the success of the protest. We were both filled with doubt. Attempted boycotts had failed in Montgomery and other cities. Because of changing times and tempers, this one seemed to have a better chance, but it was still a slender hope. We finally decided that if the boycott was sixty percent effective we would be doing all right, and we would be satisfied to have made a good start.

A little after midnight we finally went to bed, but at five-thirty the next morning we were up and dressed again. The first bus was due at six o'clock at the bus stop just outside our house. We had coffee and toast in the kitchen; then I went into the living room to watch. Right on time, the bus came, headlights blazing through the December darkness, all lit up inside. I shouted, "Martin! Martin, come quickly!" He ran in and stood beside me, his face lit with excitement. There was not one person on that usually crowded bus!

We stood together waiting for the next bus. It was empty too, and this was the most heavily traveled line in the whole city. Bus after empty bus paused at the stop and moved on. We were so excited we could hardly speak coherently. Finally Martin said, "I'm going to take the car and see what's happening other places in the city."

He picked up Ralph Abernathy and they cruised together around the city. Martin told me about it when he got home. Everywhere it was the same. A few white people and maybe one or two blacks in otherwise empty buses. Martin and Ralph saw extraordinary sights—the sidewalks crowded with men and women trudging to work; the students of Alabama State College walking or thumbing rides; taxicabs with people clustered in them. Some of our people rode mules; others went in horse-drawn buggies. But most of them were walking, some making a round trip of as much as twelve miles. Martin later wrote, "As I watched them I knew that there is nothing more majestic than the determined courage of individuals willing to suffer and sacrifice for their freedom and dignity."

Martin rushed off again at nine o'clock that morning to attend the trial of Mrs. Parks. She was convicted of disobeying the city's segregation ordinance and fined ten dollars and costs. Her young attorney, Fred D. Gray, filed an appeal. It was one of the first clear-cut cases of a Negro being convicted of disobeying the segregation laws—usually the charge was disorderly conduct or some such thing.

The leaders of the Movement called a meeting for three o'clock in the afternoon to organize the mass meeting to be held that night. Martin was a bit late, and as he entered the hall, people said to him, "Martin, we have elected you to be our president. Will you accept?"

It seemed that Rufus A. Lewis, a Montgomery businessman, had proposed Martin, and he had been unanimously elected. The people knew, and Martin knew, that the post was dangerous, for it meant being singled out to become the target of the white people's anger and vengeance. Martin said, "I don't mind. Somebody has to do it, and if you think I can, I will serve."

Then other officers were elected. Rev. L. Roy Bennett became vicepresident; Rev. E.N. French, corresponding secretary; Mrs. Erna A. Dungee, financial secretary; and E.D. Nixon, treasurer. After that they discussed what to call the organization. Someone suggested the Negro    10
Citizens' Committee. Martin did not approve, because that sounded like an organization of the same spirit as the White Citizens Council. Finally, Ralph Abernathy proposed calling the organization the Montgomery Improvement Association, the MIA, and this name was unanimously approved.

Fear was an invisible presence at the meeting, along with courage and hope. Proposals were voiced to make the MIA a sort of secret society, because if no names were mentioned it would be safer for the leaders. E.D. Nixon opposed that idea. "We're acting like little boys," he said. "Somebody's name will be known, and if we're afraid, we might just as    20
well fold up right now. The white folks are eventually going to find out anyway. We'd better decide now if we are going to be fearless men or scared little boys."

That settled that question. It was also decided that the protest would continue until certain demands were met. Ralph Abernathy was made chairman of the committee to draw up demands.

Martin came home at six o'clock. He said later that he was nervous about telling me he had accepted the presidency of the protest movement, but he need not have worried, because I sincerely meant what I said when I told him that night, "You know that whatever you do, you    30
have my backing."

Reassured, Martin went to his study. He was to make the main speech at the mass meeting that night. It was now six-thirty and—this was the way it was usually to be—he had only twenty minutes to prepare what he thought might be the most decisive speech of his life. He said afterward that thinking about the responsibility and the reporters and television cameras, he almost panicked. Five minutes wasted and only fifteen minutes left. At that moment he turned to prayer. He asked God "to restore my balance and be with me in a time when I need Your guidance more than ever."    40

How could he make his speech both militant enough to rouse people to action and yet devoid of hate and resentment? He was determined to do both.

Martin and Ralph went together to the meeting. When they got within four blocks of the Holt Street Baptist Church, there was an enormous traffic jam. Five thousand people stood outside the church listening to loudspeakers and singing hymns. Inside it was so crowded, Martin told me, the people had to lift Ralph and him above the crowd and pass them from hand to hand over their heads to the platform. The crowd and the singing inspired Martin, and God answered his prayer. Later Martin said, "That night I understood what the older preachers meant when they said, 'Open your mouth and God will speak for you.' "

First the people sang "Onward, Christian Soldiers" in a tremendous wave of five thousand voices. This was followed by a prayer and a reading of the Scriptures. Martin was introduced. People applauded; television lights beat upon him. Without any notes at all he began to speak. Once again he told the story of Mrs. Parks, and rehearsed some of the wrongs black people were suffering. Then he said, "But there comes a time when people get tired. We are here this evening to say to those who have mistreated us so long, that we are tired. Tired of being segregated and humiliated; tired of being kicked about by the brutal feet of oppression." *10*

The audience cheered wildly, and Martin said, "We have no alternative but to protest. We have been amazingly patient. . . but we come here tonight to be saved from that patience that makes us patient with anything less than freedom and justice." *20*

Taking up the challenging newspaper comparison with the White Citizens Council and the Klan, Martin said, "They are protesting for the perpetuation of injustice in the community; we're protesting for the birth of justice. . . their methods lead to violence and lawlessness. But in our protest there will be no cross-burnings, no white person will be taken from his home by a hooded Negro mob and brutally murdered. . . we will be guided by the highest principles of law and order."

Having roused the audience for militant action, Martin now set limits upon it. His study of nonviolence and his love of Christ informed his words. He said, "No one must be intimidated to keep them from riding the buses. Our method must be persuasion, not coercion. We will only say to the people 'Let your conscience be your guide.'. . . Our actions must be guided by the deepest principles of the Christian faith. . . . Once again we must hear the words of Jesus, 'Love your enemies. Bless them that curse you. Pray for them that despitefully use you.' If we fail to do this, our protest will end up as a meaningless drama on the stage of history and its memory will be shrouded in the ugly garments of shame. . . We must not become bitter and end up by hating our white brothers. As Booker T. Washington said, 'Let no man pull you so low as to make you hate him.' " *30*

*40*

Finally, Martin said, "If you will protest courageously, and yet with dignity and Christian love, future historians will say, 'There lived a great people—a black people—who injected new meaning and dignity into the veins of civilization.' This is our challenge and our overwhelming responsibility."

As Martin finished speaking, the audience rose cheering in exaltation.

And in that speech my husband set the keynote and the tempo of the Movement he was to lead, from Montgomery onward.

When we talked about it later, we pondered why, in Montgomery of all places, a movement started which had such tremendous repercussions; why here, at this moment of history, Negroes were able to unite peacefully in the cause of freedom. We found only one final explanation. Though some of the impetus came from the Supreme Court decisions, and some was due to the particularly unjust actions of the city bus company, these were not enough to explain it. Other blacks had suffered equal or greater injustices in other places and had meekly accepted them. I suggested   10
that it was due to his own leadership and to his devoted co-workers, but Martin said, "No." There was no rational explanation that would suffice. Therefore we must accept something else. The birth of the Movement could not be explained "without a divine dimension." My husband devoutly believed that there is "a creative force that works to pull down mountains of evil and level hilltops of injustice." As we have seen, he regarded himself as an instrument of this force, and he said, "God still works through history His wonders to perform." He believed that "God had decided to use Montgomery as a proving ground for the struggle and the triumph of freedom and justice in America." Martin's strong sense of history de-   20
lighted in the appropriateness of "Montgomery, the cradle of the Confederacy, being transformed into Montgomery, the cradle of freedom and justice."

That night, December 5, 1955, victory was far away; the struggle just beginning. After Martin's speech the mass meeting unanimously approved the demands Ralph Abernathy had drawn up, which had to be met before we would ride the buses again. They were very moderate: (1) Courteous treatment by bus operators must be guaranteed; (2) Passengers to be seated on a first-come, first-served basis—Negroes sitting from the back forward, whites from front to back; and (3) Negro bus   30
drivers to be employed on predominantly Negro routes.

On Wednesday, December 7, Martin headed a committee to meet with Mayor W.A. Gayle, the city commissioners, and bus company officials to discuss terms of possible settlement. He was very hopeful. The commissioners listened courteously and seemed inclined to accept our proposals on bus seating, which, in fact, were identical to those in other southern cities such as Mobile, Alabama, and Nashville, Tennessee. It is important to realize that we were *not*, at first, asking for blacks and whites to sit on the same seats. However, the attorney for the bus company, Jack Crenshaw, declared that the plan would be illegal under Montgomery's   40
segregation laws. After the meeting, he gave his real reason, when I said, "If we granted the Negroes these demands, they would go about boasting they had won a victory over the white people; and this we will not stand for."

In spite of the agreeable way in which it had been conducted, the meeting came to nothing, and we knew we were in for a long struggle. The white people were expecting the boycott to collapse on the first rainy day,

but Martin realized that the way to avoid this was through skillful organization. The first order of business was to get our people to and from work with as little inconvenience as possible. On Friday, December 9, city officials informed the Negro taxi companies that mass rides were illegal and that they would be put out of business if they continued that practice. However, by that time a motor pool of volunteer drivers had been organized, and pickup stations selected throughout the city with dispatchers to match passengers and destinations. Hundreds of people volunteered to drive. At the boycott's peak there were over three hundred cars participating. There were many memorable and inspiring occurrences during     10
that period. For example, one of the drivers was Mrs. A.W. West, who was on the board of the Montgomery Improvement Association. Every morning and afternoon this well-to-do, elderly, and elegant widow drove her green Cadillac back and forth from the black neighborhoods, filled with workers who had to get to their jobs. Eventually the MIA helped ten of the Negro churches to buy station wagons to supplement the car pool. The names of the sponsoring churches were painted on the car doors, and as they drove along, filled to capacity, the people sang hymns.

But with all we could do, thousands of people still had to walk. They walked magnificently and proudly. Somebody asked one old grandmother,     20
coming down the street, if she was not tired. She answered, "It used to be my soul was tired and my feets rested; now my feet's tired, but my soul is rested."

Without meaning to, some white women helped us by driving down to pick up their Negro maids, to make sure they got to work.

Mass meetings were held twice a week at churches in the city, to keep morale up. Thousands of people attended them, some arriving hours ahead of time to be sure of getting a seat. Martin kept a firm hand on the orators to preserve the delicate balance between inspiration and rabble-rousing. By now he was consciously emulating the Gandhian     30
technique, and many people outside of the South were beginning to realize that something new was taking place in Montgomery: black people, on their own, were creating a new instrument of social change; they were building and developing a totally new kind of structure.

The organization, all on a volunteer basis, was remarkable. The various committees—transportation, negotation, programs, fund raising—functioned surprisingly well. All the things we were doing cost a great deal of money, and at first it all came from Montgomery Negroes. Then as news of our Movement spread, contributions came in from all parts of the country and from foreign places as far away as Tokyo and     40
Switzerland.

The spirit of the black community was inspiring. There was a sort of contagion of enthusiasm. Groups from all levels were becoming involved. This was most unusual in Montgomery, where Negroes had been divided into cliques and classes and had not been able to unite on anything before. I truly believe that this beautiful demonstration of unity was in a great measure due to Martin's leadership. People believed in him and had great respect for him as a leader. Because of his training and background, the intellectuals could respect him and the genuine love of people emanated to the poorer people so they knew he was fully identified with them. He became a symbol of black unity, a link between the divergent groups.

While it primarily helped Negroes, my husband never allowed the struggle to limit itself solely to the needs of black people. He said, "What we are doing is not only for the black man, but for the white man too. The system that has banished personality and scarred the soul of the Negro has also damaged the white man's personality, giving him a false sense of superiority as it gives the Negro a false sense of inferiority. Segregation is as bad for one as for the other. So in freeing the Negro we will also free the white man of his misconceptions and his subconscious feeling of guilt toward those he wrongs."

Inevitably, and especially when reporting on the black community, the press tends to oversimplify issues and situations. In the case of coverage of the MIA, Martin became the focal point for news stories despite his own efforts to avoid it. This caused problems, quite naturally, since other people were also hard at work and sharing the dangers. At one point, saddened and discouraged by self-defeating rivalries, he was ready to resign. "I am willing to decrease," he said, "so that others may increase."

The suggestion that Martin might resign had a unifying effect on the MIA board members, most of whom understood his sincerity and also understood that his own rank was not important to him. It was only the Movement he cared about. Martin always worried about whether any element of his own leadership was divisive. He would, throughout his life, question whether someone else would be more useful to the Movement at any moment in history.

Although I had no prominent place in the boycott, it was an exciting time and I found my role an important one. At first our house was the office of the MIA. The phone rang from five o'clock in the morning until midnight; and all day long, groups of people were meeting there. It was impossible to keep Yoki on any sort of schedule, and she learned to adapt with the rest of us. I never knew how many people Martin would ask to stay for dinner, but somehow I managed to feed them. Sometimes it seemed like a loaves-and-fishes miracle.

Then as the days of December dragged on, and the white community saw we would not give up, things began to get really difficult. All efforts at negotiations broke down. The mayor and the commissioners joined the White Citizens Council, as a "lesson" to us. The sick telephone calls to our house increased. At any hour, day or night, the phone would ring and some man or woman would pour out a string of obscene epithets, of which "nigger son of a bitch" was the mildest. Often the women callers raved on about sex, accusing Martin and me of incredible degeneracies. Frequently the call ended with a threat to kill us if we didn't get out of town. As the leader and selected spokesman of the protest, Martin was the target for all the hate and frustration of the whites—as he knew he would be when he accepted the role.

But in spite of all the work and confusion and danger, the chaos of our private lives, I felt inspired, almost elated. By January Martin and I became convinced that this Movement was more than local. We felt that something was unfolding that was very important to the common struggle of oppressed people everywhere. I was very excited to be a part of a surge forward that was much bigger than Montgomery — of a nation-wide Movement whose birth was taking place before our eyes. Later we began to see that it was not only a national, but an international phenom-enon, part of a worldwide revolution of humanity, asserting the individ-   10
ual's right to freedom and self-respect.

One night in January, recalling that I had not wanted to come to Mont-gomery, I said, "Oh, Martin, how happy I am to be living in Montgomery. with you, at this moment in history."

But we could not hold that high note all the time. The threats and the real danger sometimes were very depressing. One night at a mass meeting, Martin found himself saying without premeditation, "If one day you find me sprawled and dead, I do not want you to retaliate with a single act of violence. I urge you to continue protesting with the same dignity and discipline you have shown so far."                                           20

On another day Martin came home feeling very weary. He said later that he had looked at me and the baby and thought, "They might be taken from me, or I from them, anytime." Then in the middle of the night the telephone rang. An angry voice said, "Listen, nigger, we've taken all we want from you. Before next week you'll be sorry you ever came to Montgomery."

It was just another of the abusive calls, but Martin felt he could take no more. He went into the kitchen and made himself a cup of coffee and began to think calmly of the position we were in and what the alternatives were. With his head in his hands, Martin bowed over the table and prayed   30
aloud to God, saying, "Lord, I am taking a stand for what I believe is right. The people are looking to me for leadership, and if I stand before them without strength and courage, they will falter. I am at the end of my powers. I have nothing left. I've come to the point where I can't face it alone."

Martin said to me, "At that moment I experienced the presence of the Divine as I had never experienced Him before. It seemed as though I could hear the quiet of an inner voice saying: 'Stand up for righteousness; stand up for truth; and God will be at your side forever.'"

Martin said that after that experience, he rose up sure of himself again, ready to face anything.                                                        40

When it became obvious that the boycott was not going to collapse, the city government decided on a get-tough policy. On one of those dreary January afternoons, Martin and I were eating dinner. Bob Williams, a dear friend who had been at Morehouse with Martin and was teaching music at Alabama State College, was with us; he spent a good deal of time at our house, acting as a sort of protector. Martin told Bob and me,

"You know, someone told me that the police are planning to arrest me on some trumped-up charge."

"That would be a good thing," I said. "It would make our people angry and unite them even more. It would be a great mistake, one of the mistakes they will probably make."

Both men agreed with me, and Martin decided not to try to avoid arrest. He and Bob drove downtown to pick up the church secretary, Mrs. Lillie Thomas (now Mrs. Lillie Hunter, office manager of SCLC), and then continued on to one of the parking lots that was a station for the car pool. Martin picked up three passengers and started out. At the edge of the lot a policeman stopped him and asked to see his license. As Martin was showing it, he heard another policeman say, "It's that damn King fellow."

When Martin left the lot, a motorcycle cop followed him. Of course, he drove very carefully, obeying all traffic rules. As he stopped to let his passengers out, the policeman pulled alongside and said, "Get out, King! You're under arrest for going thirty in a twenty-five-mile zone."

A patrol car pulled up and took Martin to the city jail. He was thrown into a dingy and odorous, segregated cell. Among the prisoners he recognized a teacher who had been arrested in connection with the protest. Others crowded around Martin, asking his help in getting them out. Martin said, "Fellows, before I can get you out, I've got to get out my own self."

Meanwhile, the news of his arrest spread like wildfire. There were five mass meetings going on that evening, and the arrest was announced at all of them. One of our devoted church members, Miss Viola Webb, came rushing down our block to tell me the news. She was shouting, "Mrs. King, Mrs. King, they got him. They've arrested Dr. King. Mrs. King, please get him out. Please do something."

I took the news calmly, because I had been expecting it, but I'm afraid Miss Webb thought I was unconcerned.

The first person to reach the jail was Ralph Abernathy. When he offered to post bail for Martin, the official in charge said, "You'll have to wait till tomorrow."

"I am pastor of the First Baptist Church of Montgomery," Ralph said. "Do you mean to tell me I can't sign a bond?"

"No, you can't."

"Can I see Dr. King?"

"No."

Pretty soon the deacons of the church and many other people began gathering at the jail. It must have looked ominous to the police. Nervously, the jailer hauled Martin out of his cell to a chorus from its inmates, "Don't forget us, Dr. King!"

Martin was fingerprinted and then was told, "All right, King. You're released on your own recognizance."

Martin told me later that he had been a little frightened that first time in jail. He had not even known where the jail was before, and he thought they might be taking him out to lynch him. He cheered up when he saw all his supporters waiting outside. One of the deacons drove him and Ralph around to each of the meetings, where the people were praying aloud to God to soften the jailer's heart and make him let their leader go. God had surely answered their prayers.

The following Saturday night there were thirty or forty threatening and abusive telephone calls. Finally, at two-thirty I took the receiver off the hook so we could get some sleep. When I put it back on at about seven in the morning, it rang immediately and a voice said, "My boys told me you took the phone off the hook last night."

Angrily I answered, "It's my phone, and I'll do what I like with it."

In the background Martin was saying, "Oh, darling, don't talk like that."

He would always say, "Be nice. Be kind. Be nonviolent." But I was just too tired and worn out to be nonviolent with so little sleep and so much provocation.

That Sunday, from the pulpit, Martin told the congregation, "We're getting so many unpleasant telephone calls that we're taking the receiver off the hook at night because it's the only way we can get any rest. If any of you are trying to get me, you'll know why you can't."

Our church people were becoming very concerned about me and felt I should have someone stay with me while Martin was out at meetings. When Martin told me this, I said, "I'm not afraid to be alone. I'm happy staying by myself."

We had considered the possibility of someone bombing the house. However, though the front of the house was right on the street, it was in a closely populated area, and I thought that no one would run the risk of attacking from there. In the back, there was a deep yard with a fence around it, so that no one could really get very close. The baby and I slept in back, and I was fairly confident we would be all right. Though there had been bombings in remote country towns, I did not think anybody would try it in a densely settled neighborhood in the heart of the city.

However, Martin seemed so anxious that I agreed to call our good friend and church member, Mary Lucy Williams, and ask her to sit with me the following night.

That was Monday, January 30, 1956. At about nine-thirty in the evening I had put on a robe and Mary Lucy and I were chatting in the sitting room. I heard a heavy thump on the concrete porch outside. Had I not been anticipating an attack, I might have looked out to see what it was. Instead I said, "It sounds as if someone has hit the house. We'd better move to the back."

We moved fast — not through the hall, which would have taken us nearer the sound, but straight back through the guest bedroom. We were in the middle of it when there was a thunderous blast. Then smoke and the sound of breaking glass.

Mary Lucy grabbed me and started screaming. Her screaming frightened me, and I was shaken by the impact and the noise. I hurried to my bedroom, two rooms back, where Yolanda was in her bassinet. She was all right and I automatically reached for the telephone. Then I thought, "Whom am I going to call? I'm not going to call the police in this instance."

Then the doorbell started ringing. My first thought was that it was the person who had thrown the bomb. I was trying to think of what I should do about the baby, and for a split second I got panicky. Then I shouted, "Who is it?" and a voice said, "Is anybody hurt?"

I went to the door and let in my neighbors. They were frightened and worried. All over our part of town people had heard the blast and came rushing. The windows had been blown into the living room. The floor was covered with broken glass. The porch had been split, and there was a small hole in the concrete floor. All the lights were off in the front rooms, and I got a bulb and screwed it into a socket so we could see.

Then I decided to call Ralph Abernathy's First Baptist Church, where the mass meeting was being held and where my husband was speaking. Mrs. Irene Grant, a member of the church whom I knew, answered and I told her that our house had been bombed.

I didn't think about telling her that the baby and I were safe, but I asked her to get some people to the house quickly. My thought was that our friends ought to come for protection. I did not want the police, because I could not be sure that they did not know about the bombing before I did.

I called some of our friends and finally reached Mrs. Euretta Adair, who asked, "Do you want me to come and get you?"

I remember that when Mrs. Adair arrived, she stood looking into the bassinet and talking to Yoki, who was not even crying. By that time the house was full of people, white reporters, neighbors, all sorts of people trying to find out what was happening.

A call came from the First Baptist Church to find out if we were safe. I assured them that we were, and they decided not to tell Martin until he finished his speech. But my husband noticed people rushing about looking worried and sensed that something had happened. He called to Ralph Abernathy, "Ralph, what's happened?"

Ralph couldn't speak. Martin insisted. "Ralph, you must tell me."

"Your house has been bombed."

"Are Coretta and the baby all right?"

"We're checking on that now. We think so."

In his account of that terrible night, Martin wrote, "Strangely enough, I accepted the word of the bombing calmly. My religious experience a few nights before had given me the strength to face it."

He interrupted the speech to tell the people what had happened, and he urged them all to go straight home. "Don't get panicky and lose your heads," he said. "Let us keep moving with the faith that what we are doing is right, and with the even greater faith that God is with us in the struggle."

Then Martin rushed home.

By the time he got there a big angry crowd was around the house. The police were nervously holding the people back. Mayor Gayle and Police Commissioner Clyde Sellers had just arrived. Martin hurried into the house. It was so full of people he could barely get in. He saw me and he saw the baby, and I think he was relieved to know that I had accepted it so calmly. He said, "Thank God you and the baby are all right!"

I reassured him and Martin kissed me and said, "Why don't you get dressed, darling?"

Suddenly I realized that I had been relaxing when this happened and            10
although all those people were in the house, I still had my robe on!

The situation outside the house was tense and dangerous. Though the crowd was singing, the people were angry and aroused. I remember hearing "My Country, 'Tis of Thee," but you could sense the heat of their anger. Many were armed; even the little boys had broken bottles. A policeman held back one black man who said, "You got your thirty-eight, I got mine. Let's shoot it out."

Later someone said tension was so high that if a white man had accidentally tripped over a Negro, it could have triggered the most awful riot in our history. The crowd was so wrought up that the white reporters           20
were afraid to leave to file their stories. The faces of Mayor Gayle and Commissioner Sellers were deathly pale. They went up to Martin and expressed their regret that "this unfortunate incident has taken place in our city."

Chairman C.T. Smiley of Dexter's trustee board, and principal of Booker T. Washington High School, the largest Negro high school in the city, standing beside Martin, said angrily, "Regrets are all very well, but you are responsible. It is you who created the climate for this."

More people were joining the crowd every minute. They stood swaying and muttering and shouting insults at the nervous police. At that point           30
Martin walked out on the porch. In some ways, it was the most important hour of his life. His own home had just been bombed, his wife and baby could have been killed; this was the first deep test of his Christian principles and his theories of nonviolence. Standing there, very grave and calm, he dominated those furious people. He held up his hand, and they were suddenly silent—the crowd of angry men and women, of excited children and sullen, frightened policemen in a clump by the steps—all were absolutely still. In a calm voice Martin said, "My wife and baby are all right. I want you to go home and put down your weapons. We cannot solve this problem through retaliatory violence. We must meet violence           40
with nonviolence. Remember the words of Jesus: 'He who lives by the sword will perish by the sword.' We must love our white brothers, no matter what they do to us. We must make them know that we love them. Jesus still cries out across the centuries, 'Love your enemies.' This is what we must live by. We must meet hate with love."

Then my husband's voice took on the resonance and grandeur of its full emotional power as he said, "Remember, if I am stopped, this Movement will not stop, because God is with this Movement. Go home with this glowing faith and this radiant assurance."

Many people out there were crying. I could see the shine of tears on their faces, in the strong lights. They were moved, as by a holy exaltation. They shouted, "Amen." They shouted, "God bless you. We are with you all the way, Reverend."

One person asked, "What will become of you?" Martin replied, "I have been promised protection."

Mayor Gayle and the commissioner came forward. The crowd turned, began booing and threatening. The police made it worse by shouting, "Listen to the commissioner!" The crowd yelled furiously. Martin stepped to the edge of the porch, holding up his hand, and the noise suddenly stopped, as when the conductor of an orchestra holds his baton high. Martin spoke, "Remember what I just said. Let us hear the commissioner."

Commissioner Sellers said, "We are going to do everything in our power to find out who did this dreadful thing and bring him to justice."

Mayor Gayle added, "We are offering five thousand dollars reward for information leading to his arrest."

After that the crowd began to thin out, and the people went back to their homes. A white policeman's voice was heard in the crowd saying, "If it hadn't been for that nigger preacher, we'd all be dead."

# Roger Wilkins
## A Black at the Gridiron Dinner

When it was all over, a number of men had tears in their eyes, even more had lifted hearts and spirits, but a few were so dispirited that they went upstairs to get drunk. We had just heard the President and Vice President of the United States in a unique piano duet—and to many old Gridiron Dinner veterans, it was a moving show-stopper. To a few others, it was a depressing display of gross insensitivity and both conscious and unconscious racism—further proof that they and their hopes for their country are becoming more and more isolated from those places where America's heart and power seemed to be moving.

The annual dinner of the Gridiron Club is the time when men can put on white ties and tails and forget the anxiety and loneliness that are central to the human condition and look at other men in white ties and tails and know that they have arrived or are still there.

The guests are generally grateful and gracious. But the event's importance is beyond the structures of graciousness because it shows the most powerful elements of the nation's daily press and all elements of the nation's government locked in a symbiotic embrace. The rich and the powerful in jest tell many truths about themselves and about their country. I don't feel very gracious about what they told me.

Some weeks ago, to my surprise and delight, a friend—a sensitive man of honor—with a little half-apology about the required costume, invited me to attend the dinner.

The first impression was stunning: almost every passing face was a familiar one. Some had names that were household words. Some merely made up a montage of the familiar faces and bearings of our times. There were Richard Helms and Walter Mondale and Henry Kissinger and George

138

McGovern and Joel Broyhill and Tom Wicker and William Westmoreland
and John Mitchell and Tom Clark (ironically placed, by some pixie no
doubt, next to each other on the dais) and Robert Finch and Ralph Nader,
and of course, the President of the United States.

One thing quickly became clear about those faces. Apart from Walter
Washington — who, I suppose, as Mayor had to be invited — mine was the
only face in a crowd of some 500 that was not white. There were no
Indians, there were no Asians, there were no Puerto Ricans, there were
no Mexican-Americans. There were just the Mayor and me. Incredibly,
I sensed that there were few in that room who thought that anything     10
was missing.

There is something about an atmosphere like that that is hard to define,
but excruciatingly easy for a black man to feel. It is the heavy, almost
tangible, clearly visible, broad assumption that in places where it counts,
America is a white country. I was an American citizen sitting in a
banquet room in a hotel which I had visited many times. (My last occasion for a visit to that hotel was the farewell party for the white staff
director and the black deputy staff director of the United States Commission on Civil Rights.) This night in that room, less than three miles
from my home in the nation's capital, a 60 per cent black city, I felt out   20
of place in America.

That is not to say that there were not kind men, good men, warm men
in and around and about the party, nor is it to say that anyone was personally rude to me. There were some old friends and some new acquaintances whom I was genuinely glad to see. Ed Muskie who had given a very
funny and exquisitely partisan speech (the Republicans have three problems: the war, inflation, and what to say on Lincoln's Birthday) was one
of those. I was even warmly embraced by the Deputy Attorney General,
Mr. Kleindienst, and had a long conversation with the associate director
of the FBI, Mr. DeLoach.     30

But it was not the people so much who shaped the evening. It was the
humor amidst that pervasive whiteness about what was going on in this
country these days that gave the evening its form and substance. There
were many jokes about the "Southern strategy." White people have funny
senses of humor. Some of them found something to laugh about in the
Southern strategy. Black people don't think it's funny at all. That strategy
hits men where they live — in their hopes for themselves and their dreams
for their children. We find it sinister and frightening. And let it not be
said that the Gridiron Club and its guests are not discriminating about
their humor. There was a real sensitivity about the inappropriateness of   40
poking fun that night about an ailing former President, but none about
laughing about policies which crush the aspirations of millions of citizens of this nation. An instructive distinction, I thought.

There was a joke about the amendments to the Constitution (so what
if we rescind the First Amendment, there'll still be 25 left), and about
repression (you stop bugging me, I'll stop bugging you), and there were

warm, almost admiring jokes about the lady who despises "liberal Communists" and thinks something like the Russian Revolution occurred in Washington on November 15. There was applause—explosive and prolonged—for Judges Clement Haynsworth and Julius Hoffman (the largest hands of the evening by my reckoning.)

As I looked, listened and saw the faces of those judges and of the generals and of the admirals and of the old members of the oligarchies of the House and Senate, I thought of the soft, almost beatific smile of Cesar Chavez; the serious troubled face of Vine Deloria Jr., and the handsome, sensitive faces of Andy Young and Julian Bond of Georgia. All those men and more have fought with surely as much idealism as any general ever carried with him to Saigon, with as much courage as any senator ever took with him on a fact-finding trip to a Vietnam battlefield, or even as much hope, spirit and belief in the American dream as any Peace Corps kid ever took to the Andes in Peru. But the men I have named fought for American freedom on American soil. And they were not there. But Julius Hoffman was.

As the jokes about the "Southern strategy" continued, I thought about the one-room segregated schoolhouse where I began my education in Kansas City. That was my neighborhood school. When they closed it, I was bused—without an apparent second thought—as a 5-year-old kindergartener, across town to the black elementary school. It was called Crispus Attucks.

And I thought of the day I took my daughter when she was seven along the Freedom Trail, in Boston, and of telling her about the black man named Crispus Attucks who was the first American to die in our revolution. And I remember telling her that white America would try very hard in thousands of conscious and unconscious ways both to make her feel that her people had had no part in building America's greatness and to make her feel inferior. And I remember the profoundly moving and grateful look in her eyes and the wordless hug she gave me when I told her, "Don't you believe them because they are lies." And I felt white America in that room in the Statler Hilton telling me all those things that night, and I told myself, "Don't you believe them because they are lies."

And when it came to the end, the President and the Vice President of the United States, in an act which they had consciously worked up, put on a Mr. Bones routine about the Southern strategy with the biggest boffo coming as the Vice President affected a deep Southern accent. And then they played their duets—the President playing his songs, the Vice President playing "Dixie," the whole thing climaxed by "God Bless America" and "Auld Lang Syne." The crowd ate it up. They roared. As they roared I thought that after our black decade of imploring, suing, marching, lobbying, singing, rebelling, praying and dying we had come to this: a Vice Presidential Dixie with the President as his straight man. In the serious and frivolous places of power—at the end of that decade—America was still virtually lily white. And most of the people in that room were reveling in it. What, I wondered, would it take for them to understand that men also come in colors other than white. Seeing and feeling their blindness, I shuddered at the answers that came most readily to mind.

As we stood voluntarily, some more slowly than others, when the two men began to play "God Bless America", I couldn't help remembering Judy Collins (who could not sing in Chicago) singing "Where Have All the Flowers Gone?"

So, later, I joined Nick Kotz, author of *Let Them Eat Promises* and we drank down our dreams.

I don't believe that I have been blanketed in and suffocated by such 10 racism and insensitivity since I was a sophomore in college when I was the only black invited to a minstrel spoof put on at a white fraternity house.

But then, they were only fraternity brothers, weren't they?

# Dick Gregory
## America was momma's momma

Now that I am a man, I have "given up childish ways." I realize that America is my momma and America was Momma's momma. And I am going to place the blame for injustice and wrong on the right momma. Even today, when I leave my country to appear on television and make other public appearances in foreign countries, I find it difficult to speak of the injustices I experience in this country. Because America is my momma. Even if Momma is a whore, she is still Momma. Many times I am asked if I would go to war if drafted. I always answer, "Yes, under one condition; that I be allowed to go to the front line without a gun. Momma is worth dying for, but there is nothing worth killing for. And if I ever change my opinion about killing, I will go to Mississippi and kill that sheriff who spit in my wife's face." 10

America is my momma. One Fourth of July, I want to go to the New York harbor and talk to Momma—the Statue of Liberty. I want to snatch that torch out of her hand and take her with me to the ghetto and sit her down on the street corner. I want to show her the "tired, the poor, the huddled masses yearning to breathe free." I want to show Momma what she has been doing to her children. And Momma should weep. For the grief of the ghetto is the grief of the entire American family.

142

# Black Panther Party
## Platform and Program

Between October 1 and October 15, 1966, in North Oakland, California, Huey P. Newton and Bobby Seale prepared the ten-point platform and program of the Black Panther Party. Seale made suggestions, but the platform and program were actually written by Newton, who divided them into "What We Want" and "What We Believe." The rules of the Party were set down later and added to as more were required. Today there are twenty-six rules: some for members of the Party and others for office and Party functionaries.

### WHAT WE WANT
### WHAT WE BELIEVE

*1. We want freedom. We want power to determine the destiny of our Black Community.*

We believe that black people will not be free until we are able to determine our destiny.

*2. We want full employment for our people.*

We believe that the federal government is responsible and obligated to give every man employment or a guaranteed income. We believe that if the white American businessmen will not give full employment, then the means of production should be taken from the businessmen and placed in the community so that the people of the community can organize and employ all of its people and give a high standard of living.

*3. We want an end to the robbery by the white man of our Black Community.*

143

We believe that this racist government has robbed us and now we are demanding the overdue debt of forty acres and two mules. Forty acres and two mules was promised 100 years ago as restitution for slave labor and mass murder of black people. We will accept the payment in currency which will be distributed to our many communities. The Germans are now aiding the Jews in Israel for the genocide of the Jewish people. The Germans murdered six million Jews. The American racist has taken part in the slaughter of over fifty million black people; therefore, we feel that this is a modest demand that we make.

4. *We want decent housing, fit for shelter of human beings.*                        10

We believe that if the white landlords will not give decent housing to our black community, then the housing and the land should be made into cooperatives so that our community, with government aid, can build and make decent housing for its people.

5. *We want education for our people that exposes the true nature of this decadent American society. We want education that teaches us our true history and our role in the present-day society.*

We believe in an educational system that will give to our people a knowledge of self. If a man does not have knowledge of himself and his position in society and the world, then he has little chance to relate to anything       20 else.

6. *We want all black men to be exempt from military service.*

We believe that Black people should not be forced to fight in the military service to defend a racist government that does not protect us. We will not fight and kill other people of color in the world who, like black people, are being victimized by the white racist government of America. We will protect ourselves from the force and violence of the racist police and the racist military, by whatever means necessary.

7. *We want an immediate end to POLICE BRUTALITY and MURDER of black people.*                                                                          30

We believe we can end police brutality in our black community by organizing black self-defense groups that are dedicated to defending our black community from racist police oppression and brutality. The Second Amendment to the Constitution of the United States gives a right to bear arms. We therefore believe that all black people should arm themselves for self-defense.

8. *We want freedom for all black men held in federal, state, county and city prisons and jails.*

We believe that all black people should be released from the many jails and prisons because they have not received a fair and impartial trial.       40

9. *We want all black people when brought to trial to be tried in court by a jury of their peer group or people from their black communities, as defined by the Constitution of the United States.*

We believe that the courts should follow the United States Constitution so that black people will receive fair trials. The 14th Amendment of the U.S. Constitution gives a man a right to be tried by his peer group.

A peer is a person from a similar economic, social, religious, geographical, environmental, historical and racial background. To do this the court will be forced to select a jury from the black community from which the black defendant came. We have been, and are being tried by all-white juries that have no understanding of the "average reasoning man" of the black community.

10. *We want land, bread, housing, education, clothing, justice and peace. And as our major political objective, a United Nations-supervised plebiscite to be held through)ut the black colony in which only black colonial subjects will be allowed to participate, for the purpose of determining the will of black people as to their national destiny.*

When, in the course of human events, it becomes necessary for one people to dissolve the political bands which have connected them with another, and to assume, among the powers of the earth, the separate and equal station to which the laws of nature and nature's God entitle them, a decent respect to the opinions of mankind requires that they should declare the causes which impel them to the separation.

We hold these truths to be self-evident, that all men are created equal; that they are endowed by their Creator with certain unalienable rights; that among these are life, liberty, and the pursuit of happiness. *That, to secure these rights, governments are instituted among men, deriving their just powers from the governed; that, whenever any form of government becomes destructive of these ends, it is the right of the people to alter or to abolish it, and to institute a new government, laying its foundation on such principles, and organizing its powers in such form, as to them shall seem most likely to effect their safety and happiness.* Prudence, indeed, will dictate that governments long established should not be changed for light and transient causes; and, accordingly, all experience hath shown, that mankind are more disposed to suffer, while evils are sufferable, than to right themselves by abolishing the forms to which they are accustomed. *But, when a long train of abuses and usurpations, pursuing invariably the same object, evinces a design to reduce them under absolute despotism, it is their right, it is their duty, to throw off such government, and to provide new guards for their future security.*

## RULES OF THE BLACK PANTHER PARTY

Every member of the BLACK PANTHER PARTY throughout this country of racist America must abide by these rules as functional members of this party. CENTRAL COMMITTEE members, CENTRAL STAFFS, and LOCAL STAFFS, including all captains subordinate to either national, state, and local leadership of the BLACK PANTHER PARTY will enforce these rules. Length of suspension or other disciplinary action necessary for violation of these rules will depend on national decisions by national, state or state area, and local committees and staffs where said rule or rules of the BLACK PANTHER PARTY WERE VIOLATED.

Every member of the party must know these verbatim by heart. And apply them daily. Each member must report any violation of these rules to their leadership or they are counter-revolutionary and are also subjected to suspension by the BLACK PANTHER PARTY

*The Rules are:*

1. No party member can have narcotics or weed in his possession while doing party work.

2. Any party member found shooting narcotics will be expelled from this party.

3. No party member can be DRUNK while doing daily party work.

4. No party member will violate rules relating to office work, general meetings of the BLACK PANTHER PARTY, and meetings of the BLACK PANTHER PARTY ANYWHERE.

5. No party member will USE, POINT, or FIRE a weapon of any kind unnecessarily or accidentally at anyone.

6. No party member can join any other army force other than the BLACK LIBERATION ARMY.

7. No party member can have a weapon in his possession while DRUNK or loaded off narcotics or weed.

8. No party member will commit any crimes against other party members or BLACK people at all, and cannot steal or take from the people, not even a needle or a piece of thread.

9. When arrested BLACK PANTHER MEMBERS will give only name, address, and will sign nothing. Legal first aid must be understood by all Party members.

10. The Ten-Point Program and platform of the BLACK PANTHER PARTY must be known and understood by each Party member.

11. Party Communications must be National and Local.

12. The 10-10-10-program should be known by all members and also understood by all members.

13. All Finance officers will operate under the jurisdiction of the Ministry of Finance.

14. Each person will submit a report of daily work.

15. Each Sub-Section Leaders, Section Leaders, and Lieutenants, Captains must submit Daily reports of work.

16. All Panthers must learn to operate and service weapons correctly.

17. All Leadership personnel who expel a member must submit this information to the Editor of the Newspaper, so that it will be published in the paper and will be known by all chapters and branches.

18. Political Education Classes are mandatory for general membership.

19. Only office personnel assigned to respective offices each day should be there. All others are to sell papers and do Political work out in the community, including Captains, Section Leaders, etc.

20. COMMUNICATIONS—all chapters must submit weekly reports in

writing to the National Headquarters.

21. All Branches must implement First Aid and/or Medical Cadres.

22. All Chapters, Branches, and components of the BLACK PANTHER PARTY must submit a monthly Financial Report to the Ministry of Finance, and also the Central Committee.

23. Everyone in a leadership position must read no less than two hours per day to keep abreast of the changing political situation.

24. No chapter or branch shall accept grants, poverty funds, money or any other aid from any government agency without contacting the National Headquarters.

25. All chapters must adhere to the policy and the ideology laid down by the CENTRAL COMMITTEE of the BLACK PANTHER PARTY.

26. All Branches must submit weekly reports in writing to their respective Chapters.

## 8 Points of Attention
1) Speak politely.
2) Pay fairly for what you buy.
3) Return everything you borrow.
4) Pay for anything you damage.
5) Do not hit or swear at people.
6) Do not damage property or crops of the poor, oppressed masses.
7) Do not take liberties with women.
8) If we ever have to take captives do not ill-treat them.

## 3 Main Rules of Discipline
1) Obey orders in all your actions.
2) Do not take a single needle or a piece of thread from the poor and oppressed masses.
3) Turn in everything captured from the attacking enemy.

# Harry L. Jones
## Black Humor and
## The American Way of Life

In this day when black is set forth not only as beautiful but superior to white, blue, green, or yellow, assimilated middle class Negroes are erroneously defined as those who have adopted white values, wear wigs instead of Afro bushes, want to integrate rather than separate, and work to move from inner city black ghettos to suburban white ghettos. The definition is wrong, for such a person can still have "soul." He can eat fried chicken in the quiet confines of his suburban rambler, sneak watermelons disguised as bowling balls into his house, and grow collard greens in his spacious backyard. The accurate definition of an assimilated middle class Negro is that he is a person who fails to see the joke of America and who has forgotten how to laugh. He really believes and accepts the American creed that "all men are created equal." He takes rather seriously "the threat" of George Wallace, and he believes that somehow Richard Nixon was a better choice. He feels that only a "fluke" caused the good people of Georgia to put "Axe Handle" Maddox in the gubernatorial mansion, and he waits for these good people to come to their senses and throw the rascal out, to borrow a phrase from a campaign slogan of a few years back. He goofs constantly by assuming that what is normal is anomaly and that soon things will get better. But most importantly, he has lost his real black roots, and he fails to see that the disparity between preachment and practice in America is one of the most painfully hilarious facts of black existence.

Most serious black writers suffer from having become assimilated middle class Negroes. They are serious, and, by and large, they have bought the whole American bag. Baldwin, Wright, and Ellison all suffer from the lack of humor in any of their major works. It is true that as

148

regards Negroes they never miss an opportunity to point to the distance between American preachment and practice, but their "Ain't-it-a-shame" posture seems to indicate that they think that America is for real; and that all they have to do is to expose the disparity and America will sell all it has and give to the poor. Such a view as this has deprived Negro America of writers who could speak its soul. The most successful black writers are blacks writing for whites. Even the most bitter attacks on whites, the most vitriolic pronouncements presenting so-called authoritative views from the black community, *Look Out Whitey, Black Power's Going to Get Your Mama* (a title which plays the black "dirty dozens" with whites), *Die, Nigger, Die, Black Rage,* or *Soul on Ice,* are written not for blacks in the ghetto, who don't buy books, but for suburban whites, who do. Yet no successful Negro writer has yet expressed in print the ironic humor in the fact that it is whites who make these books moderate best sellers.

Unassimiliated blacks or folk Negroes have, for three hundred years, used the bastardization of the American creed as a source of painful humor. Contrary to a current stereotype, Negroes are no more natural clowns or happy-go-lucky laughers than any other ethnic group; they are rather hard-headed realists who see it and tell it like it is. He knows the reality of his own existence in America despite the stereotype of his clownish nature and he says in his blues:

You don't know me, you don't know my mind;
When you see me laughing, laughing just to keep from crying.

A folk Negro can assuage some of his hard life through a laugh: "Man, I really don't mind them rats being in my house, but when I get home and find they done set the table like I'm a *guest*, that's too much."

After Wallace's defeat in the last presidential election, one of the stories making the rounds in the ghetto went like this:

"Man, you hear where Wallace going to run for president in 1972 with Maddox as his vice-president? They saying they ain't prejudiced, and they writing this book about how they entertained in the governors' mansions of Georgia and Alabama people like Leontyne Price, Duke Ellington, Malcolm X, and Martin Luther King."

"No, man, I ain't heard that, but that sound like a good book. What they gonna call it?"

*"Famous Niggers We Have Known."*

Through "lies," as jokes and folk stories are called in the black ghetto, like this, folk Negroes have survived for over three hundred and fifty years.

While serious Negro writers continue to be serious, Langston Hughes stands out as a singular exception to the general rule. Hughes was the one successful black writer who was aware of his folk roots and consistently made capital of folk humor. In his series about Jesse B. Semple, known

as "Simple," works which are masterpieces of folk humor, what one
discovers is that Simple isn't simple. With an ear for language, Simple
speaks a musical folk dialect, and he sprinkles it generously with what
used to be called "Harlem jive." Simple is an astute observer who sees
America clearly, and he makes some telling comments on the system. As
a symbol of everything that is real and true in the black experience, Simple
knows that Negroes are the lump that has not melted in the melting pot
culture. But Simple survives. As he remarks to the census taker:

> My mama should have named me Job instead of Jesse B. Simple. I     10
> have been underfed, underpaid, undernourished, and everything but
> undertaken — yet I am still here.

In speaking of the American space program, Simple is concerned that
there are no black astronauts:
I have not heard tell of no Negro astronaughts nowhere in space yet.
This is serious, because if one of them white Southerners gets to the
moon first COLORED NOT ADMITTED signs will go up all over
heaven as sure as God made little green apples, and Dixiecrats will
be asking the man in the moon, "Do you want your daughter to marry     20
a Nigra?" Meanwhile, the NAACP will have to go to the Supreme
Court, as usual, to get an edict for Negroes to even set foot on the moon.

Then, bringing the problem down from heaven to earth, Simple remarks,
"If white Americans can learn to fly past Venus, go in orbit, and make
telestars, it looks like to me white barbers in Ohio could learn how to cut
colored hair."
   One of the most obvious signs of Negro invisibility in America is the
television commercials about sun and fun vacations in the South, usually
sponsored by the airlines. No matter whether it is "number one to the     30
sun," "turning Florida into an airline," or someone yelling, "Come on
down," these commercials are as striking in their absence of black faces
as the Miss America contest in its absence of black bodies. Simple wants
to establish a tour service which he feels will induce Negroes to go South.
He says, "My ad would read:

> Special Rates for a Weekend.
> In a Typical Mississippi Jail.
> Get arrested now; pay later. Bail money not included. Have the time of
> your life among the Dixie White Skins. Excitement guaranteed. For
> full details contact the Savage South Tours, Inc. Jesse B. Semple, your     40
> host, wishing you hell."

Hughes was fully aware that in creating Simple, he was presenting a
prototype of the American folk Negro with his marvelous articulateness,
given the instrument of his own folk speech, with his firm grip on the
harsh realities of black existence in America, and with his devastating

satirical wit. In fact, the model for Simple was just such a folk type that Hughes met in a Harlem bar near the St. Nicholas Avenue apartment where Hughes lived in 1942. When he overheard the man telling his girl-friend about his job, making cranks in a war plant in New Jersey, Hughes asked the man what the cranks were for. The model for Simple replied, "I don't know what them cranks crank. You know white folks don't tell Negroes what cranks crank." Hughes's creation of the Simple narratives required a good ear and a handy notebook rather than an active creative imagination nurtured in a lonely garret, for the language, the ideas, and the attitudes manifested in Simple are those of the folk Negro of the urban ghettos.

For three hundred and fifty years, black humor has been a survival technique and a weapon of the weak against the strong. It has touched, and still touches, all aspects of the black experience in America. Even the blues, those songs generally thought of as sad and depressing presentations of life and love, are not always blue. Life and love would indeed be unbearable if they could not be laughed at at times. In the blues one finds generous examples of humor of comic hyperbole:

> The gal I love is chocolate to the bone.
> I done drunk so much whiskey I stagger in my sleep.
> A good-looking gal will make a bulldog gnaw his chain.
> I creep up to her window just to hear how sweet she snores.

When it treats black-white relations, black humor can be bitingly satiric. One of the oldest of the folk tales insists that Adam, Eve, Cain and Abel were all black. Shortly after he killed Abel, Cain heard a voice behind him asking where Abel was. Without looking around, Cain asked, "Am I my brother's keeper?" When he turned and discovered that it was the Lord he was talking to, his hair stood straight out and he was so scared that he turned white. And that's where the first white man came from.

Black folk songs similarly take a rather dark view of whites:

> When they get old and grey,
> When they get old and grey,
> White folks look just like monkeys,
> When they get old and grey.

Even the times in slavery when freedom was promised and subsequently denied became subjects for laughter through song:

> My old mistress promised me
> When she died she'd set me free.
> She lived so long her head got bald;
> Then she gave up the notion of dying at all.

Economic and social inequities, the white procreation and use of mulatto women and American justice as it affects blacks are all treated in the following:

> White folks live in a fine brick house.
> Lord, the yellow gal does the same.
> Poor black man lives in the big rock jail,
> But it's a brick house just the same.

So far as black humor is concerned, nothing in the American way of life is sacred or safe from being made the brunt of a joke. A little story about the winters up North even involves the Great Emancipator: "Man, it got so cold in New York last winter that Old Abe, standing down in Lincoln Square, took his hand off that poor little Negro's head and put it in his pocket." And even the child's nursery rhyme can be utilized in the cause:

> Mary had a little lamb.
> Its *fleas* were white as snow.
> For everywhere that Mary went,
> Only *white* fleas could go.

It is unfortunate that the integrationist approach to black life in America insists that equal status for Negroes must come at the loss of cultural identity. That seems a high price to pay, but since Negro folk culture is largely oral rather than literate and since writers have to sell the books they produce, it is a price that most successful "civil writers" have paid for their entrance into the mainstream of middle-class American life. So it is that the black roots in the rich cultural tradition of black humor and folklore remain mostly uncultivated. On the other hand, perhaps these writers are more to be pitied than scorned, for, as Simple says, "It is not easy, by and large, to live one hundred years in the Land of the Free, if black you be."

# Leon Williams
## Vining

"Don't tell me my bike ain't better than yours! Man, I knows my bike is better than yours."

"Yo' bike ain't better than mine. I know yo' bike ain't better than mine. How many speeds you got?"

"Listen here, my man, my bike is got to be better than yours, 'cause mine is got five speeds."

"That ain't nothing, Roe, my bike got ten speeds and it can move."

"Me too, man, I got a ten-speed; I got a ten-speed. Mine goes real fast too, but it depands on who's riding it, ya know?"

"Man, you a liar, Struss! You just told me that you had a five-speed. Now you tryin' to tell me that you got a ten-speed. I saw that bike you was riding last week, man. That ain't no ten-speed; that ain't even a five-speed, man. That was a three-speed."

"No man, that wasn't my bike. That was my brother's bike."

"What the heck is wrong with your own bike Roe?"

"Man, I just didn't want to mess up the wheels."

"What kind a ten-speed you got?"

"I got a English ten!"

"Look Struss, if your bike is so fast, how come you ain't raced nobody? Ha, Ha."

"Man I raced Morris. I raced Morris last week. We raced up Columbus Avenue an I beat him man!"

"I know you ain't beat Morris cause Morris beat me and you can't beat me Struss."

"O.K. Roe; Do you wanna race me man? I'll tell you what. I'll meet yo' behind the church on Monday at 125th St. man. I'm gonna bring my ten

10

20

153

speed and you bring yours. I'm gonna shut you up fo good my man. You
be at 125th St. an we'll race up Lenox Avenue."

"That's fine with me Struss. Since you got all your fellas here listen to
you yap, man they can prove that you said you was gonna beat me."

"Tell ya'll what. I'll judge the race."

"Look Steve, we don't need you to judge no race man! We don't need
you cause you is a bum my man! Look at yo cheap clothes man."

"Dig it Roe, I may not ride a bike as good as you, but I'll tell you this
much; I vines man. I dresses fine!"

"Man, you don't dress worth nothin. You ain't even got no gators."          10

"Who ain't got no gators? I got gators man. I got two pairs of gators."

"Last week you told me you had three pairs of gators, Steve."

"I did not tell you I had three pairs a gators man! I told you that I had
two pairs a gators and one pair a snakes my man! That's what I told you!"

"So what? You ain't got no silks. Everytime I see you, you got on those
same pair of fogy-dogy pants."

"I got silks my man. I got silks, Roe, I got blue, green, black and two
pairs of gray silks. That ain't all I got. I got about five knits man. The
jives cost me $55 each man! So don't tell me that I ain't got no vines."

"You a liar Steve. You ain't got no knits. Look at that shirt you wearing     20
now. Where'd you git it? I know where you got it man. You got it at Alex-
anders on Fordham. I seen the same jive for $4 each!"

"I don't care what you say Roe. I know what I paid fo my knit. Anyway,
my clothes is all tailor made. I got pants and coats that is tailor made.
I got plenty a skys and everything."

"What skys man? You got one sky and that ain't saying nothing."

"I got more than one sky. I got a beaver hat and a cashmere hat and and
I even got a play hat man! What you got, Roe?"

"You know I'm altogether. When I go in my bag man it's all over. I
vines better than anybody on the block man. I knows you don't really      30
think you vines better than me. You don't even wear Cons man. 'If you
wearing those sneakers that slip and slide, get the Cons with the star on
the side.' "

"Who needs Cons man? It's how much game you got that counts. You
can have all the Cons in the world man, but if you ain't got no game they
ain't going to do you no good. And you is so bad Roe, that you need to go
to the store and buy a can of game. Ha, Ha, Ha, Ha."

"I ain't talking about no game man; I is talking about vines. You have
the nerve to stand here with your hair so knotty and your nose so snotty
and tell me about game! You and your beat-up skips and hand-me-down     40
shirt! Dig it man; If I have to come out my bag to sound you down, yo
mind will be messed up!"

"Look man; I ain't gonna argue with you. I know that sneakers don't
make the man. Sneakers don't make the man! You a damn fool if you
think sneakers make the man. I'll tell you what makes the man: sneakers
don't make the man—clothes make the man!

"O.K. man. If you think clothes make the man, I'll meet you tonight in front of the church and have you a dress out man! If you dare show your ugly mug tonight I am going to scream you!"

"O.K. Roe, I'll meet you tonight at 9:30 in front of the church man. The only thing you might beat me in is your hat man. You got a leather and I ain't got no leather."

"Dig this, I'm gonna wear all my jive and you wear all yours too. I'm gonna give you a break man. I'm not even gonna wear my leather and I'm gonna beat you. I don't even need my damn leather! O.K. Steve?"

"O.K. Roe, I'll be there. We can let the fellas decide who is the coolest 10 cat. See you at 9:30 my man!"

LAZARUS *The New Colossus* ☐ ULLMAN *We Are Americans* ☐ BARONI *The Ethnic Bag* ☐ MANN *Hybridism* ☐ LA GUARDIA *A Glimpse of Racial Feeling* ☐ MALAMUD *Black is My Favorite Color* ☐ LEVENSON *Sweet Horseradish* ☐ ODETS *Awake and Sing* ☐ REMBIENSKA *A Servant Girl* ☐ BANKS *Growing Up Polish in Pittsburgh* ☐ SIU *The Sojourner* ☐ U.S. SUPREME COURT *Korematsu v. United States, 1944* ☐ NAKASHIMA *Japanese-Americans Interned During World War II* ☐ SMITH *An American Catholic Answers Back* ☐ FISHER *The Ice People* ☐

# Immigration and Assimilation:
## the others

*"I'm sorry, young man, but I'm afraid I don't speak Spanish."*

# Introduction

For the most part, the tone of this section is different from that of the others. A play like "We Are Americans" is a false and oversimplified version of immigrants coming to America. But this play is the way many of us were taught, say, in junior high, to think of "the others." Still even though the people who "escaped" into America didn't find the promise exactly as the New Colossus predicted, the America seen through their eyes is not the America of the blacks and reds and browns.

We have two selections in this section dealing with the imprisonment of American citizens of Japanese descent in World War II. Here there is anger, and justifiably so. Among other immigrant groups there is a recounting of poverty, of loneliness, of hard work, but rarely in despair.

Why was the case of the Japanese so different? Keep the "Melting Pot" image in mind. The immigrants were, for the most part, white. Some had red hair, some brown hair, some blue eyes, some hazel, but they were white. It was easier for them to fit in. The melting pot idea makes fitting in a goal, and for white immigrants it was a realistic goal.

When Sam Levenson looks back at his childhood, his memories are affectionate. He tells his tale with humor and warmth because he looks back and likes what he sees. Even Gino Baroni in "The Ethnic Bag" smiles at memories of "Italian soul food." The short story by Carolyn Banks, "Growing Up Polish in Pittsburgh," also looks back with a nostalgic smile.

Not that petty prejudices didn't exist. All of the pieces make this clear. Fiorello LaGuardia was driven to success by a "sense of injustice that was still bottomless, with a capacity for outrage that was still boundless . . . "Even Sam Levenson refers to himself as "a virtually free American."

What is different throughout this section is the element of choice. The immigrants could melt into the mainstream because they couldn't be picked out in a crowd. They didn't always decide to blend protectively into the majority. But when we talk about a ghetto in this section it is closer to what the essay, "The Sojourner," calls "a racial colony" in the sense that the immigrants weren't forced to live there but chose to. It was "an effort to create a home away from home."

"Ghetto," in the sections dealing with blacks or reds or browns, is a dirty word. The ethnic ghettoes were places which sometimes allowed the immigrants greater freedom. They could "be themselves," live as they had lived in "the old country," in the middle of cities which were frightening because they were new and different. The neighborhood boundaries in "Growing Up Polish," for example, are very clearly drawn. And when you read the letter from "A Servant Girl," you can see how much easier it would be for her to find friends in the same lonely situation as hers, other immigrants from Poland, rather than try to overcome a tremendous language barrier and join the larger society.

Life for the immigrant wasn't rosy by any means. Even within groups there was and still is prejudice and hostility. Look at the blacks in Malamud's story, "Black is My Favorite Color." The blind man in the same story is not color blind. "I can tell you're white," he says at the end of the story. Gino Baroni's article makes clear that it is precisely those people who overcame prejudice and bigotry themselves who now practice it. We don't seem to be learning from our mistakes.

America's treatment of its Japanese citizens is quite another matter. The Supreme Court documents don't rile us very much, nor are they meant to. They sound so official that the problem seems miles away. Arguments for both sides are given, but the strongest argument, the argument that brings it home, is Ted Nakashima's own account of his "resettlement." Just as "racial colony" sounds better than "ghetto," "resettlement center" sounds better than "concentration camp." But read Mr. Nakashima's description and think about what you'd call it.

# Emma Lazarus
## The New Colossus

Not like the brazen giant of Greek fame,
With conquering limbs astride from land to land;
Here at our sea-washed, sunset gates shall stand
A mighty woman with a torch, whose flame
Is the imprisoned lightning, and her name
Mother of Exiles. From her beacon-hand
Glows world-wide welcome; her mild eyes command
The air-bridged harbor that twin cities frame.

"Keep, ancient lands, your storied pomp!" cries she          10
With silent lips. "Give me your tired, your poor,
Your huddled masses yearning to breathe free,
The wretched refuse of your teeming shore.
Send these, the homeless, tempest-tossed to me.
I lift my lamp beside the golden door!"

# Samuel S. Ullman
## We Are Americans

### Characters
#### ACT ONE
Two sailors, two Italian men and two Italian women, Polish man and woman, Hungarian man and woman, Russian man and woman, Austrian, Slovak, Greek, Portuguese, Swede, a group of children, the captain of the ship.

#### ACT TWO
A group of six men and three women in American dress, a court attendant, the judge.

#### ACT ONE
TIME: *About 1905.*
PLACE: *Aboard an ocean liner nearing America.*
*Stretching across the front of the stage is a ship's railing. Behind it and looking toward audience is a fairly large group of men, women and children of various nationalities—Italian, Hungarian, Russian, Austrian, Greek, Polish, Slovak, Swede, Portuguese. Some are sitting on large bundles. The clothing the people wear represents the costumes of their homeland. A number of women wear skirts, shawls, head kerchiefs. The women are sitting on chairs. On rear wall left is painted a black smokestack. Smoke rises from it. On each side of the stage at rear is a life preserver marked—S.S. AMERICA. An American flag is at rear center. It is placed above an anchor. Two sailors are winding a length of rope into a heap. A number of flags of different nationalities decorate the stage. Bells are heard at curtain rise and during the Act.*

163

FIRST SAILOR. Well, the ship is nearing port now, I guess you'll all be glad you're arriving in America . . . though the trip wasn't bad.

SECOND SAILOR. The ocean was pretty smooth this voyage.

ITALIAN WOMAN. We'll be in America at last.

HUNGARIAN WOMAN. America . . . the United States. Farewell to Europe.

SECOND SAILOR. The Statue of Liberty will soon be in sight. That always affects immigrants coming to our country.

RUSSIAN. The Statue of Liberty *(To wife.)* Sonya, we shall soon see the wonderful Statue, the wonderful lady who stands at the gate of America    *10* with the torch of freedom held in her hand. We shall soon see her.

HIS WIFE. Yes, we shall begin life anew in America.

GREEK. In America, the land of free men and women.

FIRST SAILOR. It's a funny thing about immigrants coming to America these years. . . .

POLISH BOY. What is the Statue of Liberty, mamma?

POLISH WOMAN. You heard the gentleman, my son. She is a kind, wonderful lady who stands at the gate of this wonderful country that will be our home. She holds out her hands to the poor, oppressed peoples of the world.    *20*

RUSSIAN. To us.

POLISH WOMAN. And says to them, Here in this land, America, you will find hope for you and your children, hope for a better life.

POLISH BOY. And we will see this lady?

POLISH MAN. Yes . . . soon, my son.

POLISH WOMAN. *(Pointing to rear.)* There you see the beautiful flag of the lady of freedom . . . red, white and blue.

*(Some of the children go to the flag, repeating "red, white and blue.")*

FIRST SAILOR. I was saying . . . in the old days the immigrants spoke mostly of opportunity, success, the fortunes they were going to make;    *30* not that they don't speak of these things today. But nowadays . . .

HUNGARIAN. Now they speak of liberty, freedom, democracy.

RUSSIAN. Equality.

FIRST SAILOR. Yes.

HUNGARIAN. They are the most precious things in life, the things for which your people fought the great Revolutionary War. They are found in your wonderful Declaration of Independence.

AUSTRIAN. In America, freedom, liberty, democracy are the everyday possessions of the people. But in the Old World, people know little of these things and speak less of them.    *40*

FIRST ITALIAN MAN. My uncle Pietro from California he write to me all the time. Uncle Pietro say America is land of freedom. Come to America. Uncle Pietro come to America ten years ago. He has large farm in California. He raises fine grapes.

SECOND SAILOR. Many Italians raise grapes in California.

FIRST ITALIAN WOMAN. Grapes for wine. They bring the fine art of wine making to America from Italy.

FIRST ITALIAN MAN. Uncle Pietro is a citizen. He say it is good to be a citizen of the great United States. We become citizens, too.

SECOND ITALIAN, *(Pointing to wife.)* We come from Italy, too. My wife has uncle in New York City. He is a big builder. He come from Italy eight years ago. Uncle Angelo is citizen, too.

HIS WIFE. Angelo is rich man now. He builds roads and builds houses in New York. In Italy he was bricklayer. Uncle Angelo say America is land of opportunity.

SECOND ITALIAN MAN. I am bricklayer. Some day I will be big builder. *(He takes photograph from pocket and shows it to* FIRST ITALIAN MAN.*)* Here is picture of Uncle Angelo.

FIRST ITALIAN MAN. He looks like a real American.

SECOND ITALIAN MAN. He has a gold watch and chain. He is dressed in fine American clothes.

*(The* AUSTRIAN *standing near by looks at picture.)*

AUSTRIAN. Dressed in fine American clothes. Yes, clothes, not a uniform. People in America do not wear uniforms in time of peace. I leave Austria, my country, because I do not want to wear a uniform. I do not want to be a soldier in time of peace.

VOICES. That is true. . . . In my country, too. . . . Too many soldiers. . . . Too many soldiers in Europe.

SLOVAK. I have job waiting for me in America.

POLISH MAN. I have job waiting, too.

SLOVAK. *(Continuing.)* I go to work in Pennsylvania, in coal mine. My brother write to me in Slovakia. He say "Plenty mines, plenty factories in America." Many people from my country work in coal mines, in steel mills in Pennsylvania.

PORTUGUESE. In Portugal, I was fisherman. In America, I join fishing fleet in Atlantic Ocean. Catch cod, mackerel, halibut. Many of my people join fishing fleets in Pacific Ocean.

SWEDE. I am going to be a farmer in America. In Sweden I had a farm. But life is hard in Europe, especially when there are so many mouths to feed.

HUNGARIAN. We all know that. We all have come to America because life is so hard in Europe.

SWEDE. Many people from Sweden and Norway settled in the United States many years ago. They have farms, big farms, in state of Minnesota. They write me. They tell me the land is fertile, very fertile, and a man can buy land cheap.

*(The clanging of bells is heard offstage. Both* SAILORS *leave exit right.)*

RUSSIAN. The captain is coming. Our good captain. This is the last time he will see us.

CHILD. I like the American captain. He is so nice to us children.

FIRST ITALIAN MAN. The captain is proud of his country. He tell me that many years ago he come to America like us. . . from Europe.

POLISH WOMAN. An immigrant?

FIRST ITALIAN MAN. Yes. Now he is captain of big American ship. He says America is land of opportunity for everybody.

*(Enter* CAPTAIN *exit right, attended by two sailors who take places at rear. He is in officer's uniform. Those sitting rise.)*

CAPTAIN. Good morning, everybody. Good Morning.

ALL. Good morning, captain.

*(Some of the children go to him and take his hand. He motions to the women to sit.)*

CAPTAIN. Well, we are nearing the end of our trip. We have had a                    10
pleasant journey across. It is as good a way as any to start life in America.

CHILD. *(Taking* CAPTAIN'S *hand).* Is this the way people shake hands in America, captain?

CAPTAIN. *(Smiling.)* Yes. You are losing no time learning American ways. *(To others.)* Yes, most of you, perhaps all, will in a few years become citizens of the land you are choosing for your new home.

SLOVAK. It takes five years to become a citizen of the United States.

SWEDE. It is worth waiting for.

CAPTAIN. It is.

PORTUGUESE. I wish I could become a citizen of the United States as              20
soon as my feet touch American land.

CAPTAIN. Five years is not long. I waited, too. I came here as an immigrant forty years ago, with my parents.

HUNGARIAN WOMAN. See what you have become, a great captain of a big American ship. You make us feel good, captain. If America do so much for you, maybe. . .

CAPTAIN. America will do much for you, too, and for your children. America's children are her first care. Greater opportunities are offered children in America than anywhere else in the world. You will soon learn that. And great opportunities are offered you too.                                              30

SECOND ITALIAN MAN. I will go to school in America to learn to speak English well, to read and to write.

CAPTAIN. America wants her immigrants to become citizens. Schools are free in this country, where you can educate yourselves and learn the history of our country and its leaders, where you can learn about our Declaration of Independence, and the Constitution of the United States. Attend these schools and Americanization classes. In whatever city or state you live you will find them.

POLISH WOMAN. You are so proud of your country, captain.

CAPTAIN. I am. And I trust you will be, some day.

*(Bells are heard again.)*                                                                 40

CHILD. *(At left, pointing.)* Look! Look! Everybody. There is the tall lady.
*(All look toward right.)*

ITALIAN MAN. The Statue of Liberty.

VOICES. The Statue of Liberty! The Statue of Liberty! Hurrah! Hurrah!
*(Some remove their hats.)*

RUSSIAN. The Statue. How wonderful she looks! How wonderful! She seems to be saying "Welcome" to us.

CAPTAIN. She is saying "Welcome."

*(The women repeat "She is . . . she is.")*

POLISH MAN. Captain, while we are sailing past the wonderful Statue, could we not hear the great American national song, the one we hear so often on the boat?

SWEDE. Yes, *The Star Spangled Banner.*

VOICES. Yes. . . . Yes, captain.

CAPTAIN. Of course. Of course. An excellent idea. *(To* SAILOR.*)* Tell Officer Dunlap to have *The Star Spangled Banner* played. (SAILOR *salutes and leaves.)* An excellent idea. Yes, we will listen to the United States' national anthem as we sail past the Statue of Liberty.

RUSSIAN WOMAN. *(To child.)* There. . . . See the kind, wonderful lady of America? See her holding up her hand?

CHILD. Yes, I see her.

*(The national anthem is heard. The* CAPTAIN *places his cap across his chest. The women rise. One or two of the men do as the captain does. The others bring their hands up to a salute. The children gather near flag and salute. The curtain closes slowly as the song comes to an end.)*

CURTAIN

ACT TWO

TIME. *Five years later.*

PLACE: *A federal court. Any large city.*

*The scene is a court room. A group of six men and three women, in American dress, sits in chairs facing toward left where the* JUDGE'S *desk and chair are seen. The* JUDGE *has not yet arrived. On the desk are seen a Bible, some papers, a pile of small booklets containing the Declaration of Independence and the Constitution, and a heap of small American flags. High up on rear wall is written—* UNITED STATES COURT OF NATURALI-ZATION. *Below it are portraits of* JEFFERSON, WASHINGTON, LINCOLN. *The American Flag is in view at rear. A* COURT ATTENDANT, *dressed like a police officer, is distributing envelopes. One or two have already received theirs. They remove the enclosed papers and read them.*

ATTENDANT. The next name is Antonio Burelli.

FIRST MAN. *(Rising.)* I am Antonio. *(He takes envelope.)*

ATTENDANT. Mina Nurnburg.

(FIRST WOMAN *rises and receives an envelope.)*

FIRST WOMAN. *(Curtseying.)* Thank you, sir. *(She reads contents.)*

ATTENDANT. Maximus Zolanos.

(SECOND MAN *rises. Attendant gives him envelope which he opens.)*

THIRD MAN. *(Rising.)* And this paper, this paper really makes us citizens of the United States?

ATTENDANT. There is just one step left to your full naturalization as American citizens.

FIRST MAN. I know. We must take the oath of allegiance.

ATTENDANT. That is right. These are your second papers, the final papers of citizenship. Now you must swear an oath of allegiance to the government of the United States before the judge.

SECOND MAN. We will do that. We will be glad to swear allegiance to the United States. The United States is now our country.

VOICES. Yes. . . . The United States is our country.

ATTENDANT. Judge McDonald will be here soon to administer the oath. *(He continues calling the names.)* Stanislaus Tripp. . . Trippich.

*(He gives envelope to* FOURTH MAN.*)*

FOURTH MAN. *(Rising.)* Now that I am becoming an American citizen, I would like to change my name. . . to an American name.

ATTENDANT. You have the right to do it. The law gives you the right to change your name.

FOURTH MAN. Thank you.

ATTENDANT. Eric Gustafson.

(FIFTH MAN *rises and takes envelope.)*

FIFTH MAN. Thank you.

ATTENDANT. Nicolai Orsoffsky.

(SIXTH MAN *takes last envelope.)*

SIXTH MAN. *(Holding up envelope.)* I am an American citizen at last, an American citizen, thank God.

ATTENDANT. That takes care of everybody. *(He looks at watch.)* Judge McDonald must be here. I'll tell him you are ready to take the Oath of Allegiance.

*(He leaves exit left. For a moment all are busy reading their folded papers. Some read aloud.)*

THIRD MAN. *(Excited, pointing to paper.)* Here are the words. Look. *(The woman near him looks at paper.)* ". . . do hereby declare you to be a citizen of the United States of America." Is it not wonderful?

SECOND WOMAN. It is wonderful. And our children, too, will be citizens of the United States. It is a good thing. It is a good thing to be a citizen of the United States.

THIRD WOMAN. *(To* THIRD MAN.*)* I hear you read. You read very well. You understand the big words.

THIRD MAN. I have been going to night school, to Americanization classes, since I came to America five years ago.

SIXTH MAN. I have just begun to go. I am here five years, too. I am sorry I did not begin before.

THIRD MAN. In Europe I could not read or write. I could not write my name. Now I read American books, newspapers. I write letters to my family and friends in Europe.

FIRST WOMAN. You learn this by going to night school?

THIRD MAN. Yes, this country does much to help immigrants and foreigners to become American citizens.

SECOND WOMAN. It wants them to become citizens.

THIRD MAN. And in night school I learn also the history of this country and its great men. *(He rises and points to portraits at rear.)* Here are three great Americans, three presidents. The whole world should know about them. Do you know who they are?

THIRD WOMAN. *(Rising.)* In the middle is the great George Washington, the first president of the United States.

SECOND MAN. He is called the "Father of his country."

SIXTH MAN. *(Rising.)* On the right is the great president, Abe Lincoln. He was born very poor.

FIRST MAN. He was born in a small log cabin.

THIRD MAN. *(After a moment's pause.)* And this man on the left. . . he is President Jefferson.

FIFTH MAN. *(Rising.)* Yes, I know now. Thomas Jefferson. . . the great American who wrote the Declaration of Independence.

THIRD MAN. Yes. . . Washington, Jefferson, Lincoln. They are all great men. They believe in liberty and freedom for all the people.

*(Enter* ATTENDANT *exit left.)*

ATTENDANT. *(Announcing.)* His Honor, Judge McDonald. Please rise.

*(Everybody rises. Enter* JUDGE *exit left. He wears a black robe. He takes his seat at the desk.)*

JUDGE. Be seated, my friends.

*(All sit.)*

ATTENDANT. The naturalization papers have been distributed, your Honor.

JUDGE. Very well. . . . Before I proceed with the Oath of Allegiance, may I take a few moments to speak with you. . . about the meaning of citizenship and what this country expects of her citizens?

FOURTH MAN. *(Rising.)* I will do anything for this country. I love the United States. My sons and daughters will grow up American citizens.

JUDGE. *(Looking through some papers.)* I see that most of you have been in the country only five years. It is the shortest period of residence allowed before one can become a naturalized citizen. *(He looks through papers again.)* Yes, and many of you took out your first citizenship papers soon after you arrived in this country. That is fine.

FIFTH MAN. My brother and I take out our first papers one week after we arrive in the United States.

JUDGE. It shows you had it in your hearts to become American citizens from the beginning. It is a good start.

SIXTH MAN. We can vote when we are citizens? In Europe I never vote.

THIRD MAN. Where I come from in Europe, only rich people, people with property, have the right to vote.

JUDGE. In the United States, all citizens, rich or poor, have the right to vote, the right to choose their representatives and leaders. Ours is a government of the people, of all the people. . . a democracy.

THIRD MAN. Democracy. . . . It means a government of the people.

JUDGE. Voting for our leaders is one of many privileges a democracy gives her citizens. But citizens have their duties. Democracy expects her citizens to fulfill their duties. Do you know what the highest of these is? Nothing more or less than being a good citizen, a good American, a good man or woman.

VOICES. We will be good citizens. . . . We will be good Americans.

JUDGE. I know you will. I know you will. In this country men live not only for themselves, but for the good of all. Serve your community and your nation. Work for the good of your fellow citizens as well as for yourself. Be a good American. Make your country proud of you.                                     10

VOICES. The United States will be proud of us. The United States will be proud of us.

JUDGE. It is the highest honor you can hope for. . . that your country be proud of you. *(He moves flags and booklets on his desk to one side. The* ATTENDANT *steps to desk and takes them.)* And now, my friends, it has been my custom, for many years, just before delivering the Oath of Allegiance, to give to each new citizen *(He holds up a booklet.)* a copy of the Declaration of Independence and the Constitution of the United States, together with an American flag. (ATTENDANT *distributes them.)* Read         20
them. Study them. They are the guardians of human liberty and human rights in our country.

*(Some have opened the booklets and are reading.)*

THIRD MAN. Here in the Declaration of Independence it says, "All men are created equal."

FIRST WOMAN. Here it says, "Life, Liberty, and . . . Happiness." Such fine words.

JUDGE. And now, my friends, the day is drawing to a close. I know you are anxious to return to your families to tell them you are full fledged American citizens. As the final step in your naturalization, I will now         30
administer the Oath of Allegiance which you will repeat after me.

*(The* ATTENDANT *takes the Bible and comes before the group.)*

ATTENDANT. Please rise. *(They rise.)* Raise the right hand. *(He raises his hand. They do the same.)* And repeat after Judge McDonald.

JUDGE. *(Reading from paper.\*)* I hereby declare on oath *(Group repeats.)* that I absolutely and entirely renounce and abjure. . . *(Group repeats.)* all allegiance to any prince, state, or sovereignty. . . *(Group repeats.)* of whom I have heretofore been a subject. . . *(Group repeats.)* that I will support and defend the Constitution and the Laws of the United States of America. . . *(Group repeats.)* and that I will bear faith and allegiance         40
to the same. *(Group repeats. The* JUDGE *puts paper down on desk. The* ATTENDANT *lowers his arm.)* Ladies and gentlemen, I greet you as citizens of the United States of America.

CURTAIN

*A chorus softly sings "America" while the Oath is being administered.

# Gino Baroni
## The Ethnic Bag

The college kids are right, most of the big-city cops are pigs. And the firemen, the mailmen, the factory workers, and the priests. Poles, Italians, Germans and Slavs—PIGS. By that definition I'm a pig, too, and so are most of us from the working class.

The end of the 1960's was the end of an era, both for the country and for me personally. I was in Washington for the black revolution, and I saw things change so much. Blacks became so much more aggressive. At the same time, blacks became increasingly resentful of whites who try to work with them, and rightly so. I believe the black community should do its own thing. Of course, when blacks tell me this, I have to smile. 10 I tell them "our thing" in Italian is "cosa nostra."

As I began to realize that my role as a white clergyman in a black community had increased liabilities, I began to ask who *I* was. When I was introduced to somebody, he would ask if I was Italian. What was I supposed to answer? "No, I'm American"? "Yes, I'm Italian-American"? I realized I was still the ethnic bag, and nine years in Washington didn't change that.

Every Thanksgiving my family gathers back in Pennsylvania for a reunion. It always starts out polite. One of my brothers will say, "How are the blacks in Washington?" Pretty soon it's, "Well, we made it, why can't they?" 20 I try the academic explanations, but they never work. Then we get into a shouting match, and my mother says, "Shut up and eat the spaghetti."

I became sensitive to where the resistance to black revolution was. Why were the Nixons and Wallaces so successful? I realized that a lot of people were resisting the black revolution for a lot of reasons, and that the largest group was the white ethnics in the large industrial cities. This was my side of the street, and I had left for Washington.

I come from a working class family in a company town between Johnstown and Altoona, Pennsylvania. The town is Acosta, and the mine is Mine 120. It was one of the last areas in coal country to be organized. We moved from a shack to a company house. The company owned the electricity, the water, the outhouses. We bought everything at the company store. Remember that song, "Sixteen Tons"? My father loved that song; he sang it practically every day.

One thing I remember about Acosta is that the Episcopalians and the Jews owned the mines, the Presbyterians and Lutherans were the bosses, and the Italians and the Poles dug the coal. FDR and John L. Lewis were our idols. We had their pictures on the wall. I remember the heartbreak it caused when the two of them split up in 1940. It gave us a hell of a time. We even thought about voting for Willkie.

When it came time for me to go to high school, I was bused to Somerset, the county seat. My classmates were the sons and daughters of lawyers, doctors, and feed salesmen. All the teachers were WASPS. There was Bible-reading and hymn-singing. The atmosphere was very antiunion, antiworking class. We were taught that unions were a ruination of everything, and that God loves those who make it. There were only three of us Catholics in a class of 180. We were the outsiders; they didn't want any "lunch-buckets" in Somerset. When I took my salami sandwiches to school, the teacher fussed about the smell.

My family used to eat mushrooms, snails, gizzard, tripe, brains, and dandelions—Italian soul food. We raised rabbits and caught squirrels. Rabbit was my favorite meat. I ate it because that's what poor people ate. Now if I want these same things, I have to go to a fancy restaurant.

I often use that example to show working class audiences that although we were materially poor, psychologically and culturally we were very rich. My family and their friends had stability. My father couldn't read or write, but after one bottle of wine he thought he was related to Garibaldi. After two bottles it was Leonardo da Vinci. My father could prune trees and make wine. We used to crush the grapes with our feet. Then somebody told my father it wasn't sanitary, so he got us little white boots to wear. We also made whiskey and sold it to the Protestants. They called it "bootlegging," but today it would probably be called "income maintenance."

My family came to this country with a strong family setup, a strong work ethic, fantastic culture, and hope for life in America. People with my background will tell you now, "I was poor, but I went through the Depression, and I made it." But there was a tremendous difference between the immigrants and the blacks. Black families were scattered and their culture was ripped apart.

Working class people have been taught they are making it economically, and they have come to believe it. Now they are not so sure. They have become fearful, and the competition from the blacks scares them.

When I used to give talks on race in places like Silver Spring or Marlow Heights, most of the flak would come from barbers or policemen who came from the same background as I did. The coalminer's son has become the policeman. These guys have a nostalgia for the old neighborhood, and they are also among the most resentful of the blacks and the students. A guy works hard on a job and tends bar on the side trying to put his kid through college. Then he worries that his kid will come back looking like Mark Rudd.

The guy I'm speaking of doesn't have much social perspective. He didn't go to Harvard. If he went past high school, he went to Cleveland State or whatever trying to make it. Then he went into the service and got a job. He didn't go running off to the ghetto or VISTA or the Peace Corps. 10

This group, which is so hung up on the blacks, has yet to realize that it has many problems in common with them. When I'm with a working class group, I ask them what their problems are. They never hear it quite that way. They always answer, "The blacks," and I start getting these wild economic myths and theories. They still think their parents had it harder than the blacks. They'll tell you the blacks don't have the will or motivation. "The blacks don't want to work." "Everybody's on welfare." "They get all this free housing and medicare and scholarships for their kids."

The Kerner Commission blamed our troubles on "white racism." But 20 the Commission didn't explain racism in terms that people could understand. I've come to realize that some liberals use "white racism" as a handle to beat the working class.

The real problem is lack of social conscience on everyone's part. America is pervaded with a *Reader's Digest* mentality. People are interested in learning how to make it rather than in learning how to be a person. Go to school; learn to make it. On the spiritual end, this translates into individualism: Save your own soul, and to hell with anyone else's.

When you put materialism together with spiritual individualism, you get this person who may have a fine personal morality but who has abso- 30 lutely no social conscience. During the District riots in 1968, we had to organize a whole network of people for relief work. I would run across very respectable individuals who would ask me, in all seriousness, "Well, why *don't* we shoot the looters?"

People in the suburbs are apt to sympathize with me, living in the District, and then go on to tell me how they don't have any problems out there. It's a failure to recognize the interdependence of society. All of America has become essentially metropolitan and urban in character.

In the suburbs, you can't tell the difference between Protestants, Catholics, and Jews. They're all nice, well-meaning people. If you tell 40 them about poor Mrs. Brown who is going to be evicted because her relief check got lost in the mail and she can't pay her rent, you'll get a flood of sympathy. They'll give you as much secondhand underwear as you can carry. Someone will even give you a check.

But talk about welfare reform or social change? Then you'll get this business about lazy, no-good chiselers living off of welfare. If it's an indiv-

idual problem, they'll give you a donation, a handout, a check. But they
resist social action; they fear the poor getting organized. The same people
who call you up at Christmas offering food baskets will cut your throat
if you try for meaningful reform.

A clergyman has to resist becoming an ambulance service for the system.
I could spend all day talking to twelve or fifteen families, getting them
food or cash—charity. But we also have to talk about justice. A higher
minimum wage for the District would help ten thousand people, not just
a dozen. I would rather work for better housing and better education than
be in the handout business. It's paternalistic and demeaning. I believe      10
in self-help and self-determination.

We have to go beyond the old civil rights struggles. Here in Washington
I had gotten used to thinking black. Liberals and blacks have been
screaming "bigot" and "racist" and "pig" for so long that, politically,
someone like Spiro Agnew was bound to come along and talk about
pseudo-intellectuals. The working class can be exploited in a regressive
way, and Agnew has the touch. Working people see themselves on a
collision course with the blacks. Many are in stable communities that are
starting to fall apart. They provide buffer zones between the poor blacks
and the middle-class whites.                                                  20

It's different here, of course. Washington isn't a factory town, or even a
working class town in the usual sense. The tone is set by government,
intellectuals, and academics. It isn't an immigrant town, either, although
there are plenty of people with immigrant backgrounds in the suburbs.
One of my questions is how much identification such people have with
the old neighborhood.

The kind of neighborhood I'm talking about is found in cities like Cleveland or Milwaukee, although the percentage of working class varies from
city to city. In Gary, Indiana, I sat down with a group of priests in Glen
Park, which is talking about seceding from the rest of the city because     30
of fear of the blacks. One priest was telling me how he had experimented
with the Prayer of the Faithful. This is a petitionary prayer with responses
from the congregation. First, my friend prayed for the President. "Lord,
have mercy," said the congregation. Then he prayed for the sick, "Lord,
have mercy." Finally, he prayed for the black brothers. Silence. Not a
whisper. He had to give the response himself.

"Yah, they're uptight," this priest said to me. "They're uptight and
Agnew's right."

At the same time I feel there is an untapped energy in the working class
that could eventually lead to coalitions with the blacks. The value system  40
of the working class has a positive side: self-help and self-determination.
Blacks use different language and different words, but they don't want
handouts either. I believe that as the ethnic groups become more and
more self-confident, they will recognize that they have a lot in common
with the blacks. Maybe they will start telling Spiro Agnew, "What you're
saying about pseudo-intellectuals is fine, but what are you doing for me?"

By virtue of its size and strategic location, you can't exclude the working class from any agenda for the nation. Out of 90 million people in the northern industrial states, 40 million are Catholics, and most are working class. Like the blacks, they are burdened by the lion's share of taxes. They are dissatisfied with government services, fearful of job security, and worried about raising money to send their kids to college. We have to form coalitions around these problems. I see this as a better route than talking about brotherhood. You can't talk brotherhood to barbers, mailmen, and factory workers.

The hope lies not in intellectualizing, but in a real, live problem-solving agenda. One example of this occurred last December at the White House Hunger Conference. The blacks, chicanos, and Appalachian whites mistrusted one another so much that they formed separate caucuses. The blacks talked about "demands," the chicanos listed "goals" and the poor whites spoke about "priorities." At that point the three groups discovered that they were all interested in the same thing, and they joined forces.

I watched them try the coalition approach in Detroit, where the Poles won't vote for black politicians and vice-versa. First, the Poles and the blacks sat down separately to talk about their problems. Then they were put together, storekeepers with storekeepers, drycleaners with drycleaners. "What are your problems and what are mine?" It was the usual list: They didn't have a say, they couldn't control things. A black guy came up to me and shook his head. "I've heard it all before," he said, "hundreds of times at dozens of meetings in the black community."

But you can't go into these working class neighborhoods with guys who learned to do it in the black community, and you can't go in with white intellectuals. It will take authentic representatives of these communities to cause real change. When I sat down with a group of priests in Gary, for the first few hours all I heard was how much of a problem the blacks were. After a while I found a guy at my elbow—he had a good Polish name—who told me he had asked to be assigned to a black neighborhood. "I made a mistake," this priest told me. "I should be organizing in my own neighborhood."

So I'm hoping we can find and help support young people who see that the working class does not want to participate and be part of the democratic process. Can young people from the working class see a challenge in their own communities? Will they become city planners, housing specialists, community organizers?

I'm interested in the police thing, too. The police are among the most alienated of the working class. In the old days they were a respected part of the community. Police work was an honored career. Lately the police have become the front line in black-white confrontations. They are the flash point of the urban crisis. Yet they had little to do with making the social order they are sworn to defend. Policemen are very devout. Here in Washington I used to take a lot of criticism from them. What did I mean, taking the side of the blacks? The police were law and order.

They went to church. They obeyed the Ten Commandments.

Today you have clergy relating to the police in the worst possible way. There are priests buying guns and helmets, supporting alienation. How can we develop a new religious ministry to the police profession? If the police department is the cutting edge, how can we train police to work toward outreach rather than repression? It's the hour of crisis for the cop, and he is so much one of ours.

When I start pushing a working class group on race, I have to go back to my father. I give them the ethnic stuff, and they start giggling and laughing. I talk about pasta and kolbasi and blood pudding. Just a word  10 or two evokes so much. You can practically smell it.

I also talk about the unions and the strikes. "You may not have been singing 'We Shall Overcome,'" I tell them, "but you were singing songs in Polish, right?" Black violence? I tell them how my father had a basement full of dynamite he had stolen from the mine. He was never a Molly Maguire, but he did happen to be in the vicinity of a few bridges and tool shacks that were missing the next day. Back then, people didn't mess around with breaking windows; they played for keeps.

So the civil rights era is over. America has got to be big enough for everybody, black and white. In the 1940's the academics said America  20 was the melting pot and we were all being assimilated. They had me goofed up, too. I refused to let my family teach me Italian. We all played down ethnicity and groupiness. Now we're learning that we're a nation of groups after all.

I think those of us in the ethnic bag can learn from the blacks about the importance of cultural identity. In our eagerness to "make it," we cut ourselves off from our roots too fast. Now we are discovering that we aren't all making it. and we are learning just how important those roots are. We are beginning to celebrate our differences instead of insisting that everybody has to be the same.  30

On the other hand, I'm scared to death that we will become increasingly regressive, like Hitler's Germany, trying to recapture the past by persecuting minorities and dissenters. That speech of Hitler's in 1932 calling for "law and order" gives me the willies. The fear is there in the working class, along with the independence and the individualism. Somehow we have to translate that ethic of working hard and making it into the 1970's.

I think that the priests have a decisive role to play in the years ahead. The urban crisis occurs at a time when many of us are wondering who we are and what we can do. Here, it seems to me, is precisely the opportunity that we have been searching for. What the nation is facing is pri-  40 marily a spiritual crisis, a failure of will. As a nation we lack commitment, not technology or material resources.

In the neighborhoods I am speaking of, the parish church is the major cohesive force, sometimes the only cohesive force. Perhaps the churches can lead the working class away from guilt and fear toward a reordering of our national priorities. Perhaps we can help the nation develop a commitment to justice.

I think I see something of what is happening to the country. My shift is just one little spit of it. Here I am wondering where I am at. And where the country is at.

# Arthur Mann
## Hybridism

Some men go to the top in politics when society seems to be a going concern and the people have need of an amiable figurehead who is content to stand still. It is usual for such a leader to avoid conflict, stress harmony, and celebrate what is: to assure and reassure the electorate that they've never had it so good. Government is not supposed to be an instrument for social change, it is considered an exercise in caretaking. Such is the leadership of normalcy.

Neither by temperament nor intellect was La Guardia the sort to administer a going concern. Unable to slow down long enough to stand still, he was inclined to shock and mock the celebrators of the status quo and   *10* to celebrate only the possibilities of the future. He throve on conflict, not harmony, in situations that made reform possible. It was no accident that the Anti-Injunction Act, for which La Guardia and Senator George Norris had agitated futilely during the so-called normalcy of the 1920's, should suddenly have been passed by Congress at the beginning of the Depression. Fiorello was the kind of leader who comes into his own when a crisis in the old order creates opportunities for new directions.

Yet the laws of heredity and environment that produce a La Guardia have still to be discovered. His biographer can only call attention to his most important characteristics, infer their probable source from available   *20* evidence, and relate them to the culture in which they flourished. Three characteristics of the fifty-one-year-old man who entered City Hall in 1934 deserve special mention and elaboration: his hybridism, his ambition for power and fame, and his passion to do good.

His hybridism derives from an extraordinary mobility. Born in Greenwich Village but raised on Western Army posts and growing to maturity

178

in the Balkans, he returned to his native city at twenty-three and later spent much of his adult life in the nation's capital as a Congressman. All his life he had been learning how to live in someone else's culture and he acquired a working knowledge of half a dozen languages besides English: Italian, French, German, Yiddish, Hungarian, and Serbo-Croation. He was a true cosmopolitan, which is to say that he was at home nearly everywhere, but without the roots that bind a true insider to the group and the place in which he was born.

His parentage foreordained that he would be what sociologists call a marginal man. Achille Luigi Carlo La Guardia and his wife Irene Coen   10 emigrated to America in 1880 and returned to Italy with their children twenty years later. Theirs was a mixed marriage — Achille was a lapsed Catholic and Irene a lukewarm Jew — and while in the United States they raised their children as Episcopalians. When, in 1906, Fiorello returned to America, where everyone has an ethnic label or gets one, he considered himself an Italo-American. But his being a Protestant set him apart from his ethnic group, which was, of course, overwhelmingly Catholic.

Observers have asked why Fiorello did not identify himself as a Jew. His inheritance is again instructive. Irene Coen La Guardia, his Trieste-born mother, thought of herself as Austrian in nationality, Italian in cul-   20 ture, and Jewish only in religion. There was no Jewish community in the army towns where Fiorello grew up while his father was serving in the United States Army as a bandmaster. When Fiorello met Jews in large numbers — first as a consular agent in Fiume, than as an Ellis Island interpreter, and later as a labor lawyer on Manhattan's Lower East Side — he met Jews unlike his mother. They were Eastern European, not Mediterranean, Jews. They spoke Yiddish, their ritual was Ashkenazic, and they considered themselves a nationality and a cultural group as well as a religious body. Neither by descent nor religious upbringing was Fiorello one of them.   30

Nor was it expedient for him to be be known as Jewish when he broke into politics in the 1910's. He started out with handicaps enough against him. His aberrant appearance and unpronounceable name put him at a disadvantage to the dominant Celtic and the vanishing Anglo-Saxon types who ran the city. Nativism was rising and would shortly culminate in restrictive legislation against the new immigrants from eastern and southern Europe. It was hard enough to be an Italo-American fifty and more years ago without inviting the derisive taunt — which his enemies would hurl at him in the 1930's after his mother's origins became known — "the half-Jewish wop."   40

So he made little of his Jewish background in public but exploited his Italian name and built a political base in Little Italy from which to launch a career. By 1934 not even Primo Carnera or Benito Mussolini exceeded the Little Flower as a popular idol in the colony. What is more, after establishing his public image as a Latin, he championed a number of Jewish causes, sometimes in Yiddish, but as an understanding and compassionate *outsider*. This was smart politics in the largest Jewish city in the world (the Jews and the Italians together constituted almost 45 per cent of New York's population in the 1920's and 1930's). It was also, and nevertheless, sincere. Free from self-hatred, La Guardia was a man of mixed loyalties.

The son of Jewish and Italian immigrants who attended services in the Cathedral of Saint John the Divine, but who was married to his first wife in the rectory of Saint Patrick's and to his second wife by a Lutheran minister, was clearly the most remarkable hybrid in the history of New York City politics. Belonging, yet not fully belonging, to nearly every 10 important ancestral group in the city, including the British-descended community of Episcopalians, Fiorello was a balanced ticket all by himself.

His being marginal to many cultures had a deeper significance still. The mayor of New York, like a leader of any pluralist community, must be a political broker. This had been a familiar role to the hyphenated Congressman who started his career on the Lower East Side as a mediator between immigrant and native America, interpreting one to the other. A friend in court for the poor and the persecuted, he also had served as a go-between for reformers and professional politicians and a bridge connecting urban and rural progressives in Congress. The mayoralty 20 would enlarge the scope of previous experience. La Guardia would have to balance the demands of a variety of competing interest groups in the city, and also bargain and trade with borough, county, state, and Federal officials whose power impinged on his own as chief executive.

But an effective leader must not only mediate and negotiate, he also has to command, take the initiative, make policy, and break through channels when necessary to get things done. Such a leader seeks power, enlarges it, and enjoys its use. La Guardia was like that by 1934. One of the few pieces of sculpture the Mayor owned was a bust of Napoleon that he first put on his desk when he began to practice law at twenty- 30 eight. When he bought that object is unknown, but Bonaparte may have been his model at an even earlier age.

"Ambitious for promotion"—that is how the American Consul General of Budapest, who was given to the understatement of his New England birth and education, described his Italo-American subordinate in Fiume at the turn of the century. Commissioned a consular agent at twenty-one, Fiorello's pride of rank was inordinate. He expanded his jurisdiction whenever possible, breaking archaic rules and bringing them up to date on his own authority. The results of his innovations were often salutary, but his aggressiveness antagonized superiors. He quit in a huff after two 40 and a half years, writing in 1906 to the State Department "that the service is not the place for a young man to work up. . . . "

During World War I, as a major in command of American aviation in Italy, La Guardia was something of a virtuoso in running around, over, across, or simply straight through the protocol of two armies and one foreign government. Not having resigned his seat in Congress, he either

impressed or intimidated higher ranking officers with his political connections. And forced to improvise on America's forgotten front, he im-
provised brilliantly, whether in training pilots, conferring with cabinet
ministers, speeding up the production of planes, or rallying Italians to
their own war effort after the disaster of Caporetto. "I love him like a
brother," one Italian official exclaimed.

Many voters in America felt much the same way. Between 1914 and
1934 La Guardia ran for office twelve times, and apart from a first and
hopeless try, he lost only twice. His victories were particularly impressive
in view of the fact that New York City was virtually a one-party (Democratic) town. Elected president of the Board of Aldermen in 1919, he was
the first Republican to win a city-wide contest without Fusion backing
since the creation of Greater New York by legislative act in 1897. At one
time during the 1920's La Guardia was the sole Republican Congressman from Manhattan outside the silk-stocking district.

His most obvious asset as a campaigner was his grasp of relevant
issues and his ability to dramatize those issues, and himself as well, in
colorful language and forceful terms. And once in office he was
conscientious in serving his constituents. He was particularly popular
with immigrants and their children, who accounted for 75 per cent of
New York's population when he was rising to power. He was fighting
their battle, and his, too, for recognition and against bigotry. One of the
few ethnic groups that could not claim the multi-hyphenated Little Flower
through blood were the Polish-Americans, yet *Nowy Swiat,* a Polish-
language newspaper, looked up to him as "head of the family. . . father,
leader, judge, authority, and educator — like in the village. . . . "

But there was a Machiavellian, even diabolical, side to La Guardia's
melting-pot politics. When haranguing an audience, which he could do
in any of seven languages, he was not above exploiting its fears, insecurities,
prejudices, and hatreds. There were ways and ways of getting out the vote.
After one such harangue to an Italo-American crowd in the campaign
of 1919, he turned in pride to an associate and said: "I can outdema-
gogue the best of demagogues."

He justified such tactics by insisting that he had to fight the Tammany
Tiger with its own weapons, and it was said of the Little Flower during
his life that he was no shrinking violet. What a negative way of putting
it! Fiorello was a superbly conditioned political animal who not only
struck back when attacked but who really enjoyed the brutal struggle
for office in the Manhattan jungle. No matter what he said in public to
the contrary, La Guardia was a professional politician, bruising, cunning,
tough, and with a strong stomach for the sordid methods and grubby
details of election politics in his part of the world. "I invented the low
blow," he boasted to an aide in the 1920's. In East Harlem, which he
represented in Congress for five terms until 1932, he commanded a superb
personal organization of his own and gave lessons to Tammany at election
time in machine campaigning.

The Mayor knew how to get power, all right, and how to keep it, as his record for election and re-election proves. But why did he want it? There are very many gifted men, after all, for whom public responsibility is distasteful and whose main thrust is for money, leisure, travel, or women. Those had been the tastes of Mayor Jimmy Walker, who gladly let the Tammany bosses govern New York City while he relentlessly pursued pleasure on two continents.

Some of La Guardia's associates thought, and still think, that in reaching out for power he was compensating for feelings of inferiority deriving from a hypersensitivity to his size, his lack of formal education, and his origins. To reduce the complexity of Fiorello's behavior to an inferiority complex is too pat and too simple. His wife, who knew him as well as anyone, has dismissed the idea as preposterous. Yet it is a matter of historical record that the Little Flower *was* hypersensitive and, therefore, easily insulted and ferociously combative.

Who can forget the fury, for example, with which the Mayor banned organ-grinders from the streets of New York? Those foreign-looking men, with their broken English, farcical little monkeys, and panhandling canned music, called attention to one of several disreputable Italian stereotypes that the Little Flower had labored all his life to refute and overcome. And although he himself might joke about his height and that of other men, no one else was allowed to do so in his presence. Once, when an associate made the mistake of being playful about a pint-sized applicant for a municipal job, La Guardia lost control of himself and screamed:

"What's the matter with a little guy? What's the matter with a little guy? What's the matter with a little guy?"

The Mayor was clearly a man of explosive resentments. They were long-standing and are a key to his personality. As a boy growing up on army posts he had resented the children of officers for lording it over the children of enlisted men. Why was he not as good as they? Later, in the Foreign Service or in the Army, on the board of Alderman or in Congress, he would resent superiors he thought intellectually and morally inferior to himself. By what rights should they be placed over him? To measure one's self against others is normal for competitive men, but in La Guardia's case it was excessive. His resentfulness heightened his competitiveness and his competitiveness intensified his resentfulness, so that he was constantly in rivalry with nearly everyone he met and forever proving that he was number one.

"I think he put on a great deal of his brutalities to test people out," C. C. Burlingham, who knew La Guardia well, has shrewdly observed. "If they could stand up against him it was all right, but if they couldn't they were in bad luck."

That La Guardia was ambitious will surprise only those people who think that a stained-glass window of Saint Francis is really a sufficient monument to the Mayor's memory. Yet only a mistaken realism would conclude that there was nothing more to his nature, and to human nature in general, than the promotion of self. Ed Flynn, the Democratic boss from the Bronx who prided himself on being a realistic judge of men, made that kind of mistake. That is why Flynn was never able to understand and appreciate—or cope with—the *direction* of La Guardia's drive.

The direction was a liberal one. La Guardia wanted the power of public office not just to assert himself, it must be emphasized, but so that he could also be in a position to right social wrongs. Joining his resentments to a cause, he made a career for himself as a leader of the have-nots against the haves, or as he would have put it, the People against the Interests.

That was the image he had of himself—when he strove as a consul agent     10
and interpreter to defend the humanity of immigrants against bureaucratic mindlessness and heartlessness; when he contributed his services as a lawyer and an orator to the trade unions that began to emerge in the 1910's from the squalid sweatshops of the Lower East Side; when as an over-age aviator he went off to war to make the world safe for democracy; when as president of the Board of Aldermen he defied the governor of New York State and fought against an increase of the five-cent fare on the subway (the poor man's ride) and the repeal of the direct primary (the people's defense against bossism); when as a Republican Congressman he bolted his party to join the Progressive Party of 1924 in a crusade     20
against the credo of the day that the business of America was business, not welfare. Had La Guardia done nothing else he still would have passed the bar of American liberalism in 1934 for the anti-injunction law he co-authored two years earlier with Nebraska's Senator Norris; it was the most significant piece of labor legislation passed by Congress up to that time.

La Guardia entered City Hall with a sense of injustice that was still bottomless, with a capacity for outrage that was still boundless, with a determination to reform society that was still enormous. His social conscience was as highly developed as his instinct for the jugular in political     30
combat. The mayor's office, toward which he had reached out three times before finally capturing it, would give him the power he had wanted so long in order to realize his humanitarian goals.

The thrust of an enormous internal drive to establish his own high place in the sum of things carried La Guardia very close to the top in American politics, and in that process he found more gratification in public fame than in the pleasures of private life.

When Fiorello returned to New York in 1906 after resigning from the consular service in Fiume ("Look here, Mother," he said in explanation, "I'm going back to America to become a lawyer and make something of     40
myself."), he arrived without friends or family. His father had been dead for two years and his mother chose to remain in Europe with her married daughter. The next decade and a half were devoted to the struggle to gain a foothold in the city he would someday rule. Not until 1919, when he was thirty-six, back from the wars as a hero, and finally established in his career, did Congressman La Guardia take a wife, an exquisite young

blonde from Trieste by the name of Thea Almerigotti.

That marriage was, and would remain, the high point of La Guardia's private emotional experience. Setting up housekeeping in Greenwich Village, the couple enjoyed a semi-Bohemian life, one that was full of love and fun and music and good eating. La Guardia adored children, and in 1920 Thea gave birth to a daughter, who was named Fioretta after Fiorello's maternal grandmother. Yet La Guardia's personal happiness flickered for only a moment. Throughout 1921 he suffered the agony of watching his baby, and then his wife, waste away and die of tuberculosis. For the next eight years he threw himself into his work with an energy that can only be described as ferocious.

His second marriage in 1929 to Marie Fischer, his secretary since 1914, was a union of two mature persons. It was not blessed with children. The couple adopted a girl, Jean, in 1933 and a boy, Eric, the following year. At fifty-one, the Mayor was the foster father of very young children and had known married life for a total of only seven years.

In the nearly three decades he had lived in New York Fiorello acquired few personal friends, but rather many admirers, acquaintances, colleagues, allies, patrons, proteges, and advisers. He was too competitive to get along intimately with his equals. Only with children could he give himself completely. Hobbies he had none, other than a fondness for classical music. He was as mayor to surround himself with more intellectuals than any of his predecessors, but he had either no time or no taste for literature, not even for biography and history, and rarely read anything not directly relevant to his work. He had lived, and would continue to live, mostly for his career and, what is equally important, for the affectionate acclaim that his public personality generated in a vast but impersonal audience. New York had in 1934 a full-time mayor.

La Guardia brought other qualities to the mayoralty in addition to his hybridism, his ambition, and his compassion for the oppressed. There was his gusto for work and his slashing wit, his quick but retentive mind and his theatrical flair. He also brought a considerable experience, stretching back to 1901 when he received his commission as consul agent from John Hay, Secretary of State under the first Roosevelt. By 1934 La Guardia had spent all but six years of his majority in one Government job or another. Public service was a way of life for him.

He clearly qualified for the office sometimes described as second in difficulty only to the Presidency as an elective office in American government. And by the late 1930's Republicans of the stature of William Allen White were booming him for the Presidency itself. Twelve years after his death in 1947, Professor Rexford G. Tugwell saluted him as "a great man in the Republic" and, excepting only F.D.R. among his contemporaries, as "the best-known leader in our democracy. . . . " Many people today accept that estimate as valid.

# Fiorello La Guardia
## A Glimpse of Racial Feeling

. . . I also got my first glimpse of racial feeling born of ignorance, out there in Arizona. I must have been about ten when a street organ-grinder with a monkey blew into town. He, and particularly the monkey, attracted a great deal of attention. I can still hear the cries of the kids: "A dago with a monkey! Hey, Fiorello, you're a dago too. Where's your monkey?" It hurt. And what made it worse, along came Dad, and he started to chatter Neapolitan with the organ-grinder. He hadn't spoken Italian in many years, and he seemed to enjoy it. Perhaps, too, he considered the organ-grinder a fellow musician. At any rate, he promptly invited him to our house for a macaroni dinner. The kids taunted me for a long time after 10 that. I couldn't understand it. What difference was there between us? Some of their families hadn't been in the country any longer than mine.

# Bernard Malamud
## Black is My Favorite Color

Charity Sweetness sits in the toilet eating her two hardboiled eggs while I'm having my ham sandwich and coffee in the kitchen. That's how it goes only don't get the idea of ghettoes. If there's a ghetto I'm the one that's in it. She's my cleaning woman from Father Divine and comes in once a week to my small three-room apartment on my day off from the liquor store. "Peace," she says to me, "Father reached on down and took me right up in Heaven." She's a small person with a flat body, frizzy hair, and a quiet face that the light shines out of, and Mama had such eyes before she died. The first time Charity Sweetness came in to clean, a little more than a year and a half, I made the mistake to ask her to sit down at the kitchen table with me and eat her lunch. I was still feeling not so hot after Ornita left but I'm the kind of a man—Nat Lime, forty-four, a bachelor with a daily growing bald spot on the back of my head, and I could lose frankly fifteen pounds—who enjoys company so long as he has it. So she cooked up her two hardboiled eggs and sat down and took a small bite out of one of them. But after a minute she stopped chewing and she got up and carried the eggs in a cup in the bathroom, and since then she eats there. I said to her more than once, "Okay, Charity Sweetness, so have it your way, eat the eggs in the kitchen by yourself and I'll eat when you're done," but she smiles absentminded, and eats in the toilet. It's my fate with colored people.

Although black is still my favorite color you wouldn't know it from my luck except in short quantities even though I do all right in the liquor business in Harlem, on Eight Avenue between 110th and 111th. I speak with respect. A large part of my life I've had dealings with Negro people, most on a business basis but sometimes for friendly reasons with genuine feeling on both sides. I'm drawn to them. At this time of my life I should have one or two good colored friends but the fault isn't necessarily mine.

186

If they knew what was in my heart towards them but how can you tell that to anybody nowadays? I've tried more than once but the language of the heart either is a dead language or else nobody understands it the way you speak it. Very few. What I'm saying is, personally for me there's only one human color and that's the color of blood. I like a black person if not because he's black, then because I'm white. It comes to the same thing. If I wasn't white my first choice would be black. I'm satisfied to be white because I have no other choice. Anyway, I got an eye for color. I appreciate. Who wants everybody to be the same? Maybe it's like some kind of a talent. Nat Lime might be a liquor dealer in Harlem, but once in the jungle in New Guinea in the Second War, I got the idea when I shot at a running Jap and missed him, that I had some kind of a talent, though maybe it's the kind where you have a marvelous idea now and then but in the end what do they come to? After all, it's a strange world.

Where Charity Sweetness eats her eggs makes me think about Buster Wilson when we were both boys in the Williamsburg section of Brooklyn. There was this long block of run-down dirty frame houses in the middle of a not-so-hot white neighborhood full of pushcarts. The Negro houses looked to me like they had been born and died there, dead not long after the beginning of the world. I lived on the next street. My father was a cutter with arthritis in both hands, big red knuckles and swollen fingers so he didn't cut, and my mother was the one who went to work. She sold paper bags from a second-hand pushcart in Ellery Street. We didn't starve but nobody ate chicken unless we were sick or the chicken was. This was my first acquaintance with a lot of black people and I used to poke around on their poor block. I think I thought, brother, if there can be like this, what can't there be? I mean I caught an early idea what life was about. Anyway I met Buster Wilson there. He used to play marbles by himself. I sat on the curb across the street, watching him shoot one marble lefty and the other one righty. The hand that won picked up the marbles. It wasn't so much of a game but he didn't ask me to come over. My idea was to be friendly, only he never encouraged, he discouraged. Why did I pick him out for a friend? Maybe because I had no others then, we were new in the neighborhood, from Manhattan. Also I liked his type. Buster did everything alone. He was a skinny kid and his brother's clothes hung on him like worn-out potato sacks. He was a beanpole boy, about twelve, and I was then ten. His arms and legs were burnt out matchsticks. He always wore a brown wool sweater, one arm half unraveled, the other went down to the wrist. His long and narrow head had a white part cut straight in the short woolly hair, maybe with a ruler there, by his father, a barber but too drunk to stay a barber. In those days though I had little myself I was old enough to know who was better off, and the whole block of colored houses made me feel bad in the daylight. But I went there as much as I could because the street was full of life. In the night it looked different, it's hard to tell a cripple in the dark. Sometimes I was afraid to walk by the houses when they were dark and quiet. I was afraid there were people looking at me that I couldn't see. I liked it better when they had parties at night and everybody had a good time. The musicians played their banjos and saxophones and the houses shook with the music and laughing. The young girls, with their pretty dresses and ribbons in their hair, caught me in my throat when I saw them through the windows.

But with the parties came drinking and fights. Sundays were bad days after the Saturday night parties. I remember once that Buster's father, also long and loose, always wearing a dirty gray Homburg hat, chased another black man in the street with a half-inch chisel. The other one, maybe five feet high, lost his shoe and when they wrestled on the ground he was already bleeding through his suit, a thick red blood smearing the sidewalk. I was frightened by the blood and wanted to pour it back in the man who was bleeding from the chisel. On another time Buster's father was playing in a crap game with two big bouncy red dice, in the back of an alley between two middle houses. Then about six men started fist-fighting there, and they ran out of the alley and hit each other in the street. The neighbors, including children, came out and watched, everybody afraid but nobody moving to do anything. I saw the same thing near my store in Harlem, years later, a big crowd watching two men in the street, their breaths hanging in the air on a winter night, murdering each other with switch knives, but nobody moved to call a cop. I didn't either. Anyway, I was just a young kid but I still remember how the cops drove up in a police paddy wagon and broke up the fight by hitting everybody they could hit with big nightsticks. This was in the days before LaGuardia. Most of the fighters were knocked out cold, only one or two got away. Buster's father started to run back in his house but a cop ran after him and cracked him on his Homburg hat with a club, right on the front porch. Then the Negro men were lifted up by the cops, one at the arms and the other at the feet, and they heaved them in the paddy wagon. Buster's father hit the back of the wagon and fell, with his nose spouting very red blood, on top of three other men. I personally couldn't stand it, I was scared of the human race so I ran home, but I remember Buster watching without any expression in his eyes. I stole an extra fifteen cents from my mother's pocketbook and I ran back and asked Buster if he wanted to go to the movies. I would pay. He said yes. This was the first time he talked to me.

So we went more than once to the movies. But we never got to be friends. Maybe because it was a one-way proposition—from me to him. Which includes my invitations to go with me, my (poor mother's) movie money, Hershey chocolate bars, watermelon slices, even my best Nick Carter and Merriwell books that I spent hours picking up in the junk shops, and that he never gave me back. Once he let me go in his house to get a match so we could smoke some butts we found, but it smelled so heavy, so impossible, I died till I got out of there. What I saw in the way of furniture I won't mention—the best was falling apart in pieces. Maybe we went to the movies all together five or six matinees that spring and in the summertime, but when the shows were over he usually walked home by himself.

"Why don't you wait for me, Buster?" I said. "We're both going in the same direction."

But he was walking ahead and didn't hear me. Anyway he didn't answer.

One day when I wasn't expecting it he hit me in the teeth. I felt like crying but not because of the pain. I spit blood and said, "What did you hit me for? What did I do to you?"

"Because you a Jew bastard. Take your Jew movies and your Jew candy and shove them up your Jew ass."

And he ran away.

I thought to myself how was I to know he didn't like the movies. When I was a man I thought, you can't force it.

Years later, in the prime of my life, I met Mrs. Ornita Harris. She was standing by herself under an open umbrella at the bus stop, crosstown 110th, and I picked up her green glove that she had dropped on the wet sidewalk. It was at the end of November. Before I could ask her was it hers, she grabbed the glove out of my hand, closed her umbrella, and stepped in the bus. I got on right after her.

I was annoyed so I said, "If you'll pardon me, Miss, there's no law that you have to say thanks, but at least don't make a criminal out of me."

"Well, I'm sorry," she said, "but I don't like white men trying to do me favors."

I tipped my hat and that was that. In ten minutes I got off the bus but she was already gone.

Who expected to see her again but I did. She came into my store about a week later for a bottle of scotch.

"I would offer you a discount," I told her, "but I know you don't like a certain kind of favor and I'm not looking for a slap in the face."

Then she recognized me and got a little embarrassed.

"I'm sorry I misunderstood you that day."

"So mistakes happen."

The result was she took the discount. I gave her a dollar off.

She used to come in about every two weeks for a fifth of Haig and Haig. Sometimes I waited on her, sometimes my helpers, Jimmy or Mason, also colored, but I said to give the discount. They both looked at me but I had nothing to be ashamed. In the spring when she came in we used to talk once in a while. She was a slim woman, dark but not the most dark, about thirty years I would say, also well built, with a combination nice legs and a good-size bosom that I like. Her face was pretty, with big eyes and high cheek bones, but lips a little thick and nose a little broad. Sometimes she didn't feel like talking, she paid for the bottle, less discount, and walked out. Her eyes were tired and she didn't look to me like a happy woman.

I found out her husband was once a window cleaner on the big buildings, but one day his safety belt broke and he fell fifteen stories. After the funeral she got a job as a manicurist in a Times Square barber shop. I told her I was a bachelor and lived with my mother in a small three-room apartment on West Eighty-third near Broadway. My mother had cancer, and Ornita said she was very sorry.

One night in July we went out together. How that happened I'm still not so sure. I guess I asked her and she didn't say no. Where do you go out with a Negro woman? We went to the Village. We had a good dinner and walked in Washington Square Park. It was a hot night. Nobody was surprised when they saw us, nobody looked at us like we were against the law. If they looked maybe they saw my new lightweight suit that I bought    10 yesterday and my shiny bald spot when we walked under a lamp, also how pretty she was for a man of my type. We went in a movie on West Eighth Street. I didn't want to go in but she said she had heard about the picture. We went in like strangers and we came out like strangers. I wondered what was in her mind and I thought to myself, whatever is in there it's not a certain white man that I know. All night long we went together like we were chained. After the movie she wouldn't let me take her back to Harlem. When I put her in a taxi she asked me, "Why did we bother?"

For the steak, I wanted to say. Instead I said, "You're worth the bother."

"Thanks anyway."    20

Kiddo, I thought to myself after the taxi left, you just found out what's what, now the best thing is forget her.

It's easy to say. In August we went out the second time. That was the night she wore a purple dress and I thought to myself, my God, what colors. Who paints that picture paints a masterpiece. Everybody looked at us but I had pleasure. That night when she took off her dress it was in a furnished room I had the sense to rent a few days before. With my sick mother, I couldn't ask her to come to my apartment, and she didn't want me to go home with her where she lived with her brother's family on West 115th near Lenox Avenue. Under her purple dress she wore a black slip,    30 and when she took that off she had white underwear. When she took off the white underwear she was black again. But I know where the next white was, if you want to call it white. And that was the night I think I fell in love with her, the first time in my life though I have liked one or two nice girls I used to go with when I was a boy. It was a serious proposition. I'm the kind of a man when I think of love I'm thinking of marriage. I guess that's why I am a bachelor.

That same week I had a holdup in my place, two big men — both black — with revolvers. One got excited when I rang open the cash register so he could take the money and he hit me over the ear with his gun. I stayed in    40 the hospital a couple of weeks. Otherwise I was insured. Ornita came to see me. She sat on a chair without talking much. Finally I saw she was uncomfortable so I suggested she ought to go home.

"I'm sorry it happened," she said.

"Don't talk like it's your fault."

When I got out of the hospital my mother was dead. She was a wonderful person. My father died when I was thirteen and all by herself she kept the family alive and together. I sat shive for a week and remembered how she sold paper bags on her pushcart. I remembered her life and what she tried to teach me. Nathan, she said, if you ever forget you are a Jew a goy will remind you. Mama, I said, rest in peace on this subject. But if I do something you don't like, remember, on earth it's harder than where you are. Then when my week of mourning was finished, one night I said, "Ornita, let's get married. We're both honest people and if you love me like I love you it won't be such a bad time. If you don't like New York I'll sell out here and we'll move someplace else. Maybe to San Francisco where nobody knows us. I was there for a week in the Second War and I saw white and colored living together."

"Nat," she answered me, "I like you but I'd be afraid. My husband woulda killed me."

"Your husband is dead."

"Not in my memory."

"In that case I'll wait."

"Do you know what it'd be like—I mean the life we could expect?"

"Ornita," I said, "I'm the kind of a man, if he picks his own way of life he's satisfied."

"What about children? Were you looking forward to half-Jewish polka dots?"

"I was looking forward to children."

"I can't," she said.

Can't is can't. I saw she was afraid and the best thing was not to push. Sometimes when we met she was so nervous that whatever we did she couldn't enjoy it. At the same time I still thought I had a chance. We were together more and more. I got rid of my furnished room and she came to my apartment—I gave away Mama's bed and bought a new one. She stayed with me all day on Sundays. When she wasn't so nervous she was affectionate, and if I know what love is, I had it. We went out a couple of times a week, the same way—usually I met her in Times Square and sent her home in a taxi, but I talked more about marriage and she talked less against it. One night she told me she was still trying to convince herself but she was almost convinced. I took an inventory of my liquor stock so I could put the store up for sale.

Ornita knew what I was doing. One day she quit her job, the next she took it back. She also went away a week to visit her sister in Philadelphia for a little rest. She came back tired but said maybe. Maybe is maybe so I'll wait. The way she said it it was closer to yes. That was the winter two years ago. When she was in Philadelphia I called up a friend of mine from the Army, now a CPA, and told him I would appreciate an invitation for an evening. He knew why. His wife said yes right away. When Ornita came back we went there. The wife made a fine dinner. It wasn't a bad time and they told us to come again. Ornita had a few drinks. She looked relaxed, wonderful. Later, because of a twenty-four hour taxi strike I had to take her home on the subway. When we got to the 116th Street station she told me to stay on the train, and she would walk the couple of blocks to her house. I didn't like a woman walking alone on the streets at that time of the night. She said she never had any trouble but I insisted nothing doing. I said I would walk to her stoop with her and when she went upstairs I would go back to the subway.

On the way there, on 115th in the middle of the block before Lenox, we were stopped by three men—maybe they were boys. One had a black hat with a half-inch brim, one a green cloth hat, and the third wore a black leather cap. The green hat was wearing a short coat and the other two had long ones. It was under a street light but the leather cap snapped a six-inch switchblade open in the light.

"What you doin' with this white son of a bitch?" he said to Ornita.

"I'm minding my own business," she answered him, "and I wish you would too."

"Boys," I said, "we're all brothers. I'm a reliable merchant in the neighborhood. This young lady is my dear friend. We don't want any trouble. Please let us pass."

"You talk like a Jew landlord," said the green hat. "Fifty a week for a single room."

"No charge fo' the rats," said the half-inch brim.

"Believe me, I'm no landlord. My store is 'Nathan's Liquors' between Hundred Tenth and Eleventh. I also have two colored clerks, Mason and Jimmy, and they will tell you I pay good wages as well as I give discounts to certain customers."

"Shut your mouth, Jewboy," said the leather cap, and he moved the knife back and forth in front of my coat button. "No more black pussy for you."

"Speak with respect about this lady, please."

I got slapped on my mouth.

"That ain't no lady," said the long face in the half-inch brim, "that's black pussy. She deserve to have evvy bit of her hair shave off. How you like to have evvy bit of your hair shave off, black pussy?"

"Please leave me and this gentleman alone or I'm gonna scream long and loud. That's my house three doors down."

They slapped her. I never heard such a scream. Like her husband was falling fifteen stories.

I hit the one that slapped her and the next I knew I was laying in the gutter with a pain in my head. I thought, goodbye, Nat, they'll stab me for sure, but all they did was take my wallet and run in three different directions.

Ornita walked back with me to the subway and she wouldn't let me go home with her again.

"Just get home safely."

She looked terrible. Her face was gray and I still remembered her scream. It was a terrible winter night, very cold February, and it took me an hour and ten minutes to get home. I felt bad for leaving her but what could I do?

We had a date downtown the next night but she didn't show up, the first time.

In the morning I called her in her place of business.

"For God's sake, Ornita, if we got married and moved away we wouldn't have that kind of trouble that we had. We wouldn't come in that neighborhood any more."

"Yes, we would. I have family there and don't want to move anyplace else. The truth of it is I can't marry you, Nat. I got troubles enough of my own."

"I coulda sworn you love me."

"Maybe I do but I can't marry you."

"For God's sake, why?"

"I got enough trouble of my own."

I went that night in a cab to her brother's house to see her. He was a quiet man with a thin mustache. "She gone," he said, "left for a long visit to some close relatives in the South. She said to tell you she appreciate your intentions but didn't think it will work out."

"Thank you kindly," I said.

Don't ask me how I got home.

Once on Eighth Avenue, a couple of blocks from my store, I saw a blind man with a white cane tapping on the sidewalk. I figured we were going in the same direction so I took his arm.

"I can tell you're white," he said.

A heavy colored woman with a full shopping bag rushed after us.

"Never mind," she said, "I know where he live."

She pushed me with her shoulder and I hurt my leg on the fire hydrant. That's how it is. I give my heart and they kick me in my teeth.

"Charity Sweetness—you hear me?—come out of that goddamn toilet!"

# Sam Levenson
## Sweet Horseradish

My parents came to America by invitation. Those who had landed here before them sent back picture postcards of a lady called Miss Liberty. Printed on them were these words:

> Give me your tired, your poor,
> Your huddled masses yearning to breathe free,
> The wretched refuse of your teeming shores.
> Send these, the homeless, tempest-tost to me,
> I lift my lamp beside the golden door.

It was signed Emma Lazarus, a name that sounded familiar to my parents—perhaps some second cousin on my mother's side. So Mama and Papa packed all their belongings and left for America. After all, who was more tired, poor, huddled, yearning to be free, wretched, homeless and tempest-tost than they?

I was raised as a virtually free American in East Harlem, a section of New York that was called a slum by sightseeing guides and a depressed area by sociologists. Both were right. Our neighborhood fulfilled all the sordid requirements with honors. We were unquestionably above average in squalid tenements, putrid poolrooms, stenchy saloons, cold flats, hot roofs, dirty streets and flying garbage. Yet, paradoxically, I never felt depressed or deprived. My environment was miserable; I was not.

I was a most fortunate child. Ours was a home rich enough in family harmony and love to immunize eight kids against the potentially toxic effects of the environment beyond our door. Since the social scientists do not, as far as I know, have a clinical name for the fortunate possessors of this kind of emotional security, I might suggest they label them "the privileged poor." Poverty never succeeded in degrading our family. We were independently poor.

Our home was a battleground in the relentless struggle not only for survival (which even beasts can manage) but for survival with dignity. This was the American Revolution fourth floor back.

Mama and Papa were the leaders of this band of freedom fighters consisting of seven sons and one daughter, whose homemade weapons were hard work, family pride and, above all, faith in education as the major weapon of our liberation movement. Our watchword was a variant of the adage "Better to light a candle than curse the darkness." We did curse the darkness quite a bit, but we also lit candles, fires, lamps—and we studied by all of them.

Those were not the "good old days," but there were more victories than defeats, and each small victory was cause for a large celebration around the dinner table at the end of the day. Each member of the clan would recount his conquests at the shop or in school, with as much gesticulation as exaggeration, to the great delight of the others, who responded with much back-slapping, hysterical laughter and chants of victory. We became superb actors in an unfinished tragi-comedy called "The Battle Against Poverty." We tried by every device we could contrive to outwit the enemy—to outshout it, upstage it and confuse it by ad-libbing little pieces of business not in the script. We never played it the same way twice. Although we were not sure just how the play would end, we did have visions, not so much of a happy ending as of some happy new beginning in some special place of honor reserved for conquerors of poverty and its allies—disease and ignorance.

According to studies made by social-service agencies, a good home is defined as one in which there are love, acceptance, belonging, high moral standards, good parental example, decent food, clothing, shelter, spiritual guidance, discipline, joint enterprises, a place to bring friends, and respect for authority. Today any child, rich or poor, who lives in such a home is considered a "lucky kid." By these standards, then, I was a "lucky kid," not in spite of my home but because of it.

It is also possible—and this is not unusual among poor children—that I went on my merry way being merry simply because I did not know any better. I had no idea, for instance, that I was entitled to a bed of my own. It was obvious even to an ordinary kid like me that the more kids you slept with the more fun you had in bed. I figured that was what they meant by "bedlam." I didn't know that beds were supposed to be soft. To me "bed and board" meant one and the same thing.

I didn't feel that privacy was especially desirable. What was attractive about being alone? I thought that going to the bathroom with a friend was real friendly. It transformed a biological necessity into a social amenity.

I didn't know that a long narrow street was not an ideal baseball diamond. I was so busy playing I didn't have time to check the measurements. The butcher store was first base, the sewer second, the laundry third, and the open manhole home plate. You slid in and down, and if you didn't waste your time foolishly while you were there you could find old baseballs.

I didn't know there were good cuts of meat and bad. Our menu at mealtime offered two choices—take it or leave it—an approach that seemed to stimulate our appetites. Most meat came to our table in the form of meatballs. (I had an idea that cows laid meatballs the way chickens lay eggs.) I didn't know that meatballs were supposed to contain meat. To this day I don't like the taste of meatballs made of meat. They just don't taste like Mama's.

I didn't know we were supposed to eat fresh bread. Mama said it would give us a bellyache; stale bread was much better for us. She believed so strongly in the stale-bread theory that she even learned to bake day-old bread.

Our block had about twenty tenements; each building about thirty families (not counting sleep-in strangers); each family about 5.6 children (not counting stowaways) by government census—if the census taker could halt the increase long enough to write down the number. There are towns in the United States with smaller populations which have a post office of their own. Yet I never felt crowded in or crowded out. My neighbors never appeared as a crowd to me. To the rich all poor people look alike. To me they were individuals—not all good and kind and noble, but individuals. We knew all about them and they all about us.

I didn't know I needed some quiet place where I could do my homework. My brothers used to sit around the dining-room table in the evening doing homework en masse, noisily, bothering each other, correcting, helping. They didn't know they were doing it all wrong. Tough luck! It's too late to rectify it now that they are educated and doing nicely. I didn't know I was supposed to be obsessed by sibling rivalries, so I admired my brothers and learned a great deal from them.

I didn't know mothers were supposed to use psychology on children. I knew they used whatever was immediately available, like shaving strops, wooden ladles, or the everready palm of the hand which wise Mother Nature had shaped to fit perfectly over the rear end of a kid. Wise Mother Levenson simply applied wise Mother Nature's wisdom to us.

I didn't know that fathers were not supposed to hit kids if they were bad. Most fathers hit kids—anybody's. The kid whose father didn't hit him felt that his father either wasn't interested in him or wasn't his real father. Besides, as any honest kid will tell you under oath, there are days when kids can be quite impossible—like Monday through Sunday, for instance. Come to think of it, the only perfect kid I ever heard of was my father when he was a kid.

I didn't know I had to *feel like* doing my homework, practicing the violin, washing dishes or running errands. I just *had* to do it because everyone had to do things he really didn't feel like doing—even big people. I had a strong suspicion my father didn't feel like working twelve hours a day in a sweatshop.

I learned from experience that if there was something lacking it might turn up if I went after it, saved up for it, worked for it, but never if I just waited for it. Of course, you had to be lucky, too, but I discovered that the more I hustled the luckier I seemed to get.

As an additional safeguard against self-pity in our home, Mama kept several charity boxes marked "For the Poor." We gave to the poor regularly. It made us feel rich.

Lest all this appear as a defense of the notion that ignorance is bliss, I'd like to tell you what I *did* know. I knew that there were things I wanted badly, things I would ask for. Mama's answer to such requests usually came in two words: "Not now." (Later we came to refer to this approach as Mama's theory of postponement of pleasure.) First things first. First came the absolute *necessities* like books. Skates, sleds and bicycles would have to wait. I know Mama didn't enjoy denying us the joys of childhood. She had to, in the interest of our adulthood. "You'll have to do *without* today if you want a tomorrow *with*."

Our parents set the moral tone of the family. They expected more of some of us and less of others, but never less than they thought we were capable of. "The Levensons"—Joe, Jack, Dora, David, Mike, Bill, Albert and Sammy—were different from each other, yet very much alike, as children and as adults. As brothers we were expected to collaborate rather than compete. Each was responsible not only to himself but to his brother, and all were responsible to our parents, who were prepared to answer to the world for all of us.

Mama and Papa hoped to derive joy from their children. "May you have joy from your children" was the greatest blessing conceivable. They were the parting words on happy and sad occasions. Honor brought to parents by their children was the accepted standard for measuring success. It also became an incentive for us. Our personal success was to a great extent predicated upon the happiness we could bring to our parents. It would not be long before this idea would be completely reversed. To make our children happy was to become the *summum bonum* of family life.

I should like to tell you how my brothers and sister turned out; then we can go back to the beginning of things.

As the children of immigrants my brothers were aware of the fact that they represented the "undesirables," the "foreigners," as others had been "undesirables" in previous decades. They realized, too, that the only way to rise above undesirability was not merely to become desirable, but to become indispensable. This would require equal amounts of education and sacrifice. They filled every hour not devoted to study with part-time jobs as truant officers, book salesmen, teachers of English to foreigners— wearing out their eyes, their pants and their books, drinking black coffee to stay awake, postponing marriage, sharing clothes, colds, money and dreams. They defined freedom as the opportunity to change the circumstances of your life through your own effort, to force the hand of history rather than to remain forever enslaved by it.

Joe, the eldest, became a doctor (Fordham, 1920). Jack, next in line, became a dentist (Columbia, 1924). They were the first to break through the barbed-wire fence of poverty. Because of them it was easier for the rest of us.

Through all the bleak years that Joe spent in medical school Papa could contribute nothing but a regular allowance of moral support. Joe will tell you to this day that he sews up a wound just like his father, the tailor, did. The stitches never show. He has still retained one nasty habit, though —he bites off the thread, a trick he learned from Mama who, in turn, learned a lot from Joe. He used to show her medical pictures of man's    10 insides. "Just like a chicken," Mama observed. Joe will also tell you about the skull he brought home. The brothers placed it in the bookcase. At night they would put a lighted candle into it to scare off burglars. It worked. The one burglar who got in was so terrified he forgot his tools. We gave them to Joe, who used them on us, his first patients. (Joe told us years later that after he had explained human birth control to Papa, the only thing Papa asked was whether it could be retroactive.)

Jack, immediately after graduation from dental school, was besieged by all the moneyless tenants of our building, who provided him with the kind of professional experience money couldn't buy. After a while he    20 learned how to cope with the situation. He either told them that nothing was wrong, or that they needed a specialist—my cousin Alvin.

Papa never quite forgave Mama for having broken his record by giving him a daughter. The other fathers on the block consoled Papa. After all, it happened while he was still young and hadn't hit his stride. Our only sister's name is Dora. To this day none of us can remember where she got dressed. She is the clearing house for all news, gossip, birth announcements and recipes. Dora has been the family historian, the curator of pictures, medals, legal documents, and old silver. She knows everybody's age but her own.    30

David was the Horatio Alger kid of our family. He had only one job in all his life. At the age of sixteen he went to work as a bookkeeper for a clothing jobber. He is now a partner in the business. He has not gone out to lunch in forty years. He can't make it because during lunch hour all the poor relatives come for suits.

Michael, next in line, threw Mama completely. At about the age of fourteen he won a medal for art. An artist in the family? "From this you expect to make a living? Learn a trade!" But there was no stopping him. He studied art all day and worked in the post office all night. Mama used to leave his portion of chopped liver on a plate so that he could have "a    40 little something" before he went to bed. This unprotected delicacy standing on the table for hours brought out the wolf in the rest of us. Each one would wait till no one else was around, scoop out a little section of the liver, gulp it down, and flatten out the remainder with the palm of his hand so it would cover the same area. By the time Mike sat down to eat he could see the design on the plate through the liver.

To make matters worse, Michael refused to stay in commercial art where he could have made easy money. In the same cold bedroom where Joe had studied medicine and Jack dentistry, he painted in oils. We slept in a dense aroma of pigment and turpentine. He finally had to leave the house in order to make his struggle less painful to Mama and Papa.

At the age of twenty-three Michael Lenson (his nom de brush) won the Chaloner Prize which sent him to study in Europe for five years. The relatives sent him off with about thirty-two hand-knit sweaters and sixty-seven jars of homemade jelly. Newspaper photographers came and took pictures, and there was lots of crying and kidding. From Paris he sent me some of his prize money to buy a violin.

He worked at the Slade School, University of London, then went on to study and paint in France, Italy, Spain and the Netherlands, while exhibiting his work at the Goupil Gallery in London and in the Printemps and Automne salons in Paris. In subsequent years he has shown in such group shows as the Carnegie International, Corcoran Gallery, Museum of Modern Art, Pennsylvania Academy, Albright Gallery, Butler Institute, Art USA, and the Cleveland, Rochester, Dallas, and Newark museums to name a few. As art critic, he is now in his eleventh year with the Newark *Sunday News.*

In reviewing his last one-man show, one of the critics said: "His art is projected as a moral force . . . wherein content must serve as the vehicle for human values." This, I suspect, he learned at home before he went to Paris. His life has remained unfulfilled in only one respect—he still can't get enough chopped liver.

Bill, next in line, became a successful dental technician. At first he decided not to work for somebody else for ten hours a day—not him, boy—so he went into business and worked twelve hours a day—for himself, boy. After about forty years of this kind of "independence" he decided to work eight hours a day for somebody who works twelve hours a day. Bill, the kindest, gentlest, and most devoted to the family, died on July 3, 1965. Our magic number has been reduced forever. We are now eight minus one. It will never be the same without that one.

Albert, just ahead of me, has been at my side all my life. He had a genius for getting into trouble. He did not go looking for it. He didn't have to. It came looking for him. Somehow he was always available.

I was there when:

1. The revolving door at the Automat jammed on Albert when he was halfway through. In the presence of hundreds of people studying Albert under glass, a crew of mechanics had to release him.

2. Albert took two steps on the sidewalk to let an elderly man pass, and found himself in a cellar with a freshly delivered ton of coal for company.

3. Albert walked into the house carrying a jar of sour cream. He slipped on the freshly washed wooden planks and the jar hit the floor. Nor-

mally the cream would splash on the floor, but not for Albert. The jar
hit the floor and the cream hit the ceiling. This may not work for you even
if you try it, but for Albert this was a "natural."

Through all his disasters Albert was silent. Even as a child he never
cried. It drove Mama mad. She would shake him. "Cry, for God's sake,
cry."

He has been my librarian and secretary for years. His remarkable memory provided much of the documentation of this book.

I am the kid brother of the family. To this day when the boys get together they send me for ice cream, and I have to go. (Joe still calls me the      10
"go-getter.") As the last of so many I presented a special problem to
Mama, who in moments of anger often couldn't remember my name. She
would stare at me and call off every name but mine: "Joe, no, Jack, no . . ."
Out of sheer frustration, she would hit me. "You, what's your name?"

I became a schoolteacher and married Esther, who had waited eight
years for me to get a job. It was customary at the time to get a job first,
then a wife. I never claimed my college diploma. It cost $1.87. My cap-
and-gown graduation picture is a further commentary on those days.
Across the face are stamped the words "Proof Only."

All turned out to be quite remarkable adults. Aside from the fact that      20
a couple of them made it into various Who's Whos, they are concertgoers,
art patrons, theatergoers, book readers; they are keenly interested in their
fellow man; they react strongly against social injustice. They are civilized
people.

Now that we are all married (Joe to Kate; Jack to Florence; David to
Elizabeth; Mike to June; Bill to Freida; Albert to Helen; me to Esther; and
Dora, most unfortunately widowed twice in her lifetime, to Sam and to
Morris) and have families of our own, we often recall and try to assess
the childhood experiences that experts tell us must have been traumatic.
By current standards we were raised all wrong. Why, then, do we re-      30
member our parents' homes with affection? Did our parents have a method
of raising children or was it merely trial and error? What were their
values? Is the current crop of children happier than we were? Will they
speak as well of us as we speak of our parents? What was it they gave us,
they who said they had nothing to give?

The stories that follow may provide some of the answers.

* * * *

Ours was a life of plenty: plenty of relatives, neighbors, boarders, jani-      40
tors, landlords, holidays, cockroaches, cats, dogs, music, books, romance,
fights, parties, weddings, medals, illnesses, politicians, superstitions
and junk.

According to the Constitution we were first-class citizens, but we
could afford only second-class merchandise. We ate for years from a set
of dairy dishes on the back of which were imprinted the words "U.S.

Coast Guard Imperfect." Our neighborhood was the wastebasket of the city. We were the heirs to the shopworn, frayed, faded and castoff goods of our more affluent fellow Americans. Our household furnishings came from the poor man's antique shop, the slightly-used-as-good-as-new bargain store where we could bid on wares which were in the same fix we were.

The sign on the store window read FURNITURE, but that covered only two brass beds, a chest of drawers and a kitchen table. The rest of the merchandise consisted of accessories for gracious living such as chipped punch glasses, bronze statues of Atlas holding up an ashtray, or a bell for calling the maid.

In front of the store there stood a bushel basket full of butter-dish covers and a book rack displaying books that the owner had found in the drawers of discarded furniture. For five cents per copy anyone with a thirst for learning could start a fine basic library containing *Lives of the Mexican Generals, Chrestomathie de la Poésie Turcque, Six Unaccompanied Sonatas for Bass Viol Attributed to a Pupil of Monteverdi, The Practice of Insect Extermination, Second Edition, Letters of Admiral Breckenridge to His Nephew,* and *How to Heat an Igloo.*

Our neighborhood also had an open-air pushcart market where there were genuine bargains: overripe onions, frostbitten tomatoes, and a great variety of canned goods whose labels were burnt or missing. We called them "surprise lunches." There were large barrels of pickles (the best, as any good shopper could tell you, were always on the bottom), and even larger barrels full of bright-eyed herrings living in crowded quarters with their sisters, their cousins, their uncles and their aunts just as we did; tail ends of sturgeon, the meatier parts of which had been promoted to better neighborhoods; suits of long winter underwear suspended from high poles like effigies; and hoisted way above all was the flag of the pushcart fleet—pink bloomers full-blown in the wind. You could not try on underthings but you could buy them with the understanding that if they didn't fit after you got them home your money would be cheerfully refunded. The quality was guaranteed verbally: "It will last a lifetime, and after that you can make a skirt out of it." You could also buy tarnished crucifixes and Stars of David impiously displayed alongside trusses, hot-water bags, and remedies for the itch.

In this market you might latch onto a "reject"—a brand new item with a birth defect. If the damage was in the back where it didn't show, you paid more than if it was in the front. After all, only you would know about the hidden damage, and you could keep a secret.

At twilight the human scavengers would descend upon the market to buy up the marked down from the marked down, the foods that had been squeezed, bent, smelled and rejected. Hungry kids would never know the difference.

At the very end of a winter's day, when the peddlers were stiff with the cold, zero hour transactions such as the following were not unusual.

Lady, examining one last, tarnished teaspoon on a pushcart:
"How much?"
"A penny."
"Too much."
"Make me an offer."

In those days people did not live as long as they do today, but things
lived longer. In our house old things were not discarded but retired to a
drawer in the kitchen which we called "Mama's shame-to-throw-out
drawer." Every family had one. It contained at all times such indispen-
sables as half a pair of scissors, a toothless comb, eyeglass frames without    10
lenses, empty Vaseline jars, a knotted rubber band, the face of a clock,
a black button marked "Off," the bulb of a nasal spray, a fountain-pen
tube, a ball of tinfoil, a key to the old apartment, and a "gold" medal
which read "Best Wishes Thom McAn Shoes."

The drawer was appropriately lined with old newspaper, of which there
was always a great abundance, since news, too, did not have to be new
to be good. Mama saw no reason for buying new news when she had not
yet used up the old.

Newspapers, in fact, served many functions besides covering the news;
they also covered the floors, for instance. After the lady of the house had    20
washed her wooden floors she covered them with newspaper, wall to wall.
Many a time I came home from school to find Mama stretched out on the
floor absorbed in an editorial.

The rotogravure section was reserved for sideboard-drawer lining because its brownish-red color matched our genuine imitation mahogany.
The bottom drawer was known as the Maternity Ward. When our cat was
expecting (again), Mama shredded a newspaper with her meat chopper
and padded the drawer. Women understood such things. At our house
kittens could read before they could walk.

I inherited most of my hats from older brothers, uncles and forgetful      30
strangers, who got them that way themselves. The size was reduced to
fit my head by folding a string of newspaper under the inside leather band.

Party hats were fashioned of cleverly folded newspaper, as were generals' hats, Chinese hats, chefs' hats, kings' crowns, sailboats, bandits'
masks, megaphones, telescopes and fly-swatters.

A short, hand-rolled wad of newspaper served as a cork for bottles as
well as a packing for keyholes when privacy was desired. (Keyholes were
for looking, not for locking.)

We cut our schoolbook covers out of newspaper. My brother Mike could
work it out so that an inspiring picture of Tom Mix's horse would appear      40
smack on the front of the book.

Children were punished by being slapped on the head with a rolled-up
newspaper. I must say, though, that no father was cruel enough to swat
a kid with the Sunday paper. This might leave him punchy through the
following Thursday.

Mama and my sister Dora cut newspapers into dress patterns—for fancy dresses the society page, for daily wear the Situations Wanted.

If any parts of the newspaper survived they were stored in the cellar for months. Eventually they were sold to the junk dealer who then sold the lot to the newspaper publisher whose mother probably had lots of floors to cover.

While we did not possess the purchasing power to buy first-class merchandise, we did possess the will power to be first-class human beings. Things could become junk, but people didn't have to accept such a fate. Man could fight back. A teapot, Mama said, had no soul, but man did.

Mama had a philosopher's insight and a prophet's foresight. She foresaw the corrupting effect of vermin not only on beds but on people in the beds, the gnawing of rats not only on plaster but on the moral fiber of humans. Dirt is bad company. Dirty beds could breed dirty thoughts which could breed dirty deeds.

Mama, therefore, practiced preventive housekeeping. Capitulation to a second-class physical environment might mean the renunciation of first-class ideals. Personal honor, behavior and character could never be "marked down." Mama's search for defects in the quality of our values was far more exacting than her appraisal of a pushcart bargain. She made it pretty clear that our home was not a pushcart, and that our integrity would not be reduced. Mama insisted that we were a first-class family, and that among the few treasures she could afford in life was a clean home.

Her fight against dirt was based upon the premise that circumstance makes poor, but people make dirt, and that if everyone cleaned his own house inside and out, the whole world would be clean. If Mama had to contend with the environment, the environment would have to contend with Mama. She was the environment's problem.

Some housekeepers threw in the mop: "You want dirt? I'll show you dirt!" Mama reacted with spite. "You want dirt? Not from me. I'll show you who's boss in this house! I'll show you clean like you never saw clean. I'll kill you with cleanliness." She did, in fact, almost kill my brother Albert, who ran through a closed window onto the fire escape to watch a parade going by. Mrs. Clean had polished the window to the point where it was invisible. The day Mrs. Gordon, upstairs, forgot to clean her windows Mama was quick to remark, "Next thing you know she'll start using lipstick."

Today psychiatrists would call Mama a compulsive housekeeper. She would get up at 6 A.M. mumbling, "Here it is Monday, before you know it Tuesday, and Wednesday just around the corner, and Thursday running into Friday, and I haven't done a stitch of work yet."

Bedmaking in our house began earlier than in most, and more suddenly. It started with either three or four of us on the bedroom floor, depending on which bed Mama overturned first. If we didn't come to quickly enough we often found ourselves folded up in a mattress on the fire escape. Or Mama would pretend to be considerate. She wouldn't wake you. "You want to sleep? Sleep. Sleep. Sleep." And she would pull the sheet out from under you, start pounding the pillows with a carpet beater, and proceed to make the bed with you in it.

One morning I was sent home by my teacher: "Young man, you look sick. Go right home and tell your mother to put you to bed." I walked into the house to find Mama in her customary position—on her knees, wet rag in hand, next to a pail of sudsy-gray water. "The teacher said I'm sick and that I should lie down in bed."

Mama looked up. "In what? Are you sure you can't sit up? I just made the bed!"

Mama would sooner have been caught drunk than have anyone, espe-                    10
cially a stranger, walk in and find her house dirty. My brothers used to joke about it: "Mama's ashamed to leave dirty dishes in the sink overnight. If a burglar broke in she would be embarrassed."

At our house "The line is busy" meant that Mama was hanging out the wash. On Monday at dawn you were wakened by the twittering of hysterical sparrows trying to reply to the squealing of the clothesline pulleys. By noon all the women had hung their laundry. All light was shut out of the yard by the hundreds of garments crisscrossing each other to form an impenetrable forest of wet wash.

In that yard I picked up a working knowledge of sex. By studying the              20
wash, I could determine whether Mrs. Burn's daughters were now "big girls" by the appearance of brassieres and panties, or whether they were still "little girls" who wore woolen bloomers.

My mother had an all-male line of "union suits" (closed shop but for the trap door), with the exception of her own long nightgowns which hung down two full flights when they were wet, and my sister Dora's skirts which dripped in technicolor onto other people's white laundry.

My job on Mondays was to "run down into the yard and pick up the handkerchiefs that fell off the line before someone takes them." The reason I didn't like to go was that some window would invariably fly open          30
and an angry woman would call down to me, "What are you doing there?"

"I'm picking up my mother's handkerchiefs."

"They're mine, not your mother's." Other windows would open. The battle was on.

"They're not his and they're not yours. They're mine."

"And how do you know they're yours?"

"If I don't know mine who knows mine?"

"And I know mine."

"May I not live to see my daughter married if it's not mine."

"Don't swear for a handkerchief. It doesn't pay. It's not a tablecloth."          40

It would take days before peace was restored.

The difference between keeping things clean and keeping kids clean was that things just sat still and waited for the dirt to collect. We kids were carriers. We ran a pickup and delivery service.

If you brought dirt into the house your name was mud. A kangaroo court was in session at all times. Mama would line up the eight kids against the kitchen wall, one hand pointing at us accusingly, the other pointing up to the evidence: the mark of a rubber ball on the ceiling. What she said does not seem to make much sense now, but it did then. "I just scrubbed that ceiling on my hands and knees and now look. Who did it?"

Sometimes when we walked into the house we would get a wet rag square in the face for two reasons: one, to clean; two, to identify. "Let me see which slob it is." Mama sometimes cleaned off the grimy little faces of total strangers. "You I don't know. Out!"

If Mama didn't happen to have a rag in her hand she wiped your face with the edge of her apron which she had moistened with *your* spit. "Here, spit on this." Obviously she knew it was unsanitary for us to use other people's spit.

It wasn't that we kids loved dirt; we simply valued time more. Keeping clean used up too much of a kid's valuable minutes. There was so much to do. There was ink to be spilled, chalk to be stepped on, toothpaste to be squirted, pencil shavings to be scattered, and windows to be finger-printed.

It's hard to believe that dirt could overcome hunger, but it did.

"Ma, I'm hungry."

"Wash your hands; I'll give you a piece of bread and butter."

"I'm not hungry."

One of Mama's favorite teaching techniques was comparison — impossible us versus some paragon of elegance. "Does President Coolidge hang his dirty socks on a doorknob? Answer me! Does Rudolph Valentino leave his sneakers on his bed? Answer me! Does Chaim Weizmann chew his tie? Does the Prince of Wales throw newspaper into his mother's toilet bowl?"

When all else failed Mama made the announcement that put fear in our hearts. "All right; enough is enough. Tomorrow the Board of Health is coming to take you all away. Goodbye."

Came Monday morning however, you wouldn't have recognized us. We had to be thoroughly clean, even where it didn't show, like inside the ears "you shouldn't give me any excuses that you didn't hear what the teacher said." Our hands had to be scrubbed clean as a surgeon's notwithstanding brother Albert's claim that "I never raise my hand in class, anyhow." In school it was essential not only to spell good, but to smell good. You even had to put on a fresh, clean shirt. On lesser occasions, if you got caught putting on a clean shirt Mama would say, "Take it off before you get it dirty."

For school we had to take a bath. "Scratching, like borrowing, helps only for a while," Mama said. We reluctantly turned in our bodies to Mama and submitted to Operation Skin Removal. We resisted, connived, lied, and finally ran out of effective evasions. "It's not dirt; it's my tan from last summer" had been used too often, as had "It's too soon after my cold." We made token attempts at cleanliness by following the spray truck on the street, rubbing our faces and arms in the muddy mist it left in its wake. We walked in the rain face up. Before putting on a fresh shirt we determined whether it had long sleeves or short, and washed ourselves accordingly.

Any one of us who of his own free will just went and took a bath (like brother David who was unnaturally neat for a child) had a lot of explaining to do. "What's the matter you're taking a bath, you going to the doctor or something?"

We knew about cleanliness being next to Godliness, but taking a bath in our home was next to impossible. For six days a week our bathtub served as a storage bin for paint cans, brushes, wine jugs, umbrellas, toilet plungers, soiled laundry and a day-to-day supply of coal. Before we could be bathed, the tub had to be scoured and the bathroom sealed off. There was a broken window over the bathtub, which had never been replaced. We covered it with a board that the boys referred to as the "draft board." Since there was never a supply of water hot enough to deterge urgent cases like ours, steaming reinforcements were brought to the scene in teakettles, pots and pans. After Mama had made the elbow test (if the skin blistered it was just right), we were thrown in en masse to soak, like laundry. Since the stopper was always missing, we seated a soft, fat brother at the drain end.

Mama washed kids like she washed floors. She tore through our scalps with a horse brush soaked in naphtha soap. We screamed in pain as the acids ate into every aperture. To kill the lice she added kerosene. "Please, Ma! Enough!" Not yet. Her fingers dug into both your ears, twisting, turning, brain-washing mercilessly. You were left draped over the rim of the tub in a state of amnesia, recognizing nobody, frothing at the mouth, promising to be a good boy in the future, ready to sign any confession.

This fierce bathing ritual was another expression of Mama's constant battle against the environment. As I lay in my clean bed recovering from the ordeal by water I knew the great joy of pride in one's body. My self-esteem had been lifted. I felt important, fresh, redeemed. I was glad to be alive and very much in love with the world and my home. The sin of dirt which the street had inflicted upon me had been washed away, and I was reborn, a first-class citizen, the equal of any kid.

Years later, the older boys, who were beginning to earn money, hired a woman to come once a week to help Mama. On the day she was due, Mama got up at five-thirty, scrubbed the floors and put up fresh curtains, "Nobody should think we're pigs." When the lady arrived, Mama had hot coffee ready for her. They compared aches and pains, including a few heartaches, recipes, husbands, children and blood pressures. When she left they cried on each other's shoulders, and Mama promised to come and help her with her house real soon.

When Papa married Mama he put a ring on one of her fingers and thimbles on all the others. Without benefit of bifocals she could thread a needle in the dark with one hand, tie a knot with her teeth, and chop meat with her free hand. She pumped away at her sewing machine like a six-day bicycle rider, used up enough energy to go around the world three times, and never left home.

Long pants were belittled into short pants; old skirts became new aprons; old aprons became good as new collars; collars were reversed and re-reversed; sleeves were amputated to the elbow; cuffs were successfully transplanted and grafted onto strange pants—and the scar never showed. All garments, outer or under, public or private, mentionable or unmentionable, could be made to fit anyone. "Use it up, wear it out; make it do or do without." If your sleeves were short you got longer mittens. Padding the size of beanbags took care of sloping shoulders, and flour sacks expanded the crotches of narrow-minded undershorts. Besides, whatever Mama Levenson couldn't fill in, Father Time would: "He'll grow into it." Mama was not concerned with fashion but with nakedness. "It's good enough for now." We were never sure how long now would be.

Clothing was always en route from one kid to another. Typical conversations ran something like this:

"Ma, where's my shirt?"

"Which shirt?"

"The one that used to be Albert's jumper that used to be Jack's sport shirt that used to be Dora's blouse."

"Oh, that one? Too late. It's Albert's underwear now."

Mama hated holes the way nature abhors a vacuum. A rip was followed immediately by a patch. The colors of her patches were brilliant, and no two were alike. When brother Bill bent over, he looked like a stained-glass window.

Mama cut up the oldest blankets to patch the older ones. The old blankets were not even used. They were considered too new to be put on the beds.

Even a hole in the head was covered with a patch, not necessarily white, and certainly not sterile, but effective. The germs died of overpopulation.

The knot was a handy device for tying off poverty. If one of us kids tore his shoelace, he didn't pull out the remainder and discard it. It was cheaper to make a knot and lace the shoe only three-quarters of the way up. After the next break came more knots. The lace usually ended up outlasting the shoe.

If the top button of your shorts tore off you could pull the section where the button had been through the buttonhole, then tie a knot into it, and it would hold better than a button.

Between the hours of after supper and bedtime Mama could always be found knitting things for the family, "Here, hold out your hands." I would hold taut a skein of wool while she rolled it into a ball. She was off on a new project. Often there were mystery knittings. "A surprise for you; something you need." This was no help at all because I needed everything. It never fit the one for whom it was intended, but there were so many of us that it was bound to fit at least one.

The whole family watched in fascination as the thing began to take form. When I saw it had no fingers, I decided it was a mitten. When she left off the thumb, I decided it was a hat. When she left off the woolly knob on top, I decided it was socks after all, especially because she had measured my hand. Mama operated on the well-known scientific fact that the circumference of the fist is equal to the length of the foot. The socks Mama knitted had a heavy inner seam. It felt like walking barefoot on the blade of an ice skate. If we complained she would say, "They don't appreciate anything."

# Clifford Odets*
## Awake and Sing!

### The Characters of the Play

*All of the characters in* Awake and Sing!
*share a fundamental activity:*
*a struggle for life amidst petty conditions.*

BESSIE BERGER, *as she herself states, is not only the mother in this home but also the father. She is constantly arranging and taking care of her family. She loves life, likes to laugh, has great resourcefulness and enjoys living from day to day. A high degree of energy accounts for her quick exasperation at ineptitude. She is a shrewd judge of realistic qualities in people in the sense of being able to gauge quickly their effectiveness. In her eyes all of the people in the house are equal. She is naive and quick in emotional response. She is afraid of utter poverty. She is proper according to her own standards, which are fairly close to those of most middle-class families. She knows that when one lives in the jungle one must look out for the wild life.*

MYRON, *her husband, is a born follower. He would like to be a leader. He would like to make a million dollars. He is not sad or ever depressed.*

10

*Life is an even sweet event to him, but the "old days" were sweeter yet. He has a dignified sense of himself. He likes people. He likes everything. But he is heartbroken without being aware of it.*

HENNIE *is a girl who has had few friends, male or female. She is proud of her body. She won't ask favors. She travels alone. She is fatalistic about being trapped, but will escape if possible. She is self-reliant in the best sense. Till the day she dies she will be faithful to a loved man. She inherits her mother's sense of humor and energy.*

RALPH *is a boy with a clean spirit. He wants to know, wants to learn. He is ardent, he is romantic, he is sensitive. He is naive too. He is trying to* 10 *find why so much dirt must be cleared away before it is possible to "get to first base."*

JACOB, *too, is trying to find a right path for himself and the others. He is aware of justice, of dignity. He is an observer of the others, compares their activities with his real and ideal sense of life. This produces a reflective nature. In this home he is a constant boarder. He is a sentimental idealist with no power to turn ideal to action.*

*With physical facts — such as housework — he putters. But as a barber he demonstrates the flair of an artist. He is an old Jew with living eyes in his tired face.* 20

UNCLE MORTY *is a successful American business man with five good senses. Something sinister comes out of the fact that the lives of others seldom touch him deeply. He holds to his own line of life. When he is generous he wants others to be aware of it. He is pleased by attention — a rich relative to the* BERGER *family. He is a shrewd judge of material values. He will die unmarried. Two and two make four, never five with him. He can blink in the sun for hours, a fat tomcat. Tickle him, he laughs. He lives in a penthouse with a real Japanese butler to serve him. He sleeps with dress models, but not from his own showrooms. He plays cards for hours on end. He smokes expensive cigars. He sees every Mickey* 30 *Mouse cartoon that appears. He is a 32-degree Mason. He is really deeply intolerant finally.*

MOE AXELROD *lost a leg in the war. He seldom forgets that fact. He has killed two men in extra-martial activity. He is mordant, bitter. Life has taught him a disbelief in everything, but he will fight his way through. He seldom shows his feelings: fights against his own sensitivity. He has been everywhere and seen everything. All he wants is* HENNIE. *He is very proud. He scorns the inability of others to make their way in life, but he likes people for whatever good qualities they possess. His passionate outbursts come from a strong but contained emotional mechanism.* 40

SAM FEINSCHREIBER *wants to find a home. He is a lonely man, a foreigner in a strange land, hypersensitive about this fact, conditioned by the humiliation of not making his way alone. He has a sense of others laughing at him. At night he gets up and sits alone in the dark. He hears acutely all the small sounds of life. He might have been a poet in another time and place. He approaches his wife as if he were always offering her a delicate flower. Life is a high chill wind weaving itself around his head.*

SCHLOSSER, *the janitor, is an overworked German whose wife ran away with another man and left him with a young daughter who in turn ran away and joined a burlesque show as chorus girl. The man suffers rheumatic pains. He has lost his identity twenty years before.*

SCENE: *Exposed on the stage are the dining room and adjoining front room of the* BERGER *apartment. These two rooms are typically furnished. There is a curtain between them. A small door off the front room leads to* JACOB'S *room. When his door is open one sees a picture of Sacco and Vanzetti on the wall and several shelves of books. Stage left of this door presents the entrance to the foyer hall of the apartment. The two other bedrooms of the apartment are off this hall, but not necessarily shown.*

10

*Stage left of the dining room presents a swinging door which opens on the kitchen.*

*Awake and sing,* ye that dwell in dust:
ISAIAH—26:19

## ACT ONE

TIME. . *The present; the family finishing supper.*
PLACE. . *An apartment in the Bronx, New York City.*

RALPH. Where's advancement down the place? Work like crazy! Think they see it? You'd drop dead first.

MYRON. Never mind, son, merit never goes unrewarded. Teddy Roosevelt used to say—

HENNIE. It rewarded you—thirty years a haberdashery clerk!
[ *Jacob laughs.*]

30

RALPH. All I want's a chance to get to first base!

HENNIE. That's all?

RALPH. Stuck down in that joint on Fourth Avenue—a stock clerk in a silk house! Just look at Eddie. I'm as good as he is—pulling in two-fifty a week for forty-eight minutes a day. A headliner, his name in all the papers.

JACOB. That's what you want, Ralphie? Your name in the paper?

RALPH. I wanna make up my own mind about things . . . be something! Didn't I want to take up tap dancing, too?

BESSIE. So take lessons. Who stopped you?

40

RALPH. On what?

BESSIE. On what? Save money.

RALPH. Sure, five dollars a week for expenses and the rest in the house. I can't save even for shoe laces.

BESSIE. You mean we shouldn't have food in the house, but you'll do a jig on the street corner?

RALPH. I mean something.

BESSIE. You also mean something when you studied on the drum, Mr. Smartie!

RALPH. I don't know. . . . Every other day to sit around with the blues and mud in your mouth.

MYRON. That's how it is—life is like that—a cake-walk.

RALPH. What's it get you?

HENNIE. A four-car funeral.

RALPH. What's it for?

JACOB. What's it for? If this life leads to a revolution it's a good life.  10
Otherwise it's for nothing.

BESSIE. Never mind, Pop! Pass me the salt.

RALPH. It's crazy—all my life I want a pair of black and white shoes and can't get them. It's crazy!

BESSIE. In a minute I'll get up from the table. I can't take a bite in my mouth no more.

MYRON [*restraining her*]. Now, Mamma, just don't excite yourself—

BESSIE. I'm so nervous I can't hold a knife in my hand.

MYRON. Is that a way to talk, Ralphie? Don't Momma work hard enough all day?                                                   20

[BESSIE *allows herself to be reseated.*]

BESSIE. On my feet twenty-four hours?

MYRON. On her feet—

RALPH [*jumps up*]. What do I do—go to night-clubs with Greta Garbo? Then when I come home can't even have my own room? Sleep on a day-bed in the front room! [*Choked, he exits to front room.*]

BESSIE. He's starting up that stuff again. [*Shouts to him.*] When Hennie here marries you'll have her room—I should only live to see the day.

HENNIE. Me, too. [*They settle down to serious eating.*]

MYRON. This morning the sink was full of ants. Where they come from  30
I just don't know. I thought it was coffee grounds . . . and then they began moving.

BESSIE. You gave the dog eat?

JACOB. I gave the dog eat.

[HENNIE *drops a knife and picks it up again.*]

BESSIE. You got dropsy tonight.

HENNIE. Company's coming.

MYRON. You can buy a ticket for fifty cents and win fortunes. A man came in the store—it's the Irish Sweepstakes.

BESSIE. What?                                                        40

MYRON. Like a raffle, only different. A man came in—

BESSIE. Who spends fifty-cent pieces for Irish raffles? They threw out a family on Dawson Street today. All the furniture on the sidewalk. A fine old woman with gray hair.

JACOB. Come eat, Ralph.

MYRON. A butcher on Beck Street won eighty thousand dollars.

BESSIE. Eighty thousand dollars! You'll excuse my expression, you're bughouse!

MYRON. I seen it in the paper—on one ticket—765 Beck Street.

BESSIE. Impossible!

MYRON. He did . . . yes he did. He says he'll take his old mother to Europe . . . an Austrian—

HENNIE. Europe . . .

MYRON. Six per cent on eighty thousand—forty-eight hundred a year.

BESSIE. I'll give you money. Buy a ticket in Hennie's name. Say, you can't tell—lightning never struck us yet. If they win on Beck Street we    10 could win on Longwood Avenue.

JACOB[*ironically*]. If it rained pearls—who would work?

BESSIE. Another country heard from.

[RALPH *enters and silently seats himself.*]

MYRON. I forgot, Beauty—Sam Feinschreiber sent you a present. Since I brought him for supper he just can't stop talking about you.

HENNIE. What's that "mockie" bothering about? Who needs him?

MYRON. He's a very lonely boy.

HENNIE. So I'll sit down and bust out crying "'cause he's lonely."

BESSIE [*opening candy*]. He'd marry you one two three.    20

HENNIE. Too bad about him.

BESSIE [*naively delighted*]. Chocolate peanuts.

HENNIE. Loft's week-end special, two for thirty-nine.

BESSIE. You could think about it. It wouldn't hurt.

HENNIE [ *laughing*]. To quote Moe Axelrod, "Don't make me laugh."

BESSIE. Never mind laughing. It's time you already had in your head a serious thought. A girl twenty-six don't grow younger. When I was your age it was already a big family with responsibilities.

HENNIE [*laughing*]. Maybe that's what ails you, Mom.

BESSIE. Don't you feel well?    30

HENNIE. 'Cause I'm laughing? I feel fine. It's just funny—that poor guy sending me presents 'cause he loves me.

BESSIE. I think it's very, very nice.

HENNIE. Sure. . . swell!

BESSIE. Mrs. Marcus' Roşe is engaged to a Brooklyn boy, a dentist. He came in his car today. A little dope should get such a boy.

[*Finished with the meal,* BESSIE, MYRON *and* JACOB *rise. Both* HENNIE *and* RALPH *sit silently at the table, he eating. Suddenly she rises.*]

HENNIE. Tell you what, Mom. I saved for a new dress, but I'll take you and Pop to the Franklin. Don't need a dress. From now on I'm planning    40 to stay in nights. Hold everything!

BESSIE. What's the matter—a bedbug bit you suddenly?

HENNIE. It's a good bill—Belle Baker. Maybe she'll sing "Eli, Eli."

BESSIE. We was going to a movie.

HENNIE. Forget it. Let's go.

MYRON. I see in the papers [*as he picks his teeth*] Sophie Tucker took off twenty-six pounds. Fearful business with Japan.

HENNIE. Write a book, Pop! Come on, we'll go early for good seats.

MYRON. Moe said you had a date with him for tonight.

BESSIE. Axelrod?

HENNIE. I told him no, but he don't believe it. I'll tell him no for the next hundred years, too.

MYRON. Don't break appointments, Beauty, and hurt people's feelings. [*Bessie exits.*]

HENNIE. His hands got free wheeling. [*She exits.*]

MYRON. I don't know. . . people ain't the same. N-O. The whole world's    10
changing right under our eyes. Presto! No manners. Like the great Italian lover in the movies. What was his name? The Sheik. . . . No one remembers? [*Exits, shaking his head.*]

RALPH [*unmoving at the table*]. Jake. . .

JACOB. Noo?

RALPH. I can't stand it.

JACOB. There's an expression—"strong as iron you must be."

RALPH. It's a cock-eyed world.

JACOB. Boys like you could fix it some day. Look on the world, not on yourself so much. Every country with starving millions, no? In Germany    20
and Poland a Jew couldn't walk in the street. Everybody hates, nobody loves.

RALPH. I don't get all that.

JACOB. For years, I watched you grow up. Wait! You'll graduate from my university.

[*The others enter, dressed.*]

MYRON [*lighting*]. Good cigars now for a nickel.

BESSIE [*to* JACOB]. After take Tootsie on the roof. [*To* RALPH.] What'll you do?

RALPH. Don't know.                                                          30

BESSIE. You'll see the boys around the block?

RALPH. I'll stay home every night!

MYRON. Momma don't mean for you—

RALPH. I'm flying to Hollywood by plane, that's what I'm doing.

[*Doorbell rings.* MYRON *answers it.*]

BESSIE. I don't like my boy to be seen with those tramps on the corner.

MYRON [*without*]. Schlosser's here, Momma, with the garbage can.

BESSIE. Come in here, Schlosser. [*Sotto voce.*] Wait, I'll give him a piece of my mind. [MYRON *ushers in* SCHLOSSER *who carries a garbage can in each hand.*] What's the matter, the dumbwaiter's broken again?          40

SCHLOSSER. Mr. Wimmer sends new ropes next week. I got a sore arm.

BESSIE. He should live so long your Mr. Wimmer. For seven years already he's sending new ropes. No dumbwaiter, no hot water, no steam— In a respectable house, they don't allow such conditions.

SCHLOSSER. In a decent house dogs are not running to make dirty the hallway.

BESSIE. Tootsie's making dirty? Our Tootsie's making dirty in the hall?

SCHLOSSER [*to* JACOB]. I tell you yesterday again. You must not leave her—

BESSIE [*indignantly*]. Excuse me! Please don't yell on an old man. He's got more brains in his finger than you got—I don't know where. Did you ever see—he should talk to you an old man?

MYRON. Awful.

BESSIE. From now on we don't walk up the stairs no more. You keep it so clean we'll fly in the windows.

SCHLOSSER. I speak to Mr. Wimmer.                                      10

BESSIE. Speak! Speak. Tootsie walks behind me like a lady any time, any place. So good-bye. . . good-bye, Mr. Schlosser.

SCHLOSSER. I tell you dot—I verk verry hard here. My arms is. . . [*Exits in confusion.*]

BESSIE. Tootsie should lay all day in the kitchen maybe. Give him back if he yells on you. What's funny?

JACOB [*laughing*]. Nothing.

BESSIE. Come [*Exits.*]

JACOB. Hennie, take care. . . .

HENNIE. Sure.                                                          20

JACOB. Bye-bye.

[HENNIE *exits.* MYRON *pops head back in door.*]

MYRON. Valentino! That's the one! [*He exits.*]

RALPH. I never in my life ever had a birthday party. Every time I went and cried in the toilet when my birthday came.

JACOB [*seeing* RALPH *remove his tie*]. You're going to bed?

RALPH. No, I'm putting on a clean shirt.

JACOB. Why?

RALPH. I got a girl. . . . Don't laugh!

JACOB. Who laughs? Since when?                                        30

RALPH. Three weeks. She lives in Yorkville with an aunt and uncle. A bunch of relatives, but no parents.

JACOB. An orphan girl—tch, tch.

RALPH. But she's got me! Boy, I'm telling you I could sing! Jake, she's like stars. She's so beautiful you look at her and cry! She's like French words! We went to the park the other night. Heard the last band concert.

JACOB. Music. . .

RALPH [*stuffing shirt in trousers*]. It got cold and I gave her my coat to wear. We just walked like that, see, without a word, see. I never was so happy in all my life. It got late. . . we just sat there. She looked at me—  40
you know what I mean, how a girl looks at you—right in the eyes? "I love you," she says, "Ralph." I took her home. . . . I wanted to cry. That's how I felt!

JACOB. It's a beautiful feeling.

RALPH. You said a mouthful!

JACOB. Her name is—

RALPH. Blanche.

JACOB. A fine name. Bring her sometimes here.

RALPH. She's scared to meet Mom.

JACOB. Why?

RALPH. You know Mom's not letting my sixteen bucks out of the house if she can help it. She'd take one look at Blanche and insult her in a minute—a kid who's got nothing.

JACOB. Boychick!

RALPH. What's the diff?

JACOB. It's no difference—a plain bourgeois prejudice—but when they find out a poor girl—it ain't so kosher.                                        10

RALPH. They don't have to know I've got a girl.

JACOB. What's in the end?

RALPH. Out I go! I don't mean maybe!

JACOB. And then what?

RALPH. Life begins.

JACOB. What life?

RALPH. Life with my girl. Boy, I could sing when I think about it! Her and me together—that's a new life!

JACOB. Don't make a mistake! A new death!                                        20

RALPH. What's the idea?

JACOB. Me, I'm the idea! Once I had in *my* heart a dream, a vision, but came marriage and then you forget. Children come and you forget because—

RALPH. Don't worry, Jake.

JACOB. Remember, a woman insults a man's soul like no other thing in the whole world!

RALPH. Why get so excited? No one—

JACOB. Boychick, wake up! Be something! Make your life something good. For the love of an old man who sees in your young days his new         30
life, for such love take the world in your two hands and make it like new. Go out and fight so life shouldn't be printed on dollar bills. A woman waits.

RALPH. Say, I'm no fool!

JACOB. From my heart I hope not. In the meantime—

[*Bell rings.*]

RALPH. See who it is, will you? [*Stands off.*] Don't want Mom to catch me with a clean shirt.

JACOB [*calls*]. Come in. [*Sotto voce.*] Moe Axelrod.

[MOE *enters.*]                                        40

MOE . Hello girls, how's your whiskers? [*To* RALPH.] All dolled up. What's it, the weekly visit to the cat house?

RALPH. Please mind your business.

MOE. Okay, sweetheart.

RALPH [*taking a hidden dollar from a book*]. If Mom asks where I went—

JACOB. I know. Enjoy yourself.

RALPH. Bye-bye. [*He exits.*]

JACOB. Bye-bye.

MOE. Who's home?

JACOB. Me.

MOE. Good. I'll stick around a few minutes. Where's Hennie?

JACOB. She went with Bessie and Myron to a show.

MOE. She what?!

JACOB. You had a date?

MOE. [*hiding his feelings*]. Here—I brought you some halavah.    10

JACOB. Halavah? Thanks. I'll eat a piece after.

MOE. So Ralph's got a dame? Hot stuff—a kid can't even play a card game.

JACOB. Moe, you're a no-good, a bum of the first water. To your dying day you won't change.

MOE. Where'd you get that stuff, a no-good?

JACOB. But I like you.

MOE. Didn't I go fight in France for democracy? Didn't I get my goddam leg shot off in that war the day before the armistice? Uncle Sam give me the Order of the Purple Heart, didn't he? What'd you mean, a no-good?    20

JACOB. Excuse me.

MOE. If you got an orange I'll eat an orange.

JACOB. No orange. An apple.

MOE. No oranges, huh?—what a dump!

JACOB. Bessie hears you once talking like this she'll knock your head off.

MOE. Hennie went with, huh? She wantsa see me squirm, only I don't squirm for dames.

JACOB. You came to see her?

MOE. What for? I got a present for our boy friend, Myron. He'll drop dead when I tell him his gentle horse galloped in fifteen to one. He'll die.    30

JACOB. It really won? The first time I remember.

MOE. Where'd they go?

JACOB. A vaudeville by the Franklin.

MOE. What's special tonight?

JACOB. Someone tells a few jokes. . . and they forget the street is filled with starving beggars.

MOE. What'll they do—start a war?

JACOB. I don't know.

MOE. You oughta know. What the hell you got all the books for?

JACOB. It needs a new world.    40

MOE. That's why they had the big war—to make a new world, they said —safe for democracy. Sure every big general laying up in a Paris hotel with a half dozen broads pinned on his mustache. Democracy! I learned a lesson.

JACOB. An imperial war. You know what this means?

MOE. Sure, I know everything!

JACOB. By money men the interests must be protected. Who gave you such a rotten haircut? Please [*fishing in his vest pocket*], give me for a cent a cigarette. I didn't have since yesterday—

MOE [*giving one*]. Don't make me laugh. [*A cent passes back and forth between them,* MOE *finally throwing it over his shoulder.*] Don't look so tired all the time. You're a wow—always sore about something.

JACOB. And you?

MOE. You got one thing—you can play pinochle. I'll take you over in a game. Then you'll have something to be sore on.

JACOB. Who'll wash dishes?                                                    10

[MOE *takes deck from buffet drawer.*]

MOE. Do 'em after. Ten cents a deal.

JACOB. Who's got ten cents?

MOE. I got ten cents. I'll lend it to you.

JACOB. Commence.

MOE [*shaking cards*]. The first time I had my hands on a pack in two days. Lemme shake up these cards. I'll make 'em talk.

[JACOB *goes to his room where he puts on a Caruso record.*]

JACOB. You should live so long.

MOE. Ever see oranges grow? I know a certain place—One summer I     20
laid under a tree and let them fall right in my mouth.

JACOB [*off, the music is playing; the card game begins*]. From "L'Africana". . . a big explorer comes on a new land—"O Paradiso." From act four this piece. Caruso stands on a ship and looks on a Utopia. You hear? "Oh paradise! Oh paradise on earth! Oh blue sky, oh fragrant air—"

MOE. Ask him does he see any oranges?

[BESSIE, MYRON *and* HENNIE *enter.*]

JACOB. You came back so soon?

BESSIE. Hennie got sick on the way.

MYRON. Hello, Moe. . .                                                        30

[ MOE *puts cards back in pocket.*]

BESSIE. Take off the phonograph, Pop. [ *To* HENNIE.] Lay down. . . I'll call the doctor. You should see how she got sick on Prospect Avenue. Two weeks already she don't feel right.

MYRON. Moe. . . ?

BESSIE. Go to bed, Hennie.

HENNIE. I'll sit here.

BESSIE. Such a girl I never saw! Now you'll be stubborn?

MYRON. It's for your own good, Beauty. Influenza—

HENNIE. I'll sit here.                                                        40

BESSIE. You ever seen a girl should say no to everything. She can't stand on her feet, so—

HENNIE. Don't yell in my ears. I hear. Nothing's wrong. I ate tuna fish for lunch.

MYRON. Canned goods. . .

BESSIE. Last week you also ate tuna fish?

HENNIE. Yeah, I'm funny for tuna fish. Go to the show—have a good time.

BESSIE. I don't understand what I did to God. He blessed me with such children. From the whole world—

MOE. [*coming to aid of* HENNIE.] For Chris' sake, don't kibitz so much!

BESSIE. You don't like it?

MOE [*aping*]. No, I don't like it.

BESSIE. That's too bad, Axelrod. Maybe it's better by your cigar store friends. Here we're different people.

MOE. Don't gimme that cigar store line, Bessie. I walked up five flights— 10

BESSIE. To take out Hennie. But my daughter ain't in your class, Axelrod.

MOE. To see Myron.

MYRON. Did he, did he, Moe?

MOE. Did he what?

MYRON. "Sky Rocket"?

BESSIE. You bet on a horse!

MOE. Paid twelve and a half to one.

MYRON. There! You hear that, Momma? Our horse came in. You see, it happens, and twelve and a half to one. Just look at that! 20

MOE. What the hell, a sure thing. I told you.

BESSIE. If Moe said a sure thing, you couldn't bet a few dollars instead of fifty cents?

JACOB [*laughs*]. "Aie, aie, aie."

MOE [*at his wallet*]. I'm carrying six hundred "plunks" in big denominations.

BESSIE. A banker!

MOE. Uncle Sam sends me ninety a month.

BESSIE. So you save it?

MOE. Run it up. Run-it-up-Axelrod, that's me. 30

BESSIE. The police should know how.

MOE [*shutting her up*]. All right, all right—Change twenty, sweetheart.

MYRON. Can you make change?

BESSIE. Don't be crazy.

MOE. I'll meet a guy in Goldman's restaurant. I'll meet 'im and come back with change.

MYRON [*figuring on paper*]. You can give it to me tomorrow in the store.

BESSIE [*acquisitive*]. He'll come back, he'll come back!

MOE. Lucky I bet some bucks myself. [*In derision to* HENNIE.] Let's 40 step out tomorrow night, Par-a-dise. [*Thumbs his nose at her, laughs mordantly and exits.*]

MYRON. Oh, that's big percentage. If I picked a winner every day . . .

BESSIE. Poppa, did you take Tootsie on the roof?

JACOB. All right.

MYRON. Just look at that—a cake-walk. We can make—

BESSIE. It's enough talk. I got a splitting headache. Hennie, go in bed. I'll call Dr. Cantor.

HENNIE. I'll sit here . . . and don't call that old Ignatz 'cause I won't see him.

MYRON. If you get sick Momma can't nurse you. You don't want to go to a hospital.

JACOB. She don't look sick, Bessie, it's a fact.

BESSIE. She's got fever. I see in her eyes, so he tells me no. Myron, call Dr. Cantor.

[MYRON *picks up phone, but* HENNIE *grabs it from him.*]                    10

HENNIE. I don't want any doctor. I ain't sick. Leave me alone.

MYRON. Beauty, it's for your own sake.

HENNIE. Day in and day out pestering. Why are you always right and no one else can say a word?

BESSIE. When you have your own children—

HENNIE. I'm not sick! Hear what I say? I'm not sick! Nothing's the matter with me! I don't want a doctor.

[BESSIE *is watching her with slow progressive understanding.*]

BESSIE. What's the matter?

HENNIE. Nothing, I told you!                                                   20

BESSIE. You told me, but—[*A long pause of examination follows.*]

HENNIE. See much?

BESSIE. Myron, put down the . . . the . . . [*He slowly puts the phone down.*] Tell me what happened. . . .

HENNIE. Brooklyn Bridge fell down.

BESSIE [*approaching*]. I'm asking a question. . . .

MYRON. What's happened, Momma?

BESSIE. Listen to me!

HENNIE. What the hell are you talking?

BESSIE. Poppa—take Tootsie on the roof.                                       30

HENNIE [*holding* JACOB *back*]. If he wants he can stay here.

MYRON. What's wrong, Momma?

BESSIE [*her voice quivering slightly*]. Myron, your fine Beauty's in trouble. Our society lady . . .

MYRON. Trouble? I don't under—is it—?

BESSIE. Look in her face. [*He looks, understands and slowly sits in a chair, utterly crushed.*] Who's the man?

HENNIE. The Prince of Wales.

BESSIE. My gall is bursting in me. In two seconds—

HENNIE [*in a violent outburst*]. Shut up! Shut up! I'll jump out the      40
window in a minute! Shut up! [*Finally she gains control of herself, says in a low, hard voice:*] You don't know him.

JACOB. Bessie . . .

BESSIE. He's a Bronx boy?

HENNIE. From out of town.

BESSIE. What do you mean?

HENNIE. From out of town!!

BESSIE. A long time you know him? You were sleeping by a girl from the office Saturday nights? You slept good, my lovely lady. You'll go to him. . . he'll marry you.

HENNIE. That's what you say.

BESSIE. That's what I say! He'll do it, take *my* word he'll do it!

HENNIE. Where? [*To* JACOB.] Give her the letter.

[JACOB *does so.*]

BESSIE. What? [*Reads.*] "Dear sir: In reply to your request of the 14th inst., we can state that no Mr. Ben Grossman has ever been connected 10 with our organization . . . " You don't know where he is?

HENNIE. No.

BESSIE [*walks back and forth*]. Stop crying like a baby, Myron.

MYRON. It's like a play on a stage. . . .

BESSIE. To a mother you couldn't say something before. I'm old-fashioned—like your friends I'm not smart—I don't eat chop suey and run around Coney Island with tramps. [*She walks reflectively to buffet, picks up a box of candy, puts it down, says to* MYRON:] Tomorrow night bring Sam Feinschreiber for supper.

HENNIE. I won't do it.                                                    20

BESSIE. You'll do it, my fine beauty, you'll do it!

HENNIE. I'm not marrying a poor foreigner like him. Can't even speak an English word. Not me! I'll go to my grave without a husband.

BESSIE. You don't say! We'll find for you somewhere a millionaire with a pleasure boat. He's going to night school, Sam. For a boy only three years in the country he speaks very nice. In three years he put enough in the bank, a good living.

JACOB. This is serious?

BESSIE. What then? I'm talking for my health? He'll come tomorrow night for supper. By Saturday they're engaged.                             30

JACOB. Such a thing you can't do.

BESSIE. Who asked your advice?

JACOB. Such a thing—

BESSIE. Never mind!

JACOB. The lowest from the low!

BESSIE. Don't talk! I'm warning you! A man who don't believe in God— with crazy ideas—

JACOB. So bad I never imagined you could be.

BESSIE. Maybe if you don't talk so much it wouldn't happen like this. You with your ideas—I'm a mother. I raise a family, they should have 40 respect.

JACOB. Respect? [*Spits.*] Respect! For the neighbors' opinion! You insult me, Bessie!

BESSIE. Go in your room, Papa. Every job he ever had he lost because he's got a big mouth. He opens his mouth and the whole Bronx could fall in. Everybody said it—

MYRON. Momma, they'll hear you down the dumbwaiter.

BESSIE. A good barber not to hold a job a week. Maybe you never heard charity starts at home. You never heard it, Pop?

JACOB. All you know, I heard, and more yet. But Ralph you don't make like you. Before you do it I'll die first. He'll find a girl. He'll go in a fresh world with her. This is a house? Marx said it—abolish such families.

BESSIE. Go in your room, Papa.

JACOB. Ralph you don't make like you!

BESSIE. Go lay in your room with Caruso and the books together.

JACOB. All right!                                                                    10

BESSIE. Go in the room!

JACOB. Some day I'll come out, I'll—[*Unable to continue, he turns, looks at* HENNIE, *goes to his door and there says with an attempt at humor:*] Bessie, some day you'll talk to me so fresh . . . I'll leave the house for good! [*He exits.*]

BESSIE [*crying*]. You ever in your life seen it? He should dare! He should just dare say in the house another word. Your gall could bust from such a man. [*Bell rings*, MYRON *goes.*] Go to sleep now. It won't hurt.

HENNIE. Yeah?

[MOE *enters, a box in his hand.* MYRON *follows and sits down.*]                   20

MOE [*looks around first—putting box on table*]. Cake. [*About to give* MYRON *the money, he turns instead to* BESSIE.] Six fifty, four bits change . . . come on, hand over half a buck. [*She does so. Of* MYRON.] Who bit him?

BESSIE. We're soon losing our Hennie, Moe.

MOE. Why? What's the matter?

BESSIE. She made her engagement.

MOE. Zat so?

BESSIE. Today it happened . . . he asked her.

MOE. Did he? Who? Who's the corpse?                                                  30

BESSIE. It's a secret.

MOE. In the bag, huh?

HENNIE. Yeah. . .

BESSIE. When a mother gives away an only daughter it's no joke. Wait, when you'll get married you'll know. . . .

MOE [*bitterly*]. Don't make me laugh—when I get married! What I think a women? Take 'em all, cut 'em in little pieces like a herring in Greek salad. A guy in France had the right idea—dropped his wife in a bathtub fulla acid. [*Whistles.*] Sss, down the pipe! Pfft—not even a corset button left!                                                                           40

MYRON. Corsets don't have buttons.

MOE [*to* HENNIE]. What's the great idea? Gone big time, Paradise? Christ, it's suicide! Sure, kids you'll have, gold teeth, get fat, big in the tangerines—

HENNIE. Shut your face!

MOE. Who's it—some dope pullin' down twenty bucks a week? Cut your throat, sweetheart. Save time.

BESSIE. Never mind your two cents, Axelrod.

MOE. I say what I think—that's me!

HENNIE. That's you—a lousy fourflusher who'd steal the glasses off a blind man.

MOE. Get hot!

HENNIE. My God, do I need it—to listen to this mutt shoot his mouth off?

MYRON. Please. . . .

MOE. Now wait a minute, sweetheart, wait a minute. I don't have to take that from you.                                                                    10

BESSIE. Don't yell at her!

HENNIE. For two cents I'd spit in your eye.

MOE [*throwing coin to table*]. Here's two bits.

[HENNIE *looks at him and then starts across the room.*]

BESSIE. Where are you going?

HENNIE [*crying*]. For my beauty nap, Mussolini. Wake me up when it's apple blossom time in Normandy. [*Exits.*]

MOE. Pretty, pretty—a sweet gal, your Hennie. See the look in her eyes?

BESSIE. She don't feel well. . . .

MYRON. Canned goods. . .                                                     20

BESSIE. So don't start with her.

MOE. Like a battleship she's got it. Not like other dames—shove 'em and they lay. Not her. I got a yen for her and I don't mean a Chinese coin.

BESSIE. Listen, Axelrod, in my house you don't talk this way. Either have respect or get out.

MOE. When I think about it. . . maybe I'd marry her myself.

BESSIE [*suddenly aware of* MOE]. You could—What do you mean, Moe?

MOE. You ain't sunburnt—you heard me.

BESSIE. Why don't you, Moe? An old friend of the family like you. It would be a blessing on all of us.                                           30

MOE. You said she's engaged.

BESSIE. But maybe she don't know her own mind. Say, it's—

MOE. I need a wife like a hole in the head. . . . What's to know about women, I know. Even if I asked her. She won't do it! A guy with one leg—it gives her the heebie-jeebies. I know what she's looking for. An arrow-collar guy, a hero, but with a wad of jack. Only the two don't go together. But I got what it takes . . . plenty, and more where it comes from. . . . [*Breaks off, snorts and rubs his knee.*]

[*A pause. In his room* JACOB *puts on Caruso singing the lament from "The Pearl Fishers."*]                                                       40

BESSIE. It's right—she wants a millionaire with a mansion on Riverside Drive. So go fight with City Hall. Cake?

MOE. Cake.

BESSIE. I'll make tea. But one thing—she's got a fine boy with a business brain. Caruso! [*Exits into the front room and stands in the dark, at the window.*]

MOE. No wet smack . . . a fine girl . . . She'll burn that guy out in a month. [MOE *retrieves the quarter and spins it on the table.*]

MYRON. I remember that song. . . beautiful. Nora Bayes sang it at the old Proctor's Twenty-third Street—"When It's Apple Blossom Time in Normandy.". . .

MOE. She wantsa see me crawl—my head on a plate she wants! A snowball in hell's got a better chance. [*Out of sheer fury he spins the quarter in his fingers.*]

MYRON [*as his eyes slowly fill with tears*]. Beautiful . . .

MOE. Match you for a quarter. Match you for any goddam thing you got. [*Spins the coin viciously.*] What the hell kind of house is this it ain't got an orange!! 10

SLOW—CURTAIN

ACT TWO

SCENE I

*One year later, a Sunday afternoon. The front room.* JACOB *is giving his son* MORDECAI (UNCLE MORTY) *a haircut, newspapers spread around the base of the chair.* MOE *is reading a newspaper, leg propped on a chair.* RALPH, *in another chair, is spasmodically reading a paper,* UNCLE MORTY *reads colored jokes. Silence, then* BESSIE *enters.* 20

BESSIE. Dinner's in half an hour, Morty.

MORTY [*still reading jokes*]. I got time.

BESSIE. A duck. Don't get hair on the rug, Pop. [*Goes to window and pulls down shade.*] What's the matter the shade's up to the ceiling?

JACOB [*pulling it up again*]. Since when do I give a haircut in the dark? [*He mimics her tone.*]

BESSIE. When you're finished, pull it down. I like my house to look respectable. Ralphie, bring up two bottles seltzer from Weiss.

RALPH. I'm reading the paper. 30

BESSIE. Uncle Morty takes a little seltzer.

RALPH. I'm expecting a phone call.

BESSIE. Noo, if it comes you'll be back. What's the matter? [*Gives him money from apron pocket.*] Take down the old bottles.

RALPH [*to JACOB*]. Get that call if it comes. Say I'll be right back. [JACOB *nods assent.*]

MORTY [*giving change from vest*]. Get grandpa some cigarettes.

RALPH. Okay. [*Exits.*]

JACOB. What's new in the paper, Moe?

MOE. Still jumping off the high buildings like flies—the big shots who lost all their cocoanuts. Pfft! 40

JACOB. Suicides?

MOE. Plenty can't take it—good in the break, but can't take the whip in the stretch.

MORTY [*without looking up*]. I saw it happen Monday in my building. My hair stood up how they shoveled him together—like a pancake—a bankrupt manufacturer.

MOE. No brains.

MORTY. Enough . . . all over the sidewalk.

JACOB. If someone said five-ten years ago I couldn't make for myself a living, I wouldn't believe—

MORTY. Duck for dinner?

BESSIE. The best Long Island duck.

MORTY. I like goose.

BESSIE. A duck is just like a goose, only better.

MORTY: I like goose.                                                    10

BESSIE. The next time you'll be for Sunday dinner I'll make a goose.

MORTY [*sniffs deeply*]. Smells good. I'm a great boy for smells.

BESSIE. Ain't you ashamed? Once in a blue moon he should come to an only sister's house.

MORTY. Bessie, leave me live.

BESSIE. You should be ashamed!

MORTY. Quack quack!

BESSIE. No, better to lay around Mecca Temple playing cards with the Masons.

MORTY [*with good nature*]. Bessie, don't you see Pop's giving me a    20
haircut?

BESSIE. You don't need no haircut. Look, two hairs he took off.

MORTY. Pop likes to give me a haircut. If I said no he don't forget for a year, do you, Pop? An old man's like that.

JACOB. I still do an A-1 job.

MORTY [*winking*]. Pop cuts hair to fit the face, don't you, Pop?

JACOB. For sure, Morty. To each face a different haircut. Custom built, no ready made. A round face needs special—

BESSIE [*cutting him short*]. A graduate from the B.M.T. [*Going.*] Don't forget the shade. [*The phone rings. She beats* JACOB *to it.*] Hello?    30
Who is it, please? . . . Who is it, please? . . . Miss Hirsch? No, he ain't here. . . . No, I couldn't say when. [*Hangs up sharply.*]

JACOB. For Ralph?

BESSIE. A wrong number.

[JACOB *looks at her and goes back to his job.*]

JACOB. Excuse me!

BESSIE [*to* MORTY]. Ralphie took another cut down the place yesterday.

MORTY. Business is bad. I saw his boss Harry Glicksman Thursday. I bought some velvets . . . they're coming in again.                      40

BESSIE. Do something for Ralphie down there.

MORTY. What can I do? I mentioned it to Glicksman. He told me they squeezed out half the people. . . .

[MYRON *enters dressed in apron.*]

BESSIE. What's gonna be the end? Myron's working only three days a week now.

MYRON. It's conditions.

BESSIE. Hennie's married with a baby . . . money just don't come in. I never saw conditions should be so bad.

MORTY. Times'll change.

MOE. The only thing'll change is my underwear.

MORTY. These last few years I got my share of gray hairs. [*Still reading jokes without having looked up once.*] Ha, ha, ha—Popeye the sailor ate spinach and knocked out four bums.

MYRON. I'll tell you the way I see it. The country needs a great man now—a regular Teddy Roosevelt.

MOE. What this country needs is a good five-cent earthquake.                    10

JACOB. So long labor lives it should increase private gain—

BESSIE [*to* JACOB]. Listen, Poppa, go talk on the street corner. The government'll give you free board the rest of your life.

MORTY. I'm surprised. Don't I send a five-dollar check for Pop every week?

BESSIE. You could afford a couple more and not miss it.

MORTY. Tell me jokes. Business is so rotten I could just as soon lay all day in the Turkish bath.

MYRON. Why'd I come in here? [*Puzzled, he exits.*]

MORTY [*to* MOE]. I hear the bootleggers still do business, Moe.          20

MOE. Wake up! I kissed bootlegging bye-bye two years back.

MORTY. For a fact? What kind of racket is it now?

MOE. If I told you, you'd know something.

[HENNIE *comes from bedroom.*]

HENNIE. Where's Sam?

BESSIE. Sam? In the kitchen.

HENNIE [*calls*]. Sam. Come take the diaper.

MORTY. How's the Mickey Louse? Ha, ha, ha. . .

HENNIE. Sleeping.

MORTY. Ah, that's life to a baby. He sleeps—gets it in the mouth—          30
sleeps some more. To raise a family nowadays you must be a damn fool.

BESSIE. Never mind, never mind, a woman who don't raise a family—
a girl—should jump overboard. What's she good for? [*To* MOE—*to change the subject.*] Your leg bothers you bad?

MOE. It's okay, sweetheart.

BESSIE [*to* MORTY]. It hurts him every time it's cold out. He's got four legs in the closet.

MORTY. Four wooden legs?

MOE. Three.

MORTY. What's the big idea?                                                        40

MOE. Why not? Uncle Sam gives them out free.

MORTY. Say, maybe if Uncle Sam gave out less legs we could balance the budget.

JACOB. Or not have a war so they wouldn't have to give out legs.

MORTY. Shame on you, Pop. Everybody knows war is necessary.

MOE. Don't make me laugh. Ask me—the first time you pick up a dead one in the trench—then you learn war ain't so damn necessary.

MORTY. Say, you should kick. The rest of your life Uncle Sam pays you ninety a month. Look, not a worry in the world.

MOE. Don't make me laugh. Uncle Sam can take his *seventy* bucks and—[*Finishes with a gesture.*] Nothing good hurts. [*He rubs his stump.*]

HENNIE. Use a crutch, Axelrod. Give the stump a rest.

MOE. Mind your business, Feinschreiber.

BESSIE. It's a sensible idea.

MOE. Who asked you?

BESSIE. Look he's ashamed.                                              10

MOE. So's your Aunt Fanny.

BESSIE [*naively*]. Who's got an Aunt Fanny? [*She cleans a rubber plant's leaves with her apron.*]

MORTY. It's a joke!

MOE. I don't want my paper creased before I read it. I want it fresh. Fifty times I said that.

BESSIE. Don't get so excited for a five-cent paper—our star boarder.

MOE. And I don't want no one using my razor either. Get it straight. I'm not buying ten blades a week for the Berger family. [*Furious, he limps out.*]                                                             20

BESSIE. Maybe I'm using his razor too.

HENNIE. Proud!

BESSIE. You need luck with plants. I didn't clean off the leaves in a month.

MORTY. You keep the house like a pin and I like your cooking. Any time Myron fires you, come to me, Bessie. I'll let the butler go and you'll be my housekeeper. I don't like Japs so much—sneaky.

BESSIE. Say, you can't tell. Maybe any day I'm coming to stay.

[HENNIE *exits.*]

JACOB. Finished.                                                       30

MORTY. How much, Ed. Pinaud? [*Disengages self from chair.*]

JACOB. Five cents.

MORTY. Still five cents for a haircut to fit the face?

JACOB. Prices don't change by me. [*Takes a dollar.*] I can't change—

MORTY. Keep it. Buy yourself a Packard. Ha, ha, ha.

JACOB [*taking large envelope from pocket*]. Please, you'll keep this for me. Put it away.

MORTY. What is it?

JACOB. My insurance policy. I don't like it should lay around where something could happen.                                                40

MORTY. What could happen?

JACOB. Who knows, robbers, fire. . . they took next door. Fifty dollars from O'Reilly.

MORTY. Say, lucky a Berger didn't lose it.

JACOB. Put it downtown in the safe. Bessie don't have to know.

MORTY. It's made out to Bessie?

JACOB. No, to Ralph.

MORTY. To Ralph?

JACOB. He don't know. Some day he'll get three thousand.

MORTY. You got good years ahead.

JACOB. Behind.

[RALPH *enters.*]

RALPH. Cigarettes. Did a call come?

JACOB. A few minutes. She don't let me answer it.

RALPH. Did Mom say I was coming back?

JACOB. No.                                                                    10

[MORTY *is back at new jokes.*]

RALPH. She starting that stuff again? [BESSIE *enters.*] A call come for me?

BESSIE [*waters pot from milk bottle*]. A wrong number.

JACOB. Don't say a lie, Bessie.

RALPH. Blanche said she'd call me at two—was it her?

BESSIE. I said a wrong number.

RALPH. Please, Mom, if it was her tell me.

BESSIE. You call me a liar next. You got no shame—to start a scene in front of Uncle Morty. Once in a blue moon he comes—             20

RALPH. What's the shame? If my girl calls I wanna know it.

BESSIE. You made enough mish mosh with her until now.

MORTY. I'm surprised, Bessie. For the love of Mike tell him yes or no.

BESSIE. I didn't tell him? No!

MORTY [*to* RALPH]. No!

[RALPH *goes to a window and looks out.*]

BESSIE. Morty, I didn't say before—he runs around steady with a girl.

MORTY. Terrible. Should he run around with a foxie-woxie?

BESSIE. A girl with no parents.

MORTY. An orphan?                                                             30

BESSIE. I could die from shame. A year already he runs around with her. He brought her once for supper. Believe me, she didn't come again, no!

RALPH. Don't think I didn't ask her.

BESSIE. You hear? You raise them and what's in the end for all your trouble?

JACOB. When you'll lay in a grave, no more trouble. [*Exits.*]

MORTY. Quack quack!

BESSIE. A girl like that he wants to marry. A skinny consumptive-looking . . . six months already she's not working—taking charity from      40
an aunt. You should see her. In a year she's dead on his hands.

RALPH. You'd cut her throat if you could.

BESSIE. That's right! Before she'd ruin a nice boy's life I would first go to prison. Miss Nobody should step in the picture and I'll stand by with my mouth shut.

RALPH. Miss Nobody! Who am I? Al Jolson?

BESSIE. Fix your tie!

RALPH. I'll take care of my own life.

BESSIE. You'll take care? Excuse my expression, you can't even wipe your nose yet! He'll take care!

MORTY [to BESSIE]. I'm surprised. Don't worry so much, Bessie. When it's time to settle down he won't marry a poor girl, will you? In the long run common sense is thicker than love. I'm a great boy for live and let live.

BESSIE. Sure, it's easy to say. In the meantime he eats out my heart. You know I'm not strong.                                                                    10

MORTY. I know . . . a pussy cat . . . ha, ha, ha.

BESSIE. You got money and money talks. But without the dollar who sleeps at night?

RALPH. I been working for years, bringing in money here—putting it in your hand like a kid. All right, I can't get my teeth fixed. All right, that a new suit's like trying to buy the Chrysler Building. You never in your life bought me a pair of skates even—things I died for when I was a kid. I don't care about that stuff, see. Only just remember I pay some of the bills around here, just a few. . . and if my girl calls me on the phone I'll talk to her any time I please. [He exits. HENNIE applauds.]          20

BESSIE. Don't be so smart, Miss America! [To MORTY.] He didn't have skates! But when he got sick, a twelve-year-old boy, who called a big specialist for the last $25 in the house? Skates!

JACOB [just in. Adjusts window shade]. It looks like snow today.

MORTY. It's about time—winter.

BESSIE. Poppa here could talk like Samuel Webster, too, but it's just talk. He should try to buy a two-cent pickle in the Burland Market without money.

MORTY. I'm getting an appetite.

BESSIE. Right away we'll eat. I made chopped liver for you.          30

MORTY. My specialty!

BESSIE. Ralph should only be a success like you, Morty. I should only live to see the day when he rides up to the door in a big car with a chauffeur and a radio. I could die happy, believe me.

MORTY. Success she says. She should see how we spend thousands of dollars making up a winter line and winter don't come—summer in January. Can you beat it?

JACOB. Don't live, just make success.

MORTY. Chopped liver—ha!

JACOB. Ha! [Exits.]          40

MORTY. When they start arguing, I don't hear. Suddenly I'm deaf. I'm a great boy for the practical side. [He looks over to HENNIE who sits rubbing her hands with lotion.]

HENNIE. Hands like a raw potato.

MORTY. What's the matter? You don't look so well. . . no pep.

HENNIE. I'm swell.

MORTY. You used to be such a pretty girl.

HENNIE. Maybe I got the blues. You can't tell.

MORTY. You could stand a new dress.

HENNIE. That's not all I could stand.

MORTY. Come down to the place tomorrow and pick out a couple from the "eleven-eighty" line. Only don't sing me the blues.

HENNIE. Thanks. I need some new clothes.

MORTY. I got two thousand pieces of merchandise waiting in the stock room for winter.

HENNIE. I never had anything from life. Sam don't help.                    10

MORTY. He's crazy about the kid.

HENNIE. Crazy is right. Twenty-one a week he brings in—a nigger don't have it so hard. I wore my fingers off on an Underwood for six years. For what? Now I wash baby diapers. Sure, I'm crazy about the kid too. But half the night the kid's up. Try to sleep. You don't know how it is, Uncle Morty.

MORTY. No, I don't know. I was born yesterday. Ha, ha, ha. Some day I'll leave you a little nest egg. You like eggs? Ha?

HENNIE. When? When I'm dead and buried?

MORTY. No, when *I'm* dead and buried. Ha, ha, ha.                         20

HENNIE. You should know what I'm thinking.

MORTY. Ha, ha, ha, I know.

[MYRON *enters.*]

MYRON. I never take a drink. I'm just surprised at myself, I—

MORTY. I got a pain. Maybe I'm hungry.

MYRON. Come inside, Morty. Bessie's got some schnapps.

MORTY. I'll take a drink. Yesterday I missed the Turkish bath.

MYRON. I get so bitter when I take a drink, it just surprises me.

MORTY. Look how fat. Say, you live once. . . . Quack, quack. [*Both exit.* MOE *stands silently in the doorway.*]                                30

SAM [*entering*]. I'll make Leon's bottle now!

HENNIE. No, let him sleep, Sam. Take away the diaper.

[*He does. Exits.*]

MOE [*advancing into the room*]. That your husband?

HENNIE. Don't you know?

MOE. Maybe he's a nurse you hired for the kid—it looks it—how he tends it. A guy comes howling to your old lady every time you look cock-eyed. Does he sleep with you?

HENNIE. Don't be so wise!

MOE [*indicating newspaper*]. Here's a dame strangled her hubby with    40
wire. Claimed she didn't like him. Why don't you brain Sam with an axe some night?

HENNIE. Why don't you lay an egg, Axelrod?

MOE. I laid a few in my day, Feinschreiber. Hardboiled ones too.

HENNIE. Yeah?

MOE. Yeah. You wanna know what I see when I look in your eyes?

HENNIE. No.

MOE. Ted Lewis playing the clarinet—some of those high crazy notes! Christ, you coulda had a guy with some guts instead of a cluck who stands around boilin' baby nipples.

HENNIE. Meaning you?

MOE. Meaning me, sweetheart.

HENNIE. Think you're pretty good.

MOE. You'd know if I slept with you again.

HENNIE. I'll smack your face in a minute.

MOE. You do and I'll break your arm. [*Holds up paper.*] Take a look. 10 [*Reads.*] "Ten-day luxury cruise to Havana." That's the stuff you coulda had. Put up at ritzy hotels, frenchie soap, champagne. Now you're tied down to "Snake-Eye" here. What for? What's it get you?. . . a two by four flat on 108th Street. . . a pain in the bustle it gets you.

HENNIE. What's it to you?

MOE. I know you from the old days. How you like to spend it! What I mean! Lizard-skin shoes, perfume behind the ears. . . . You're in a mess, Paradise! Paradise—that's a hot one—yah, crazy to eat a knish at your own wedding.

HENNIE. I get it—you're jealous. You can't get me.

MOE. Don't make me laugh. 20

HENNIE. Kid Jailbird's been trying to make me for years. You'd give your other leg. I'm hooked? Maybe, but you're in the same boat. Only it's worse for you. I don't give a damn no more, but you gotta yen makes you—

MOE. Don't make me laugh.

HENNIE. Compared to you I'm sittin' on top of the world.

MOE. You're losing your looks. A dame don't stay young forever.

HENNIE. Your a liar. I'm only twenty-four.

MOE. When you comin' home to stay?

HENNIE. Wouldn't you like to know? 30

MOE. I'll get you again.

HENNIE. Think so?

MOE. Sure, whatever goes up comes down. You're easy—you remember —two for a nickel—a pushover! [*Suddenly she slaps him. They both seemed stunned.*] What's the idea?

HENNIE. Go on. . . break my arm.

MOE [*as if saying "I love you"*] . Listen, lousy.

HENNIE. Go on, do something!

MOE. Listen—

HENNIE. You're so damn tough! 40

MOE. You like me. [*He takes her.*]

HENNIE. Take your hand off! [*Pushes him away.*] Come around when it's a flood again and they put you in the ark with the animals. Not even then—if you was the last man!

MOE. Baby, if you had a dog I'd love the dog.

HENNIE. Gorilla! [*Exits.* RALPH *enters.*]

RALPH. Were you here before?

MOE [*sits*]. What?

RALPH. When the call came for me?

MOE. What?

RALPH. The call came.

[JACOB *enters.*]

MOE [*rubbing his leg*]. No.

JACOB. Don't worry, Ralphie, she'll call back.

RALPH. Maybe not. I think somethin's the matter.

JACOB. What?                                                          10

RALPH. I don't know. I took her home from the movie last night. She asked me what I'd think if she went away.

JACOB. Don't worry, she'll call again.

RALPH. Maybe not, if Mom insulted her. She gets it on both ends, the poor kid. Lived in an orphan asylum most of her life. They shove her around like an empty freight train.

JACOB. After dinner go see her.

RALPH. Twice they kicked her down the stairs.

JACOB. Life should have some dignity.

RALPH. Every time I go near the place I get heart failure. The uncle    20
drives a bus. You oughta see him—like Babe Ruth.

MOE. Use your brains. Stop acting like a kid who still wets the bed. Hire a room somewhere—a club room for two members.

RALPH. Not that kind of proposition, Moe.

MOE. Don't be a bush leaguer all your life.

RALPH. Cut it out!

MOE. [*on a sudden upsurge of emotion*]. Ever sleep with one? Look at 'im blush.

RALPH. You don't know her.

MOE. I seen her—the kind no one sees undressed till the undertaker   30
works on her.

RALPH. Why give me the needles all the time? What'd I ever do to you?

MOE. Not a thing. You're a nice kid. But grow up! In life there's two kinds—the men that's sure of themselves and the ones who ain't! It's time you quit being a selling-plater and got in the first class.

JACOB. And you, Axelrod?

MOE [*to* JACOB]. Scratch your whiskers! [*To* RALPH.] Get independent. Get what-it-takes and be yourself. Do what you like.

RALPH. Got a suggestion?

[MORTY *enters, eating.*]                                              40

MOE. Sure, pick out a racket. Shake down the cocoanuts. See what that does.

MORTY. We know what it does—puts a pudding on your nose! Sing Sing! Easy money's against the law. Against the law don't win. A racket is illegitimate, no?

MOE. It's all a racket—from horse racing down. Marriage, politics, big business—everybody plays cops and robbers. You, you're a racketeer yourself.

MORTY. Who? Me? Personally I manufacture dresses.

MOE. Horse feathers!

MORTY [ *seriously*] . Don't make such remarks to me without proof. I'm a great one for proof. That's why I made a success in business. Proof— put up or shut up, like a game of cards. I heard this remark before—a rich man's a crook who steals from the poor. Personally, I don't like it. It's a big lie!

MOE. If you don't like it, buy yourself a fife and drum—and go fight     10
your own war.

MORTY. Sweatshop talk. Every Jew and Wop in the shop eats my bread and behind my back says, "a sonofabitch." I started from a poor boy who worked on an ice wagon for two dollars a week. Pop's right here—he'll tell you. I made it honest. In the whole industry nobody's got a better name.

JACOB. It's an exception, such success.

MORTY. Ralph can't do the same thing?

JACOB. No, Morty, I don't think. In a house like this he don't realize even the possibilities of life. Economics comes down like a ton of coal     20
on the head.

MOE. Red rover, red rover, let Jacob come over!

JACOB. In my day the propaganda was for God. Now it's for success. A boy don't turn around without having shoved in him he should make success.

MORTY. Pop, you're a comedian, a regular Charlie Chaplin.

JACOB. He dreams all night of fortunes. Why not? Don't it say in the movies he should have a personal steamship, pyjamas for fifty dollars a pair and a toilet like a monument? But in the morning he wakes up and for ten dollars he can't fix the teeth. And millions more worse off in the     30
mills of the South—starvation wages. The blood from the worker's heart. [MORTY *laughs loud and long.*] Laugh, laugh. . . tomorrow not.

MORTY. A real, a real Boob McNutt you're getting to be.

JACOB. Laugh, my son. . . .

MORTY. Here is the North, Pop.

JACOB. North, south, it's one country.

MORTY. The country's all right. A duck quacks in every pot!

JACOB. You never heard how they shoot down men and women which ask a better wage? Kentucky 1932?

MORTY. That's a pile of chopped liver, Pop.                              40

[BESSIE *and others enter.*]

JACOB. Pittsburgh, Passaic, Illinois—slavery—it begins where success begins in a competitive system.

[MORTY *howls with delight.*] .

MORTY. Oh, Pop, what are you bothering? Why? Tell me why? Ha ha ha. I bought you a phonograph. . . stick to Caruso.

BESSIE. He's starting up again.

MORTY. Don't bother with Kentucky. It's full of moonshiners.

JACOB. Sure, sure—

MORTY. You don't know practical affairs. Stay home and cut hair to fit the face.

JACOB. It says in the Bible how the Red Sea opened and the Egyptians went in and the sea rolled over them. [*Quotes two lines of Hebrew.*] In this boy's life a Red Sea will happen again. I see it!

MORTY. I'm getting sore, Pop, with all this sweatshop talk.

BESSIE. He don't stop a minute. The whole day, like a phonograph.    10

MORTY. I'm surprised. Without a rich man you don't have a roof over your head. You don't know it?

MYRON. Now you can't bite the hand that feeds you.

RALPH. Let him alone—he's right!

BESSIE. Another county heard from.

RALPH. It's truth. It's—

MORTY. Keep quiet, snotnose!

JACOB. For sure, charity, a bone for an old dog. But in Russia an old man don't take charity so his eyes turn black in his head. In Russia they got Marx.    20

MORTY [*scoffingly*]. Who's Marx?

MOE. An outfielder for the Yanks.

[MORTY *howls with delight.*]

MORTY. Ha ha ha, it's better than the jokes. I'm telling you. This is Uncle Sam's country. Put it in your pipe and smoke it.

BESSIE. Russia, he says! Read the papers.

SAM. Here is opportunity.

MYRON. People can't believe in God in Russia. The papers tell the truth, they do.

JACOB . So you believe in God. . . you got something for it? You! You    30
worked for all the capitalists. You harvested the fruit from your labor? You got God! But the past comforts you? The present smiles on you, yes? It promises you the future something? Did you found a piece of earth where you could live like a human being and die with the sun on your face? Tell me, yes, tell me. I would like to know myself. But on these questions, on this theme—the struggle for existence—you can't make an answer. The answer I see in your face. . . the answer is your mouth can't talk. In this dark corner you sit and you die. But abolish private property!

BESSIE [*settling the issue*]. Noo, go fight City Hall!

MORTY. He's drunk!    40

JACOB. I'm studying from books a whole lifetime.

MORTY. That's what it is—he's drunk. What the hell does all that mean?

JACOB. If you don't know, why should I tell you.

MORTY [*triumphant at last*]. You see? Hear him? Like all those nuts, don't know what they're saying.

JACOB . I know, I know.

MORTY. Like Boob McNutt you know! Don't go in the park, Pop—the squirrels'll get you. Ha, ha, ha. . .

BESSIE. Save your appetite, Morty. [*To* MYRON.] Don't drop the duck.

MYRON. We're ready to eat, Momma.

MORTY [*to* JACOB]. Shame on you. It's your second childhood.

[*Now they file out.* MYRON *first with the duck, the others behind him.*]

BESSIE. Come eat. We had enough for one day. [*Exits.*]

MORTY. Ha, ha, ha. Quack, quack. [*Exits.*]

[JACOB *sits there trembling and deeply humiliated.* MOE *approaches him and thumbs the old man's nose in the direction of the dining room.*]    10

MOE. Give 'em five. [*Takes his hand away.*] They got you pasted on the wall like a picture, Jake. [*He limps out to seat himself at the table in the next room.*]

JACOB. Go eat, boychick. [RALPH *comes to him.*] He gives me eat, so I'll climb in a needle. One time I saw an old horse in summer. . . he wore a straw hat. . . the ears stuck out on top. An old horse for hire. Give me back my young days. . . give me fresh blood. . . arms. . . give me—

[*The telephone rings. Quickly* RALPH *goes to it.* JACOB *pulls the cirtains and stands there, a sentry on guard.*]

RALPH. Hello? . . . Yeah, I went to the store and came right back, right    20
after you called. [*Looks at* JACOB.]

JACOB. Speak, speak. Don't be afraid they'll hear.

RALPH. I'm sorry if Mom said something. You know how excitable Mom is. . . . Sure! What?. . . Sure, I'm listening. . . . Put on the radio, Jake. [JACOB *does so. Music comes in and up, a tango, grating with an insistent nostalgic pulse. Under the cover of the music* RALPH *speaks more freely.*] Yes. . . yes. . . What's the matter? Why're you crying? What happened? [*To* JACOB.] She's putting her uncle on. Yes? . . . Listen, Mr. Hirsch, what're you trying to do? What's the big idea? Honest to God. I'm in no mood for joking! Lemme talk to her! Gimme Blanche! [*Waits.*]    30
Blanche? What's this? Is this a joke? Is that true? I'm coming right down! I know, but—You wanna do that?. . . I know, but—I'm coming down. . . tonight! Nine o'clock. . . sure. . . sure. . . sure. . . [*Hangs up.*]

JACOB. What happened?

MORTY [*enters*]. Listen, Pop. I'm surprised you didn't—[*He howls, shakes his head in mock despair, exits.*]

JACOB. Boychick, what?

RALPH. I don't get it straight. [*To* JACOB.] She's leaving. . . .

JACOB. Where?

RALPH. Out West— To Cleveland.    40

JACOB. Cleveland?

RALPH. . . . In a week or two. Can you picture it? It's a put-up job. But they can't get away with that.

JACOB. We'll find something.

RALPH. Sure, the angels of heaven'll come down on her uncle's cab and whisper in his ear.

JACOB. Come eat. . . . We'll find something.

RALPH. I'm meeting her tonight, but I know—

[BESSIE *throws open the curtain between the two rooms and enters.*]

BESSIE. Maybe we'll serve for you a special blue plate supper in the garden?

JACOB. All right, all right.

[BESSIE *goes over to the window, levels the shade and on her way out, clicks off the radio.*]

MORTY [*within*]. Leave the music, Bessie.

[ *She clicks it on again, looks at them, exits.*]                         10

RALPH. I know. . . .

JACOB. Don't cry, boychick. [*Goes over to* RALPH.] Why should you make like this? Tell me why you should cry, just tell me. . . . [JACOB *takes* RALPH *in his arms and both, trying to keep back the tears, trying fearfully not to be heard by the others in the dining room, begin crying.*] You mustn't cry. . . .

[*The tango twists on. Inside the clatter of dishes and the clash of cutlery sound.* MORTY *begins to howl with laughter.*]


CURTAIN

SCENE II

*That night. The dark dining room.*

AT RISE JACOB *is heard in his lighted room, reading from a sheet, declaiming aloud as if to an audience.*


JACOB. They are there to remind us of the horrors—under those crosses lie hundreds of thousands of workers and farmers who murdered each other in uniform for the greater glory of capitalism. [*Comes out of his room.*] The new imperialist war will send millions to their death, will     30 bring prosperity to the pockets of the capitalist—aie, Morty—and will bring only greater hunger and misery to the masses of workers and farmers. The memories of the last world slaughter are still vivid in our minds. [*Hearing a noise he quickly retreats to his room.* RALPH *comes in from the street. He sits with hat and coat on.* JACOB *tentatively opens the door and asks:*] Ralphie?

RALPH. It's getting pretty cold out.

[JACOB *enters room fully, cleaning hair clippers*]. We should have steam till twelve instead of ten. Go complain to the Board of Health.

RALPH. It might snow.                                                      40

JACOB. It don't hurt . . . extra work for men.

RALPH. When I was a kid I laid awake at nights and heard the sounds of trains . . . far-away lonesome sounds . . . boats going up and down the river. I used to think of all kinds of things I wanted to do. What was it, Jake? Just a bunch of noise in my head?

JACOB [*waiting for news of the girl*]. You wanted to make for yourself a certain kind of world.

RALPH. I guess I didn't. I'm feeling pretty, pretty low.

JACOB. You're a young boy and for you life is all in front like a big mountain. You got feet to climb.

RALPH. I don't know how.

JACOB . So you'll find out. Never a young man had such opportunity like today. He could make history.

RALPH. Ten p.m. and all is well. Where's everybody?

JACOB. They went.

RALPH. Uncle Morty too? 10

JACOB. Hennie and Sam he drove down.

RALPH. I saw her.

JACOB [*alert and eager*]. Yes, yes, tell me.

RALPH. I waited in Mount Morris Park till she came out. So cold I did a buck'n wing to keep warm. She's scared to death.

JACOB. They made her?

RALPH. Sure. She wants to go. They keep yelling at her — they want her to marry a millionaire, too.

JACOB. You told her you love her?

RALPH. Sure. "Marry me," I said. "Marry me tomorrow." On sixteen 20 bucks a week. On top of that I had to admit Mom'd have Uncle Morty get me fired in a second. . . . Two can starve as cheap as one!

JACOB. So what happened?

RALPH. I made her promise to meet me tomorrow.

JACOB. Now she'll go in the West?

RALPH. I'd fight the whole goddam world with her, but not her. No guts. The hell with her. If she wantsa go — all right — I'll get along.

JACOB. For sure, there's more important things than girls. . . .

RALPH. You said a mouthful . . . and maybe I don't see it. She'll see what I can do. No one stops me when I get going. . . . [*Near to tears, he* 30 *has to stop.* JACOB *examines his clippers very closely.*]

JACOB. Electric clippers never do a job like by hand.

RALPH. Why won't Mom let us live here?

JACOB. Why? Why? Because in a society like this today people don't love. Hate!

RALPH. Gee, I'm no bum who hangs around pool parlors. I got the stuff to go ahead. I don't know what to do.

JACOB. Look on me and learn what to do, boychick. Here sits an old man polishing tools. You think maybe I'll use them again! Look on this failure and see for seventy years he talked, with good ideas, but only in 40 the head. It's enough for me now I should see your happiness. This is why I tell you — DO! Do what is in your heart and you carry in yourself a revolution. But you should act. Not like me. A man who had golden opportunities but drank instead a glass tea. No . . . [*A pause of silence.*]

RALPH [*listening*]. Hear it? The Boston air mail plane. Ten minutes late. I get a kick the way it cuts across the Bronx every night.

[*The bell rings:* SAM, *excited, disheveled, enters.*]

JACOB. You came back so soon?

SAM. Where's Mom?

JACOB. Mom? Look on the chandelier.

SAM. Nobody's home?

JACOB. Sit down. Right away they're coming. You went in the street without a tie?

SAM. Maybe it's a crime.

JACOB. Excuse me.

RALPH. You had a fight with Hennie again?                                    10

SAM. She'll fight once. . . some day. . . . [*Lapses into silence.*]

JACOB. In my day the daughter came home. Now comes the son-in-law.

SAM. Once too often she'll fight with me, Hennie. I mean it. I mean it like anything. I'm a person with a bad heart. I sit quiet, but inside I got a —

RALPH. What happened?

SAM. I'll talk to Mom. I'll see Mom.

JACOB. Take an apple.

SAM. Please . . . he tells me apples.

RALPH. Why hop around like a billiard ball?

SAM. Even in a joke she should dare say it.                                    20

JACOB. My grandchild said something?

SAM. To my father in the old country they did a joke . . . I'll tell you: One day in Odessa he talked to another Jew on the street. They didn't like it, they jumped on him like a wild wolf.

RALPH. Who?

SAM. Cossacks. They cut off his beard. A Jew without a beard! He came home — I remember like yesterday how he came home and went in bed for two days. He put like this the cover on his face. No one should see. The third morning he died.

RALPH. From what?                                    30

SAM. From a broken heart . . . Some people are like this. Me too. I could die like this from shame.

JACOB. Hennie told you something?

SAM. Straight out she said it — like a lightning from the sky. The baby ain't mine. She said it.

RALPH. Don't be a dope.

SAM. For sure, a joke.

RALPH. She's kidding you.

SAM. She should kid a policeman, not Sam Feinschreiber. Please . . . you don't know her like me. I wake up in the nighttime and she sits    40 watching me like I don't know what. I make a nice living from the store. But it's no use — she looks for a star in the sky. I'm afraid like anything. You could go crazy from less even. What I shall do I'll ask Mom.

JACOB. "Go home and sleep," she'll say. "It's a bad dream."

SAM. It don't satisfy me more, such remarks, when Hennie could kill in the bed. [JACOB *laughs.*] Don't laugh. I'm so nervous — look, two times I weighed myself on the subway station. [*Throws small cards to table.*]

JACOB [*examining one*]. One hundred and thirty-eight—also a fortune. [*Turns it and reads.*] "You are inclined to deep thinking, and have a high admiration for intellectual excellence and inclined to be very exclusive in the selection of friends." Correct! I think maybe you got mixed up in the wrong family, Sam.

[MYRON *and* BESSIE *now enter.*]

BESSIE. Look, a guest! What's the matter? Something wrong with the baby? [*Waits.*]

SAM. No.

BESSIE. Noo?

SAM [*in a burst*]. I wash my hands from everything.

BESSIE. Take off your coat and hat. Have a seat. Excitement don't help. Myron, make tea. You'll have a glass tea. We'll talk like civilized people [MYRON *goes.*] What is it, Ralph, you're all dressed up for a party? [*He looks at her silently and exits. To* SAM.] We saw a very good movie, with Wallace Beery. He acts like life, very good.

MYRON [*within*]. Polly Moran too.

BESSIE. Polly Moran too—a woman with a nose from here to Hunts Point, but a fine player. Poppa, take away the tools and the books.

JACOB. All right. [*Exits to his room.*]

BESSIE. Noo, Sam, why do you look like a funeral?

SAM. I can't stand it. . . .

BESSIE. Wait. [*Yells.*] You took up Tootsie on the roof.

JACOB [*within*]. In a minute.

BESSIE. What can't you stand?

SAM. She said I'm a second fiddle in my own house.

BESSIE. Who?

SAM. Hennie. In the second place, it ain't my baby, she said.

BESSIE. What? What are you talking?

[MYRON *enters with dishes.*]

SAM. From her own mouth. It went like a knife in my heart.

BESSIE. Sam, what're you saying?

SAM. Please, I'm making a story? I fell in the chair like a dead.

BESSIE. Such a story you believe?

SAM. I don't know.

BESSIE. How you don't know?

SAM. She told me even the man.

BESSIE. Impossible!

SAM. I can't believe myself. But she said it. I'm a second fiddle, she said. She made such a yell everybody heard for ten miles.

BESSIE. Such a thing Hennie should say—impossible!

SAM. What should I do? With my bad heart such a remark kills.

MYRON. Hennie don't feel well' Sam. You see, she—

BESSIE. What then?—a sick girl. Believe me, a mother knows. Nerves.

Our Hennie's got a bad temper. You'll let her she says anything. She takes after me—nervous. [*To* MYRON.] You ever heard such a remark in all your life? She should make such a statement! Bughouse.

MYRON. The little one's been sick all these months. Hennie needs a rest. No doubt.

BESSIE. Sam don't think she means it—

MYRON. Oh, I know he don't, of course—

BESSIE. I'll say the truth, Sam. We didn't half the time understand her ourselves. A girl with her own mind. When she makes it up, wild horses wouldn't change her.                                                10

SAM. She don't love me.

BESSIE. This is sensible, Sam?

SAM. Not for a nickel.

BESSIE. What do you think? She married you for your money? For your looks? You ain't no John Barrymore, Sam. No, she liked you.

SAM. Please, not for a nickel.

[JACOB *stands in the doorway.*]

BESSIE. We stood right here the first time she said it. "Sam Fein-schreiber's a nice boy," she said it, "a boy he's got good common sense, with a business head." Right here she said it, in this room. You sent her   20
two boxes of candy together, you remember?

MYRON. Loft's candy.

BESSIE. This is when she said it. What do you think?

MYRON. You were just the only boy she cared for.

BESSIE. So she married you. Such a world . . . plenty of boy friends she had, believe me!

JACOB. A popular girl . . .

MYRON. Y-e-s.

BESSIE. I'll say it plain out—Moe Axelrod offered her plenty—a servant, a house . . . she don't have to pick up a hand.                                30

MYRON. Oh, Moe? Just wild about her . . .

SAM. Moe Axelrod? He wanted to—

BESSIE. But she didn't care. A girl like Hennie you don't buy. I should never live to see another day if I'm telling a lie.

SAM. She was kidding me.

BESSIE. What then? You shouldn't be foolish.

SAM. The baby looks like my family. He's got Feinschreiber eyes.

BESSIE. A blind man could see it.

JACOB. Sure . . . sure. . . .

SAM. The baby looks like me. Yes . . .                                          40

BESSIE. You could believe me.

JACOB. Any day . . .

SAM. But she tells me the man. She made up his name too?

BESSIE. Sam, Sam, look in the phone book—a million names.

MYRON. Tom, Dick and Harry.

[JACOB *laughs quietly, soberly.*]

BESSIE. Don't stand around, Poppa. Take Tootsie on the roof. And you don't let her go under the water tank.

JACOB. Schmah Yisroeal. Behold! [*Quietly laughing he goes back into his room, closing the door behind him.*]

SAM. I won't stand he should make insults. A man eats out his—

BESSIE. No, no, he's an old man—a second childhood. Myron, bring in the tea. Open a jar of raspberry jelly.

[MYRON *exits.*]

SAM. Mom, you think—?

BESSIE. I'll talk to Hennie. It's all right.　　　　　　　　　　　　10

SAM. Tomorrow, I'll take her by the doctor.

[RALPH *enters.*]

BESSIE. Stay for a little tea.

SAM. No, I'll go home. I'm tired. Already I caught a cold in such weather. [*Blows his nose.*]

MYRON[ *entering with stuffs*] . Going home?

SAM. I'll go in bed. I caught a cold.

MYRON. Teddy Roosevelt used to say, "When you have a problem, sleep on it."

BESSIE. My Sam is no problem.　　　　　　　　　　　　20

MYRON. I don't mean . . . I mean he said—

BESSIE. Call me tomorrow, Sam.

SAM. I'll phone supper time. Sometime I think there's something funny about me.

[MYRON *sees him out. In the following pause Caruso is heard singing within.*]

BESSIE. A bargain! Second fiddle. By me he don't even play in the orchestra—a man like a mouse. Maybe she'll lay down and die 'cause he makes a living?

RALPH. Can I talk to you about something?　　　　　　　　　　　　30

BESSIE. What's the matter—I'm biting you?

RALPH. It's something about Blanche.

BESSIE. Don't tell me.

RALPH. Listen now—

BESSIE. I don't wanna know.

RALPH. She's got no place to go.

BESSIE. I don't want to know.

RALPH. Mom, I love this girl. . . .

BESSIE. So go knock your head against the wall.

RALPH. I want her to come here. Listen, Mom, I want you to let her 40 live here for a while.

BESSIE. You got funny ideas, my son.

RALPH. I'm as good as anyone else. Don't I have some rights in the world? Listen, Mom, if I don't do something, she's going away. Why don't you do it? Why don't you let her stay here for a few weeks? Things'll pick up. Then we can—

BESSIE. Sure, sure. I'll keep her fresh on ice for a wedding day. That's what you want?

RALPH. No, I mean you should—

BESSIE. Or maybe you'll sleep here in the same bed without marriage.

[ JACOB *stands in his doorway, dressed.*]

RALPH. Don't say that, Mom. I only mean . . .

BESSIE. What you mean, I know . . . and what I mean I also know. Make up your mind. For your own good, Ralphie. If she dropped in the ocean I don't lift a finger.

RALPH. That's all, I suppose.                                                    10

BESSIE. With me it's one thing—a boy should have respect for his own future. Go to sleep, you look tired. In the morning you'll forget.

JACOB. "Awake and sing, ye that dwell in dust, and the earth shall cast out the dead." It's cold out?

MYRON. Oh, yes.

JACOB. I'll take up Tootsie now.

MYRON [*eating bread and jam*]. He come on us like the wild man of Borneo, Sam. I don't think Hennie was fool enough to tell him the truth like that.

BESSIE. Myron!                                                    20

[*A deep pause.*]

RALPH. What did he say?

BESSIE. Never mind.

RALPH. I heard him. I heard him. You don't needa tell me.

BESSIE. Never mind.

RALPH. You trapped that guy.

BESSIE. Don't say another word.

RALPH. Just have respect? That's the idea?

BESSIE. Don't say another word. I'm boiling over ten times inside.

RALPH. You won't let Blanche here, huh. I'm not sure I want her. You    30
put one over on that little shrimp. The cat's whiskers, Mom?

BESSIE. I'm telling you something!

RALPH. I got the whole idea. I get it so quick my head's swimming. Boy, what a laugh! I suppose you know about this, Jake?

JACOB. Yes.

RALPH. Why didn't you do something?

JACOB. I'm an old man.

RALPH. What's that got to do with the price of bonds? Sits around and lets a thing like that happen! You make me sick too.

MYRON [*after a pause*]. Let me say something, son.                            40

RALPH. Take your hand away! Sit in a corner and wag your tail. Keep on boasting you went to law school for two years.

MYRON. I want to tell you—

RALPH. You never in your life had a thing to tell me.

BESSIE [*bitterly*]. Don't say a word. Let him, let him run and tell Sam. Publish in the papers, give a broadcast on the radio. To him it don't matter nothing his family sits with tears pouring from the eyes. [*To* JACOB] What are you waiting for? I didn't tell you twice already about the dog? You'll stand around with Caruso and make a bughouse. It ain't enough all day long. Fifty times I told you I'll break every record in the house. [*She brushes past him, breaks the records, comes out.*] The next time I say something you'll maybe believe it. Now maybe you learned a lesson.

[*Pause.*]

JACOB [*quietly*]. Bessie, new lessons. . . not for an old dog.

[MOE *enters.*]

MYRON. You didn't have to do it, Momma.

BESSIE. Talk better to your son, Mr. Berger! Me, I don't lay down and die for him and Poppa no more. I'll work like a nigger? For what? Wait, the day comes when you'll be punished. When its too late you'll remember how you sucked away a mother's life. Talk to him, tell him how I don't sleep at night. [*Bursts into tears and exits.*]

MOE [*sings*]. "Good-bye to all your sorrows. You never hear them talk about the war, in the land of Yama Yama. . . . "

MYRON. Yes, Momma's a sick woman, Ralphie.

RALPH. Yeah?

MOE. We'll be out of the trenches by Christmas. Putt, putt, putt . . . here, stinker. . . . [*Picks up Tootsie, a small, white poodle that just then enters from the hall.*] If there's reincarnation in the next life I wanna be a dog and lay in a fat lady's lap. Barrage over? How 'bout a little pinochle, Pop?

JACOB. Nnno.

RALPH [*taking dog*]. I'll take her up. [*Conciliatory.*]

JACOB. No, I'll do it. [*Takes dog.*]

RALPH [*ashamed*]. It's cold out.

JACOB. I was cold before in my life. A man sixty-seven. . . . [*Strokes the dog.*] Tootsie is my favorite lady in the house. [*He slowly passes across the room and exits. A settling pause.*]

MYRON. She cried all last night—Tootsie—I heard her in the kitchen like a young girl.

MOE. Tonight I could do something. I got a yen . . . I don't know.

MYRON [*rubbing his head*]. My scalp is impoverished.

RALPH. Mom bust all his records.

MYRON. She didn't have to do it.

MOE. Tough tit! Now I can sleep in the morning. Who the hell wantsa hear a wop air his tonsils all day long!

RALPH [*handling the fragment of a record*]. "O Paradiso!"

MOE [*gets cards*]. It's snowing out, girls.

MYRON. There's no more big snows like in the old days. I think the whole world's changing. I see it, right under our very eyes. No one hardly remembers any more when we used to have gaslight and all the dishes had little fishes on them.

MOE. It's the system, girls.

MYRON. I was a little boy when it happened—the Great Blizzard. It snowed three days without a stop that time. Yes, and the horse cars stopped. A silence of death was on the city and little babies got no milk . . . they say a lot of people died that year.

MOE [*singing as he deals himself cards*].

> "Lights are blinking while you're drinking,
> That's the place where the good fellows go.
> Good-bye to all your sorrows,
> You never hear them talk about the war,
> In the land of Yama Yama.
> Funicalee, funicala, funicalo. . . . "

10

MYRON. What can I say to you, Big Boy?

RALPH. Not a damn word.

MOE [*goes "ta ra ta ra" throughout.*]

MYRON. I know how you feel about all those things, I know.

RALPH. Forget it.

MYRON. And your girl . . .

RALPH. Don't soft soap me all of a sudden.

MYRON. I'm not foreign born. I'm an American, and yet I never got close to you. It's an American father's duty to be his son's friend.

20

RALPH. Who said that—Teddy R.?

MOE [*dealing cards*]. You'r breaking his heart, "Litvak."

MYRON. It just happened the other day. The moment I began losing my hair I just knew I was destined to be a failure in life . . . and when I grew bald I was. Now isn't that funny, Big Boy?

MOE. It's a pisscutter!

MYRON. I believe in Destiny.

MOE. You get what-it-takes. Then they don't catch you with your pants down. [*Sings out.*] Eight of clubs. . . .

MYRON. I really don't know. I sold jewelry on the road before I married. It's one thing to—Now here's a thing the druggist gave me. [*Reads.*] "The Marvel Cosmetic Girl of Hollywood is going on the air. Give this charming little radio singer a name and win five thousand dollars. If you will send—"

30

MOE. Your old man still believes in Santy Claus.

MYRON. Someone's got to win. The government isn't gonna allow everything to be a fake.

MOE. It's a fake. There ain't no prizes. It's a fake.

MYRON. It says—

RALPH [*snatching it*]. For Christ's sake, Pop, forget it. Grow up. Jake's right—everybody's crazy. It's like a zoo in this house. I'm going to bed.

40

MOE. In the land of Yama Yama . . . [*Goes on with ta ra.*]

MYRON. Don't think life's easy with Momma. No, but she means for your good all the time. I tell you she does, she—

RALPH. Maybe, but I'm going to bed.

[*Downstairs doorbell rings violently.*]

MOE [*ring*]. Enemy barrage begins on sector eight seventy-five.

RALPH. That's downstairs.

MYRON. We ain't expecting anyone this hour of the night.

MOE. "Lights are blinking while you're drinking, that's the place where the good fellows go. Good-bye to ta ra tara ra," etc.

RALPH. I better see who it is.

MYRON. I'll tick the button. [*As he starts, the apartment doorbell begins ringing, followed by large knocking.* MYRON *goes out.*]

RALPH. Who's ever ringing means it.

[*A loud excited voice outside.*]      10

MOE. "In the land of Yama Yama, Funicalee, funicalo, funic—"

[MYRON *enters followed by* SCHLOSSER *the janitor.* BESSIE *cuts in from the other side.*]

BESSIE. Who's ringing like a lunatic?

RALPH. What's the matter?

MYRON. Momma . . .

BESSIE. Noo, what's the matter?

[*Downstairs bell continues.*]

RALPH. What's the matter?

BESSIE. Well, well . . . ?      20

MYRON. Poppa . . .

BESSIE. What happened?

SCHLOSSER. He shlipped maybe in de snow.

RALPH. Who?

SCHLOSSER [*to* BESSIE]. Your fadder fall off de roof. . . . Ja.

[ *A dead pause.* RALPH *then runs out.*]

BESSIE [*dazed*]. Myron. . . Call Morty on the phone. . . call him.

[MYRON *starts for phone.*] No. I'll do it myself. I'll. . . do it.

[MYRON *exits.*]

SCHLOSSER [*standing stupidly*]. Since I was in dis country. . . I was    30 pudding out de ash can. . . The snow is vet. . . .

MOE [*to* SCHLOSSER]. Scram.

[SCHLOSSER *exits.*]

[BESSIE *goes blindly to the phone, fumbles and gets it.* MOE *sits quietly, slowly turning cards over, but watching her.*]

BESSIE. He slipped. . . .

MOE [*deeply moved*]. Slipped?

BESSIE. I can't see the numbers. Make it, Moe, make it. . . .

MOE. Make it yourself. [*He looks at her and slowly goes back to his game of cards with shaking hands.*]      40

BESSIE. Riverside 7—. . . [*Unable to talk she dials slowly. The dial whizzes on*].

MOE. Don't. . . make me laugh. . . . [*He turns over cards.*]

CURTAIN

ACT THREE

*A week later in the dining room.* MORTY, BESSIE *and* MYRON *eating. Sitting in the front room is* MOE *marking a "dope sheet," but really listening to the others.*

BESSIE. You're sure he'll come tonight—the insurance man?

MORTY. Why not? I shtupped him a ten-dollar bill. Everything's hot delicatessen.

BESSIE. Why must he come so soon?

MORTY. Because you had a big expense. You'll settle once and for all.    10
I'm a great boy for making hay while the sun shines.

BESSIE. Stay till he'll come, Morty. . . .

MORTY. No, I got a strike downtown. Business don't stop for personal life. Two times already in the past week those bastards threw stink bombs in the showroom. Wait! We'll give them strikes—in the kishkas we'll give them. . . .

BESSIE. I'm a woman. I don't know about policies. Stay till he comes.

MORTY. Bessie—sweetheart, leave me live.

BESSIE. I'm afraid, Morty.

MORTY. Be practical. They made an investigation. Everybody knows    20
Pop had an accident. Now we'll collect.

MYRON. Ralphie don't know Papa left the insurance in his name.

MORTY. It's not his business. And I'll tell him.

BESSIE. The way he feels. [*Enter* RALPH *into front room.*] He'll do something crazy. He thinks Poppa jumped off the roof.

MORTY. Be practical, Bessie. Ralphie will sign when I tell him. Everything is peaches and cream.

BESSIE. Wait for a few minutes. . . .

MORTY. Look, I'll show you in black and white what the policy says. *For God's sake, leave me live!* [*Angrily exits to kitchen. In parlor,* MOE    30
*speaks to* RALPH, *who is reading a letter.*]

MOE. What's the letter say?

RALPH. Blanche won't see me no more, she says. I couldn't care very much, she says. If I didn't come like I said. . . . She'll phone before she leaves.

MOE. She don't know about Pop?

RALPH. She won't ever forget me she says. Look what she sends me . . . a little locket on a chain . . . if she calls I'm out.

MOE. You mean it?

RALPH. For a week I'm trying to go in his room. I guess he'd like me    40
to have it, but I can't. . . .

MOE. Wait a minute! [*Crosses over.*] They're trying to rook you—a freeze-out.

RALPH. Who?

MOE. That bunch stuffin' their gut with hot pastrami. Morty in particular. Jake left the insurance—three thousand dollars—for you.

RALPH. For me?

MOE. Now you got wings, kid. Pop figured you could use it. That's why . . .

RALPH. That's why what?

MOE. It ain't the only reason he done it.

RALPH. He done it?

MOE. You think a breeze blew him off?

[HENNIE *enters and sits.*]

RALPH. I'm not sure what I think.

MOE. The insurance guy's coming tonight. Morty "shtupped" him.          10

RALPH. Yeah?

MOE. I'll back you up. You're dead on your feet. Grab a sleep for yourself.

RALPH. No!

MOE. Go on! [*Pushes boy into room.*]

SAM [*whom* MORTY *has sent in for the paper*]. Morty wants the paper.

HENNIE. So?

SAM. You're sitting on it. [*Gets paper.*] We could go home now, Hennie! Leon is alone by Mrs. Strasberg a whole day.

HENNIE. Go on home if you're so anxious. A full tub of diapers is          20 waiting.

SAM. Why should you act this way?

HENNIE. 'Cause there's no bones in ice cream. Don't touch me.

SAM. Please, what's the matter. . . .

MOE. She don't like you. Plain as the face on your nose. . .

SAM. To me, my friend, you talk a foreign language.

MOE. A quarter you're lousy. [SAM *exits*] Gimme a buck, I'll run it up to ten.

HENNIE. Don't do me no favors.

MOE. Take a chance. [*Stopping her as she crosses to doorway.*]          30

HENNIE. I'm a pushover.

MOE. I say lotsa things. You don't know me.

HENNIE. I know you—when you knock 'em down you're through.

MOE [*sadly*]. You still don't know me.

HENNIE. I know what goes in your wise-guy head.

MOE. Don't run away. . . . I ain't got hydrophobia. Wait. I want to tell you. . . . I'm leaving.

HENNIE. Leaving?

MOE. Tonight. Already packed.

HENNIE. Where?          40

MORTY [*as he enters followed by the others*]. My car goes through snow like a dose of salts.

BESSIE. Hennie, go eat. . . .

MORTY. Where's Ralphie?

MOE. In his new room. [*Moves into dining room.*]

MORTY. I didn't have a piece of hot pastrami in my mouth for years.

BESSIE. Take a sandwich, Hennie. You didn't eat all day .... [*At window.*] A whole week it rained cats and dogs.

MYRON. Rain, rain, go away. Come again some other days. [*Puts shawl on her.*]

MORTY. Where's my gloves?

SAM [*sits on stool*]. I'm sorry the old man lays in the rain.

MORTY. Personally, Pop was a fine man. But I'm a great boy for an honest opinion. He had enough crazy ideas for a regiment.

MYRON. Poppa never had a doctor in his whole life. . . .

[*Enter* RALPH.]                                                            10

MORTY. He had Caruso. Who's got more from life?

BESSIE. Who's got more? . . .

MYRON. And Marx he had.

[MYRON *and* BESSIE *sit on sofa.*]

MORTY. Marx! Some say Marx is the new God today. Maybe I'm wrong. Ha ha ha . . . Personally I counted my ten million last night. . . . I'm sixteen cents short. So tomorrow I'll go to Union Square and yell no equality in the country! Ah, it's a new generation.

RALPH. You said it!

MORTY. What's the matter, Ralphie? What are you looking funny?    20

RALPH. I hear I'm left insurance and the man's coming tonight.

MORTY. Poppa didn't leave no insurance for you.

RALPH. What?

MORTY. In your name he left it—but not for you.

RALPH. It's my name on the paper.

MORTY. Who said so?

RALPH [ *to his mother*]. The insurance man's coming tonight?

MORTY. What's the matter?

RALPH. I'm not talking to you. [ *To his mother.*] Why?              30

BESSIE. I don't know why.

RALPH. He don't come in this house tonight.

MORTY. That's what *you* say.

RALPH. I'm not talking to you, Uncle Morty, but I'll tell you, too, he don't come here tonight when there's still mud on a grave. [*To his mother.*] Couldn't you give the house a chance to cool off?

MORTY. Is this a way to talk to your mother?

RALPH. Was that a way to talk to your father?

MORTY. Don't be so smart with me, Mr. Ralph Berger!

RALPH. Don't be so smart with *me*.

MORTY. What'll you do? I say he's coming tonight. Who says no?    40

MOE [*suddenly, from the background*]. Me.

MORTY. Take a back seat, Axelrod. When you're in the family—

MOE. I got a little document here. [*Produces paper.*] I found it under his pillow that night. A guy who slips off a roof don't leave a note before he does it.

MORTY [*starting for* MOE *after a horrified silence*]. Let me see this note.

BESSIE. Morty, don't touch it!

MOE. Not if you crawled.

MORTY. It's a fake. Poppa wouldn't—

MOE. Get the insurance guy here and we'll see how—[*The bell rings.*] Speak of the devil . . . Answer it, see what happens.

[MORTY *starts for the ticker.*]

BESSIE. Morty, don't!

MORTY [*stopping*]. Be practical, Bessie.

MOE. Sometimes you don't collect on suicides if they know about it.

MORTY. You should let . . . You should let him. . . .        10

[ *A pause in which* ALL *seem dazed. Bell rings insistently.*]

MOE. Well, we're waiting.

MORTY. Give me the note.

MOE. I'll give you the head off your shoulders.

MORTY. Bessie, you'll stand for this? [*Points to* RALPH.] Pull down his pants and give him with a strap.

RALPH [*as bell rings again*]. How about it?

BESSIE. Don't be crazy. It's not my fault. Morty said he should come tonight. It's not nice so soon. I didn't—

MORTY. I said it? Me?        20

BESSIE. Who then?

MORTY. You didn't sing a song in my ear a whole week to settle quick?

BESSIE. I'm suprised. Morty, you're a big liar.

MYRON. Momma's telling the truth, she is!

MORTY. Lissen. In two shakes of a lamb's tail, we'll start a real fight and then nobody won't like nobody. Where's my fur gloves? I'm going downtown. [*To* SAM.] You coming? I'll drive you down.

HENNIE [*to* SAM *who looks questioningly at her*]. Don't look at me. Go home if you want.

SAM. If you're coming soon, I'll wait.        30

HENNIE. Don't do me any favors. Night and day he pesters me.

MORTY. You made a cushion—sleep!

SAM. I'll go home. I know . . . to my worst enemy I don't wish such a life—

HENNIE. Sam, keep quiet.

SAM [*quietly; sadly*]. No more free speech in America? [*Gets his hat and coat.*] I'm a lonely person. Nobody likes me.

MYRON. I like you, Sam.

HENNIE [*going to him gently; sensing the end*]. Please go home, Sam. I'll sleep here. . . . I'm tired and nervous. Tomorrow I'll come home.  40 I love you. . . . I mean it. [*She kisses him with real feeling.*]

SAM. I would die for you. . . . [SAM *looks at her. Tries to say something, but his voice chokes up with a mingled feeling. He turns and leaves the room.*]

MORTY. A bird in the hand is worth two in the bush. Remember I said it. Good night. [*Exits after* SAM.]

[HENNIE *sits depressed.* BESSIE *goes up and looks at the picture calendar again.* MYRON *finally breaks the silence.*]

MYRON. Yesterday a man wanted to sell me a saxophone with pearl buttons. But I—

BESSIE. It's a beautiful picture. In this land, nobody works. . . . Nobody worries. . . . Come to bed, Myron. [*Stops at the door, and says to* RALPH.] Please don't have foolish ideas about the money.

RALPH. Let's call it a day.

BESSIE. It belongs for the whole family. You'll get your teeth fixed—

RALPH: And a pair of black and white shoes?                                10

BESSIE. Hennie needs a vacation. She'll take two weeks in the mountains and I'll mind the baby.

RALPH. I'll take care of my own affairs.

BESSIE. A family needs for a rainy day. Times is getting worse. Prospect Avenue, Dawson, Beck Street—every day furniture's on the sidewalk.

RALPH. Forget it, Mom.

BESSIE. Ralphie, I worked too hard all my years to be treated like dirt. It's no law we should be stuck together like Siamese twins. Summer shoes you didn't have, skates you never had, but I bought a new dress every week. A lover I kept—Mr. Gigolo! Did I ever play a game of cards   20
like Mrs. Marcus? Or was Bessie Berger's children always the cleanest on the block?! Here I'm not only the mother, but also the father. The first two years I worked in a stocking factory for six dollars while Myron Berger went to law school. If I didn't worry about the family who would? On the calendar it's a different place, but here without a dollar you don't look the world in the eye. Talk from now to next year—this is life in America.

RALPH. Then it's wrong. It don't make sense. If life made you this way, then it's wrong!

BESSIE. Maybe you wanted me to give up twenty years ago. Where   30
would you be now? You'll excuse my expression—a bum in the park!

RALPH. I'm not blaming you, Mom. Sink or swim—I see it. But it can't stay like this.

BESSIE. My foolish boy . . .

RALPH. No, I see every house lousy with lies and hate. He said it, Grandpa—Brooklyn hates the Bronx. Smacked on the nose twice a day. But boys and girls can get ahead like that, Mom. We don't want life printed on dollar bills, Mom!

BESSIE. So go out and change the world if you don't like it.

RALPH. I will! And why? 'Cause life's different in my head. Gimme the   40
earth in two hands. I'm strong. There . . . hear him? The air mail off to Boston. Day or night, he flies away, a job to do. That's us and it's no time to die.

[*The airplane sound fades off as* MYRON *gives alarm clock to* BESSIE *which she begins to wind.*]

BESSIE. "Mom, what does she know? She's old-fashioned!" But I'll tell you a big secret: My whole life I wanted to go away too, but with children a woman stays home. A fire burned in *my* heart too, but now it's too late. I'm no spring chicken. The clock goes and Bessie goes. Only my machinery can't be fixed. [*She lifts a button : the alarm rings on the clock; she stops it, says "Good night" and exits.*]

MYRON. I guess I'm no prize bag. . . .

BESSIE [*from within*]. Come to bed, Myron.

MYRON [*tears page off calendar*]. Hmmm . . . [*Exits to her.*]

RALPH. Look at him, draggin' after her like an old shoe.

MOE. Punch drunk. [*Phone rings.*] That's for me. [*At phone.*] Yeah 10 . . . Just a minute. [*To* RALPH.] Your girl . . .

RALPH. Jeez, I don't know what to say to her.

MOE. Hang up?

[RALPH *slowly takes phone.*]

RALPH. Hello. . . . Blanche, I wish. . . . I don't know what to say. . . . Yes . . . Hello? . . . [*Puts phone down.*] She hung up on me. . . .

MOE. Sorry?

RALPH. No girl means anything to me until . . .

MOE. Till when?

RALPH. Till I can take care of her. Till we don't look out on an airshaft. 20 Till we can take the world in two hands and polish off the dirt.

MOE. That's a big order.

RALPH. Once upon a time I thought I'd drown to death in bolts of silk and velour. But I grew up these last few weeks. Jake said a lot.

MOE. Your memory's okay?

RALPH . But take a look at this. [ *Brings armful of books from* JACOB's *room—dumps them on table.*] His books, I got them too—the pages ain't cut in half of them.

MOE. Perfect.

RALPH. Does it prove something? Damn tootin'! A ten-cent nail-file 30 cuts them. Uptown, downtown, I'll read them on the way. Get a big lamp over the bed. [*Picks up one.*] My eyes are good. [*Puts book in pocket.*] Sure, inventory tomorrow. Coletti to Driscoll to Berger—that's how we work. It's a team down the warehouse. Driscoll's a show-off, a wiseguy, and Joe talks pigeons day and night. But they're like me, looking for a chance to get to first base too. Joe razzed me about my girl. But he don't know why. I'll tell him. Hell, he might tell me something I don't know. Get teams together all over. Spit on your hands and get to work. And with enough teams together maybe we'll get steam in the warehouse so our fingers don't freeze off. Maybe we'll fix it so life won't be printed 40 on dollar bills.

MOE. Graduation Day.

RALPH. [*starts for door of his room, stops*]. Can I have . . . Grandpa's note?

MOE. Sure you want it?

RALPH. Please—[MOE *gives it.*] It's blank!

MOE. [*taking note back and tearing it up*]. That's right.

RALPH. Thanks! [*Exits.*]

MOE. The kid's a fighter! [*To* HENNIE.] Why are you crying?

HENNIE. I never cried in my life. [*She is now.*]

MOE [*starts for door. Stops*]. You told Sam you love him. . . .

HENNIE. If I'm sore on life, why take it out on him?

MOE. You won't forget me to your dyin' day—I was the first guy. Part of your insides. You won't forget. I wrote my name on you—indelible ink!

HENNIE. One thing I won't forget—how you left me crying on the bed like I was two for a cent!                                                             10

MOE. Listen, do you think—

HENNIE. Sure. Waits till the family goes to the open air movie. He brings me perfume. . . . He grabs my arms—

MOE. You won't forget me!

HENNIE. How you left the next week?

MOE. So I made a mistake. For Chris' sake, don't act like the Queen of Roumania!

HENNIE. Don't make me laugh!

MOE. What the hell do you want, my head on a plate? Was my life so happy? Chris', my old man was a bum. I supported the whole damn   20
family—five kids and Mom. When they grew up they beat it the hell away like rabbits. Mom died. I went to the war; got clapped down like a bedbug; woke up in a room without a leg. What the hell do you think, anyone's got it better than you? I never had a home either. I'm lookin' too!

HENNIE. So what?

MOE. So you're it—you're home for me, a place to live! That's the whole parade, sickness, eating out your heart! Sometimes you meet a girl—she stops it—that's love. . . . So take a chance! Be with me, Paradise. What's to lose?

HENNIE. My pride!                                                            30

MOE [*grabbing her*]. What do you want? Say the word—I'll tango on a dime. Don't gimme ice when your heart's on fire!

HENNIE. Let me go!

[*He stops her.*]

MOE. WHERE?!

HENNIE. What do you want, Moe, what do you want?

MOE. You!

HENNIE. You'll be sorry you ever started—

MOE. You!

HENNIE. Moe, lemme go—[*Trying to leave.*] I'm getting up early—   40
lemme go.

MOE. No! . . . I got enough fever to blow the whole damn town to hell. [*He suddenly releases her and half stumbles backwards. Forces himself to quiet down.*] You wanna go back to him? Say the word. I'll know what to do. . . .

HENNIE [*helplessly*]. Moe, I don't know what to say.

MOE. Listen to me.

HENNIE. What?

MOE. Come away. A certain place where it's moonlight and roses. We'll lay down, count stars. Hear the big ocean making noise. You lay under the trees. Champagne flows like—[*Phone rings.* MOE *finally answers the telephone.*] Hello? . . . Just a minute. [*Looks at* HENNIE.]

HENNIE. Who is it?

MOE. Sam.

HENNIE [*starts for phone, but changes her mind*]. I'm sleeping. . . .

MOE [*in phone*]. She's sleeping. . . . [*Hangs up. Watches* HENNIE *who 10 slowly sits.*] He wants you to know he got home O.K. . . . What's on your mind?

HENNIE. Nothing.

MOE. Sam?

HENNIE. They say it's a palace on those Havana boats.

MOE. What's on your mind?

HENNIE [*trying to escape*]. Moe, I don't care for Sam—I never loved him—

MOE. But your kid—?

HENNIE. All my life I waited for this minute.                                    20

MOE [*holding her*]. Me too. Made believe I was talkin' just bedroom golf, but you and me forever was what I meant! Christ, baby, there's one life to live! Live it!

HENNIE. Leave the baby?

MOE. Yeah!

HENNIE. I can't . . .

MOE. You can!

HENNIE. No. . . .

MOE. But you're not sure!

HENNIE. I don't know.                                                            30

MOE. Make a break or spend the rest of your life in a coffin.

HENNIE. Oh, God, I don't know where I stand.

MOE. Don't look up there. Paradise, you're on a big boat headed south. No more pins and needles in your heart, no snake juice squirted in your arm. The whole world's green and when you cry it's because you're happy.

HENNIE. Moe, I don't know. . . .

MOE. Nobody knows, but you do it and find out. When you're scared the answer's zero.

HENNIE. You're hurting my arm.

MOE. The doctor said it—cut off your leg to save your life! And they   40 done it—one thing to get another.

[*Enter* RALPH.]

RALPH. I didn't hear a word, but do it, Hennie, do it!

MOE. Mom can mind the kid. She'll go on forever, Mom. We'll send money back, and Easter eggs.

RALPH. I'll be here.

MOE. Get your coat. . . get it.

HENNIE. Moe!

MOE. I know. . . but get your coat and hat and kiss the house good-bye.

HENNIE. The man I love. . . [MYRON *entering.*] I left my coat in Mom's room. [*Exits.*]

MYRON. Don't wake her up, Beauty. Momma fell asleep as soon as her head hit the pillow. I can't sleep. It was a long day. Hmmm. [*Examines his tongue in a buffet mirror.*] I was reading the other day a person with a thick tongue is feebleminded. I can do anything with my tongue. Make it thick, flat. No fruit in the house lately. Just a lone apple. [*He gets apple and paring knife and starts paring.*] Must be something wrong with me— I say I won't eat but I eat. [HENNIE *enters dressed to go out.*] Where you going, little Red Riding Hood?

HENNIE. Nobody knows, Peter Rabbit.

MYRON. You're looking very pretty tonight. You were a beautiful baby too. 1910, that was the year you was born. The same year Teddy Roosevelt come back from Africa.

HENNIE. Gee, Pop; you're such a funny guy.

MYRON. He was a boisterous man, Teddy. Good night. [*He exits, paring apple.*]

RALPH. When I look at him, I'm sad. Let me die like a dog, if I can't get more from life.

HENNIE. Where?

RALPH. Right here in the house! My days won't be for nothing. Let Mom have the dough. I'm twenty-two and kickin'! I'll get along. Did Jake die for us to fight about nickels? No! "Awake and sing," he said. Right here he stood and said it. The night he died, I saw it like a thunderbolt! I saw he was dead and I was born! I swear to God, I'm one week old! I want the whole city to hear it—fresh blood, arms. We got 'em. We're glad we're living.

MOE. I wouldn't trade you for two pitchers and an outfielder. Hold the fort!

RALPH. So long.

MOE. So long.

[*They go and* RALPH *stands full and strong in the doorway, seeing them off, as the curtain slowly falls.*]

CURTAIN

# Aleksandra Rembienska
## A Servant Girl

Dear Auntie: I received your letter on February 20 and I write you on February 25. Dear auntie, you wrote 3 letters and I know nothing about them; I received only this one. O dear auntie, you write to me that I either don't wish to write or that I have forgotten [you]. O dear auntie, I will not forget until my death. I write letters, one to auntie and the other to my parents. Perhaps somebody has intercepted those letters at the post-office and does not give them to you. Now, dear auntie, I inform you that I am in good health, thanks to our Lord God, which I wish also to you, dear auntie. May God help you the best; may I always hear that you are doing well; I shall be very glad then.

And now, dear auntie, I inform you that I am in the same place in service with an English [-speaking] master and mistress who don't know a word of Polish, and I don't know English; so we communicate with gestures and I know what to do, that's all. I know the work and therefore I don't mind much about the language. But, dear auntie, I went intentionally into an English household in order that I may learn to speak English, because it is necessary, in America, as the English language reigns. I am in good health, only I am a little ill with my feet, I don't know what it is, whether rheumatism or something else. I walk very much, because from 6 o'clock in the morning till 10 o'clock in the evening I have work and I receive $22 a month, and I have 7 persons, and 16 rooms to clean, and I cook; everything is on my head.

And now, dear auntie, please don't be angry with me for not answering directly, for I have no time, neither in the day nor the evening. I am always busy. And now, dear auntie, I thank you very much for the news, for now I know everything. You ask about that young man, what happened. Nothing happened, only it is so that I did not wish to marry him, because I

255

don't wish to marry at all; I will live alone through this my life to the end. He is a good fellow, nothing can be said, his name is Thomas Zylowski. He wants it to be in summer, after Easter, but I don't think about marrying, I will suffer alone to the end of this world.

O dear auntie, I write you that I have nothing to write, only I ask you for a quick answer. And now I beg you, auntie, write me what happened with [two illegible names of boy and girl]. I wish you a merry holiday of Easter time. O dear God, why cannot I be with auntie and divide the egg together with parents and brothers and sisters! When I recall all this, I would not be sorry if I had to die right now.                              10

# Carolyn Banks
## Growing Up
## Polish in Pittsburgh

The section of the city was called "Polish Hill." It consisted of narrow streets and row houses, brick pavements gradually being replaced by concrete sidewalks. A few slat fences were left, but these, too, were going, and in their stead, aluminum chain-link fences were being raised.

There was a hospital on the hill which loomed over the rest of the neighborhood. Its psychiatric ward, on the top floor, was commonly referred to as the "crazy house," and children used to line up at the fence, staring up at the top floor, waiting to see one of the patients. At the slightest sign of movement on any of the floors, they would run, screaming happily, home to safety and normalcy, the smell of *kishka* or *kielbasi* reaching 10 from kitchen to hall and all through the house. On Mondays, bleach and ammonia in every staircase welled up from some hundred whitewashed cellars.

Beyond the hospital, enemy lines. Names like Carrozza, Damiano. Pizza houses, not ours, not our own.

Most of the people in our section spoke Polish, and all of the older children understood the language when they heard it but they didn't speak it. In the market on Saturday morning, over the smell of fruit and fresh-killed meat, a steady mumble of Polish rose. The market was a favorite gathering place. It was the only store in the three-block shopping district 20 which covered its floors with sawdust. The older children would slide in it, and the little ones, hanging onto a coat sleeve or hem, would make tentative marks with their shoes, circles, lines, little ditches. My own never realized dream, to be free of my mother, free of all grown-ups, free to storm and slide up the aisles, a whirl of chips flying, the dust clouds in my wake falling evenly on every bottle, every jar, every tissue-wrapped lemon and apple and orange.

257

But secular pleasures, even those only imagined, were few. The real center of the neighborhood was the church. Everyone, even the drunkards like Diana Rzemieniewska's father, went to church on Sunday mornings. The ones who went earliest were considered saintliest, while the ones who went to the noon Mass were virtually atheists. My parents went, usually, to 6 a.m. Mass with my grandmother and Aunt Clara, while I went to "Children's Mass" at 8:30. All of my classmates were there, unwilling too, weary, but all of us kneeling starch-straight because of the nuns stationed every third row. Sometimes I pretended to be sick, so that I could sit, but during the sermon we all sat, and I would read almost all of the gospels in my Missal before the priest had finished reciting and preaching. Even though we went to church every week, few of us seemed to know when to sit, when to stand, when to kneel. We always had to look at each other or to look at the nun in the first row. Then rise, or sit, or whatever, so that it never happened all at once, in all the times I'd been to church. I always promised myself that I would learn the routine so thoroughly that the class would look at me before rising, before kneeling. And yet it was always the good girls, like Maryann Wrobleska, the girls who never talked in school and who never got their hands hit with the ruler by the nuns, who were never slow to decide when during the Mass to do whatever needed to be done. Despite my promises to myself I was always off in daydream or in the midst of some one of the gospels.

May was the cruelest month, the month of Mary. It began with a procession through the streets. The boys carried a large plaster statue of the Virgin and the girls followed, emptying baskets of rose petals along the way, all of us singing over and again a long, strangely sad Polish hymn, *Podgura Dolina,* I think it was called. I know that I hated the whole thing, and I think it was a safe guess that all of us did, the boys in crisp navy suits, the girls in starched white dresses and knee-length white socks. Old tapestry banners recalling miracles were held high, usually by the older men in the Sacred Heart Society: Lourdes, Fatima, Guadalupe. The smell of incense in the streets was fleeting except to those in procession. We grew dizzy as we walked, as we sang, as we cast the petals of flowers in the warm spring streets. The neighborhood people would come down from their porches and stand at the curb. Some would lean out of upstairs windows. The old women would cry a little and try to sing with us, but always much too slowly.

Except for May, evenings in the church were given over to these old women, who would go in groups to say the Rosary. Since few of the *babkas* had even attempted English, it was said in Polish. In any language the words would have been indistinguishable. When the priest had hurried through his part of the prayer, the tired, soft chirping began, all at once, dwindling slowly, with each of the women praying at a different pace. Wrinkled and sad, most of them fat and dressed in dark colors, they huddled over their beads down at the small side altar. My grandmother was one of these.

The only occasion in church that I enjoyed (although I managed to look every bit as put upon as my friends) fell on the Saturday before Easter. The girls would come in *babushkas* and light jackets carrying baskets of food to be blessed for the Easter morning meal. We would kneel close to the center aisle with the baskets on the floor beside the pews. Filled with the sweet smell of Polish sausage and home-baked raisin bread, the church seemed less forbidding: perhaps, too, because the agonies of Lent had passed and we no longer had to spend each Friday afternoon making Stations of the Cross and because the purple shrouds which covered all of the statuary had at last been taken up. Absent, too, was the regiment of nuns, so that we could sit or slouch as we chose. And then the priest would appear, heralded by two altar boys waving censors, filling the air with the familiar church incense, covering, temporarily, the warm and alien kitchen smells.

We would kneel, then, as straight as if the nuns were yet behind us, and up the aisle the priest would walk, muttering ecclesiastically, swinging a silver shaker of sorts, splashing the baskets and the company with tepid holy water. We would regain ourselves, shuffle out, complain together in the churchyard, and swagger home to beg the now sanctified raisin bread, eggs, or sausage. Each family kept a store of unblessed food, too, though nothing could equal the share in the baskets. But never once could we touch, let alone eat, the food which had been blessed before Easter morning.

The younger women, a group which included our mothers, did not go to Rosary, nor did they participate in our devotions. Instead, they played Bingo in the church basement. I went only twice, and, although I was bored by it, I was jealous of the girls who went regularly because they seemed so much more grown up than I. And so I always begged to go.

My mother never won anything except an Aunt Jemima cookie jar, but my Aunt Clara won almost every time she played: towels, doilies, and a salt and pepper set. Once, on one of the two nights I had been allowed to go, she won the $50 jackpot. She told me to place the see-through plastic chips on her card, but I was slow, too slow, and eventually she took over. I was almost asleep, my head pressed against the narrow table, when she called out, "Biiiiin-gooo!" We danced the polka in the streets that night on the way home and the next day my aunt bought a turkey, as big as our Thanksgiving turkeys were, and we had a huge family dinner at my grandmother's, to celebrate. Aunt Clara told all of my aunts and uncles and cousins that I had brought her luck and I got to pull the wishbone with her, although, as usual, she won. She always won. I had seen her pull the wishbone with my cousin Stash, and with my father. She always won, at everything. She even won a toaster, once, in the church raffle. Each child had to sell five books of tickets, which was pretty easy, since relatives usually bought a whole book. But Aunt Clara won the toaster and she was the only one in the whole family who bought just a single ticket. It was she to whom the Blessed Virgin once miraculously appeared. It was, in fact, the Virgin's only appearance in western Pennsylvania.

My Aunt Clara had never been my favorite. I remember her sitting on the front steps in the summertime drinking beer, setting the bottle on the steps beside her after each swig. I used to worry that my friends would see her, but if they did they never told me. She was a very loud woman and her teeth were laced with gold. She laughed a lot, throwing her head back so that all of the fillings would show. When she hugged me she squeezed too tight and her breath smelled of beer. I would squirm to get away from her but she always hugged me more than she hugged anyone else. At least I thought so.                                                                            10

Her rooms were next door to us, small and cluttered with her winnings and her handiwork. She crocheted for people in the neighborhood, pillowcases, hankies, things like that. All of our sheets had been bordered by Aunt Clara, and she made my mother's finest tablecloth, reserved for Christmas and Easter dinners. Most of my aunts and uncles bought doilies from her to give as wedding presents and to use in their homes. My parents did not use doilies except for one long one across the dining room buffet, and so, in our house, all of the doilies which Aunt Clara had given us were upstairs in the third drawer of my parents' chest of drawers, wrapped in white tissue and smelling faintly of lavender sachet. But     20 Clara's rooms had lots of doilies and long crocheted strips with tasseled edges hanging from the window frames and on the door between her bedroom and sitting room. There were many religious statues — the Infant of Prague, the Virgin in her various guises, a small wooden statue of St. Joseph — with sanctuary candles burning red and blue before them, and on the wall at the entrance, a white enamel holy water font. Her rooms were hot and the holy water was always lukewarm. I loved to dab it on my forehead when I came in, and so I never really minded having to make the Sign of the Cross when we went there, even though we didn't do it at home, only at church or at my grandmother's and at Aunt Clara's.     30

On the day that the Virgin appeared my aunt had finished a blue tablecloth. Every year on that day, June 12, she used that cloth, and uses it today. "It was blue, and blue is her color," my aunt told everyone later. "I should have known, because I never made a blue one before, that she would come." When she called on my mother that night she did not behave as if she knew the Virgin was coming. Instead, my aunt came an hour before the Bingo was to start, as she always did, settled in the green armchair with a loud, deep sigh, as she always did, and, pulling off her shoes, began to rub her feet, which she did only when she had spent the day delivering her needlework.                                                                       40

"Please, can I go?" I asked my mother.

"Not tonight, Karolcza," she said, and before they left they each kissed my cheek for luck.

May devotions ended, I had nothing to do that night. My father worked a crossword and listened to the radio and I went to bed early.

In a fuzzy way I remember hearing my name, Karolcza, being called in my sleep. This had happened only once before, on a New Year's Eve four years back. I heard my name, and then, over bells and whistles that sounded like the noon whistle at the mills, I heard my mother say, "It's 1946!" She told me that I said, "Oh," and rolled across the bed, never really waking. This time, though, she didn't allow me to fall asleep again. Instead, she stood me upright beside the bed and switched on the overhead light. I started to cry and she handed me a pile of clothes.

"No, no, don't cry," she sat on the bed and began unbuttoning my pajama top, "you must get dressed. Karolcza, your aunt has seen the Virgin." Then she shouted down the stairs, telling my father, in Polish, to hurry. My mother only spoke to my grandmother in Polish all of the time. To my father and to my aunt she spoke English, except when she said something to them which I was not to know. She turned to me and said something, still in her mother's tongue. "It's still night," I told her, but she went into the bathroom and began running the water. She came out with a washcloth and, as she passed it over my face, I realized that the Virgin had come to Polish Hill.

My father opened the front door and I was startled to see the street filled with people, all of them hurrying toward the hospital. I had never seen so many people, not even during the day. I could remember waking at night and looking out the window. It was so quiet at night and no one was ever out. Now, it looked as though church had just let out, no, more than that, as if the 6 o'clock, the 8:30, the 10 o'clock, the noon Masses had all let out at once. I saw many children I knew and called to them as they were hurried along. Loretta Mozdien waved to me and her mother smacked her. Maryann Wrobleska walked as though she were about to take communion, her hands folded in prayer, eyes front and solemn. I am reminded of that night now when I see movies involving the evacuation of villages, war movies, science fiction movies. We walked, now, up the hill, as quickly as we could without leaving my grandmother behind. She began to recite the rosary aloud, *Matka boska, swieta Maria,* those soft, chirping phrases, and my parents joined in, and the people behind us joined in, and soon the street was a moving, murmuring mass of people praying. Then someone began to sing the May Day hymn, and the May procession was reenacted there on the hill, but with no need now of the plaster statue, the torn banners.

"Aunt Clara saw her?" I asked my mother when we stopped to let my grandmother catch her breath.

"I would have seen her, too, but I left before Clara did. I won a cookie jar. I guess that was the Virgin's way of appearing to me."

"A cookie jar?" but we were on the move again and my question was lost in the singing, louder now as we neared the hospital.

There must have been a thousand people at the top of the hill. Some of the men wore sweaters over pajama tops and trousers. Women were there in housecoats and pincurls, and some of the children still wore their pajamas entire, with a shawl or coat thrown over them. Though it was

June, it was cool and a wind had been lifting the dust in the streets all
evening, as though it might storm. The wind had died now, or perhaps it
had been trampled in the crowd, but it was a chill. We sang and stared up
into the night sky. Now and then a voice would break through and shout,
"I see her," in Polish, "there she is," and all of the people would clap
their hands and sing louder and faster and then make the Sign of the Cross.
Inside the hospital, people were silhouetted against the windows. We
could see nurses in white standing with the crowd for a time, but usually
they would go back inside, I guess so others could come out. The children
who came to taunt the crazy people, they were here, but neither laughing      10
nor afraid. I looked for our priests, expecting to see one of them in the
crowd, his trouser legs peeping out from under a hastily donned cassock.
     "Maybe," I said to my mother, "one of the crazy people got out up there."
     My grandmother grabbed my arm and shook me, but my mother spoke
to her. My grandmother gave me an evil look, spat upon the ground,
crossed herself with great indignation, and resumed the song.
     "Well maybe one of them did," I said, and my mother led me away
from my grandmother, who was now beating on her breast, her fist
clenched, eyes shut, begging forgiveness for her errant grandchild.
     I looked up beyond the building, trying to find my first star. I could      20
find none to wish on. No, I must gaze upon the Virgin. I tried to focus on
the building, but saw the building only, with people black against the
light within, people on every floor, even the top. Perhaps I was possessed
by the devil. The nuns had told us of such people and of some who turned
to stone for eating meat on Friday and who swallowed their tongue for
taking communion in a state of mortal sin. Perhaps I was in a state of
mortal sin, perhaps the Virgin had come to all but me. I sang louder and
louder, raised my voice until it grew thick in my throat, but still did not
see her.
     A fire engine appeared, quite suddenly. It came slowly, as fire trucks      30
are driven in parades, but with its headlights on, the fire bell clanging.
A man called through a megaphone, "Go home, go home. There is nothing
here to see." And someone shouted, "Protestant!" The crowd laughed and
cheered and applauded. But the singing had stopped. The firemen trained
a huge light on the building and it ran up the side like a roach. The light
hovered at the rooftop, then began to move, slowly, along the edge. The
roof was indeed empty. "You see, there's nothing there," shouted the man
with the megaphone, "there is nothing there!"
     My Aunt Clara's voice came shrill through the crowd. I could not see
her, but her voice was clear as she shouted, "It is a miracle. She would      40
not let them shine those lights on her! It is a miracle!" Her opinion of the
Virgin's departure was immediately accepted. The Virgin was Catholic.
The Virgin of Guadalupe, of Lourdes, of Fatima, Polish. Of course the
Protestants could not see her. So it was that my grandmother translated Clara's words to two of her friends who spoke no English. They
nodded, grave with knowledge. Everyone took up the cry, "Miracle!"

"Okay, folks," the man, whose voice had taken on the huskiness which my own had when I'd tried to sing too loudly, tried again, "take your miracle home with you. Go on home." The light still shone on the empty roof.

Suddenly my mother's voice grew loud at my side, "I won a cookie jar!" she shouted, as if to say, "Explain that away if you can."

"That's right," my father hollered, shaking his fist, "that's right, she did!"

"Okay, people," the fireman had not heard, "you can see she's gone now, so go on back, go back home now." The huge truck began to move, turtle-slow, down the street, and everyone began to back from it, from the man with the megaphone, from the building. We backed, too, like all the rest, not turning our eyes from the hospital, but shuffling backward, staring at the spot where She had been, trying not to trip or lose balance, not to shove or be shoved, but trying, too, not to relinquish that which was especially ours, the Virgin of Polish Hill, my own Aunt Clara's Virgin.

I saw Raymond Bielski some twenty feet away and he made a foolish face at me. I kept, somehow, from laughing. Like my parents and my aunt, like my grandmother, I would be solemn. I hope his mother slapped him when he called to me, "Hey, hey Carol!" but I did not, I swear, hear him for the Virgin.

# Paul C. P. Siu
## The Sojourner

### THE "SOJOURNER" DEFINED

About forty years ago Simmel wrote in his *Soziologie* an analysis of an ideal type, with reference to race and culture contacts, which he called "der Fremde." Sociologists in America and abroad have done much significant work implicitly and explicitly on the general subject of the social type that results from race and culture contacts. Park, particularly, coined a term which he saw fit to use in the study of the kind of relationship between racial hybrids and "the two worlds in both of which he is more or less a stranger"—"the marginal man."

I am proposing to isolate another deviant type, for which I employ the term "sojourner." The sojourner, to be sure, is characteristically not a marginal man; he is different from the marginal man in many aspects. The essential characteristic of the sojourner is that he clings to the culture of his own ethnic group as in contrast to the bicultural complex of the marginal man. Psychologically he is unwilling to organize himself as a permanent resident in the country of his sojourn. When he does, he becomes a marginal man.

Both the marginal man and the sojourner are types of stranger—in Simmel's sense, products of the cultural frontier. No doubt, in many instances, the sojourner has something in common with the marginal man. It is convenient, therefore, to define the "sojourner" as a stranger who spends many years of his lifetime in a foreign country without being assimilated by it. The sojourner is par excellence an ethnocentrist. This is the case of a large number of immigrants in America and also of Americans who live abroad. The Chinese laundryman, for example, is a typical sojourner, and so is the American missionary in China. The concept may

10

20

be applied to a whole range of foreign residents in any country to the extent that they maintain sojourner attitudes. The colonist, the foreign trader, the diplomat, the foreign student, the international journalist, the foreign missionary, the research anthropologist abroad, and all sorts of migrant groups in different areas of the globe, in various degree, may be considered sojourners in the sociological sense.

In the new country the sojourner has indeed gone through a series of adjustments to his present environment, and he is very likely to be an agent of cultural diffusion between his homeland and the country of his sojourn. The sojourner, however, can hardly be assimilated. The essence of assimilation, according to Park and Burgess, is "a process of interpenetration and fusion in which person and group acquire the memories, sentiments and attitudes of other persons or groups, and by sharing their experience and history, are incorporated with them in common cultural life." It seems that the sojourner, on the contrary, tends to be isolated instead.

The characterization of the sojourner given by Simmel is not that of the man "who comes today and goes tomorrow but rather of the man who comes today and stays tomorrow." The concept, let me repeat, is applied only in the general context of race and culture contacts; it has no reference to, for example, a New Yorker who moves to San Francisco.

Social situations relative to this general problem in different countries in our time often set people apart, hindering the process of assimilation or at least making it very slow. The social adjustments and activities of the sojourner, to be sure, vary in detail in particular situations. There are, however, some general and essential characteristics which must be ascribed to the sojourner.

## THE JOB

Perhaps it is logical to consider first what it is that makes the sojourner go abroad and stay on. Apparently he knows why he migrates. It may be a religious mission, a commercial interest, an economic adventure, a military campaign, an academic degree, a journalist assignment, a political refuge, or what not. In spite of the seemingly heterogeneous motives and aims, there is, however, something common to all of them; the intrinsic purpose of the sojourn is to do a job and do it in the shortest possible time. The sojourner seldom organizes his life beyond the accomplishing of this end. The term "job" used here is to indicate a deviation from the term "career." Career is to be conceived as lifelong work, but the job can be only a part of one's career. It is quite clear in some of the cases. A foreign student, for instance, may stay several years in order to get his degree, but his school work is only the beginning of his career. A research anthropologist may visit and revisit a primitive society, but it is clear that his project may not be his lifelong career. A religious mission, on the other hand, is relatively harder to identify as a job or a career because missionary workers tend to stay abroad longer—some until retirement,

others several years—and each has a particular reason or reasons for the decision to stay or to leave. The hope and dream of an economic adventurer is, of course, to make a fortune, and the length of the sojourn depends upon his success or failure in the adventure. His job, like that of the missionary, may be finished in several years or may be prolonged for decades. Generally speaking, it seems that the time element varies according to individual situations, but the job itself is essentially a means to an end. The sojourner may not necessarily like his job and enjoy working at it. It is rather that he is fighting for social status at home. The job, therefore, is tied up with all sorts of personal needs for new experience, se-    10
curity, prestige, etc.

Although the sojourner plans to get through with the job in the shortest possible time, yet he soon finds himself in a dilemma as to whether to stay abroad or to return home. Naturally this problem is related to the success or failure of the job—he would not like to return home without a sense of accomplishment and some sort of security. But this state is psychologically never achieved. In due time the sojourner becomes vague and uncertain about the termination of his sojourn because of the fact that he has already made some adjustments to his new environment and acquired an old-timer's attitudes. "You promised me to go abroad for only three years,"    20
complained the wife of a Chinese laundryman in a letter to him, "but you have stayed there nearly thirty years now!"

This feature of staying on indefinitely is indeed interesting. In his effort to make his job a success, the sojourner stays on long enough to make changes in his life-organization, so that he is no longer the same person; in other words, he has developed a mode of living peculiar to his present situation. He has no desire for full participation in the community life of his adopted land. In other words, his activities tend to be within the limit of his own interest—the job. He tends to think of himself as an outsider and feels content as a spectator in many of the community affairs. If he    30
does take part in certain activities, they are likely to be either matters relating to his job or matters concerning his homeland's social welfare, politics, etc. Essentially his activities in the community are symbiotic rather than social. The public seldom thinks of him other than in relation to his job. He therefore is an individual who performs a function rather than a person with a social status. He is a person only to the people of his own ethnic group or to a social circle related to his job.

Related to the symbiotic level of the sojourner's activities is another feature which is what may be called the "alien" element of the job. Whatever it is, it is something foreign to the natives. It is either something    40
transplanted by the sojourner from his homeland or something new invented by him in his struggle for existence abroad. In America the Chinese laundry, the Italian fruit stand, the Greek ice-cream parlor, and the Jewish clothing store are inventions by which these immigrant groups survive in the highly competitive urban community. So, too, the Christian church, the hospital, the oil refinery, the modern school, and the archeological

excavation are indeed new elements which may disturb the social order of the folk society into which they are introduced.

Because of the alien element in the job, at least for the time being, the sojourner is not considered as a competitor of the natives. Paradoxically he often finds himself a keen competitor of the people of his own ethnic group.

## THE IN-GROUP TENDENCY

On the basis of common interests and cultural heritage the sojourner tends to associate with people of his own ethnic group. He and his country- 10
men, if there are enough of them, very likely live together in a racial colony or cultural area. "Little Tokyo," "Little Sicily," "Greek Town," and "China-town" in this country, for example, are their ghettos. An interesting jour-nalistic account of 3,600 Americans in Saudi Arabia shows that the colony is completely on American standards; the Arab world surrounding it is spoken as a "land of Wajid Mafe"—meaning "the land of plenty of nothing."

The formation of the cultural colony reveals symbiotic segregation, on the one hand, and social isolation, on the other hand. Whether the so-journer lives with or apart from the people of his own ethnic group, as 20
long as his social life ties up with all sorts of activities in the racial colony there is a tendency for forming in-group relationships. The desire to live together becomes not only social need but also a natural thing. The colony in its process of development does not always grow in one space, and often segregation may take the form of scattering around an area and maintaining only a center or several centers of social activities. The center of activites is very likely to be developed into a segregated colony if a large number of the same ethnic group can maintain themselves locally. The crucial factor, therefore, is the industrial and social potentiality of the metropolis. Chinatown in Chicago, for instance, originated in 1872 30
in a lonely laundry shop located between Clark and Madison streets. Several decades later it grew to be the third largest Chinese colony in this country, with scores of stores and hundreds of laundry shops and chop suey houses scattered all about the metropolitan area. It grew because Chicago itself developed from a frontier fort into the second largest city in the country.

In the smaller cities where we found one or more chop suey restaurants and scores of Chinese laundry shops, we found also, at the periphery of the central business district, one or more Chinese stores which are the centers of activity for the local Chinese population. To be sure, the store may not have originated as such an enterprise. It could be a former laun- 40
dry shop converted into a store as the local Chinese population increased, which, because of its position became a shopping center where homeland merchandise is offered. Occasionally local people of the ethnic group con-gregate there for social affairs and recreation. This is the situation, for instance, in Richmond, Virginia, and Indianapolis, Indiana. In still smaller cities, like Battle Creek, Michigan, and Portland, Maine, there is no Chi-

nese store, but the local Chinese usually congregate in the rear of a down-town laundry shop where facilities for recreation and personal contacts are available. The local colony has not grown, because the local population of the ethnic group has remained too small.

Essentially the colony is an instrument to establish or to re-establish some sort of primary-group relationships in the matrix of homeland culture—an effort to create a home away from home. Whatever activities the sojourner may participate in, in the community at large, in private life he tends to live apart from the natives and to share with his countrymen in striving to maintain homeland culture. His best friends are people of 10 his ethnic group, and they entertain one another at their homes. They share their pride and aspirations, hopes and dreams, prejudices, and dilemmas and express their opinions about the country of their sojourn. The following narrative tells vividly what may be called a sojourner's attitude.                                                                                 ,

Our attitude toward the Americans was a mixed one. We envied them a little; they had a country they could call their own. It was, moreover, a fairly nice country; not like Russia, but, in the long run, not a bad one. It could have been a very good country if Russians had settled it a few centuries ago; now it was too late; the Americans had 20 to content themselves with what they had.

During our American hours and enforced association with the natives we are compelled to speak their language, a most difficult and unpleasant tongue, hard and harsh, forbidding and unyielding, lacking the softness and elasticity of our own Russian language. As soon as our working day was over and we had shed our overalls, we became Russians. We went to our Russian affairs; we assembled in Russian homes around Russian samovars; ate Russian food, drank Russian tea (the tea was, unfortunately, made in New York) and discussed Russian affairs in Russian language. 30

One of our main topics was this country, and we most definitely did not like it. This country was definitely inferior to Russia—even to Russia when we left there.

Although this is a Russian story, yet it describes the general reaction of all immigrant groups which happen to be minorities in a foreign country. This sort of attitude seems to prevail in the mind of the sojourner and that is why he has to seek his countrymen as neighbors and friends. Home and family life, perhaps, show most interestingly how the sojourner can maintain his homeland cultural heritage abroad. Food habits seem to be 40 the most persistent. The Chinese invented chop suey to suit the Americans' appetite while he enjoyed typical home dishes such as *chia-chang-yu-pien* (steamed pork with imported shrimp sauce) which most Americans dislike. Homeland tongues, art, sentiments, and primary-group attitudes fortify the sojourner in his effort to maintain homeland culture—although there are variations among different ethnic groups within one country and in different countries. The American missionary, for instance, can keep his homeland culture intact better than most of the immigrant groups in America. He is more successful in isolating his children from the native influences, sending them to an American school and living in a segregated area. Pearl Buck illustrated this point very well.

The American home I know very well, partly from close observation of homes during the years that I have been living in my own country but as much from my own typically American home in China. My parents were American, patriotic to the core, and simply and honestly convinced, as most Americans are, that the American home is the best in the world. To them American home life was even a part of the Christian religion which they felt it their duty and privilege to preach to the Chinese. I do not believe it ever occurred to my parents in the goodness of their saintly hearts to ask themselves whether or not the Chinese had a sort of home life which was perhaps as valuable in its way as ours, or at least better suited to China than ours was.

Our home, therefore, was kept absolutely and carefully American. We had American furniture and American food, though all of us children liked Chinese food better, and only as a concession to our pleading did we have an occasional Chinese meal. Beyond that we satisfied our craving by partaking heartily of the servants' meals before our own and listening in guilty silence to our mother worrying over our small appetites. We got up in the morning and had prayers and ate porridge and eggs for breakfast, and studied our American lessons, and on Sunday a Christian church bell rang and we went to church, and the only difference was that the Christians in that church were Chinese instead of American. We were trained in all the ways of American homemaking, and spiritually we were kept close not to the Chinese about us but to our own loved land thousands of miles away that we had never known except through our parents' eyes and words.

But the Chinese immigrant in the United States cannot isolate his children so successfully as the American missionary in China can. The Chinese immigrant has to send his children to American schools. The Chinese child, therefore, is more likely to become a marginal man. The following story illustrates the intrinsic characteristic of the cultural pattern and the problem it creates.

The relationship between father and children in our family, as in most Chinese families, is of a very formal nature. I never think of cracking jokes with daddy. ...

Respect we children always observe—for instance, by carefully calling an older sister "second older sister" and never the familiar "Jade Lotus" which only those older than she can use. The practical result of the system is that the youngest in the family has no one with whom he can be familiar. Nothing is so effective in keeping this present adolescent quiet as to remind him that he is the smallest; therefore he can say nothing imprudent to anyone else; nor can he safely call anything his own.

It can be seen that there is little room for individuality in a Chinese family such as ours. We are early instructed that we must never bring disgrace to the family name, and that individual achievement is less significant than the resulting family glory. The individual claims his significance largely from the family to which he belongs. For instance, in Chinatown, introductions usually are no sooner under way than one is asked (if one is young), "Who is your honorable father?" The Chinese attempt to submerge individuality leads to tremendous family conflict here in the United States. My adolescent years were spent in trying to adjust a newly learned American cultural pattern to a rigid established Chinese standard. It is revolutionary to hear one's college professor say, "Parents should understand their children instead of demanding just obedience." Disaster results when adolescents return home and try to educate parents to this new idea. I have never tried to do exactly this with my father, for I am sure that he will never understand his children, though the goal of his whole life's work has unquestionably been their welfare.

The happiest adjustment in this conflict between individual expression versus parental control I have found to lie in expression outside of the family circle, acquiescence within. Such adjustment has not been made without pain and tears, for other children of the family as well as myself. In all fairness to daddy, I must say that if he demands respect, it is not because he is in any way egotistical, but because lack of respect for parents results in confusion of proper relationship. . . .

I have never been in China. My Chinese heritage, which I hold so dear, has been transmitted to me almost solely by my father in the cultural pattern which he has stamped upon me; singularly, how he imposed it does not seem to matter any more.

Both of the foregoing cases show parents who obviously have sojourners' attitudes, trying to maintain their homeland cultural heritage; the child in the former case, however, does not suffer from cultural conflict, while the child in the latter case does. These differences, it seems, are due to the different situations in China and in America. What makes the differences in detail in race and culture relation in these two countries is indeed very interesting. It is not, however, the purpose of this paper to undertake such an analysis. My attempt so far has been to show how the sojourner behaves as an individual, with reference to his job, then to describe his activities as a person among people of his own ethnic group, and, finally, in the following section, I will attempt to show his relation to the country of his sojourn and his homeland. Indeed, he is not typically a sojourner unless he has maintained his homeland tie.

## MOVEMENT BACK AND FORTH

The sojourner stays on abroad, but he also never loses his homeland tie. In the beginning he ventured to take up residence in a foreign country with a definite aim. Soon he found that the job was taking much longer than he had expected. His original plan, as a matter of fact, has been complicated by new social values and social attitudes. As a means to an end, a new orientation has been adopted; he stays several years, and, when opportunity permits, he takes a trip home for a visit. The trip is an accomplishment, but the job can never be finished. Again he has to go abroad. In his lifetime several trips are made back and forth, and in some cases     10
the career is terminated only by retirement or death.

In the preceding section, we have stated that the sojourner wants the job done in the shortest possible time. Obviously, achievement of this objective depends largely upon his ability, on the one hand, and his chance or luck, on the other hand. Each individual is not exactly like another, and yet we have a whole range of cases in which differences can be described and compared in terms of the type of job, homeland background, race and cultural situation abroad, and personal adjustments in response to these circumstances.

Typical examples of the movement back and forth are the missionary's     20
furlough and the immigrant's trip home. This movement is characterized by ethnocentrism in the form of social isolation abroad and social expectation and status at home. In other words, one has gained some sort of recognition of his accomplishment by his friends and relatives both at home and abroad. While staying abroad, the sojourner keeps his home tie by writing letters, exchanging gifts, and participating in home social and political affairs. In contrast to his role on his job, these activities seem to be purely on the basis of convention, and there is nothing to indicate the element of expediency, as in the activities of his job. The return trip is the result of a social expectation of members of his primary group     30
as much as of his individual effort; their sentiments and attitudes make his trip meaningful. The trip shows that he is a person to be admired, to be appreciated, to be proud of, and to be envied.

To illustrate the movement back and forth, the following case selected from the Chinese group is especially significant because it seems to be nearly a perfect cycle of the sojourner's career, with the usual sequence of trips taken every few years. Moreover, the pattern of behavior is carried from father to son. It seems to represent a life-cycle comparable to that of the marginal man.

Mr. C. came to America in 1919 at the age of 19, two years after his     40
marriage in his native village in China. Soon after his arrival he began to work with his father and two cousins in a laundry shop uptown. Their laundry shop was established about twenty-five years ago by his father and two partners. It had been very prosperous and was in need of helpers badly. A young man working with them was a great

help. "The work was hard," said Mr. C., as he recalled his experience in the bygone days, "I almost wanted to give up. But what else could I do? After all, the old men were working just as hard as I was. What could we Chinese do in this country? You don't know even how to speak their language [ English]. . . ."

The newcomer was encouraged to attend the Sunday school conducted by one of the churches in town, for some of his young clansmen were also pupils there and they went together. The church maintained Sunday school classes every Sunday afternoon especially for the Chinese, teaching them English and Bible lessons. For the first time Mr. C., a country boy from China, met his Sunday school teacher, Mrs. J., a housewife. He attended the class steadily for several years. Gradually he could speak English to his customers but was not converted. He admitted that his English was not adequate and he was not able to read newspapers (English papers). "Who ever thought of staying in this country so long?" Mr. C. recalled that he expected to return to China in a few years and stay home for good. And that was why he had no incentive to learn more English. In fact he had no time to study at that time, as the business was very good and they had to work day and night except Sunday.

Besides his acquaintance with the church people and his impersonal business contacts with his customers in the laundry shop, Mr. C.'s social activities were largely among his clansmen and his fellow-countrymen in Chinatown. He became an active member in C. clan. Later he joined the Kuomintang (Chinese Nationalist party), became active in the Chung Wah Association (usually known to Americans as the Benevolent Association), and was interested in social welfare in his native village as well as in China. He liked to have his name in the Chinese newspapers every now and then.

In 1925 the laundry shop was sold, and the father and son went back to China. The old man thought it was time for him to retire, and it was his fourth trip back home. But Mr. C. could have stayed here longer. Why had he to leave too? He said he was afraid something might happen to his father on the way; the old man was too old and was taking a large sum of money with him. Of course his wife wrote and urged him to come home too, for they had no children as yet. The real reason, which Mr. C. did not tell explicitly, was that he and his father thought that they had enough money to live in style in China even if Mr. C. decided not to return to America again. The family was known in their native district as being well-to-do even before Mr. C. came to America to join his father in 1919. His father was a good provider and "home builder" in all the years. They had lands and business investments and a good semi-Western-style house in the native village. At this time, they took home with them about forty thousand dollars.

In the year after the father and son reached home, the C. family married away Mr. C.'s younger sister. It became known in the whole district; people said that the dowry for the young bride consisted of 25 American gold dollars and a full possession of teakwood furniture, dozens of dresses, and, what was more, a slave maid.

Later, Mr. C. invested a large sum of money in a textile enterprise in the city of Canton. Unfortunately it turned out to be a complete failure, for which Mr. C. blamed the dishonesty of cousins and the incompetency of the management.

The spending was excessive and the loss was unexpected. Mr. C. had to come to America again and again worked in another laundry shop with one of his relatives, and the business was very good. In a few years he was able to save enough to make another trip. In 1929 his family urged him to return. At this time his father had died and his mother wanted to see him before her passing away.

Mr. C. was soon in China but he did not plan to stay for good. He came again after a year of staying with his family. Complaining that it is "too easy to spend all money in China," he said he gave his mother a birthday banquet, inviting the whole village. He also helped the village to re-establish the village school; the old school was disorganized. He would have to send his son to school soon. "He was too young yet," Mr. C. said, "but I would not let my son grow up without a school to attend. So for the good of the village as well as mine there had to be a school for the children. I spent over a thousand dollars for it, but if I did not take the lead, no one seemed to care to do it."

"And when I arrived in this country again," Mr. C. continued, "it was 1930 and it was the coming of the great depression. Life was hard here too but not as bad as in China. The people had been so poor that it sickened my heart. When I was in China, friends and relatives all came for money, one way or the other. It was hard to deal with them without hurting their feelings. They did not believe that I had spent almost all my money. After all, I had to keep some to support my family and for my trip back here."

"This is a wonderful country," said Mr. C., in response to a question about his feeling toward America. "Everything is orderly according to the law. Look at their industry—I don't know when China can follow it up. After all, we Chinese are just staying here temporarily. We are just outsiders. Outsiders, particularly of the nonwhite race, have not much of a chance. Some Americans are very nice to you, but deep in their hearts you are still, they know, different from their own. So we should hope that China would be prosperous and strong some day and we can go home and do something else instead of working as slaves in the laundry shop and chop suey house."

From 1930 to 1940 Mr. C. had been in partnership with someone in two chop suey restaurant businesses. At the beginning, Mr. C. worked as a cook for two or three years; later he became a waiter. The business was very poor because of the depression. Both of the restaurants in which he was in partnership failed and, finally, he was employed as a waiter in one of the best chop suey restaurants in Chinatown.

It was about 1940 and Mr. C. was thinking of taking another trip home or of arranging for his son to come to this country. It was a hard decision to make at the time, for he had not much money. Alas! World War II broke out and it blocked Mr. C's plan. Worse still, he lost contact with his family after the Japanese took Hong Kong and Canton. When the war was over, in 1946, Mr. C. learned that his mother was dead and his wife very sick, and that his son was under the care of relatives. His relatives wrote and urged him to return for a reunion.

Mr. C. was with his family again as soon as he could arrange his trip. Soon after he was home, his wife died. Then he took his son to Hong Kong, where the youth was sent to a missionary school. At this time, he married a woman twenty years younger than he. He said he bought a house for his young bride and stayed with her only four months. Then he had to leave for America again.

After Mr. C. reached here, he returned to his old job in the restaurant. A few months later, he heard that his second wife had given birth to a baby girl. At the present time (1948), Mr. C. is very much interested in getting his son over to this country. He was told that he could apply for American citizenship so that he could get his wife into this country nonquota. His son, however, cannot come nonquota, for when the youth was born his father was not naturalized—nor is he naturalized yet. It seems that Mr. C. cares mostly to have his son in this country; like most of his countrymen, his wife's coming has not been in his mind. He is not going to apply for citizenship now. At least he has not made up his mind.

We have in this case a representation of the stages of adjustment: first, Mr. C. has learned to be an individual who must do his "job" while, socially, he joins his countrymen in isolation in the racial colony and plans to return to the old country when it is possible; second, he soon finds himself in an anomalous position with reference to his homeland and the country of his sojourn; third, he projects a hope that someday he may accomplish his aim, but meanwhile he goes home for a visit, and the cycle closes when he makes his final trip home and retires. Comparable with the case of Mr. C. is that of an American couple who went to China soon after their marriage, took furloughs every few years, lived in a segregated compound among fellow-missionaries, sent their children back to America for education, and then, finally, came back themselves for retirement after fifty years. They follow the same general pattern—accommodation, isolation, and unassimilation.

The problem here is to inquire into the situation that makes the sojourner stay on abroad. Again each individual case varies in detail according to the situation. After a period of residence abroad, one is likely to be confronted with personal problems both directly and indirectly affecting his plan. In attempting to solve some of the problems, he sooner or later finds himself in the midst of constant emotional conflicts. As time goes on, he becomes, unconsciously perhaps, more of a sharer in the racial colony, developing a mode of living which is totally characteristic neither of his home nor of the dominant group. That is why so many sojourners do not take the trip, particularly among the migrant groups. A study of the large congregation of aged persons in Chinatown reveals an interesting angle of the situation which deserves a careful analysis in detail in another paper. From a sample of individual cases we find, first, men who could never save enough money to take the trip. The main reason is largely due to personal disorganization as a result of gambling, prostitution, or drug addiction. Others had large sums of money once or twice in their lives but were forced to stay on because of immigration difficulties. These are the men who reside in America illegally, and, even if they had money enough to take a trip home, they would not do so unless their economic security could be assured. One of the ways to play safe would be to secure a return permit from the United States Immigration Authority so that, in case his plan failed at home, he could come to America again. But there has been no immigration provision to adjust the status of most of the illegal entry cases until recently. These, together with other personal problems, often cause the sojourner to stay on for twenty, thirty, forty, or more years without taking a single trip back home—or perhaps only one trip—and there is no hope for the final one. As they are now old, poor, and sick, they become indifferent. Sometimes when a man is asked how long he has been in this country, his answer reflects self-scorn: "Only five or six weeks—is that enough?" In reality a week means seven years. If he says he has been here "five weeks," it means thirty-five years. When asked whether he has been back to China for a visit, he may mix good humor with pity in replying: "I have indeed sent letters home several times but have never sent my person!"

The second category of the nondeparture cases—which constitute only a small portion of the Chinese—are those who have their wives and children with them in this country. The return trip in such cases involves the attitudes of different members of the family; particularly, there are the problems of the second generation. Other factors, such as economic difficulties, business commitments, political unrest, etc., may prevent departure. However, the mere fact that one has never made his return trip is by no means proof that he is not a sojourner. He is, in fact, very much the same as his countrymen who do make the trips. Although he must forego the satisfaction of a homeland reunion such as his more fortunate countrymen and friends have enjoyed, yet the return to the racial colony for retirement is to some degree a substitute for a home away from home. So the old, poor, and sick seek refuge in the racial colony; their business and residence usually are located near it. Even those who have made interracial marriages return eventually to the racial colony. The same situation, no doubt—although in different degree—has developed among other ethnic groups: "The world at large was cold and strange, his contact with it being confined to an abstract and rational intercourse. But within the Ghetto he felt free. His contacts with fellow-Jew were warm, spontaneous, and intimate."

Another situation connected with this problem of homeland tie is the phenomenon of mass migration due to war and political persecution, which often results in such disturbed conditions at home that return became impossible. Under such circumstances people perhaps arrive at a new orientation and adjustment. The political refugees, the White Russians, the German Jews, and the so-called "displaced persons," for    10
instance, moved into a developed country and became its minorities. In a report on recent immigration from Europe to the United States, Professor Davie states that among the 1,600 recent political refugees, 96.5 per cent replied that they would remain in this country and only 3.5 per cent of them indicated that they would return to their respective countries when the situation permitted them to do so. It is significant to note, however, that in this small proportion there are many professional people and also people from countries where the political system has not been so radically uprooted.

This is the place to raise the question whether the state of Israel is the    20
work of the sojourner. Here is perhaps a unique example of the fact that a people can maintain a cultural heritage in the ghetto and return to the place where it originated two thousand years afterward without feeling strange. The Jews have been sojourners for centuries. The social solidarity of the ghetto as well as international political change, perhaps, made the movement possible.

Marco Polo, whose traveling was famous both at home and abroad, returned finally to Italy after many years in the court of Cathay as a sojourner. The sojourner may make several trips back and forth, he may make only one trip, or he may not make any trip at all. Nevertheless,    30
those who do not make the trip may remain unassimilated just as much as those who do make it. Psychologically the sojourner is a potential wanderer, as Simmel puts it, who has not quite gotten over the freedom of coming and going.

Being a potential wanderer, the sojourner is a skeptic on the subject of homeownership. If he does own real estate, he tends to think of it as a business proposition, and he does not suffer a sense of loss when he sells it. His furniture tends to be either such as he can dispose of without too much sacrifice or things he has treasured and would like to keep wherever and whenever he moves. If he secures any valuables, they are    40
likely to be portable objects.

## METHODOLOGICAL NOTE

The concept of "sojourner" developed from my unsuccessful effort, about ten years ago, to analyze materials gathered when employing the concept "marginal man." None of the Chinese laundrymen I studied could be considered as a marginal man. Consequently it became necessary to look at the subject matter differently. After a few years of pondering over both Chinese and non-Chinese materials, I was convinced that he should be treated as a deviant type from the concept of the stranger which Simmel described with such peculiar insight. I was also inspired by Stonequist, who stated that "some of the members of the subordinate or minority group are able to live within their own culture, or at least to live in them sufficiently not to be greatly disturbed by the culture of the dominant group." The term "sojourner," however, was first impressed on my mind from reading Glick's "The Chinese Migrant in Hawaii," since he used the terms "sojourner's attitudes" and "settler's attitudes."

The sojourner seems to be primarily a social type of the urban community. In the folk society the sojourner probably tends to be more isolated in private life but more active and more influential. The more it is a folk group, however, the more difficult it is for the sojourner to live in it. One of the most interesting projects on this general problem would be a study of the activities of the sojourner in the folk society in comparison with his behavior in the urban community. Studies of different minority groups within a given society in comparison with a particular minority group in different countries would be promising. Comparative studies of this sort would put the research sociologists in a strategic position to systematize their knowledge of the social types that results from race and culture contacts and conflicts.

Sociologists generally agree that the first-generation immigrants, occidental as well as oriental, would not be completely assimilated anyway. It is, therefore, a question of the degree of assimilation or isolation among a whole range of individual cases which, although different from one another in detail, yet are similar to one another in general characteristics. Eventually, we have to consider the borderline cases which are neither typically sojourner nor typically marginal man. It will be necessary to study the similarities and differences between the two types, using the concepts as extreme poles, and to classify them categorically and inquire into the situation in which the variation derived.

It seems that, in dealing with the problem of social type, the typological technique should be more profitable and promising than any other method. As Burgess states:

The method of typology has proved particularly appropriate for the collection, classification, and analysis of cases. It is, in fact, a large part of the case-study method so far as it consists in grouping cases under a given class or classes and then developing a new class for any negative case, i.e., one that does not fall under any previously postulated class.

At the present time our knowledge of social types resulting from race

and culture contacts is only fragmentary, and there are large areas un-
explored. To achieve a systematic knowledge of the type, one of the best
ways is through comparative studies of the types of situation. Race and
ethnic differences and conflicts are types of social bond related to the
growth of personality and institutions.

Probably another angle of this problem is another type which has arisen
in times of mass migration, when people have moved into new territories
as a result of military invasion and colonial expansion. There the newcomers become the dominant group, politically if not culturally. The
building of empires and mass emigration seems to create another type of   10
stranger—the settler. He moves to a country where there is, more or less,
a frontier and where the natives have had their own culture but not anything that we may call civilization. At the beginning the social process
seems to be predominantly the phenomena of conflict and accommodation. Between the newcomers and the natives and among groups of newcomers, the intergroup relation would eventually bring some sort of unity
through a long process of acculturation. Those who were the pioneers
were the settlers. The settler has no problem of assimilation. It seems
that in terms of conflict and accommodation the settler may be defined
in a sociological sense. The sojourner, on the other hand, is not usually   20
a product of mass migration but rather a member of a minority group
whose cultural heritage is subjected to either social isolation or assimilation.

# KOREMATSU v. UNITED STATES
## U.S. Supreme Court, 1944

MR. JUSTICE BLACK delivered the opinion of the Court.

The petitioner, an American citizen of Japanese descent, was convicted in a federal district court for remaining in San Leandro, California, a "Military Area," contrary to Civilian Exclusion Order No. 34 of the Commanding General of the Western Command, U.S. Army, which directed that after May 9, 1942, all persons of Japanese ancestry should be excluded from that area. No question was raised as to petitioner's loyalty to the United States. The Circuit Court of Appeals affirmed, and the importance of the constitutional question involved caused us to grant certiorari. 10

It should be noted, to begin with, that all legal restrictions which curtail the civil rights of a single racial group are immediately suspect. That is not to say that all such restrictions are unconstitutional. It is to say that courts must subject them to the most rigid scrutiny. Pressing public necessity may sometimes justify the existence of such restrictions; racial antagonism never can.

In the instant case prosecution of the petitioner was begun by information charging violation of an Act of Congress, of March 21, 1942, 56 Stat. 173, which provides that

" . . . whoever shall enter, remain in, leave, or commit any act in any 20 military area or military zone prescribed, under the authority of an Executive order of the President, by the Secretary of War, or by any military commander designated by the Secretary of War, contrary to the restrictions applicable to any such area or zone or contrary to the order of the Secretary of War or any such military commander, shall, if it appears that he knew or should have known of the existence and extent of the restric-

279

tions or order and that his act was in violation thereof, be guilty of a misdemeanor and upon conviction shall be liable to a fine of not to exceed $5,000 or to imprisonment for not more than one year, or both, for each offense."

Exclusion Order No. 34, which the petitioner knowingly and admittedly violated was one of a number of military orders and proclamations, all of which were substantially based upon Executive Order No. 9066, 7 Fed. Reg. 1407. That order, issued after we were at war with Japan, declared that "the successful prosecution of the war requires every possible protection against espionage and against sabotage to national-defense material, national-defense premises, and national-defense utilities. . . . "

One of the series of orders and proclamations, a curfew order, which like the exclusion order here was promulgated pursuant to Executive Order 9066, subjected all persons of Japanese ancestry in prescribed West Coast military areas to remain in their residences from 8 p.m. to 6 a.m. As is the case with the exclusion order here, that prior curfew order was designed as a "protection against espionage and against sabotage." In Kiyoshi Hirabayashi v. United States, 320 U.S. 81, we sustained a conviction obtained for violation of the curfew order. The Hirabayashi conviction and this one thus rest on the same 1942 Congressional Act and the same basic executive and military orders, all of which orders were aimed at the twin dangers of espionage and sabotage.

The 1942 Act was attacked in the Hirabayashi case as an unconstitutional delegation of power; it was contended that the curfew order and other orders on which it rested were beyond the war powers of the Congress, the military authorities and of the President, as Commander in Chief of the Army; and finally that to apply the curfew order against none but citizens of Japanese ancestry amounted to a constitutionally prohibited discrimination solely on account of race. To these questions, we gave the serious consideration which their importance justified. We upheld the curfew order as an exercise of the power of the government to take steps necessary to prevent espionage and sabotage in an area threatened by Japanese attack.

In the light of the principles we announced in the Hirabayashi case, we are unable to conclude that it was beyond the war power of Congress and the Executive to exclude those of Japanese ancestry from the West Coast war area at the time they did. True, exclusion from the area in which one's home is located is a far greater deprivation than constant confinement to the home from 8 p.m. to 6 a.m. Nothing short of apprehension by the proper military authorities of the gravest imminent danger to the public safety can constitutionally justify either. But exclusion from a threatened area, no less than curfew, has a definite and close relationship to the prevention of espionage and sabotage. The military authorities, charged with the primary responsibility of defending our shores, concluded that curfew provided inadequate protection and ordered exclusion. They did so, as pointed out in our Hirabayashi opinion, in accordance with Congressional authority to the military to say who should, and who should not, remain in the threatened areas.

In this case the petitioner challenges the assumptions upon which we rested our conclusions in the Hirabayashi case. He also urges that by May 1942, when Order No. 34 was promulgated, all danger of Japanese invasion of the West Coast had disappeared. After careful consideration of these contentions we are compelled to reject them.

Here, as in the Hirabayashi case, *supra,* at page 99, ". . . we cannot reject as unfounded the judgment of the military authorities and of Congress that there are disloyal members of that population, whose number and strength could not be precisely and quickly ascertained. We cannot say that the war-making branches of the Government did not have ground for believing that in a critical hour such persons could not readily be isolated and separately dealt with, and constituted a menace to the national defense and safety, which demanded that prompt and adequate measures be taken to guard against it."

Like curfew, exclusion of those of Japanese origin was deemed necessary because of the presence of an unascertained number of disloyal members of the group, most of whom we have no doubt were loyal to this country. It was because we could not reject the finding of the military authorities that it was impossible to bring about an immediate segregation of the disloyal from the loyal that we sustained the validity of the curfew order as applying to the whole group. In the instant case, temporary exclusion of the entire group was rested by the military on the same ground. The judgment that exclusion of the whole group was for the same reason a military imperative answers the contention that the exclusion was in the nature of group punishment based on antagonism to those of Japanese origin. That there were members of the group who retained loyalties to Japan has been confirmed by investigations made subsequent to the exclusion. Approximately five thousand American citizens of Japanese ancestry refused to swear unqualified allegiance to the United States and to renounce allegiance to the Japanese Emperor, and several thousand evacuees requested repatriation to Japan.

We uphold the exclusion order as of the time it was made and when the petitioner violated it. Cf. Chastleton Corporation v. Sinclair, 264 U.S. 543, 547; Block v. Hirsh, 256 U.S. 135, 154, 155. In doing so, we are not unmindful of the hardships imposed by it upon a large group of American citizens. Cf. Ex parte Kumezo Kawato, 317 U.S. 69, 73. But hardships are part of war, and war is an aggregation of hardships. All citizens alike, both in and out of uniform, feel the impact of war in greater or lesser measure. Citizenship has its responsibilities as well as its privileges, and in time of war the burden is always heavier. Compulsory exclusion of large groups of citizens from their homes, except under circumstances of direct emergency and peril, is inconsistent with our basic governmental institutions. But when under conditions of modern warfare our shores are threatened by hostile forces, the power to protect must be commensurate with the threatened danger.

It is argued that on May 30, 1942, the date the petitioner was charged with remaining in the prohibited area, there were conflicting orders outstanding, forbidding him both to leave the area and to remain there. Of course, a person cannot be convicted for doing the very thing which it is a crime to fail to do. But the outstanding orders here contained no such contradictory commands.

There was an order issued March 27, 1942, which prohibited petitioner and others of Japanese ancestry from leaving the area, but its effect was specifically limited in time "until and to the extent that a future proc-        10
lamation or order should so permit or direct." 7 Fed. Reg. 2601. That "future order", the one for violation of which petitioner was convicted, was issued May 3, 1942, and it did "direct" exclusion from the area of all persons of Japanese ancestry, before 12 o'clock noon, May 9; furthermore it contained a warning that all such persons found in the prohibited area would be liable to punishment under the March 21, 1942 Act of Congress. Consequently, the only order in effect touching the petitioner's being in the area on May 30, 1942, the date specified in the information against him, was the May 3 order which prohibited his remaining there, and it was that same order, which he stipulated in his trial that he had violated,        20
knowing of its existence. There is therefore no basis for the argument that on May 30, 1942, he was subject to punishment, under the March 27 and May 3rd orders, whether he remained in or left the area.

It does appear, however, that on May 9, the effective date of the exclusion order, the military authorities had already determined that the evacuation should be effected by assembling together and placing under guard all those of Japanese ancestry, at central points, designated as "assembly centers," in order "to insure the orderly evacuation and resettlement of Japanese voluntarily migrating from military area No. 1 to restrict and regulate such migration." Public Proclamation No. 4, 7 Fed. Reg. 2601.        30
And on May 19, 1942, eleven days before the time petitioner was charged with unlawfully remaining in the area, Civilian Restrictive Order No. 1, 8 Fed. Reg. 982, provided for detention of those of Japanese ancestry in assembly or relocation centers. It is now argued that the validity of the exclusion order cannot be considered apart from the orders requiring him, after departure from the area, to report and to remain in an assembly or relocation center. The contention is that we must treat these separate orders as one and inseparable; that, for this reason, if detention in the assembly or relocation center would have illegally deprived the petitioner of his liberty, the exclusion order and his conviction under it cannot stand.        40

We are thus being asked to pass at this time upon the whole subsequent detention program in both assembly and relocation centers, although the only issues framed at the trial related to petitioner's remaining in the prohibited area in violation of the exclusion order. Had petitioner here left the prohibited area and gone to an assembly center we cannot say either as a matter of fact or law, that his presence in that center would have resulted in his detention in a relocation center. Some who did report to the assembly center were not sent to relocation centers, but were released upon condition that they remain outside the prohibited zone until the military orders were modified or lifted. This illustrates that they pose different problems and may be governed by different principles. The lawfulness of one does not necessarily determine the lawfulness of the others. This is made clear when we analyze the requirements of the separate provisions of the separate orders. These separate requirements were that those of Japanese ancestry (1) depart from the area; (2) report to and temporarily remain in an assembly center; (3) go under military control to a relocation center there to remain for an indeterminate period until released conditionally or unconditionally by the military authorities. Each of these requirements, it will be noted, imposed distinct duties in connection with the separate steps in a complete evacuation program. Had Congress directly incorporated into one Act the language of these separate orders, and provided sanctions for their violations, disobedience of any one would have constituted a separate offense. Cf. Blockburger v. United States, 284 U.S. 299, 304. There is no reason why violations of these orders, insofar as they were promulgated pursuant to congressional enactment, should not be treated as separate offenses.

The Endo case [Ex parte Mitsuye Endo, 323 U.S. 283], graphically illustrates the difference between the validity of an order to exclude and the validity of a detention order after exclusion has been effected.

Since the petitioner has not been convicted of failing to report or to remain in an assembly or relocation center, we cannot in this case determine the validity of those separate provisions of the order. It is sufficient here for us to pass upon the order which petitioner violated. To do more would be to go beyond the issues raised, and to decide momentous questions not contained within the framework of the pleadings or the evidence in this case. It will be time enough to decide the serious constitutional issues which petitioner seeks to raise when an assembly or relocation order is applied or is certain to be applied to him, and we have its terms before us.

Some of the members of the Court are of the view that evacuation and detention in an Assembly Center were inseparable. After May 3, 1942, the date of Exclusion Order No. 34, Korematsu was under compulsion to leave the area not as he would choose but via an Assembly Center. The Assembly Center was conceived as a part of the machinery for group evacuation. The power to exclude includes the power to do it by force if necessary. And any forcible measure must necessarily entail some degree of detention or restraint whatever method of removal is selected. But whichever view is taken, it results in holding that the order under which petitioner was convicted was valid.

It is said that we are dealing here with the case of imprisonment of a citizen in a concentration camp solely because of his ancestry, without evidence or inquiry concerning his loyalty and good disposition towards the United States. Our task would be simple, our duty clear, were this a case involving the imprisonment of a loyal citizen in a concentration camp because of racial prejudice. Regardless of the true nature of the assembly and relocation centers—and we deem it unjustifiable to call them concentration camps with all the ugly connotations that term implies—we are dealing specifically with nothing but an exclusion order. To cast this case into outlines of racial prejudice, without reference to the real military dangers which were presented, merely confuses the issue. Korematsu was not excluded from the Military Area because of hostility to him or his race. He was excluded because we are at war with the Japanese          10 Empire, because the properly constituted military authorities feared an invasion of our West Coast and felt constrained to take proper security measures, because they decided that the military urgency of the situation demanded that all citizens of Japanese ancestry be segregated from the West Coast temporarily, and finally, because Congress, reposing its confidence in this time of war in our military leaders—as inevitably it must—determined that they should have power to do just this. There was evidence of disloyalty on the part of some, the military authorities considered that the need for action was great, and time was short. We cannot— by availing ourselves of the calm perspective of hindsight—now say          20 that at that time these actions were unjustified.

Affirmed.

MR. JUSTICE ROBERTS. I dissent, because I think the indisputable facts exhibit a clear violation of Constitutional rights.

This is not a case of keeping people off the streets at night as was Kiyoshi Hirabayashi v. United States, 320 U.S. 181, nor a case of temporary exclusion of a citizen from an area for his own safety or that of the community, nor a case of offering him an opportunity to go temporarily out of an area where his presence might cause danger to himself or to his          30 fellows. On the contrary, it is the case of convicting a citizen as a punishment for not submitting to imprisonment in a concentration camp, based on his ancestry, and solely because of his ancestry, without evidence or inquiry concerning his loyalty and good disposition towards the United States. If this be a correct statement of facts disclosed by this record, and facts of which we take judicial notice, I need hardly labor the conclusion that Constitutional rights have been violated.

The Government's argument, and the opinion of the court, in my judgment, erroneously divide that which is single and indivisible and thus make the case appear as if the petitioner violated a Military Order, sanc-          40 tioned by an Act of Congress, which excluded him from his home, by refusing voluntarily to leave and, so, knowingly and intentionally, defying the order and the Act of Congress.

The petitioner, a resident of San Leandro, Alameda County, California, is a native of the United States of Japanese ancestry who, according to the uncontradicted evidence, is a loyal citizen of the nation.

A chronological recitation of events will make it plain that the petitioner's supposed offense did not, in truth, consist in his refusal voluntarily to leave the area which included his home in obedience to the order excluding him therefrom. Critical attention must be given to the dates and sequence of events. . . .

The predicament in which the petitioner thus found himself was this: He was forbidden, by Military Order, to leave the zone in which he lived; he was forbidden, by Military Order, after a date fixed, to be found within that zone unless he were in an Assembly Center located in that zone. *10* General DeWitt's report to the Secretary of War concerning the programme of evacuation and relocation of Japanese makes it entirely clear, if it were necessary to refer to that document, — and, in the light of the above recitation, I think it is not, — that an Assembly Center was a euphemism for a prison. No person within such a center was permitted to leave except by Military Order.

In the dilemma that he dare not remain in his home, or voluntarily leave the area, without incurring criminal penalties, and that the only way he could avoid punishment was to go to an Assembly Center and submit himself to military imprisonment, the petitioner did nothing. . . . *20*

We cannot shut our eyes to the fact that had the petitioner attempted to violate Proclamation No. 4 and leave the military area in which he lived he would have been arrested and tried and convicted for violation of Proclamation No. 4. The two conflicting orders, one which commanded him to stay and the other which commanded him to go, were nothing but a cleverly devised trap to accomplish the real purpose of the military authority, which was to lock him up in a concentration camp. The only course by which the petitioner could avoid arrest and prosecution was to go to that camp according to instructions to be given him when he reported at a Civil Control Center. We know that is the fact. Why should we set *30* up a figmentary and artificial situation instead of addressing ourselves to the actualities of the case?

These stark realities are met by the suggestion that it is lawful to compel an American citizen to submit to illegal imprisonment on the assumption that he might, after going to the Assembly Center, apply for his discharge by suing out a writ of habeas corpus, as was done in the Endo case, *supra.* The answer, of course, is that where he was subject to two conflicting laws he was not bound, in order to escape violation of one or the other, to surrender his liberty for any period. Nor will it do do to say that the detention was a necessary part of the process of evacuation, and so we are here *40* concerned only with the validity of the latter.

MR. JUSTICE MURPHY, dissenting.

This exclusion of "all persons of Japanese ancestry, both alien and non-alien," from the Pacific Coast area on a plea of military necessity in the absence of martial law ought not to be approved. Such exclusion goes over "the very brink of constitutional power" and falls into the ugly abyss of racism.

In dealing with matters relating to the prosecution and progress of a war, we must accord great respect and consideration to the judgments of the military authorities who are on the scene and who have full knowledge of the military facts. The scope of their discretion must, as a matter of necessity and common sense, be wide. And their judgments ought not to be overruled lightly by those whose training and duties ill-equip them to deal intelligently with matters so vital to the physical security of the nation.

At the same time, however, it is essential that there be definite limits    10
to military discretion, especially where martial law has not been declared. Individuals must not be left impoverished of their constitutional rights on a plea of military necessity that has neither substance nor support. Thus, like other claims conflicting with the asserted constitutional rights of the individual, the military claim must subject itself to the judicial process of having its reasonableness determined and its conflicts with other interests reconciled. "What are the allowable limits of military discretion, and whether or not they have been overstepped in a particular case, are judicial questions." Sterling v. Constantin, 287 U.S. 378, 401.

The judicial test of whether the Government, on a plea of military    20
necessity, can validly deprive an individual of any of his constitutional rights is whether the deprivation is reasonably related to a public danger that is so "immediate, imminent, and impending" as not to admit of delay and not to permit the intervention of ordinary constitutional processes to alleviate the danger. United States v. Russell, 13 Wall. 623, 627, 628; Mitchell v. Harmony, 13 How. 115, 134, 135; Raymond v. Thomas, 91 U.S. 712, 716. Civilian Exclusion Order No. 34, banishing from a prescribed area of the Pacific Coast "all persons of Japanese ancestry, both alien and non-alien," clearly does not meet that test. Being an obvious racial discrimination, the order deprives all those within its scope of the    30
equal protection of the laws as guaranteed by the Fifth Amendment. It further deprives these individuals of their constitutional rights to live and work where they will, to establish a home where they choose and to move about freely. In excommunicating them without benefit of hearings, this order also deprives them of all their constitutional rights to procedural due process. Yet no reasonable relation to an "immediate, imminent, and impending" public danger is evident to support this racial restriction which is one of the most sweeping and complete deprivations of constitutional rights in the history of this nation in the absence of martial law.

It must be conceded that the military and naval situation in the spring    40
of 1942 was such as to generate a very real fear of invasion of the Pacific Coast, accompanied by fears of sabotage and espionage in that area. The military command was therefore justified in adopting all reasonable means necessary to combat these dangers. In adjudging the military action taken in light of the then apparent dangers, we must not erect too high or too meticulous standards; it is necessary only that the action have

some reasonable relation to the removal of the dangers of invasion, sabotage and espionage. But the exclusion, either temporarily or permanently, of all persons with Japanese blood in their veins has no such reasonable relation. And that relation is lacking because the exclusion order necessarily must rely for its reasonableness upon the assumption that *all* persons of Japanese ancestry may have a dangerous tendency to commit sabotage and espionage and to aid our Japanese enemy in other ways. . . .

Justification for the exclusion is sought, instead, mainly upon questionable racial and sociological grounds not ordinarily within the realm of expert military judgment, supplemented by certain semi-military conclu-   10
sions drawn from an unwarranted use of circumstantial evidence. . . .

The main reasons relied upon by those responsible for the forced evacuation, therefore, do not prove a reasonable relation between the group characteristics of Japanese Americans and the dangers of invasion, sabotage and espionage. The reasons appear, instead, to be largely an accumulation of much of the misinformation, half-truths and insinuations that for years have been directed against Japanese Americans by people with racial and economic prejudices—the same people who have been among the foremost advocates of the evacuation. A military judgment based upon such racial and sociological considerations is not entitled to the   20
great weight ordinarily given the judgments based upon strictly military considerations. Especially is this so when every charge relative to race, religion, culture, geographical location, and legal and economic status has been substantially discredited by independent studies made by experts in these matters.

MR. JUSTICE JACKSON, dissenting. . . .

But the "law" which this prisoner is convicted of disregarding is not found in an act of Congress, but in a military order. Neither the Act of Congress nor the Executive Order of the President, nor both together,   30
would afford a basis for this conviction. It rests on the orders of General DeWitt. And it is said that if the military commander had reasonable military grounds for promulgating the orders, they are constitutional and become law, and the Court is required to enforce them. There are several reasons why I cannot subscribe to this doctrine.

It would be impracticable and dangerous idealism to expect or insist that each specific military command in an area of probable operations will conform to conventional tests of constitutionality. When an area is so beset that it must be put under military control at all, the paramount consideration is that its measures be successful, rather than legal. The armed   40
services must protect a society, not merely its Constitution. The very essence of the military job is to marshal physical force, to remove every obstacle to its effectiveness, to give it every strategic advantage. Defense measures will not, and often should not, be held within the limits that bind civil authority in peace. No court can require such a commander in such circumstances to act as a reasonable man; he may be unreasonably

cautious and exacting. Perhaps he should be. But a commander in temporarily focusing the life of a community on defense is carrying out a
military program; he is not making law in the sense the courts know the
term. He issues orders, and they may have a certain authority as military
commands, although they may be very bad as constitutional law.

But if we cannot confine military expedients by the Constitution, neither
would I distort the Constitution to approve all that the military may deem
expedient. That is what the Court appears to be doing, whether consciously or not. I cannot say, from any evidence before me, that the orders
of General DeWitt were not reasonably expedient military precautions,     10
nor could I say that they were. But even if they were permissible military
procedures, I deny that it follows that they are constitutional. If, as the
Court holds, it does follow, then we may as well say that any military
order will be constitutional and have done with it. . . .

I should hold that a civil court cannot be made to enforce an order
which violates constitutional limitations even if it is a reasonable exercise
of military authority. The courts can exercise only the judicial power, can
apply only law, and must abide by the Constitution, or they cease to be
civil courts and become instruments of military policy.

Of course the existence of a military power resting on force, so vagrant,    20
so centralized, so necessarily heedless of the individual, is an inherent
threat to liberty. But I would not lead people to rely on this Court for a
review that seems to me wholly delusive. The military reasonableness of
these orders can only be determined by military superiors. If the people
ever let command of the war power fall into irresponsible and unscrupu-
lous hands, the courts wield no power equal to its restraint. The chief
restraint upon those who command the physical forces of the country, in
the future as in the past, must be their responsibility to the political judgments of their contemporaries and to the moral judgments of history.

My duties as a justice as I see them do not require me to make a mili-    30
tary judgment as to whether General DeWitt's evacuation and detention
program was a reasonable military necessity. I do not suggest that the
courts should have attempted to interfere with the Army in carrying out
its task. But I do not think they may be asked to execute a military expedient that has no place in law under the Constitution. I would reverse
the judgment and discharge the prisoner.

# Ted Nakashima
## Japanese-Americans Interned During World War II

Unfortunately in this land of liberty, I was born of Japanese parents; born in Seattle of a mother and father who have been in this country since 1901. Fine parents, who brought up their children in the best American way of life. My mother served with the Volunteer Red Cross Service in the last war—my father, an editor, has spoken and written Americanism for forty years.

### THE NAKASHIMAS

Our family is almost typical of the other unfortunates here at the camp. The oldest son, a licensed architect, was educated at the University of  10
Washington, has a master's degree from the Massachusetts Institute of Technology, and is a scholarship graduate of the American School of Fine Arts in Fontainebleau, France. He is now in camp in Oregon with his wife and three-months-old child. He had just completed designing a much-needed defense housing project at Vancouver, Washington.

The second son is an M.D. He served his internship in a New York hospital, is married, and has two fine sons. The folks banked on him, because he was the smartest of us three boys. The army took him a month after he opened his office. He is now a lieutenant in the Medical Corps, somewhere in the South.  20

I am the third son, the dumbest of the lot, but still smart enough to hold down a job as an architectural draftsman. I have just finished building a new home and had lived in it three weeks. My desk was just cleared of work done for the Army Engineers, another stack of 391 defense houses was waiting (a rush job), when the order came to pack up and leave for this resettlement center called "Camp Harmony."

289

Mary, the only girl in the family, and her year-old son, "Butch," are with our parents—interned in the stables of the Livestock Exposition Buildings in Portland.

### A RESETTLEMENT CENTER
Now that you can picture our thoroughly American background, let me describe our new home.

The resettlement center is actually a penitentiary—armed guards in towers with spotlights and deadly tommy guns, fifteen feet of barbed-wire fences, everyone confined to quarters at nine, lights out at ten o'clock. The guards are ordered to shoot anyone who approaches within twenty feet of the fences. No one is allowed to take the two-block-long hike to the latrines after nine, under any circumstances.

The apartments, as the army calls them, are two-block-long stables, with windows on one side. Floors are. . . two-by-fours laid directly on the mud, which is everywhere. The stalls are about eighteen by twenty-one feet; some contain families of six or seven persons. Partitions are seven feet high, leaving a four-foot opening above. The rooms aren't too bad, almost fit to live in for a short while.

The food and sanitation problems are the worst. We have had absolutely no fresh meat, vegetables or butter since we came here. Mealtime queues extend for blocks; standing in a rainswept line, feet in the mud, waiting for the scant portions of canned wieners and boiled potatoes, hash for breakfast or canned wieners and beans for dinner. Milk only for the kids. Coffee or tea dosed with saltpeter and stale bread are the adults' staples. Dirty, unwiped dishes, greasy silver. a starchy diet, no butter, no milk, bawling kids, mud, wet mud that stinks when it dries, no vegetables—a sad thing for the people who raised them in such abundance. Memories of a crisp head of lettuce with our special olive oil, vinegar, garlic and cheese dressing.

Today one of the surface sewage-disposal pipes broke and the sewage flowed down the streets. Kids play in the water. Shower baths without hot water. Stinking mud and slops everywhere.

Can this be the same America we left a few weeks ago?

### WHY WON'T AMERICA LET US BE AMERICANS?
As I write, I can remember our little bathroom—light coral walls. My wife painting them, and the spilled paint in her hair. The open towel shelving and the pretty shower curtains which we put up the day before we left. How sanitary and clean we left it for the airlines pilot and his young wife who are now enjoying the fruits of our labor.

It all seems so futile, struggling, trying to live our old lives under this useless, regimented life. The senselessness of all the inactive manpower. Electricians, plumbers, draftsmen, mechanics, carpenters, painters, farmers—every trade—men who are able and willing to do all they can to lick the Axis. Thousands of men and women in these camps, energetic, quick, alert, eager for hard, constructive work, waiting for the army to do something for us, an army that won't give us butter.

I can't take it! I have 391 defense houses to be drawn. I left a fine American home which we built with our own hands. I left . . . good friends, friends who would swear by us. I don't have enough of that Japanese heritage *ga-man*—a code of silent suffering and ability to stand pain.

Oddly enough I still have a bit of faith in army promises of good treatment and Mrs. Roosevelt's pledge of a future worthy of good American citizens. I'm banking another $67 of income tax on the future. Sometimes I want to spend the money I have set aside for income tax on a bit of butter or ice cream or something good that I might have smuggled through the gates, but I can't do it when I think that every dollar I can put into "the fight to lick the Japs," the sooner I will be home again. I must forget my stomach.

What really hurts most is the constant reference to us evacués as "Japs." "Japs" are the guys we are fighting. We're on this side and we want to help.

Why won't America let us?

# Alfred E. Smith
## An American Catholic
## Answers Back

I summarize my creed as an American Catholic. I believe in the worship of God according to the faith and practice of the Roman Catholic Church. I recognize no power in the institutions of my Church to interfere with the operations of the Constitution of the United States or the enforcement of the law of the land. I believe in absolute freedom of conscience for all men and in equality of all churches, all sects, and all beliefs before the law as a matter of right and not as a matter of favor. I believe in the absolute separation of Church and State and in the strict enforcement of the provisions of the Constitution that Congress shall make no law respecting an establishment of religion or prohibiting the free exercise thereof. I  10 believe that no tribunal of any church has any power to make any decree of any force in the law of the land, other than to establish the status of its own communicants within its own church.

I believe in the support of the public school as one of the cornerstones of American liberty. I believe in the right of every parent to choose whether his child shall be educated in the public school or in a religious school supported by those of his own faith. I believe in the principle of noninterference by this country in the internal affairs of other nations and that we should stand steadfastly against any such interference by whomsoever it may be urged. And I believe in the common brotherhood of man under  20 the common fatherhood of God.

In this spirit I join with fellow Americans of all creeds in a fervent prayer that never again in this land will any public servant be challenged because of the faith in which he has tried to walk humbly with his God.

# Craig Fisher
## The Ice People

The Arctic is the harshest land I've ever seen. The wind tears at you—
60 MPH is not unusual. The temperature is often 40, 50 degrees below
zero. And most of the land is snow-covered from September to June. This
bleak whiteness stretches from the Arctic Circle to the top of the earth.
It would not seem possible that this lonely land could sustain life, but the
most adaptable creature on earth does live there—Man. Man ... who
came out of Siberia, across the Bering Land Bridge, perhaps six to ten
thousand years ago. Stocky, compact, of Mongoloid origin, his very existence was determined by his ability to hunt, and to adapt to this overwhelming environment. Because his life was an endless struggle to wrest    10
food from this barren land, he also had to live with the constant anxiety
of starvation—for often the sealhunt was unsuccessful ... the caribou
or sea duck elusive.

These influences, over hundreds of generations, produced a people who
even today possess unique characteristics. They emerged as a wondrously
ingenious and highly flexible people. Though they totaled perhaps 75
thousand, they lived in small groups, with strong family ties, but few
feelings of tribe and none of nation. So personal freedom and individuality
was greatly respected and aggression of any kind abhorred. Leadership
was then limited to an informal grouping around the man who was most    20
able in the hunt—the man who owned the boat, ran the walrus hunt.

With hunting as the only, and a most precarious, source of food—the
hunting range, and the game itself, was shared—or in times of famine
only the best hunters would survive. So a bond of obligation and trust
was formed between these hunting families. A bond that persists in family
groups throughout the Arctic even today. Hunting evolved as a way for

a man to prove his manhood as well as to provide food for his family and companions.

Generations ago the people took root in the Eskimo character and moved with the flow of game and the season, locating themselves where the hunting was best. This, and the sharing concept, meant land ownership was unimportant. Each person had a share in the land, and of the game on it. The concept of personal property scarcely existed.

Pitted against the awesome power of a frozen wilderness, all of these adaptations helped the Eskimo. Not only to survive, but to prosper and make a home in the frozen Arctic from Russian Siberia, across Alaska   10
and Canada to Greenland, an immense distance of eight thousand ice-covered miles.

This then is a unique environment, one which demands that the Eskimo concentrate on minute details of his surroundings if he is to survive. He must be able to recognize subtle landmarks in a vast expanse, to judge the thickness of the ice as his sled moves across it and remember everything that strikes his senses, so that his journey will be safe—and successful.

Perhaps the Eskimo language itself suggests his great abilities of observation and perception. There are, for example, dozens of words for different types of snow, describing how hard or soft, suitable for sled   20
runners, useful as building blocks. But there is no Eskimo concept for time—no word to express "wasting time, saving time"—for time never had that kind of relevance in traditional Eskimo culture.

Another adaptability is physical. The Eskimo can withstand cold better than you or I. But no one quite knows why. This is just one of the questions the International Biological Program Study of Eskimos hopes to answer: whether the Eskimo's tolerance is genetic—or whether each man becomes acclimatized within his own lifetime.

Actually, the Eskimo has ingeniously fashioned clothing so efficient in keeping him warm he is carrying around a semi-tropical environment   30
with him. The Eskimo was a product of the land and his own ingenuity, completely self-sustaining, free and independent. But he is free no longer.

The first white man who gave him steel knives, and rifles in payment for services or furs, undermined his independence by creating needs that could only be satisfied by the outside world. Although explorers, whalers, fur traders, missionaries brought into the Arctic diseases that decimated the Eskimo population—they also brought numberless things that the Eskimo saw, and craved—to make his life more secure, easier or more pleasant, even though the white man himself was not always thought too bright.   40

But as the Eskimo acquired these goods, he lost many of his age-old abilities and skills necessary for survival and came more and more to depend upon the goods—and upon the white man.

Now the white man decided where to set up the trading posts. The government decided where to put schools and hospitals. The churches decided his religion. They all decided his future and fate. The Eskimo

moved from hunting to barter to welfare. This impact has become particularly wrenching in the past twenty years. The Eskimo still craves the
necessities and the conveniences—from a hospital to a snowmobile. But
he faces many problems in today's white world simply because he is an
Eskimo. Although the Eskimo is individually competitive in physical
games, his culture for thousands of years dictated that he should not be
outwardly aggressive—but that's a necessary trait for leadership in business or politics. The Eskimo's free, independent nature comes into immediate conflict when he moves to town and takes a job—and here too the
strongest drive he knows—love of the land and hunting—cannot be satis-         10
fied when he has a regular job with regular hours.

Most Eskimos today are dissatisfied with their lives—few think of
themselves as winners in the struggle between the cultures—but believe
they are powerless to change it.

What are the options open to an Eskimo today? Must he sacrifice his
culture to buy a snowmobile; can he live near a hospital, and a school;
hold a regular job and yet still hunt? Is there a place for a man who wishes
to live a traditional life?

Today's Eskimo lives in villages and towns—he hasn't lived in an Igloo
for twenty years. His old living ways, habits and customs are disappear-         20
ing. Ministers replace the ancient shamans—hunting is just to augment
food purchased at the store. Manufactured clothes replace homemade fur
clothing almost everywhere. Although he still speaks his native tongue
here in Canada, and in Greenland, even his language is dying out in Alaska.
Despite the fact that most Eskimos now do live in villages and towns,
the living's still not easy. Here in Anaktuvak Pass there is no sewer system and no piped water. Water comes from the creek and must be boiled
before drinking. This is common in Eskimo villages throughout the Arctic.
There is no regular electric service—gasoline powers the washing machines and batteries power the radios. Fewer than half the villages have         30
electric power. Housing, in Alaska, consists mostly of one room shacks—
some still made of sod. Of 75 hundred native dwellings, 71 hundred need
replacement. Our government is now beginning to construct some low
cost housing, as Canada and Greenland did some time ago. But the most
difficult problem of living in the villages is that there are no jobs. In order
to work the Eskimo must leave the villages for the larger towns—or the
major cities.

But the job situation really isn't much better here, and most Eskimos
are disoriented and unhappy in cities and feel they don't belong. More
and more Ekimos are moving into *big* villages—described by one an-         40
thropologist as emotional sinks and usually a dirty sink at that. They
move here to be near the school and the hospital, a bigger store, and what
jobs do exist. In these larger towns, in Alaska and in Canada, as well as
Greenland, the business community, the government, the schools, are
dominated by whites—who have little knowledge of the classical Eskimo
culture. Their behavior and attitudes toward Eskimos range from con-

cern and sympathy to bigotry and exploitation. It's difficult for the Eskimo people to live in these towns. They'd rather be back here on the land, not in large communities of strangers. The white prejudice is continual. They face a loss of personal freedom and are buffeted by all kinds of intense pressures. Even the game is often too far away to be conveniently hunted, without abandoning their jobs.

Most Eskimo wage earners work at mechanical and non-technical jobs, when they are available. The average westerner is appalled at the thought of 10 percent unemployment. The Eskimo understands 80 percent unemployment as a fact of life. His annual income averages less than $1,000    10 a year. A few Eskimos, particularly in Alaska, are being trained in highly technical skills at which they excel. Although there is now one Eskimo air-traffic-controller, the Eskimo professional, the trained and educated doctor, chemist or lawyer just doesn't exist. Naturally some of the old skills persist and can be utilized. When our French and British ancestors were still living in caves and painting their bodies, Eskimo artists were carving delicate figures of seal and duck in ivory and stone. This now proves to be something of an economic resource, particularly in Canada where Eskimo artists earned $4,000,000 last year . . . and did so in a manner that gave them pride in their Eskimo heritage. But not    20 enough Eskimos are skilled artists to exert a dynamic impact on the economy of all the people. Today for most of the Eskimos their income does not come from menial jobs, nor hunting, nor art—but from some form of government welfare.

From birth to death—the governments of all three countries exert tremendous influences over the Eskimo people—often dictating where, how and in what conditions they are to live. The Eskimo accepts all this rather pragmatically because he knows it's better than starvation.

If there is one benefit the white man has brought the Eskimo it is health. Although still comparatively short, his lifespan is now longer than it's    30 ever been. His greatest killing disease, tuberculosis, has been nearly wiped out. The TB rate is lower here in Igloolik, Canada than it is in Washington, D.C.—and this is typical throughout the Arctic. Though still too high, the infant mortality rate has been cut by almost 50 percent. Today half the population is *under* eighteen. And now the governments are offering to young Eskimo mothers some form of family planning. But the children continue to come, and schools are bulging. The teachers working with Eskimo students, in Greenland, Canada, and Alaska have much in common. They are most often young women, somewhat inexperienced as teachers—and almost totally inexperienced in working with    40 minority group children. Most will stay in the Arctic less than two years. So no matter how dedicated, just as they begin to understand the Eskimo child's background and problems, they leave. And, of course, some never understand. This creates problems for the child that will haunt him all his life.

The Eskimo youngster grows up straddling two cultures—not really educated in either one—so, frustrated he strives to master and be a part of the western culture, yet aches to retain his own traditions and heritage. But there is no question as to the impact of the white—as the Eskimo says, "the dominant" culture.

The manner in which young Eskimos dress is perhaps the most visual example, the same from Alaska to here in Greenland. But while clothes are western—goals often are not. Eskimo girls mimic the clothes and mannerisms of their white contemporaries; they even reject Eskimo boys in favor of white boys, but a recent study suggests they show little desire to make a good marriage and raise a family.     10

The influence of the white man on the Eskimo is as great as the influence of the natural environment. And, in a sense, the Eskimo has adapted to the white culture as he once did to his environment. This may be explained by the Eskimo word, "arunamat" (a-roon-a-mut) which describes his attitude toward a calamity in nature. It translates "because nothing can be done" and implies "so accept the situation without regret." Some experts believe that the opposite is necessary. That the white man should adapt more to the Eskimos if the Eskimo is to survive in both worlds.

The influence of an alien culture is evident even in the few places left     20
where seal hunting is still done by kayak—the kayak has almost totally disappeared in Alaska and Canada. This is the Northeast coast of Greenland. The people here are so remote that when they were first discovered they thought they were the only people on earth, and that the whole world was made of ice. Yet, even here, a powerboat is now used to carry the kayak to the hunting area, radios are used to keep track of storms, rifles have been common for fifty years—even though the harpoon is used too. Even the value of his catch—the seal—is influenced in a uniquely western way. The Eskimo hunts the adult seal for food and to sell the fur. But recently there has been an outcry against the slaughter of seals. This is     30
actually against the killing of newborn seals, which is done mostly by commercial white hunters in sub-Arctic hunting grounds. Actually the newborn seals are white—and so can be dyed to look like some other fur. But the Eskimo sells the adult sealskin which is easily recognizable—and so its price is now greatly reduced. But for the Eskimo here, it is their only source of income. So they continue to hunt the seal in frail boats through frigid, ice-choked water. The rifle is used to wound the animal—but it is still the harpoon which brings it in. Although he may cling to the older ways, his options today are limited. He must, by choice or by force, shape his life to the new world around him.     40

Most of the "big villages" of the Arctic are much alike. Kotzebue, Alaska's population is about 2,000. Kotzebue typifies the changing atmosphere of the Eskimos today. Five years ago there were 50 dogteams here. The two or three that remain today are for the amusement of tourists. Pick-up trucks and motor bikes go barreling along the gravel main street, past wooden homes that were built by the wage economy. But be-

hind some shacks you can still see fish drying; on the roof the caribou
head that is the sign that a hunter lives here. One such hunter is John
Schaefer, Sr. He's always been a hunter and he treasures his independence. He is not regularly employed. He typifies the old way of life . . .
his sons the new. He's an outstanding hunter and so is able to continue
the traditional way of life better than most men—and because his wife
has a part-time job as cook at the school. So they do have some income—
which is also augmented by their grown sons. Mrs. Schaefer speaks of
another way of life when her family was younger:

> "The way we made a living when we were younger was by trapping,    10
> fishing, and we never had oil. We had to use wood and nowadays they
> won't even buy fur. My husband used to trap mink in the wintertime,
> and that way we had what little we could get for the children like
> milk. Most of the food we ate was wild."

And much of the food they eat today is still wild, for Mr. Schaefer goes
hunting or fishing every week. His compelling drive to hunt is shared
by his son Ross:

> "Well, hunting is very important for me 'cause I love the outdoors.    20
> I have to get out every week, just to enjoy it, to relax. My dreams were
> to become a he-man when I was young. My dad took me out hunting
> only because I was always working and I had learned how to hunt
> from him there, which is real good. We live somewhat off the land. We
> get caribou meat, ducks and geese but still that's just part of our meal,
> and we have to buy the other groceries and meat and that costs a lot
> of money. It's important to go out and earn a wage. Also, we enjoy the
> comforts of life, too. Snow-go and boat and you need money to buy that,
> and you're not going to get by when you go out and hunt and trap.
> This new generation of children are totally ignorant of what the knowl-    30
> edge that I was able to get from my father where you can go out and
> hunt and know where you are all the time, and always come back.
> Whereas these kids here, I've taken my little brothers out and we'd
> go out to the lakes hunting muskrat or whatever, just for the heck of it
> I'd ask them, Where are we? Which way is home? The only way they'd
> know was they could hear the siren or hear dogs barking or seeing
> planes going over toward Kotzebue. And it's bad for them because
> later on they will go out and hunt and they won't know how to do it.
> It's sad that all this will probably die out."

His brother Bob adds:                                                    40

> "I'd rather ride a motorcycle like this or a snowmobile than walk
> behind a dog team. But if I had my choice I would go back to the old
> way of living, just hunting and fishing. It's impossible today. That's

the problem I have right now, trying to live in both worlds at the same time. I'm in between right now and trying to combine both is a big problem. I was never taught anything Eskimo or anything about Eskimo tradition in school. They teach just what the white man knows and they do a lousy job of it. In fact they don't have anything to do with the Eskimo culture in school. The attitude is that the teachers are superior and the white man is superior to the Eskimo and that's what they teach and that's what the Eskimo children feel."

Ross feels:

"That the teachers have a poor attitude toward these native stu- 10 dents. They tend to be impatient with them, I think, and a lot of them are very cruel to them."

Mrs. Schaeffer's response is that:

"There are so many children to each teacher that they don't have time, you know, to get to those that really need help. That's how come my son  hasn't learned very much, either that or he's just slow. But they said he's not dumb, he could learn if he wanted to, but when I ask him why he don't do his work, he said he don't know how to do it  20 and the teacher won't help him."

Henry Schaeffer:

"The way the teachers treat us and the way they are now, I don't care much for school."

Major Schaeffer feels that:

"The education process has taken something away from the people. 30 It's been, a new way of life has been forced on the people without bringing out the good parts of their heritage."

And Ross Schaeffer sums it up by saying:

"I would like to have my son grow up in a way that I did, where I could take him out hunting. That way I think he'll have a broader view of how to accept responsibility later on, you know, by himself, where he makes his own decisions."

The Schaefer's decisions are to try to take the best of both worlds. Bob,  40 and Ross too, both work during the summer for the airlines that service Kotzebue, while they finish college. They see the need for education— while recognizing the problems the Eskimo student faces. They wish to earn a wage while retaining as much of their Eskimo heritage as possible—

and the story of the Schaefer family is the story of all the Eskimo people.

Throughout the Arctic the same patterns keep re-appearing. The Eskimo child, beginning in the earliest grades, is not being prepared to go into the world of the Eskimo nor of the white. The teachers, the administrators, the school systems — whether run by the Bureau of Indian Affairs, or state-run in Alaska — whether Canadian or Danish — are exceedingly similar. They face the same problems and try to solve them with the same techniques. They are well-meaning, but seem unable to comprehend what the Eskimo wants and needs.

Dr. Arthur Hippler, a cultural anthropologist at the University of Alaska,      10
speaks of some of the problems the Eskimo youngster faces in school:

> "If you think that the child comes into a classroom situation and he's faced with something that's uncomfortable or difficult for him, that doesn't necessarily have to mean that the child feels inferior or backward. But, if also the teacher, and all of the teachers for the past, for say a hundred years or so, have been telling Eskimo children and their parents that they're inferior, backward and stupid, trying to make them play a game according to a set of rules that they're not accustomed to, you can get to the point where a child really feels as though there's    20 something wrong with him for not being able to play a game for which he's probably not prepared."

Mr. Lester Richesin, a high school guidance counselor in Alaska, could well be speaking for teachers throughout the Arctic:

> "The schools make a great attempt to reach the Eskimo people. It's a very difficult thing to bridge the gap you might say, from the Eskimo culture to modern America, but, I believe, the Bureau of Indian Affairs is working extremely hard in trying to bridge that gap."    30

But when young Eskimo students all across the Arctic are asked about education, they offer another opinion. One student, George Charles, says:

> "Well, I don't know who sets up the standards for the weeding out of the type of teachers we get, especially in the villages. And, speaking as a native, for my people, I felt that some of these people really didn't belong there. They had a very condescending attitude ; they spoke to the people as if they were very stupid. And then the students themselves, when they run into a teacher like that, why it really hurts emotionally and the kids lose self-confidence."    40

Arthur Hippler agrees that:

> "Until very recently, and still in many places in the State of Alaska, Alaskan native students, Eskimos, are being taught out of *Dick and*

*Jane* readers . . . "see Spot run. . . ." Well, any Alaskan Eskimo kid knows that you don't do with dogs the strange looking things that they do with dogs in *Dick and Jane* books. And so much of it is completely irrelevant."

Another student, Katie Beals, confirms this:

> "So here we were, or I was, in this class not being able to understand that much of English, beginning to, but not that well yet, and learning how to read was something else . . . also because the books were all    10
> *Dick and Jane* sort of things, and they were sometimes very scary because they were, the situations in them were, foreign to what our situation was at home. For instance, the grandparents in the book live on a farm and my grandparents stayed with us, and either they would have to do something terrible to be sent away or we would have to do something terrible to make them go away."

The administration, according to Richesin, admits they "have a tendency to stay with the customary type of teaching and in so doing we hesitate to go to the side, you might say, and take them where they are and try    20
to teach them as far as they are able to go."

But despite this recognition of faulty theory, most teachers are reluctant or unable to change specific teaching practices. For example, teaching the Eskimo language is an area of profound disagreement between Eskimos and the school system of all three countries.

> "It's only recently," says Arthur Hippler, "after a tremendous struggle to start to teach literacy in the native language, that they're finally beginning to initiate a few minor pilot programs. In fact, it's been a well-known long-time pedagogical fact that people really do learn how    30
> to read and write best in their own native tongue and that this had a transference effect into learning a second language."

Lester Richesin adds:

> "I seriously doubt if very many of the Eskimo people are anxious for the schools to start teaching their children in the Eskimo language."

An Alaskan state legislator, Willy Hensley, feels that:

> "Not only should we teach the Eskimo language in the schools and    40
> the culture and traditions and folklore of the Eskimo, I think it ought to be done by Eskimo teachers. And I know the arguments about, you know, whether there's any value in trying to preserve a culture. I just know that there's no sense in trying to break down something that has allowed a people to exist for thousands of years."

But there are virtually no Eskimo teachers anywhere in the Arctic— the Eskimo language is ignored, the curriculum is still geared for white children not Eskimo children. The result is a fearfully high drop-out rate. More than a third of the students drop out of grammar school, from 65 to 95 percent drop out of high school, and of the handful that go on to college, nearly 90 percent don't graduate. It would seem hard statistics like this should convince educators that there are indeed horrendous problems in the system.

But Richesin feels:                                                          10

". . . very confident in being able to handle the job that I have and I feel frustrated you might say, when I go out of my way to talk to a student who has dropped out and I leave his home thinking that I'll see him tomorrow, and then tomorrow comes and he doesn't show. This is frustrating but, of course, you have your gains, too. In that you let the word be known to a certain student that I want to see you and he has been dropped out for a while and you look up the same day and there he is. So, you win some and you lose some."

Katie Beals reminds us:                                                      20

"Teachers' attitudes are very important because the students can pick it up; a condescending attitude or prejudiced attitude toward them, they really can. And the hardest thing for a teacher to realize is that it shows."

Willy Hensley adds:

"When you have school officials, teachers and administrators who aren't particularly concerned or who don't really understand the cul-    30 ture of these children that they're working with, you know, it's almost a hopeless case. For some reason they think that the best approach is to completely assimilate and integrate, as far as I'm concerned obliter- ate, the native culture, which I don't think is necessary. It's a very difficult psychological thing, I think, for the Eskimo kids to feel that the whole system is saying that their culture isn't useful, that their language isn't useful, and I think it comes to the point where the stu- dent feels that he's a second-class citizen, a lower person than a white person. And in my opinion, I feel that you can't really build a human being until, he respects himself and who he is. To me, it's a waste of   40 people to make them believe that they're not as good as someone else, or their culture isn't."

The Eskimo of the past is caught in midflight in his surge into the present, a dramatic change in the life style of a people. The question now is whether the thrust can be sustained. Major Schaeffer's comment is this:

"For the next few years it's getting to be pretty hard, without jobs for the people. Yet, we are, we're going ahead and educating them for jobs and there are no jobs available. We're going to have a lot of frustration and, a lot of social problems. This frustration has a lot to do with the high alcohol and suicide rate of the Eskimo people. It's the biggest cause of it. The people themselves who are having these problems can't tell you why because they don't understand; a lot of times they can't voice their own frustrations. The future is based on economy, if we have jobs for the people then the transition is going to be fairly smooth, but, it doesn't look like we'll have that many jobs for a few    10 years.

Probably fewer than 20 percent of the Eskimo working age population are regularly employed—not because they don't wish to work—but because there are so few jobs. In the Arctic, there is, no agriculture, little mining and timbering that uses local people, and not much industry at all. And most of these factors cannot change in the future.

Of the Eskimos that are employed, nearly all work either for some government agency or for a white-owned concern. About the only Eskimo-owned business ventures are the co-ops which may be the one hope for    20 the Eskimos, economic future. In Greenland there is a hunters association and a fishing cooperative. But most Arctic locations don't have enough game for commerical purposes—particularly during the winter. In Canada though, most of the villages have organized an arts co-op to fashion handicrafts for tourists and art for the connoisseur. The Canadian co-ops set the pattern for the whole Arctic.

In Alaska, there are Eskimo owned and run salmon fishing cooperatives. Although the co-op idea began years ago with the BIA setting up small stores in the villages—only recently have the local people actually run the co-ops themselves.    30

On the Kuskokwin River, the salmon processing and freezer barge—named Yut Pitchkot—"of the people"—is tangible proof to the villagers in the co-op that theirs is a going concern. And it is the co-op members themselves who own the barge and share in the profits of the corporation. But unfortunately the co-op idea is feasible in only certain industries ... so its impact at present is limited.

It could be that the area of greatest potential impact on the Eskimo of Alaska and Canada is the oil industry. It's true that in terms of money— some billions of dollars would be pumped into the Arctic—but many white economists—as well as the Eskimo question whether any real    40 amounts of oil money would trickle down to the Eskimo—and he is terribly fearful of the potential ecological damage to the land he uses daily for hunting and fishing. We discussed the oil issue with two Alaska state legislators. Mr. Blodgett told us:

"I am convinced, beyond a question of a doubt that this is going to mean jobs for people, all people, of every race, color and creed in Alaska, including our Eskimo people."

But Willy Hensley lacks Blodgett's confidence:

"I think for a little while we may have some jobs for the people up there, but the road itself, as far as I know, isn't going to any particular Indian or Eskimo community on the slope. The idea's strictly to make way for the pipeline . . . . "

Their dialogue is revealing:                                                          10

BLODGETT:
"When the pipeline comes in there will be some change in the immediate vicinity, of the pipeline to the environment."

HENSLEY:
"I think in the long run it'll be just like any other industrialization, in any part of the country where you have aboriginal people. I think the potential for disaster to the country is there."

BLODGETT:                                                                             20
"Alaska will never be the same. It's a new ballgame."

HENSLEY:
"You have roads moving in . . . railroads, pipelines, that only mean that the traditional way of life of the people up there's going to be threatened."

BLODGETT:
"Too many people that like to call themselves conservationists are in fact preservationists; they don't want to disturb anything—leave it     30
as it is."

HENSLEY:
"They're going to probably pollute the rivers unless there's very tight control over it, and that'll mean there goes the fish."

BLODGETT:
"Now I am a conservationist, I am not a preservationist."

HENSLEY:                                                                              40
"The people up there, no matter how much money they make they still live off the land essentially. A great portion of the food comes from the caribou, from the fish, you know, from the muskrat, ducks, geese, and whale."

BLODGETT:

"We set aside vast areas of our state for preserves, wilderness areas, parks and recreational areas."

HENSLEY:

"Although we know that we can't continue subsistence economy for the indefinite future, and are going to have to accept some industrialization, we're fearful that at some point in time in the future we will not be able to utilize the land like we have been. And, in my opinion, this great dependence on the land and love for the land was what made the Indian fight for so long—and here in Alaska, to me this whole prob- *10* lem of who owns the land, what use it's going to make, be made of it, is an extension of the "westward" movement. This is just the last big wide open space that's been occupied by native people. Of course they settled the problem there with guns and bows and arrows. We have to live today and we're fighting this politically and legally, and natu- rally we feel we're fighting for our lives."

The other major impact on the Alaskan Eskimo—also surrounded by controversy—is the native Alaskan's claim to the land. When the United States purchased Alaska from Russia—for two cents an acre—Congress said that the native people should not be "disturbed" in the possession of *20* lands used, occupied or claimed by them—but that they wouldn't get title to the land until Congress passed the proper legislation. One hundred and three years after the purchase, Congress is now considering, "the proper legislation."

But opinions vary on what is proper. Alaska is as big as Texas, California and Montana combined—five hundred and six thousand square miles. The natives want forty million acres of it, and $500 million payment for the rest with royalty payments for mineral rights. But they probably won't get this.

If the natives don't think the final version is fair, they could tie-up the *30* land in court battles for years—which they may do.

"The future of Alaska and the future of the Eskimo and Indian people," Hensley believes, "is contingent on what happens in the attempt to re- solve the land issue. It can be either very bleak or it can offer a great deal of promise."

Arthur Hippler adds that "there may be a positive possibility if the land claim settlement is a large one; if the natives get a large amount of money, it just might be that they'll be able to create an educational system that will really give them what they need, prepare them for what they have to be prepared for and do it in a way that they'll be able to accept and *40* understand and deal with."

Some native opinions, voiced at an Eskimo demonstration, are these:

"I'm an Eskimo and I'm proud of what I am. Hopefully, if we do get a good land settlement with the land claims problems that we have,

the cash settlement and royalties that we'll hopefully get out of this
settlement will be sufficient. Then we can be able to work for ourselves,
determine our own future, and with more educated native Alaskans
hopefully we can excel, compete and get ahead in this modern society.
And, I think that through more education the Eskimos will get to the
point when they can take care of themselves without relying on some
one else to do it for them."

And Harvey Anderson's:

"All the Eskimos are faced with problems that they never did have      10
when the white man came up here. It's here and it's going to stay here,
and you can't help it. To adjust to it you have to have something to go
by, and education's the answer, I think."

One student expresses his desire to help his people:

"I am currently studying sociology and elementary education in college. I would like to come back and teach because these children here
need native teachers . . . not only for them to have someone to relate
to, but to really help them learn. To make them realize that education    20
is important because we have no other way to turn but towards this
white-oriented society. I hate to say it but we have no choice because
our Eskimo way of life has to change with our society. The white culture will probably be the dominant. But as long as there's caribou,
seal and beluga, I think. . . the Eskimo will always go out and get it
for his own use. I think that in our cultural festivals, like in Point Hope,
people enjoy the kill they get, the muskrat, the whale. I don't think
they'll die out. . . It's pretty hard to stop something like that. . . It'll
always be in the people."

Major Schaefer sums it up:                                                30

"The Eskimo people have been hunters and fishermen for hundreds
of years and have been able to survive in a harsh country. Well, in the
past it's been a matter of physical survival. Now it's economic. It was
much easier for them to survive under hard physical conditions, but
now it's a matter of getting a job. The mental strains are more and
they produce a lot of frustration. I'm sure that given a little time, we'll
be able to change and, I think we'll still survive."

Katie Beals echoes him:                                                   40

"I think the idea of losing one's culture, you never really do that
you know, because some days I'm absolutely the most Eskimo person
you ever met, because I remember some of the ways I did when I was

a kid and I hang on to them. So, I don't really think it's losing one's culture, I really don't think so . . . because as long as I'm alive, there's part of Eskimo still happening."

WATTERS *Melville's "Isolatoes"* ☐ TWERSKY *Being Blind* ☐ SCHORR *. . . And Children of the Nation First* ☐ BONTEMPS *A Summer Tragedy* ☐ NURSING HOME PATIENT *An Old Lady Dies* ☐ PRYOR *Where We Put the Aged* ☐ SMART *An Old Woman's Story* ☐ GLAZER *The Mill Was Made of Marble · Too Old to Work · Automation* ☐ COLES *The Lives of Migrant Farmers* ☐ U.S. CONSTITUTION *Article XIX* ☐ FLEXNER *Early Steps Toward Equal Education* ☐ ROSS *Homosexual Revolution* ☐ JOHNSON *Kent's Fifth Victim* ☐

# Isolatoes:
the expatriates among us

# Introduction

What's an Isolato? The word may puzzle you at first. Herman Melville, an American writer who often coined new words, is responsible for this one as well. You've probably heard of *Moby Dick*, perhaps Melville's greatest work. Maybe you've read it, maybe you've seen the film. The crew of the Pequod, who sailed the ocean n search of the great white whale, were the first men to be called Isolatoes: alone, adrift, cut off, *isolated.*

The first essay in this section, "Melville's 'Isolatoes,'" is what we call a scholarly article. The journal from which it is taken, *PMLA*, is addressed not to the general reader, but to a specialized audience, those who study language and literature more closely than most of us. The article may stump you at first, just as the very term "Isolato" may have puzzled you. We have chosen the article for three reasons. The first and most obvious one is that we found Melville's term the most apt to describe "the expatriates among us" and we necessarily had to give credit where credit was due. Another reason is that the scholarly community to which it is addressed is, ironically, a pretty well isolated group. If you examine the language Mr. Watters uses, the learning which he presupposes, you will see that language, the *way* in which the piece is written, serves to draw boundaries around itself—

311

the audience is defined, outsiders are warned away. But these reasons are not the most important for the choice. It is far more important that you meet the Isolatoes as Melville saw them. Look at them, at the key words and phrases that are used to describe them. For example, they are said to be "set apart from normal human relationships." Look at Melville's own words, "not acknowledging the common continent of men but each an Isolato living on a separate continent of his own." As you move through this section, try to apply those statements to the people and the situations that you meet.

In the selection from "The Sound of the Walls" we have a man isolated by his blindness. Even though he finds community in his relationship with a woman, he has been cut-off for so long that he distrusts it. For a while he thinks "she had looked for something different and had found it in a blind man such as I. But the infatuation wouldn't last." Even after they are married, he registers surprise, "To have found Esther and to be marrying her in this house!"

The approach in " . . . And the Children of the Nation First" is factual. It is interesting to note that although the article is written primarily to convey information, the effect is moving *despite* the language.

Perhaps the writer of "An Old Woman's Story" knew this and tried to approximate a factual approach in her fiction to achieve an even greater emotional appeal. You will discover that just as poor children are Isolatoes, so are old people.

In addition to "An Old Woman's Story," we have another short story dealing with the elderly, Arna Bontemp's "A Summer Tragedy." These are balanced by David Pryor's "Where We Put the Aged," a more recent reportorial examination of the same problem.

Now perhaps the title of this section makes better sense. You can see that a minority, as we have been using the term through most of this book, need not be racial or ethnic. Isolation and alienation can be conferred by economic as well as physical deprivation. Nor need a minority necessarily mean the smaller number. Women aren't, in the true meaning of the word, a minority. But they, too, have suffered discrimination and isolation. The selection from *A Century of Struggle* may surprise you since you have grown up in an age where women have had token equality. But it has been largely token, make-believe. It's been a long battle and the mighty rise of Women's Lib groups all over the country has shown that it isn't over yet.

Homosexuals are a minority forced by an often frightened majority into isolation. Only recently have they sought recognition as whole and productive members of our society, but such recognition is a long time off. The article by Nancy L. Ross tells us that even today "homosexuals employed by the government fear to declare themselves lest they lose their jobs."

"Kent's Fifth Victim" is a current report of a kind of Isolato. You may have read it in your local newspaper. If not, you may have a lot to say when you finish it.

Ironically, what joins the people in the Isolatoes section is their separation, their aloneness. They are, as Watters described in the first essay, "alienated from the human community," some by choice, some by circumstance. If all of us *really* believed that "all men are created equal, that they are endowed by their Creator with certain unalienable rights, that among these are life, liberty and the pursuit of happiness," circumstances like those endured by the Isolatoes wouldn't arise. But they do.

# Reginald E. Watters
## Melville's "Isolatoes"

The unhappy fate of the man whom choice or chance has alienated
from the human community greatly interested Hawthorne, as is well
known. The theme held a similar fascination for Melville—even before he
became acquainted with many of Hawthorne's tales. The probable discussions subsequently with his friend and neighbor, however, may well
have strengthened his interest in the Ishmael *motif*. As might be expected,
Melville explored the moral and philosophical implications of the theme,
and out of them he evolved a doctrine of racial and social community as
an ideal to set opposite the isolated individual. This positive doctrine
need concern us here, however, only in so far as it is implicit in his de-       10
lineation of individuals who, because of birth or achievement or action or
character—a white jacket of some kind, in short—were set apart from
normal human relationships. These persons may appropriately be called
"Isolatoes." a term coined by Melville himself in describing the crew of
the Pequod: "They were nearly all Islanders ... 'Isolatoes' too, I call such,
not acknowledging the common continent of men, but each Isolato living
on a separate continent of his own." In each of his books one character
at least is just such an exile, either by accident or volition.

Many of the Isolatoes are presented as involuntary outcasts from the
human community. In *Typee* the narrator is estranged because he had       20
moved in a different sphere of life from the "dastardly and mean-spirited
wretches" who mainly composed the crew. And later, in the valley with
the natives, he was again a person set apart from the common life of his
neighbors. In *Omoo* the narrator is also isolated as "a man of education."
Taji's similar exclusion in *Mardi* is explained in a passage which is probably also autobiographical:

314

. . . Aboard of all ships in which I have sailed, I have invariably been known by a sort of drawing-room title. . . . . It was because of something in me that could not be hidden; stealing out in an occasional polysyllable; an otherwise incomprehensible deliberation in dining; remote, unguarded allusions to Belles-Lettres affairs; and other trifles. . . .

Taji found no one among the crew "with whom to mingle sympathies" except Jarl, who himself was experiencing "that heart-loneliness which overtakes most seamen as they grow aged." In *White Jacket,* the notorious garment symbolized, among other things, the wearer's conspicuous difference and detachment from all but a few members of the crew. Redburn's naivete, landlubberliness, and odd clothes made him "a sort of Ishmael in the ship." The narrator in *Moby Dick* begins by calling himself Ishmael, having been made one, he says, by circumstances. But from the moment when he felt that Queequeg, himself a wanderer in an alien land, was "a human being just as I am," his initial isolation began to thaw. The thorough Ishmael in this novel, as we shall see, is Captain Ahab.

Isabel, in *Pierre,* is another involuntary Isolato. As a child she had had to discover for herself that she even belonged to the general community of humanity, so harshly had she been treated by the people among whom she lived. She wrote to Pierre eventually because she could no longer "endure to be an outcast in the world." Israel Potter, through no fault of his own, became another Ishmael, wandering from youth to age in the wilderness of estrangement from his native land.

Melville's poetry presents others in the same role. As Weaver says, "the most recurring note" of *Clarel* is a "parched desire for companionship," a yearning for spiritual brotherhood. *John Marr and Other Sailors,* published only three years before Melville's death, contains the last of his involuntary Isolatoes. The old seaman, John Marr, cannot establish "sympathetic communion" with the prairie settlers among whom he had gone to live. He lacked the "common inheritance" upon which such familiarity rests—the shared experiences of a common past. When he once reminisced of his life at sea he was silenced with "Friend, we know nothing of that here."

All these individuals, through the accidents of birth or upbringing or circumstances or temperament, found themselves lacking the requirements for familiar social intercourse with their fellows. Some of them escape at last into a social environment congenial to themselves. Some of them succumb as involuntary victims. But none of them succeed in adjusting themselves to the social group which disowned them.

Perhaps because of the greater possibilities for tragedy, Melville was more profoundly interested in those whose isolation was voluntarily chosen or preferred. No doubt every man, on occasion, must imitate Father Mapple's "act of spiritual isolation" in pulling up the rope ladder to the pulpit to signify "his spiritual withdrawal for the time from all outward worldly ties and connexions." But in Melville's opinion prolonged isolation either chills the heart or corrupts the mind—or both.

Melville's two greatest voluntary Isolatoes, Ahab and Pierre, have hyp-
notized some readers into a mistaken conception of his general attitude
towards individualism. According to F. L. Pattee, Melville "was a Nietzschean when Nietzsche was but a schoolboy. Be hard, smite down, trample,
be a superman, or else be yourself trampled—that was the law of Nature,—
of God if there be a God." R. H. Gabriel views Melville as "the supreme
individualist of the nineteenth century," and Ahab as "the personification
of Melville's individualism."

Although occasionally Ahab could regret the cold isolation his mono-
mania produced, most of the time he deliberately preferred his solitude,          10
deliberately spurned as far as possible the assistance of other agents,
human and non-human. Proudly he boasted: "Ahab stands alone among
all the millions of the peopled earth, nor gods nor men his neighbors!"
He challenges the immortal gods to "swerve" him from his chosen course.
He also curses "that mortal interdebtedness which will not do away with
ledgers. I would be free as air; and I'm down in the whole world's
books. . . . " In his pride he resents his debts to the carpenter "for a bone
to stand on" and to his ancestors and parents "for the flesh in the tongue
I brag with." He tramples on human science as symbolized in the quadrant,
and later makes his own compass. He is even glad his mates do not share        20
his fierce hatred of the whale, lest his own hate might be lessened thereby.
His vanity makes him crave to be first in sighting Moby Dick, and when
he succeeds he boasts: "*I* only; none of ye could have raised the White
Whale first." He will acknowledge no ties of neighborliness to his fellow
Nantucketer, the captain of the Rachel, who cites the Golden rule in vainly
begging Ahab to help search for the lost boy. Indeed, Ahab's first thought
on hearing of the Rachel's encounter with Moby Dick is a fear that some
other person might have killed the whale. He craved not the mere
destruction of an evil but the egocentric delight in his own destroying it.
When he thinks of his fellow men, they are as projections of himself,          30
subordinated to his selfish purpose: "Ye are not other men, but my arms
and legs; and so obey me." In his last speech he reveals nothing but self-
centered egotism: my ship, my crew, "my topmost greatness," "my topmost
grief," "I grapple with thee," and so on. Not a word of remorse, not a word
of sympathy for the men he had brought to death.

The fate Melville assigned to this "Nietzschean" individualist was not
even partial victory, but total defeat. Professor Gabriel misinterprets the
outcome when he writes: "In the end Ahab saved his soul, maintained
inviolate his personal integrity, by going down in unconquered defeat
while Moby Dick swam on for other Ahabs to pursue." The man left to       40
continue the chase, had he so desired, was Ishmael, who had found values
in this "wolfish world" which Ahab was blind to; and Ishmael was saved
by the captain of the Rachel, whose searchings were prompted by love.
Ahab did not save even his soul—in his own opinion, at least—since as
he darts the last harpoon he cries: "From hell's heart I stab at thee; for
hate's sake I spit my last breath at thee." The Pequod itself, "like Satan,

would not sink to hell till she had dragged a living part of heaven [ the skyhawk] along with her." The delight Father Mapple had promised to the man "who against the proud gods and commodores *of this earth,* ever stands forth his own inexorable self" never descended upon Ahab, for he not only opposed the powers of earth but defied those of heaven.

Not Pattee nor Gabriel but Professor Matthiessen gives the true interpretation:

> Melville created in Ahab's tragedy a fearful symbol of the self-inclosed individualism that, carried to its furthest extreme, brings disaster both upon itself and the group of which it is a part. He provided also an 10 ominous glimpse of what was the result when the Emersonian will to virtue became in less innocent natures the will to conquest.

Pierre was like Ahab in two ways: he was determined to eradicate an evil, and he was proudly self-reliant. He was ready to sacrifice his whole social group (mother, fiancée, relatives, friends, dependents—everybody) to achieve something which he, like Ahab, considered necessary and good. Pierre's desire to bestow upon Isabel the spiritual, emotional, and material benefits of her patrimony was undoubtedly admirable; so was Ahab's desire to annihilate evil in the universe as symbolized by Moby Dick. The 20 issue can be stated simply: Is a man justified in severing most of his human relationships to pursue a personal idea—particularly when that ideal may involve ambiguity or error?

When Isabel's letter frightened away "the before undistrusted moral beauty of the world" Pierre cried:

> Myself am left, at least. . . . With myself I front thee! Unhand me all fears. . . . Henceforth I will know nothing but Truth. . . . Fate, I have a choice quarrel with thee. . . . I will lift my hand in fury, for am I not struck?. . . Thou Black Knight, that with visor down, thus confrontest 30 me, and mockest at me; lo! I strike through my helm, and will see thy face, be it Gorgon!. . . I will be impious, for piety hath juggled me. . . . From all idols, I tear all veils. . . .

Such assertive self-dedication echoes not only Ahab's egotism but the very imagery in his "pasteboard masks" speech. In the process of rectifying the wrong, moreover, Pierre again followed Ahab. Not till the last possible moment did Ahab confide in anyone his purpose in the Pequod's voyage. Pierre concealed his purpose from the world also, even from his beloved Lucy. He even hid from Isabel, who shared his major secret, the identity of Lucy and the full desperateness of their plight. Because he considered 40 himself "driven out an infant Ishmael into the desert," he had little faith in either his companions or humanity at large. After his first interview with Isabel, for instance, he felt a desire to shun every human habitation, human activity, or even "remembrances and imaginings that had to do with common and general humanity." His repudiation was complete.

Unlike Ahab, however, Pierre found his action at least partly justified

by his subsequent experiences. His mother's family pride, the Reverend
Falsgrave's worldliness, and his Cousin Glen's materialism—all thrust
him away from his social group. But Pierre's own pride, like Ahab's,
made him loath to lean on anyone:

> Pierre was proud. . . . A proud man likes to feel himself in himself,
> and not by reflection in others. He likes to be not only his own Alpha
> and Omega, but to be distinctly all the intermediate gradations.

Finally, Pierre resembles Ahab in not believing that his defiance and       10
renunciation would save even his individual soul from the total defeat:

> Had I been heartless, now, disowned, and spurningly portioned off the
> girl at Saddle Meadows, then had I been happy through a long life on
> earth, and perchance through a long eternity in heaven! Now, 'tis merely
> hell in both worlds. Well, be it hell.

In truth, the Melville hero who does save his soul is not Ahab or Pierre
or Taji but Billy Budd, who lived and died, not in isolation, not in hate
or self-assertion, but in community and love and sacrifice.                 20
    Many minor self-determined Isolatoes are scattered through Melville's
works. In *Clarel,* Mortmain and Vine are two examples; Ungar is another,
a man specifically described as "a wandering Ishmael from the West."
The John Paul Jones of *Israel Potter* is as ruggedly individualistic as Ahab.
He calls himself "an untrammeled citizen and sailor of the universe," and
agrees to serve his native country only under "unlimited orders: a separate,
supreme command; no leader and no counsellor but himself." He even
prefers to sleep in a chair alone than to share a bed. In *The Confidence
Man,* Frank Goodman calls the Missourian "an Ishmael" and explains
his "philosophy of disesteem for man" as springing from "a certain low-    30
ness, if not sourness, of spirits inseparable from sequestration." Melville
devotes a short story to the life of a Jimmy Rose, who sequestered himself
from friends as well as creditors after his financial collapse, until, "in his
loneliness, [ he] had been driven half mad." The Dansker in *Billy Budd*
contributed much to the tragedy of Billy's fate because he preferred the
isloation of his aloof and guarded cynicism to the frankness of friendship.
    The most complete and moving portrait among the minor Isolatoes,
however, is that of Bartleby the Scrivener. He simply and sweetly "preferred not to" when asked to participate in the normal life and duties of
his new employer's office. Bartleby was a man who was "by nature and      40
misfortune prone to a pallid hopelessness." After years as a clerk in the
Dead Letter office, where he had sorted for the flames the unsuccessful
attempts of men to communicate with one another—where he had, in
short, witnessed the breakdown of social fellowship—he would not or
could not adapt himself to the necessary usages of society. Melville ends
the sketch with the cry: "Ah Bartleby! Ah humanity!" Both the man and

mankind lose by such Ishmaelism—an opinion antithetical to Emerson's panegyric: "the great man is he who in the midst of the crowd keeps with perfect sweetness the independence of solitude."

In fact, none of Melville's Isolatoes find much comfort in Emersonian self-reliance. The involuntary ones, at least, are not self-sufficient individualists who lean only on the impalpable Over-soul, but rather lonely men in search of a human shoulder. In *Moby Dick* Ishmael succeeded in such a quest. Queequeg's fellowship "redeemed" his heart: "I felt a melting in me. No more my splintered heart and maddened hand were turned against the wolfish world." Queequeg's race and color might have made  10
him an Ishmael, but he is revealed as the direct opposite of Ahab. To save a stranger who had mocked at him he risks his life; Ahab would not pause to help a Nantucket neighbor. Queequeg insisted that Ishmael decide the futures of both by choosing a ship, but Ahab silenced all interference in his risking the ship and his crew. Finally, Queequeg invited Ishmael to share equally in his religious worship, but Ahab harangued the corposants with his foot upon Fedallah.

Not only Queequeg but the other harpooners, the mates, and the crew found values hidden to Ahab, because they shared common duties, common dangers, and common feelings. They subordinated their egoes  20
to assist their fellow man, Ahab: "all the individualities of the crew," their virtues and vices, "were welded into oneness." "I, Ishmael, was one of that crew; my shouts had gone up with the rest. . . . A wild, mystical, sympathetical feeling was in me; Ahab's quenchless feud seemed mine." The harpooners protected one another with whalespades from snapping sharks. Daggoo and Queequeg willingly risked their lives to save Tashtego when he was engulfed in the sinking whale's head. Human interdependence was further impressed upon the crew in such operations as the one employing the "monkey-rope," in which the man on board ship staked his very life on protecting the man who worked on the slippery whale along-  30
side from falling into the shark-filled sea. Ahab took no such risks for his fellows, felt no such responsibilities for their safety. The crew found other values in such ordinary duties as the squeezing by hand of spermaceti globules. This act produced in Ishmael "a strange sort of insanity," wherein he found himself squeezing his co-workers' hands.

> I forgot all about our horrible oath; in that inexpressible sperm, I washed my hands and my heart of it....Such an abounding, affectionate, friendly loving feeling did this avocation beget . . . [ that I longed to say] —Oh! my dear fellow-beings, why should we longer  40
> cherish any social acerbities . . . let us squeeze hands all round; nay, let us squeeze ourselves into each other; let us squeeze ourselves universally into the very milk and sperm of kindness.

The same "strange sort of insanity" characterized the negro Pip, who, as even Ahab recognized, was "full of the sweet things of love and gratitude." Pip begged Ahab to use him to replace the leg lost to Moby Dick, and promised never to desert Ahab as Stubb did Pip. But Ahab remained unswerved by Pip's abounding affection, which he called something "too curing for my malady." Ahab persisted in his demoniac isolation of spirit, while he bent other men to his will; yet he found neither happiness nor success. Although all the crew except Ishmael died, they did not die like Ahab, alone in hate and selfish concentration of purpose, but rather with brave fidelity and conscious of their humanity. Even the materialistic Flask thought of his mother!

Not admiration for their self-reliance but the deepest pity for their 10 loneliness dominated Melville's attitude towards his Isolatoes. As Bartleby's employer put it: "What miserable friendlessness and loneliness are here revealed! His poverty is great; but his solitude, how horrible!" The horror of loneliness is expressed again and again by Melville. In his first novel, *Typee,* he cites as a social crime far worse than wars, hangings, or even cannibalism, "the horrors we inflict, upon these wretches, whom we mason up in cells of our prisons, and condemn to perpetual solitude in the very heart of our population." Pip, who was deserted for many hours after his jump from the whaleboat, went insane less from fear than from his discovery, as a "lonely castaway" in the "shoreless ocean," 20 that "the awful lonesomeness is intolerable. The intense concentration of self in the middle of such a heartless immensity, my God! who can tell it?" Even Ahab, when in "The Symphony" chapter his "intense concentration of self" is momentarily diffused by a trace of human sympathy— even Ahab acknowledges the human horror of loneliness:

> When I think of this life I have led; the desolation of solitude it has been; the masoned, walled-town of a captain's exclusiveness, which admits but small entrance to any sympathy from the green country without—oh, weariness! heaviness! Guinea-coast slavery of solitary 30 command!

Denied even the privilege common to "the meanest shipwrecked captains" of going down with his ship, he dies with only one emotion other than his consuming hatred: "Oh, lonely death on lonely life!"

Melville's abounding pity for all his Isolatoes, the voluntary no less than the involuntary, no doubt issued from his own love of companionship, often thwarted as that may have been. He was himself no lover of solitude, though he probably experienced something of the involuntary Isolato's plight on shipboard because of his different upbringing. But no 40 man who repudiated fellowship in a preference for privacy would have chosen to spend many months in the confinement of a whaler, especially after already experiencing crews' quarters on Atlantic crossings. John Marr's reminiscences about the jovial companionship he once knew on ships suggest a similar indulgence by Melville himself. The letters Melville wrote to Duyckinck and especially to Hawthorne give overt evidence of what conversation, sympathy, appreciation, fraternity, meant to him. Even before meeting Hawthorne he had responded to the "depth of tenderness . . . boundless sympathy . . . omnipresent love" which he had detected in *The Mosses*. And when he received Hawthorne's "joy-giving" letter about *Moby Dick* he felt a oneness of himself and his neighbor—"ineffable socialities . . . infinite fraternity of feeling."

Frank Goodman's remark in *The Confidence Man* suggests what Melvill considered to be the prime cause of voluntary Ishmaelism:

> . . . . Misanthropy, springing from the same roof with disbelief in re-    10
> ligion, is twin with that . . . ; for, set aside materialism, and what is an
> atheist, but one who does not, or will not, see in the universe a ruling
> principle of love; and what a misanthrope, but one who does not, or
> will not, see in man a ruling principle of kindness? . . .

Except momentarily, Ahab expunges kindness from his heart, yet demands of God: "Come in thy lowest form of love, and I will kneel and kiss thee; but . . . come as mere supernal power [ and I remain indifferent] ." Yet he would not recognize that "lowest form of love" when it was displayed through humanity (Pip and Starbuck), through the serenity of the    20
ocean, and even through the gentleness of Moby Dick himself on the first day of the chase—when the whale merely splintered Ahab's leg but spared every man who took to boats after him, except Ahab's "evil shadow" Fedallah. Ahab would not recognize what was so plain to Starbuck: "All good angels mobbing thee with warnings:—what more wouldst thou have?"

Whether or not Melville himself could "see in the universe a ruling principle of love," he at least believed such a principle was essential to humanity and to religion. As Braswell says, "Christ's doctrine of love and his promise of immortality were among the lasting influences in Melville's    30
life." Melville called the Sermon on the Mount "that greatest real miracle of all religions . . . an inexhaustible soul-melting stream of tenderness and loving-kindness." In *Mardi* he presented Serenia as an ideal land which practiced the teachings of that sermon. In this Land of Love all men, rich and poor, masters and servants, were called brothers. They all united in a "fond, filial, reverential feeling" for Alma [ Christ], whose "great command is Love." Love is the greatest human virtue, as Melville suggests in *Billy Budd*—not rationality or self-reliance; and although men can think alone they must love together.

Throughout his works, then, Melville displayed his belief that happi-    40
ness is not obtainable by the individual in isolation, but may be found in shared experiences—in a community of thought and action and purpose. The man whose solitude is thrust upon him is to be deeply pitied. The man whose isolation is self-imposed through repudiation of his social ties creates sorrow for himself and pain for others. In his criticism of the voluntary Isolato—the man who would forsake the common continent

of humanity to maroon himself on his own island — Melville may conceivably have had in mind John Donne's memorable metaphor: "No man is an *Iland*, intire of it selfe; every man is a peece of the *Continent*, a part of the *maine*."

# Jacob Twersky
## Being Blind

Esther's conviction that her mother would not understand about us seemed reasonable, of course. Did I expect her to be glad about us? Nevertheless, I also thought that Esther was using her as an excuse.

She had come to New York only once since I had known Esther, and that had been early in the summer. I had not met her then. I was relieved when she left. Now I both wanted and dreaded to meet her. But she did not come. She worked in a store in Washington. She was busy, too, helping out relatives in various ways. And I wondered whether there might not be still another reason.

"You're not discouraging your mother from visiting you, are you?" I asked one day.

"What makes you think that?" Esther said. "I love my mother very much."

"Why don't you go visit her on a weekend?"

"Would you come with me?"

"That would be a little too much, moving in on her for the weekend. I ought to meet her first. Anyway, you ought to talk to her about us a good deal first."

"Yes. I wish we could just go without preliminaries. I want you to meet my brother and sister too and everybody. I miss them so much."

"Well, why don't you go yourself, if you miss them so much. I'll survive a day or two without you."

"But I'd keep thinking about you all the time."

"Did you leave home just because you wanted to study singing here, or were you a little tired of people too?"

"I did want to get away—it's pretty dull in Washington. Wouldn't you really mind very much if I went to see them?"

"I've been telling you I want you to go, haven't I?"

"I'll see. Maybe I'll go soon."

Esther did, however, write her mother a long letter that day—she said she was telling her everything. On an evening two or three days afterward, her mother phoned. She pleaded and demanded that Esther stop seeing me, that she come home to talk things over. After that call I no longer wanted her to go and felt we ought to get married secretly, but I had doubts and thought she should reach a decision herself, and I said nothing to influence her.                                                                    10

Esther's mother called again, promising or threatening to come to New York as soon as she could, but Saturday afternoon, Morton, Esther's brother, phoned that he was in the city. Esther told him to come right over. She did not say I was there. She laughed as she hung up.

"Mother is sending the man of the family to take care of everything. You'll like my brother."

"He wants to talk to you privately. I'll go to my place."

"You're staying here."

"But it'll be embarrassing for him."

"Maybe, but you're not going to run away. You have to help me."            20

"What am I supposed to do with him?"

"Nothing. Just be here."

She started straightening out the place. I walked back and forth through the rooms.

"Sit down, for goodness' sake."

I sat down. She laughed.

"Yes, it's quite a joke," I said.

"You don't understand," she said. "Morty is just not the type you send on a mission like this. You can't imagine anyone more sweet and gentle. And do you know what he says? He says he's been here since yesterday,      30 just got around to thinking of calling me. He's a pharmacist, you know. He's here on business, you see—buying for his company. He just got off the train, he means, and after he sees us he'll get right back on again."

"I guess your mother thinks he has a lot of influence with you."

"She knows better. She must be out of her mind worrying about me—poor Mother."

"Apparently you don't need my help with him. Couldn't I meet you and him later at a restaurant? It's a long trip to Washington—you can't send him right back."

She came over and leaned down to me.                                        40

"I know this isn't easy for you," she said.

When Morton knocked at the door, I felt myself stiffening. Esther exclaimed delightedly over him. Morton and I shook hands. Neither of us knew what to say. We sat down on the couch, and Esther drew over a chair for herself. She asked him about the family and about his child. I sat smoking.

"Where do you carry your wallet now when you come to New York?" she asked him.

"Where I always do," he said. "She thinks it's funny that I carry two wallets," he explained to me. "One of them is stuffed with paper, and anyone who wants to pick my pocket can have it."

"The one with money in it," she said, "he keeps pinned in his back pocket."

"It's a good idea," I said, trying not to smile.

"I notice you have some new hardware, Esther," he said. "When are you holding a sale?"

"You and Mother don't have any appreciation for antiques and nice things. Only Daddy did."

"I don't see many antiques in this room." He turned to me. "She's got some nice things, but most of the stuff is junk. Don't you think so?"

"I don't know anything about antiques," I said.

We were silent.

"Morty," she said, "did Mother show you the letter?"

"Yeah."

"Then you know something about what Jake is like. We love each other and we're going to get married. That's all there is to it."

"Yeah, that's fine. Can I see the rest of your place?"

They walked out of the room and through the kitchen and into the room where the piano was. They spoke low, only the murmur of their voices reaching me. The cat climbed on the couch and snuggled against me. I pushed it away. I walked to the open window. A smell of cellars came up from the yard. I could hear vendors calling and children shouting in the distance, and I concentrated on the sounds, not wishing to hear the voices behind me.

I heard their steps returning and I returned to the couch and lit another cigarette.

"Morty is taking us out to dinner," Esther said. "It would be nice if we could all go to a show or somewhere afterward, but he has to rush right back to his wife and child. He just can't stay away from them."

She walked out of the room to change her dress. Morton said he often went fishing in Chesapeake Bay on Saturday or Sunday. That was the life, he said. He also took in the games of the Redskins and of the Senators when he could. We talked and the tightness in me eased.

He told funny stories in the restaurant. When we walked out into the street he hailed a cab to take him to the station. . . .

Her mother came to New York during the next week. She stayed at Esther's place. I did not meet Esther the day her mother came. In the evening I tried to work in my room, but the sounds from the movie theater and my neighbors were particularly grating. I put the radio on, turned it off shortly, and just sat slumped in the armchair. I kept wanting to phone Esther, but the thought of her mother discouraged me. I saw them talking, arguing. Esther was not having an easy time, I thought, but I'd only make it worse if I called. Later I saw them getting ready for bed. Esther would sleep on the couch and her mother in the bed. Her poor mother, I thought. She was a good woman, worked hard, was worried about her daughter. And didn't she have reason to be worried? I sympathized with her, but also felt hostile toward her.

The phone rang, and it was Esther. She wanted to know what I was doing. She sounded as though she had been crying.

"Go to bed," she said. "Did you eat in one of those greasy joints around your way? You should have had dinner with Vic or gone to Brooklyn."

"I thought you and your mother would be asleep by now," I said.

"She's gone to bed. Did you think I could go to sleep without saying goodnight to you?"

"I guess we better not talk long. You'd be keeping her up."

"I don't care. But I'll talk softly. Will you hear me? Is it very noisy there tonight?"

"I'll hear you, darling."

Next evening I waited before the building where Esther went for her voice lessons. Her mother had gone with her to her lesson. They would be coming out soon and we would go to a restaurant. I leaned against the building. People were hurrying by.

Was her mother expecting a very blindish-looking blind man? But what difference did it make? She wouldn't see me anyway—she'd only be able to see my blindness.

People came out of the building. I listened for Esther's step. I did not hear it. I dried the dampness from my palm on the lining of my pocket. In a moment she and her mother came out and I turned to them. Her mother took my hand. I felt her pity for me. Esther put her arm through mine and we started for the restaurant. Her mother spoke rapidly, nervously, as we walked. She said I was a wonderful young man. She said she did not like New York. She criticized Esther for not practicing her singing enough.

At dinner she worried that I would put my hand in the butter, that I would upset my glass of water.

"Does he want any more bread?" she asked.

"I don't know," Esther said angrily. "Ask him. He's not deaf. And he knows if he wants bread or not. He knows at least that much."

I smiled and said I'd have some more bread. Her mother buttered a piece for me and handed it to me.

"I should've spoken directly to you," she said. "I'll learn. It's just that—"

"It's just that she doesn't think," Esther interrupted.

"What's the matter with you, Esther?" I said.

"She's been like that with me ever since I came," her mother said.

"And all she's done is talk about my junk, as she calls it, and how I'm wasting my time with my singing."

"I think there definitely is something wrong with her," her mother said.

"Now this singing of hers. If she's going to be a singer—fine. That's up to her. I'd be just as happy if she wouldn't be one. She did so well in law school and had a good government job. But if she's going to be a singer, why doesn't she work at it? That's what she came here to do. Her teacher says she could be a marvelous singer."

"Oh, stop, Mother. He's sick of hearing about my singing."

I protested I was not, and her mother continued. She complained also about Esther's flat and the neighborhood it was in. She was complaining about everything, I thought, except what she most wanted to complain about. The poor woman. But she grew calmer, tried to put me at ease. Esther's tone became affectionate toward her.

Her mother wished to see my parents, and, since she was not going to stay long in the city, we went to Brooklyn the following evening. We all sat in the living room, Davy too. Esther's mother began unburdening herself to my parents, especially to Father. She spoke of her hardships after her husband's death, of the hopes she had had for Esther. And she spoke of my blindness, sympathizing with my parents and me and saying that it hurt her terribly to see me as I was, and she wept. Father tried to console her. Mother also tried, but her own voice was tearful.

What was she doing to Mama and Papa? Why couldn't she let them alone? I remained silent with an effort, but I walked over to Mother. Esther's mother rose and hugged me.

"You'll be my son too," she said. "Is it strange that I want you to see? But I'll get used to your not seeing. It won't hurt so much after a while."

A few days after her mother returned to Washington, Esther went there too. She had promised her mother to make the visit, and her sister and her relatives were anxious to see her. I doubt that I would have gone with her if she had asked me, but I was hurt that she had not asked. Her mother had made her squeamish about me, I thought. She'd come back even more squeamish.

She was gone more than a weekend. I phoned her several times from my room. Afterward it seemed that the warmth of her voice had been put on, or at least not completely sincere. I hated the room, the hotel.

Maybe she'd have nothing more to do with me when she came back, I thought. No, it would go on for a time. She was infatuated with me. A bizarre infatuation. She had looked for something different and had found it in a blind man such as I. But the infatuation wouldn't last. She was coming to her senses. Anyway, no matter how she felt about me, she had to drop me. I'd be a drag on her if she became a singer, or even if she didn't.

What would I do after she dropped me? I asked myself one night. I'd get away from the rotten city, I thought. If I stayed around I'd go crawling to her sooner or later, and she'd take me back after a fashion, to see me now and then. I'd have to go far away. But where would I get a job? Would another college take me? How about another blind school? That was it, a blind school—perhaps I could get into one far away. I belonged in a blind school. I'd rest in it. What did I care about anything?

The night that Esther was coming back I went down to where she lived
to meet her in front of the house. Laughter and jarring music came from
the bar two doors down the street. It was late—the rest of the street was
still. She would drive up in a cab from the station because she had a heavy
suitcase with her. I had helped her pack the suitcase. I waited, but no car
stopped in front of the house. She was coming back this late at night
because she and her mother had visited relatives in Baltimore today and
she had not been able to leave till after supper. I cursed her relatives. I
examined my watch. Why wasn't she here yet? What had happened now?
Maybe the train had been early—she had got here before me and was       10
upstairs. I hurried up the stoop, pushed open the door that had one of its
glass panes missing, ran up the flights of stairs, breathing in the dust.
I had a key to her door, but I knocked. I knocked again, then went down
the stairs. Maybe she wasn't coming back tonight—she had changed her
mind. But wouldn't she have let me know? She knew I'd be waiting here
for her. Downstairs I leaned against the cracked wall in the vestibule.
Presently I went out into the street again.

The train was late—that was all. Relax, I told myself. But why the
devil hadn't she started back earlier? My anger gathered against her.
I walked up and down before the house. Whenever anyone passed, I felt     20
my mouth hardening. Get into the vestibule, I told myself. They'd be
coming out of the bar soon to stare at me. Let them come. The hell with
all of them.

I rested against the rusty rail of the stoop. It was over an hour since I
had come to the house. The street was quieter. A car came toward the
house, stopped. "Darling!" Esther called. I walked slowly to the cab. She
kissed me. In the vestibule she threw her arms about me.

"I thought your train would never come in," I said.

"Didn't you get my message?"

She had had to take a later train. She had phoned from the station in     30
Baltimore, but I had not been in my room. She was furious with the man
at the desk at my hotel for not having given me the message.

"My poor darling," she said, "waiting for me all this time. Why didn't
you wait up in the apartment?"

"I don't like your apartment much."

I started up the stairs with the suitcase. "Wait," she told me when we
were about halfway to her floor. She was worried about her cat. She had
left it in the care of an old man who lived on the ground floor. The old
man always took good care of her cat in her absence. "The old man sleeps
all day," she said. "Maybe he isn't sleeping now. Do you think I should    40
pick her up now?"

"Damn your cat," I said.

I continued up the stairs and she followed me. She held me close again
in her flat.

"Don't be angry with me," she said. "I missed you so much! I'll never
go away without you again."

I kissed her. Suddenly I pushed her away.

"You're tired," I said. "Sit down."

"I'm not at all tired, honey." I sat down on the couch and she sat down next to me. "I was tired on the train, but now I feel fine."

"Good. Then I can ask you something. When are we getting married?"

"Whenever you say."

"Make it this week, next week, as soon as possible. Let your mother know."

"I didn't think you wanted it to be that soon. I have to talk to you about it, but must we do it now?"

"Yes, now."

"You really want to marry me right away?"

"No, I don't. I'm just talking to hear myself talk. Why wouldn't I want to marry you right away?"

"There are lots of reasons. I'm such a mess. One reason is that I'm still not clear about my singing. I know you're sick of hearing about it, but—"

"Why do you keep saying I'm sick of hearing about your damn singing?"

"You're angry with me because I went away. I knew you would be. You'll be angry with me all the time when I'll have to go away on singing trips."

"I'm not angry with you for going away, and I won't be angry about your singing trips."

"Won't you? And I'll have to deal with all kinds of people. You won't like that either. You won't like it that I'll have any kind of a life apart from yours. You'll be a very demanding husband, I'm afraid."

"You've thought it all out, haven't you? Have your mother and sister and the others helped you? You're quite clear in your mind now. What's there to talk about?"

"Won't you even promise that you'll try to be understanding?"

I got up and walked across the room.

"Honey, I didn't want to talk about it now," she said.

"You want us to wait awhile before we get married—is that it? You'll decide whether you want to be a singer. If you decide you do, you won't marry me."

"I didn't say that!"

"Why wait then?"

"I want to be fair to you. I don't want to be so mixed up when we're married."

"And you want your people to accept me more before we're married. Is that right?"

"Yes. You do understand."

"Yeah, I understand. You have a million excuses and you always will. Perhaps you don't know what you want, but you're finding out you don't want me."

"It isn't true!"

"I've had enough," I said.

"I knew you'd get sick of me."

She started to cry.

"Look, you're tired," I said, "and I'm getting you all upset. I better go."

She threw herself, sobbing, on the couch. I walked into the kitchen and then into the other room. Antiques, I thought. Junk. What I had to do was clear out of this junk shop right now. It was over—it had to be over soon. I clenched my fists and stood still, listening to her sobs. I turned and hurried over to her and gripped her shoulder.

"Listen to me," I said. "We're getting married right away. You'll go on with your singing lessons after we're married. You'll decide then about    10
being a singer. That's the way it's going to be."

She grasped my hand and drew me to her. . . .

We were married in Father's synagogue. Before the ceremony, as the people gathered in the synagogue and the living quarters, as the voices and the merriment increased, I felt that it was all strange, dreamlike. To have found Esther and to be marrying her in this house!

My brothers and friends surrounded me. Mother was everywhere, bustling, happy. Esther, in accordance with the custom for a bride, sat in a room apart. Her mother, brother, and some other relatives were with her. People went in to see her. I kept going in, as though to assure myself    20
she was really there. Her voice was calm, but she clung to my hand. I pictured her loveliness. Her mother several times looked me over to make certain that my tie was still straight, that my suit was not wrinkled, that I had not dropped cigarette ashes on it.

Esther and her mother and my mother and I went down to the study. The *Chassidim* were singing in the synagogue. A number of them shook my hand. I felt the warmth of all of them toward me. Yesterday too, the day of the Sabbath, I had felt this warmth. I had been at the Sabbath service as a bridegroom, to be called up to the Torah with special recognition, to be welcomed as a responsible man, as an equal.    30

In the study there was a group of rabbis with Father, distant relatives and close friends of his. Father led Esther and me to the desk, and we signed the marriage contract.

"Now it is signed, dear children," Father said. "In a few minutes you will be married."

"God bless them," one of the other rabbis said.

"It is the prayer of all of us," another said.

Esther's mother and mine wept softly. I took Esther's hand. Father explained to her mother what was to be done next, and she and Esther went out of the study. My brothers entered and came up to me.    40

I walked between Mother and Father out into the synagogue to the *chuppah*, the marriage canopy, held up on poles by four of the *Chassidim*. Esther was led to it from the other side. Our fingers touched under the *chuppah*. Father began the service in the stillness. His voice broke. One of the other rabbis took up the prayers.

To end the ceremony a wineglass was put down by my foot. I was to shatter the glass under my heel. It would symbolize that Jews even at their merriest must remember the destruction of the Temple, must remember human suffering. It would symbolize the beginning of a new life too, and might bring good luck. I stamped down on the glass. It shattered loudly.

*"Mazel tov! Mazel tov!"*

People were congratulating us, wishing us well. Relatives and friends crowded around us. Esther and I kissed each other. I hugged Mother and Esther's mother. The *Chassidim* started to sing, joined hands and danced.

* * *

Apartments were still hard to find, but as if the shattering of the wineglass at the wedding were indeed bringing us good luck, we easily found one we wanted not far from the college. Esther gave some of her antiques and art objects away, but there was still a good deal of packing to do in her flat. We wrapped statuettes and paintings and vases and other of her smaller things in newspaper and stowed them in cartons. It seemed that most of the floor space in the flat became taken up with cartons.

"I've certainly married a woman of property," I said. "I guess we'll fix our new apartment up to rival any museum."

"Our new apartment will be lovely," she said. "Haven't I given all the junk away? You wouldn't want our place to look like any old apartment, would you?"

"I guess not," I said hesitantly.

"I won't buy more junk — I promise. I won't even buy beautiful things like those I've kept, till we can afford to. We have to buy so many other things now. Darling, we will have a lovely home. Don't be angry with me for taking all this with me."

I kissed her.

"I'm not angry, honey. I know our home will be lovely, no matter what it looks like."

"But it will look beautiful too. You just wait and see."

In our new apartment I put up curtains and shelves at her direction. Out of new pine boards I also made bookcases and a record cabinet and she painted them. She worked hard at various tasks about the place, but in showing it off to guests she seemed proudest of the bookcases and the record cabinet.

We had gatherings of our friends frequently. Sometimes Esther sang for us, or one of her friends played the piano. At first I took the role of host very seriously, mixing drinks and in general exerting myself in an effort to be helpful, entertaining. But shortly I began to relax, letting Esther do more of the serving of refreshments or asking the guests to serve themselves, and I became less concerned whether anyone was bored.

I wanted Esther to quit her job at the concert agency, but she refused, even for some time after we knew we were going to have a child. When she did quit, she also gave up her singing lessons.

"I'm not going to be a singer," she said one night. "I'm not going back to my lessons after the baby is born."

"That's how you feel now," I said. "You'll have to go back because you haven't thought it through yet."

"Haven't I? Well, you can think what you want to. I'm just not going to try to be a singer any more. I'm happy knowing it. I'll sing to friends if they want to hear me, and I'll sing to you and the baby. That's all the singing I'm going to do."

"You have plenty of time to change your mind. Go to sleep now."

"Honey, I think the baby is going to be a girl. Will you be disappointed?" 10

"I believe so. Can't you make it twins?"

"It'll be so nice to dress her and fix her hair before the mirror when she gets a little older. Will you really be disappointed in a beautiful little girl?"

"Of course not, darling."

We held each other and talked about the baby.

I was finding it harder those days to travel in the streets alone efficiently. I could not concentrate enough on it. Esther and the child we were going to have were on my mind. I was also finishing writing a novel—a novel about blind people—and sometimes I did a bit of the writing in my 20 mind as I walked. Perhaps too my reflexes had slowed down. I knocked into things. Brakes screeched at me as I crossed streets. I fell over an open cellar door.

Once, hurrying home, I cracked into a post on our street, cutting myself above the eye. I pressed my handkerchief over the cut a moment and hurried on, not wishing to be seen by any of our neighbors. I let myself quietly into the apartment. I'd wash up before Esther could see me. But she stepped out into my path in the hall.

"What have you done to yourself?"

"It's nothing. It only looks a little bad." 30

She led me into the bathroom and cleaned the cut. "It really isn't so bad," she said. She cleaned a spot of blood from my face too. "Why don't you carry a cane?" she demanded. "When are you going to stop being so proud and stupid? Don't you ever think of me and the baby?"

"Stop making a fuss. It was just a little accident."

"Next time it can be a big accident. You're selfish—that's what you are."

"I'll be damned if I'll go groping around like some old blindish blind man."

"Oh, don't talk to me!" 40

She walked into the kitchen. She had fussed about a cane before, I told myself. She'd be all right soon. I followed her into the kitchen.

"Is supper ready yet?"

"No."

"How do you feel?"

"A lot you care. I don't want to talk to you. You make me so angry."

"It was just a little accident."

I walked up the hall into the living room. Sure she was right about me, I told myself. I had to start carrying a damn cane. Hadn't I always known I'd start sometime? I had to do it now. I walked up and down in the living room. Esther came in.

"You can have something before supper if you're hungry."

"Honey, if you're not tired later we'll go buy a cane."

She was very pleased.

I took the cane with me next day when I went out. It was decidedly a help. In succeeding days I even began to feel at ease about being seen with the cane by people who knew me.

It takes a long time and a great deal of help from others to learn to accept blindness, and perhaps one can never fully accept it. My blindness mattered to me less now than ever before. My past was falling into a pattern with the present, giving my life clear meaning, making my blindness more acceptable. But I was also afraid—the meaning I saw might yet somehow be destroyed.

On a summer morning Esther and I drove in a cab to the hospital. She wasn't in much pain, she said. We reported at the desk in the hospital. A nurse took Esther away. The woman behind the desk showed me to a chair in a room off the lobby. People stirred in the room.

"In about half an hour," the woman told me, "you can go up to see your wife. I'll call you. Don't look so worried. Nothing will happen for quite some time."

The doctor, when I spoke to him on the phone before we left the apartment, had also said there would be a long wait. But Esther would be all right, I told myself. She was going to have a baby—that was all. The worried prospective father—the woman out there knew the type well. I had to relax.

Half an hour passed. I was not called. I waited a few minutes more and walked out to the desk.

"Yes," the woman said, "your wife is probably much more comfortable now. I'll show you to the elevator."

When I stepped out of the elevator a nurse met me and took me to Esther. I sat down by the bed.

"It's a little worse," Esther said. "If it gets very bad I want you to go away."

"Didn't they give you something for the pain?"

"Maybe they will later. It's up to the doctor. He'll be here soon."

She had not wanted her mother to know when she would be going into the hospital.

"It would be good to have your mother around now."

"She'll be giving up enough of her time when she comes to help with the baby."

"I could call her. She could get here today sometime."

"You're being silly. It's just that you're so worried, honey. What good could Mother do me now? She'd only make me nervous. I don't want anyone here except you, but I don't want you here either if it gets very bad or takes a very long time."

"Don't be afraid. It'll happen quickly and easily."

When the doctor came I felt that I was in the way, and I walked out of the room and down the corridor a little and stood against the wall there. Shortly he came out of the room and came up to me.

"She'll have a difficult time. She may not have the child until tomorrow."

"Is anything wrong?"

"Nothing serious. You better go home for a while. She's worried about you and that doesn't help."

I went back to her, told her I would be with Vic and that he and I would be here later. I left the hospital and went to the Mathematics Institute where Vic worked. We had coffee in a drugstore. He phoned his wife and she met us and I returned with them to the hospital. We stayed with Esther and then sat in the waiting room. We were permitted to go up to her again early in the evening, but only for a few minutes. She pressed me to her tremulously before we left.

I stayed with Vic and my sister-in-law. I slept on the couch in their living room. I had not truly prayed perhaps in years, but I prayed that night with all my heart. I phoned the hospital during the night and early in the morning. There was no change, I was told. We went back to the hospital to wait there.

Shortly before noon the woman behind the desk in the lobby ran into the room where we were sitting and took my hand in both of hers.

"Your wife's fine and you have a little girl now. You can go up to see them soon."

Esther had the baby with her when we went up. She said she really was feeling fine and that the baby was wonderful.

"She's not like other newborn children," she said. "Touch her head. She how long her hair already is? It's blond, but it'll get darker like yours. Her face is much more like mine, though."

"That's fortunate," I said, touching the baby's half-closed hand.

The doctor breezed into the room. He left in a moment, but I followed him, calling to him.

"I want to talk to you," I said to him gruffly in the corridor. "Why did it take so long?"

"These things happen," he said. "The child was turned around."

"Is my wife perfectly all right now?"

"Yes, certainly."

"And the baby?"

"A normal healthy baby."

I knew it was foolish to ask about the baby's eyes, but I had to be completely assured.

"And the baby's eyes?"

"The eyes?"

"Yes. Are they all right?"

"Of course."

"You can really tell so soon that they're all right?"

"They're perfect."

I visited Esther and the baby usually twice a day while they were in the hospital. I came with my parents or brothers or alone. I knew the way from the lobby to Esther's room, but one nurse or another generally hurried up to me as I stepped out of the elevator.

Sometimes I brought with me the mail that had come in the morning and that had not been identified or read to me yet. One day Esther told me excitedly that one of the letters I had just handed her was from a publisher I had submitted my novel to. "Wouldn't it be wonderful if they accepted it?" she said. She opened the letter. "They have accepted it!" The baby woke, crying. Esther soothed her.

"You sure have a lucky old dad, Laura," I said.

I felt I would go on being lucky, and I felt encouraged to believe that I would write with growing insight into people and blindness.

When Esther was ready to come home with the baby, my mother-in-law and I went to the hospital together. In the cab going home I held the baby. My mother-in-law gave me a number of instructions on how to do it. Esther protested.

"Bessie and I get along fine," I said. "I simply turn off my hearing aid."

"You'll have her believing you have one."

My mother-in-law was paying attention to the baby. "She's smiling right up at you," she told me. "I guess her daddy knows how to hold her. Esther says you're going to help out with the diapering and everything. You really can do just about everything."

"Keep saying that," I said. "You may convince yourself. You want to hold Laurie awhile?"

She took her happily.

My mother-in-law stayed with us some ten days, becoming ever fonder of the baby and learning to be more and more natural with me. Doubtless it helped her that I had grown more at ease with her. She visited us regularly after this stay.

Laurie was always natural with me. Understandable as it was, it nevertheless amazed me. She was quite content when I bathed her or gave her her bottle, perhaps almost as content as with Esther, though she often took exception to anyone else doing things for her. She didn't know yet that I was blind, I told myself. She'd lose her confidence in me soon enough. When she started crawling about, she did not move out of Esther's path, but did out of mine, though I had never bumped into her, or she made a sound to let me know where she was. Now she definitely knew that I was blind, I thought. Still, save for her intelligent concern that I might bump into her or step on her, her confidence in me was unchanged.

She began showing me her toys by thrusting them into my hand. To show them to Esther she merely held them up. For a time she thought that women and children alone could see, scurrying out of the way of men or thrusting her toys into the hands of those she liked, though I was the only blind man she had ever seen.

She learned of various ways in which blindness made me different, but she continued to regard the difference as unimportant. Mommy read with her eyes, Dad with his fingers. She imitated us both, bowing her head over a printed page, running her hands over a page of Braille, till she understood that because she could see she must read only as Mommy did. But to write she was sometimes allowed either to scratch with Mommy's pen or bang on Dad's typewriter. She knew that Dad could not help her draw with a pencil or a crayon—anyway he couldn't do it well—but he could build houses and ships with her easily out of blocks. He could play ball with her too, but she couldn't make too much noise then, because he had to hear the ball bounce. If it rolled under the bed he didn't like it, even though he was especially good at finding things that got lost under the bed.

She liked me to stand at the bottom of the sliding board in the park to catch her as she slid down. She was about a year old when she started helping me carry my briefcase to the door as I left for the college. When I returned, she ran to meet me.

In the house in Brooklyn Laurie followed my mother about. Mother gave her bowls of water to stir with a spoon, a whiskbroom to brush the sofa and pillows with. She said she had always wanted a little girl herself. Laurie also liked to run up and down in the synagogue and to bring her toys to my father in the study. Father's ailments caused him increasing pain—sometimes as he played with Laurie he stopped short a moment, making no sound, or gasping for breath.

Father was anxious for Davy to be married, as though fearful that he might not live to see it. Davy was engaged to a girl he had met at Brooklyn College. He finished his studies at the Yeshiva and became an assistant rabbi in a large synagogue. Then—he was only twenty-two—they were married. Afterward Father's strength failed rapidly. He was taken to the hospital. He seemed to be getting better there, and he spoke cheerfully about his children, regarding them all now as set for a good life, but early one evening Davy phoned us from the hospital, his voice full of sorrow. Father had died.

Esther called in a neighbor to stay with Laurie, and we started for Brooklyn. On the subway train I did not want to talk about Father.

"He was very ill, honey," Esther said. "He was in very great pain."

I did not answer her. She tried a number of times more to console me, and I either said nothing or answered shortly, and then we were both silent.

In the house in Brooklyn we waited for Father to be brought home. He was carried into the synagogue, and we all went down the stairs to him. There was a strong smell of melting wax, and *Chassidim* were praying.

A group of them would pray through the entire night by him. He lay under a prayer shawl, and one of the congregation put my hand on the prayer shawl over one of the dead hands. I was afraid to feel it—I scarcely touched it. Mother sobbed uncontrollably. I told Esther to take her back upstairs. I walked into the study and touched Father's chair behind the desk and wept.

I went upstairs with my brothers. Men and women of the congregation kept coming up to extend their condolences. When they stopped coming and it was quiet, save for the murmur of the praying in the synagogue, Mother wanted to make tea for us.

"Say you want some," Esther whispered to me. "It'll give her something to do."

We had the tea. It grew late—our neighbor could not stay much longer with Laurie. Vic and Davy and their wives would spend the night with Mother, but I wished to remain with her too.

"Hen will drive you home," I told Esther. "It's late. You better go now."

"You go with her," Mother said. "I'm not afraid here."

Esther touched my hand timidly. I thought of her and Laurie alone in our apartment and I stood up to go with her. In Hen's car we talked about Father and Mother. Mother would be all right.

The funeral was next day in accordance with the traditional quick burial requirement. We left Laurie at the home of a friend. After the service in the synagogue we drove a long time in one of the hired limousines, and then we stood out in the openness. I touched the coffin as it was carried past me. Presently I heard the earth falling on the wood—the rattling hollow sound.

Mother lived with Davy and his wife. When Davy accepted a rabbinical position out of town, she moved into an apartment of her own near the house we had lived in. She felt at home in the old neighborhood—she did not want to leave it. She saw all of us often at our homes and at hers. She was not lonely, she said. She wanted many grandchildren, she told us.

Esther and I continued to grow closer, to understand each other better and feel more deeply for each other, but I could not believe that she had no regrets about marrying me.

"You might have become a famous singer if you hadn't married me," I said one evening.

"I was really taking my singing very seriously when I met you, wasn't I?" she said. "I don't know what I was taking seriously. I was lost about everything."

"You would've found yourself."

"Not without you. I'm very happy now, darling."

"Don't you ever still think of becoming a singer? We'd work it out."

"I don't want to become one. Can't you understand that?"

"But there must be something to make you sorry you married me."

"Oh, be still. You just want me to keep telling you there isn't."

I smiled and caressed her.

Laurie and I also learned to understand each other better, but with her too I had my fears. Would she someday look down upon me and pity me for my blindness, instead of being natural or intelligently sympathetic about it? Would she be ashamed of me, or ashamed for me?

Once—she was three years old then—she climbed into my lap and wanted me to tell her the story of how I became blind.

"She asked why you couldn't see," Esther said. "I told her you had a special kind of sickness when you were a little boy. Children don't get that sickness any more, do they?"

"No," I said, "not any more."                                              10

"Tell the story, Daddy," Laurie urged.

"I had that special sickness, honey, and then I couldn't see—that's all there is to that story."

"You lived far away. Tell that, Daddy."

"I lived far away over the ocean. There was a little girl there with a ponytail like yours, but not as soft and pretty."

"I have a lovely dress on too. Touch it. It's blue."

"Yes, it's very lovely."

She settled herself more comfortably against me.

"What was the little girl doing far away over the ocean?" she asked.     20

"Well, once upon a time she and her mom and dad went into the woods to pick blueberries. It was a very nice day and—"

"Oh, I don't like that story, Dad. Tell about the little boy who couldn't see."

"Why?"

"Because I want to hear it."

"He was a little boy like other little boys, but he was blind. There's nothing to tell."

"He was sad."

"Why?"                                                                     30

"Because he was blind."

"Yes, he was sad a little."

She turned to look up at me.

"My daddy is sad."

"No, Laurie darling, I'm not. You know why? It's because I have you and Mommy and that makes me very happy. Do you understand?"

"Yes."

"She does," Esther said, coming over to us.

"If she doesn't," I said, "she certainly will."

I drew Esther to me. I held them both close.                              40

# Alvin L. Schorr
## ... And Children of the
## Nation First

In 1963, of the 69 million children in the United States who lived in families, 15.6 million were poor.

Depending upon one's definition of poverty, the number of poor children can be enlarged or diminished. It may be well, therefore, to be explicit about what this particular figure means. The portion of income that a family uses for food may be regarded as a rough indicator of its prosperity. That is, as total income goes up, a smaller and smaller percentage is devoted to food. The poorest families spend a third or more of their income on food; other families generally spend a smaller proportion. The point at which total income is less than three times the cost of the basic nutritional requirements of a family (of specified size and ages) may be viewed as the brink of poverty. Basic requirements are determined here—some will think too stringently—by the economy food plan developed by the Department of Agriculture. The economy food plan is for "temporary or emergency use when funds are low." In the long run it cannot provide an adequate diet. It is by this standard that almost one fourth of the children in the United States are counted as poor.

These are the primitive elements of a standard of living: food, clothing, shelter, and medical care. How do American children make out in these simplest terms? Even poor families find defenses against lack of food. If total income is inadequate, food costs may be met first (along with rent and utilities) and other needs sacrificed. Mothers may starve themselves in order to feed their children adequately. A series of studies makes it clear, nevertheless, that inadequate diet follows upon inadequate income. For example, a Cleveland study of 100 families with 446 children traced the following results to "low income . . . only": two thirds of the families

339

had substantial deficits of two or more basic nutrients (calcium, vitamins A or C); most of the teenagers might count on only one cup of milk a day; half the families had only one serving of fruit or vegetables a day—or none.

About the extent to which children are inadequately clothed, comparatively little is known. From time to time one reads about children kept out of school for lack of clothes, but scientific precision would require that we know how many. Quite possibly clothing of sound quality has become comparatively easy to come by and the least acute of the deficits that poor children suffer. Rather more is known about the housing of children. In 1960 about 10 million children lived in houses that lacked a proper toilet, bath, or hot water. About 4 million lived in housing that census enumerators called dangerous.

As for medical care, the President's Task Force on Manpower Conservation estimates that one third of all youths turning eighteen are unqualified for induction into the Armed Forces. The majority of rejectees "appear to be victims of inadequate education and insufficient health services." The Task Force report suggests that children's poverty and poor health reinforce each other; the National Health Survey substantiates this. Telephone consultations between parents and physicians are common when children are ill. The average child in families with an annual income over $4,000 was the subject of one or more such consultations a year; among families with less than $2,000, fewer than one child in five benefited from a telephone consultation in a given year. Similarly, poorer children averaged fewer visits to a doctor's or dentist's office. A child in a family with over $4,000 in annual income is almost twice as likely as a poorer child to have visited a dentist. Three out of four of the poorer children have never seen a dentist.

Mention must be made of the tangible effects of poverty on the family in which a child lives. Although the precise relationship of family breakdown and poverty is debatable, it is clear that poor families suffer more. Of the children counted as poor, one out of three lives in a family without a father—as compared with one out of twenty-three children not counted as poor who live in such a family. Six hundred thousand poor children escape "poverty by living . . . with relatives whose combined income is adequate for all." Teenagers apparently spin off from their families—because nothing keeps them or perhaps because they are a burden. At any rate, there are fewer teenagers in poor families than seems reasonable in relation to the number of younger children. Uncounted young children have been given up entirely by their families for primarily financial reasons and drift from home to home or enter the care of social agencies.

It is apparent that the 15.6 million children about whom we are concerned make out badly by the most primitive standards. It should not be supposed that the scales are balanced in other ways. A bit of modern folklore surrounds the prevalence of television sets in poor homes. Certainly television is widely regarded as a necessity. For example, a sociologist asked parents in desperate circumstances how they managed to have television. One had had her telephone removed but kept the television set. "You can count on TV any old time," she said, "but if you want to talk to somebody on the phone he's got to be there." A father of five sold most of his furniture but kept the bed, chairs, and television set. He said "he felt he should have kept [the books] for his children but decided that it was more important for them to have TV." Nevertheless, probably a third of poor children are without television.

The reasons why poor children are even more severely deprived of recreation, personal care, and so forth hardly need mention. First, if food and shelter use up all the money, none is left. Second, not enough money makes for wasteful management. Purchases are made in dribbles, or on credit which costs more in the long run, and evictions and repossessions pile new costs upon others. Third, those who suffer from malnutrition and inadequate housing have physiological cause for managing poorly. Technical data are available on the manner in which health and competence are affected. A bit of personal testimony will make the point. Having lived his years in the desert of hunger and homelessness, George Orwell wrote in 1933:

> Hunger reduces one to an utterly spineless, brainless condition, more like the aftereffects of influenza than anything else . . . Complete inertia is my chief memory of hunger.

We have dealt so far largely with the commodities that poor children lack. Another cost of poverty to children is that they live among poor people, whether on the farm, in the heart of the city, or in suburban enclaves. Characteristically these areas are poorer in public services. The free public schools are not so well supported. Their teachers are not so well trained and come and go more frequently. The supply of physicians and dentists is comparatively low, for they locate where paying patients are to be found and where they can themselves benefit from good public services. And voluntary agencies, if they have been established at all, have difficulty in raising funds in poor communities. Their finances may keep pace with rising costs but not with growing needs or a growing clientele. Thus, poor children are deprived not only by lack of income but by lack of access to services meant to be universal.

In short, poor children in the United States are poorly sheltered, many of them do not eat adequately, and their medical care is insufficient. Their right to an intact family is compromised. Their recreational and personal needs are not met. They do not even benefit from proper education. It would be hardly worth saying these things if we could bear to keep them in mind. The children suffering from each of these deficiencies must be numbered in the millions. On the average, families with poor children have about three fifths of the income required to escape poverty. How does one account for such deprivation among children today—thirty years after the report of the Committee on Economic Security—in a land overflowing with prosperity?

## SOURCES OF CHILDHOOD POVERTY

For the moment, we shall speak of the sources of poverty superficially, noting employment and unemployment but not asking why a man failed in competition with other men, noting family breakdown but not asking why his particular family was affected. Poor children may be classified roughly into three groups—one third live in homes headed by men who have regular work, one third in the homes of men who do not, and one third in homes headed by women.

Most poor children live in a home headed by a man. For these families    10
work would unequivocally seem to be the route to a decent income. But in 1963, 1.5 million families with a father regularly employed were poor; they included 5.2 million children. Thus responsibility for a third of the children who are poor must be charged to employment that does not, even with full time devoted to it, provide an income adequate to family needs. The problem of minimum income is compound. On one hand, it is a problem of the poorly paid occupations—laborer, farmer, and so forth. On the other hand, a modest income of, say, $4,000 does not, for urban families of six or more, escape the standard we have described as poverty. Unfortunately men who work in poorly paid occupations tend,    20
generally speaking, to have larger families.

In 1963 another third of the poor children lived in the families of men who had worked part-time, less than a full year, or not at all. When asked, about two out of five of those who had been continuously unemployed during the year referred to illness or disability. Who is disabled depends, of course, upon how badly workers are wanted. In any case, an unemployment rate that hovers about 4 per cent constitutes an obvious risk of poverty for children. For the unemployed (that is, those able to work and seeking work), the Committee on Economic Security proposed programs of unemployment insurance. However, not everyone is covered and most    30
state programs provide for at most six months of benefit payments. Of those unemployed for five weeks or more, only about half receive unemployment insurance payments. The average weekly payment is $36—an amount insufficient to keep a family with children from being classified as poor.

Four million children, or somewhat less than a third of those who are poor, live in families headed by women. The income deficit in these families is larger than in those headed by men. On the average, they have only about half the income required to escape poverty. Work may constitute an acceptable route to income for families headed by women but depends    40
on a number of considerations—the age and number of children, availability of child care, previous training of the mother. In fact, early in 1964 more than a third of the mothers heading poor families were at work or seeking work. Children in families without a father thus suffer to some extent from the same difficulties as families with a father—low wages and a labor market in which only the best prepared can count on finding

work. Moreover, a husband earning little may look to his wife to supplement his wages, but a divorced or widowed woman relies perforce on herself. Even with full employment and a high minimum wage, a substantial number of children in families headed by women would remain poor. Some women could not, would not, or should not leave their children for the day. The exigencies of children's daily needs limit the types of work their mothers can do. Women do not, in general, have the work habits or skills that men do.

Survivors' insurance was intended to provide a floor of income for children whose fathers died. However, partly because some fathers have not achieved coverage under social security, survivors' insurance is currently paid to only about 70 per cent of paternal orphans. Of those who do receive payments, almost a third (550,000 children) must nevertheless be counted as poor—a reflection on the amounts of payments. Aid to Families with Dependent Children (AFDC) was also intended to meet the needs of children without fathers, whether orphaned or not. However, only about 40 to 50 per cent of such poor children receive AFDC at any given moment; and payments are made in such low amounts that most children receiving aid would be counted as poor anyway.

We have now totted up the children who are poor and the programs that were meant to succor them. Obviously the need for a vigorous peacetime economy with high wages and full employment is at the heart of the matter. Diligence and wisdom are being invested to develop the necessary techniques, and we propose no contribution in this area. But time passes for children while we are achieving the objectives we do visualize. For these casualties of (what is the clinical euphemism?) frictional unemployment and of the crude economic techniques of the moment, for children without a father, and for children poor for miscellaneous reasons, a variety of income maintenance programs is required. But if we are not without resources of this sort—and we are not—why do current programs fall short by 15.6 million children?

We have observed about each of the relevant programs that it reaches only half to three fourths of the children for whom it is specifically designed. Moreover, payments are not high enough to preclude poverty for the children reached. Unfortunately this problem does not arise merely from an oversight. Public assistance incurs a set of problems we shall discuss later. The other programs are social insurance programs, with benefits roughly related to contributions that were, when they were made, based on income. Benefits are not generally planned to replace all income; in principle, other resources will also be available. To make a minimum benefit high enough to eliminate poverty among beneficiaries would, if other payments were scaled upward in accordance with the insurance principle, entail an extremely expensive program. The dilemma has been resolved by compromise, by providing formulas for calculating benefits that give some advantage to those who are poor but not sufficient advantage to eradicate poverty.

For example, about half of those unemployed receive no unemployment insurance at all. Studies show that these are families whose incomes were lower to begin with and which are more likely to contain children. Similarly, families with a father who earned little receive the lowest survivors' benefits. Savings and other private resources are most likely to be available to those whose incomes were higher and who now receive higher benefits. Thus the advantage on one side and disadvantage on the other are compounded, and the compromise between insurance and meeting need has an effect in no way intended. This effect has been put as follows by Robert Lampman:

> Our system of income maintenance, which now pays out $35 billion in benefits per year, is aimed more at the problem of income insecurity of the middle class and at blocking returns to poverty than in facilitating exits from poverty for those who have never been out of poverty.

The discussion so far echoes the conventional American (one is tempted to say, conventional Calvinist) syllogism: Work means income. Unemployment means lack of income. Protect against lack of income by protecting against unemployment. But hidden from view is a striking demographic fact—namely, that three out of four poor youths can make one or both of these statements: "I did not live with my father or even a man I could call father"; and "My family has five or more children." Thus most poor children are readily described in terms of social risk; they are vulnerable to low income because of a family characteristic. (Possibly the risks we accept are regarded as economic and those we do not yet accept are called social.) From the point of view of these three out of four children, current programs fail to meet their needs because major risks to them are not even in principle covered. In truth, either the economic or the social explanation, taken independently, is oversimple. We shall see how closely interwoven are large families, broken families, and poor earning ability.

That three out of four poor children belong to one or another of these poverty-vulnerable family types means that we cannot rely solely on the healing processes of a vigorous economy. If one overlooks the problem of the moment (the moment that is a lifetime for some children), rising wage levels and concomitant improvement of the social insurances can be expected steadily to reduce the number of children who are poor. On the other hand, the number of children in poverty-vulnerable families is on the rise.

Fundamental shifts in American patterns of marriage and birth are involved in the increase in vulnerable children. Young men and women are marrying earlier and having children earlier. In 1959, men were two years younger when first married and at the birth of their first child than in 1940; women were 1.3 years younger. If children are born earlier in marriage, more children are likely to be caught in their parents' divorce. In fact, the number so caught has been rising steadily and now approaches half a million a year. About three fourths of divorced men remarry; the rate is higher among younger men. For this and other reasons, support payments are not easy to procure upon divorce. Thus the children of divorce are increasing in number, but the money available to them is limited.

Official figures account for only legal divorce, but informal family breakdown is increasing in the same way. The number of mothers with low income (under $2,000 a year), without a man in the home, and still of child-bearing age (under thirty-five) increased by one fifth between 1949 and 1959. In other words, the number of young, husbandless mothers with less than $2,000 income increased; yet $2,000 was worth less at the end of the ten-year period. Mothers without husbands generally have more children in their lifetime than mothers with husbands; thus the disadvantage that accrues to large families is added to their burden.

It may be worth recognizing that socially orphaned children—children of divorce and separation—are a product of widely approved, basic American values. We are very much a marrying and a child-bearing people. We seem to be unaware that people have lived satisfying lives without a mate and a child. We also require that love be personally satisfying. When it does not turn out that way, we divorce or separate and try again if we can. Former generations did not know even as luxuries the things we regard as necessities. To obtain the things we must have we move, with pain sometimes but without a real alternative, in search of jobs or better jobs. In the ensuing movement and change, we experience satisfaction, but also shock and maladjustment. When we do not achieve our objectives, we feel unmanned or unfeminine and unvalued.

This set of values gives to many children homes in which they are cherished and surrounded by material possessions. It is fundamentally the same set of values that leaves other children with no father. Socially orphaned children are the casualties of a family pattern oriented to quality of relationship, to happiness, and to material possessions, just as cherished children are its successes. To understand this is to understand a phenomenon that may be controlled but is not likely to be rooted out. Family breakdown may continue to increase; there is no sign on the horizon that it is likely to decline.

We can now sum up the sources of childhood poverty. Work does not pay enough. There is not enough full-time work for all; or, as some prefer to say, not everyone has the capacity and training to command full-time work. The programs we have established do not protect all the children they set out to protect. For the children protected, benefit levels are frequently not high enough to avoid poverty. Many children are deprived of a father and many live in families too large for their income. Against these two contingencies that handicap three out of four poor children we do not have a program of social insurance, even in principle.

Numbers and generalizations inevitably lack immediacy. It may help to let a handful of visible children stand proxy for the 15 or 16 million.

# Arna Bontemps
## A Summer Tragedy

Old Jeff Patton, the black share farmer, fumbled with his bow tie. His fingers trembled and the high stiff collar pinched his throat. A fellow loses his hand for such vanities after thirty or forty years of simple life. Once a year, or maybe twice if there's a wedding among his kinfolks, he may spruce up; but generally fancy clothes do nothing but adorn the wall of the big room and feed the moths. That had been Jeff Patton's experience. He had not worn his stiff-bosomed shirt more than a dozen times in all his married life. His swallow-tailed coat lay on the bed beside him, freshly brushed and pressed, but it was as full of holes as the overalls in which he worked on weekdays. The moths had used it badly. Jeff twisted his  10 mouth into a hideous toothless grimace as he contended with the obstinate bow. He stamped his good foot and decided to give up the struggle.

"Jennie," he called.

"What's that, Jeff?" His wife's shrunken voice came out of the adjoining room like an echo. It was hardly bigger than a whisper.

"I reckon you'll have to he'p me wid this heah bow tie, baby," he said meekly. "Dog if I can hitch it up."

Her answer was not strong enough to reach him, but presently the old woman came to the door, feeling her way with a stick. She had a wasted, dead-leaf appearance. Her body, as scrawny and gnarled as a string bean,  20 seemed less than nothing in the ocean of frayed and faded petticoats that surrounded her. These hung an inch or two above the tops of her heavy unlaced shoes and showed little grotesque piles where the stockings had fallen down from her negligible legs.

"You oughta could do a heap mo' wid a thing like that'n me—beingst as you got yo' good sight."

"Looks like I oughta could," he admitted. "But my fingers is gone democrat on me. I get all mixed up in the looking glass an' can't tell wicha way to twist the devilish thing."

346

Jennie sat on the side of the bed and old Jeff Patton got down on one knee while she tied the bow knot. It was a slow and painful ordeal for each of them in this position. Jeff's bones cracked, his knee ached, and it was only after a half dozen attempts that Jennie worked a semblance of a bow into the tie.

"I got to dress maself now," the old woman whispered. "These is ma old shoes an' stockings, and I ain't so much as unwrapped ma dress."

"Well, don't worry 'bout me no mo', baby," Jeff said. "That 'bout finishes me. All I gotta do now is slip on that old coat 'n ves' an' I'll be fixed to leave."

Jennie disappeared again through the dim passage into the shed room. Being blind was no handicap to her in that black hole. Jeff heard the cane placed against the wall beside the door and knew that his wife was on easy ground. He put on his coat, took a battered top hat from the bedpost and hobbled to the front door. He was ready to travel. As soon as Jennie could get on her Sunday shoes and her old black silk dress, they would start.

Outside the tiny log house, the day was warm and mellow with sunshine. A host of wasps were humming with busy excitement in the trunk of a dead sycamore. Gray squirrels were searching through the grass for hickory nuts and blue jays were in the trees, hopping from branch to branch. Pine woods stretched away to the left like a black sea. Among them were scattered scores of log houses like Jeff's, houses of black share farmers. Cows and pigs wandered freely among the trees. There was no danger of loss. Each farmer knew his own stock and knew his neighbor's as well as he knew his neighbor's children.

Down the slope to the right were the cultivated acres on which the colored folks worked. They extended to the river, more than two miles away, and they were today green with the unmade cotton crop. A tiny thread of a road, which passed directly in front of Jeff's place, ran through these green fields like a pencil mark.

Jeff, standing outside the door, with his absurd hat in his left hand, surveyed the wide scene tenderly. He had been forty-five years on these acres. He loved them with the unexplained affection that others have for the countries to which they belong.

The sun was hot on his head, his collar still pinched his throat, and the Sunday clothes were intolerably hot. Jeff transferred the hat to his right hand and began fanning with it. Suddenly the whisper that was Jennie's voice came out of the shed room.

"You can bring the car round front whilst you's waitin'," it said feebly. There was a tired pause; then it added, "I'll soon be fixed to go."

"A'right, baby," Jeff answered. "I'll get it in a minute."

But he didn't move. A thought struck him that made his mouth fall open. The mention of the car brought to his mind, with new intensity, the trip he and Jennie were about to take. Fear came into his eyes; excitement took his breath. Lord, Jesus!

"Jeff . . . O Jeff," the old woman's whisper called.

He awakened with a jolt. "Hunh, baby?"

"What you doin'?"

"Nuthin. Jes studyin'. I jes been turnin' things round'n round in ma mind."

"You could be gettin' the car," she said.

"Oh yes, right away, baby."

He started round to the shed, limping heavily on his bad leg. There were three frizzly chickens in the yard. All his other chickens had been killed or stolen recently. But the frizzly chickens had been saved somehow. That was fortunate indeed, for these curious creatures had a way of de-    10
vouring "Poison" from the yard and in that way protecting against con-
jure and black luck and spells. But even the frizzly chickens seemed now
to be in a stupor. Jeff thought they had some ailment; he expected all three
of them to die shortly.

The shed in which the old T-model Ford stood was only a grass roof
held up by four corner poles. It had been built by tremulous hands at a
time when the little rattletrap car had been regarded as a peculiar treasure.
And, miraculously, despite wind and downpour it still stood.

Jeff adjusted the crank and put his weight upon it. The engine came
to life with a sputter and bang that rattled the old car from radiator to    20
taillight. Jeff hopped into the seat and put his foot on the accelerator.
The sputtering and banging increased. The rattling became more violent.
That was good. It was good banging, good sputtering and rattling, and it
meant that the aged car was still in running condition. She could be depended on for this trip.

Again Jeff's thought halted as if paralyzed. The suggestion of the trip
fell into the machinery of his mind like a wrench. He felt dazed and weak.
He swung the car out into the yard, made a half turn and drove around
to the front door. When he took his hands off the wheel, he noticed that
he was trembling violently. He cut off the motor and climbed to the ground    30
to wait for Jennie.

A few minutes later she was at the window, her voice rattling against
the pane like a broken shutter.

"I'm ready, Jeff."

He did not answer, but limped into the house and took her by the arm.
He led her slowly through the big room, down the step and across the
yard.

"You reckon I'd oughta lock the do'?" he asked softly.

They stopped and Jennie weighed the question. Finally she shook her
head.                                                                          40

"Ne' mind the do'," she said. "I don't see no cause to lock up things."

"You right," Jeff agreed. "No cause to lock up."

Jeff opened the door and helped his wife into the car. A quick shudder
passed over him. Jesus! Again he trembled.

"How come you shaking so?" Jennie whispered.

"I don't know," he said.

"You mus' be scairt, Jeff."

"No, baby, I ain't scairt."

He slammed the door after her and went around to crank up again. The motor started easily. Jeff wished that it had not been so responsive. He would have liked a few more minutes in which to turn things around in his head. As it was, with Jennie chiding him about being afraid, he had to keep going. He swung the car into the little pencil-mark road and started off toward the river, driving very slowly, very cautiously.

Chugging across the green countryside, the small battered Ford seemed tiny indeed. Jeff felt a familiar excitement, a thrill, as they came down the first slope to the immense levels on which the cotton was growing. He could not help reflecting that the crops were good. He knew what that meant, too; he had made forty-five of them with his own hands. It was true that he had worn out nearly a dozen mules, but that was the fault of old man Stevenson, the owner of the land. Major Stevenson had the odd notion that one mule was all a share farmer needed to work a thirty-acre plot. It was an expensive notion, the way it killed mules from overwork, but the old man held to it. Jeff thought it killed a good many share farmers as well as mules, but he had no sympathy for them. He had always been strong, and he had been taught to have no patience with weakness in men. Women or children might be tolerated if they were puny, but a weak man was a curse. Of course, his own children—

Jeff's thought halted there. He and Jennie never mentioned their dead children any more. And naturally he did not wish to dwell upon them in his mind. Before he knew it, some remark would slip out of his mouth and that would make Jennie feel blue. Perhaps she would cry. A woman like Jennie could not easily throw off the grief that comes from losing five grown children within two years. Even Jeff was still staggered by the blow. His memory had not been much good recently. He frequently talked to himself. And, although he had kept it a secret, he knew that his courage had left him. He was terrified by the least unfamiliar sound at night. He was reluctant to venture far from home in the daytime. And that habit of trembling when he felt fearful was now far beyond his control. Sometimes he became afraid and trembled without knowing what had frightened him. The feeling would just come over him like a chill.

The car rattled slowly over the dusty road. Jennie sat erect and silent, with a little absurd hat pinned to her hair. Her useless eyes seemed very large, very white in their deep sockets. Suddenly Jeff heard her voice, and he inclined his head to catch the words.

"Is we passed Delia Moore's house yet?" she asked.

"Not yet," he said.

"You must be drivin' mighty slow, Jeff."

"We might just as well take our time, baby."

There was a pause. A little puff of steam was coming out of the radiator of the car. Heat wavered above the hood. Delia Moore's house was nearly half a mile away. After a moment Jennie spoke again.

"You ain't really scairt, is you, Jeff?"

"Nah, baby, I ain't scairt."

"You know how we agreed—we gotta keep on goin'."

Jewels of perspiration appeared on Jeff's forehead. His eyes rounded, blinked, became fixed on the road.

"I don't know," he said with a shiver. "I reckon it's the only thing to do."

"Hm."

A flock of guinea fowls, pecking in the road, were scattered by the passing car. Some of them took to their wings; others hid under bushes. A blue jay, swaying on a leafy twig, was annoying a roadside squirrel. Jeff held an even speed till he came near Delia's place. Then he slowed down noticeably.

Delia's house was really no house at all, but an abandoned store building converted into a dwelling. It sat near a crossroads, beneath a single black cedar tree. There Delia, a cattish old creature of Jennie's age, lived alone. She had been there more years than anybody could remember, and long ago had won the disfavor of such women as Jennie. For in her young days Delia had been gayer, yellower and saucier than seemed proper in those parts. Her ways with menfolks had been dark and suspicious. And the fact that she had had as many husbands as children did not help her reputation.

"Yonder's old Delia," Jeff said as they passed.

"What she doin'?"

"Jes sittin' in the do'," he said.

"She see us?"

"Hm," Jeff said. "Musta did."

That relieved Jennie. It strengthened her to know that her old enemy had seen her pass in her best clothes. That would give the old she-devil something to chew her gums and fret about, Jennie thought. Wouldn't she have a fit if she didn't find out? Old evil Delia! This would be just the thing for her. It would pay her back for being so evil. It would also pay her, Jennie thought, for the way she used to grin at Jeff—long ago when her teeth were good.

The road became smooth and red, and Jeff could tell by the smell of the air that they were nearing the river. He could see the rise where the road turned and ran along parallel to the stream. The car chugged on monotonously. After a long silent spell, Jennie leaned against Jeff and spoke.

"How many bale o' cotton you think we got standin'? she said.

Jeff wrinkled his forehead as he calculated.

" 'Bout twenty-five, I reckon."

"How many you make las' year?"

"Twenty-eight," he said. "How come you ask that?"

"I's jes thinkin'," Jennie said quietly.

"It don't make a speck o' difference though," Jeff reflected. "If we get much or if we get little, we still gonna be in debt to old man Stevenson when he gets through counting up agin us. It's took us a long time to learn that."

Jennie was not listening to these words. She had fallen into a trance-like meditation. Her lips twitched. She chewed her gums and rubbed her gnarled hands nervously. Suddenly she leaned forward, buried her face in the nervous hands and burst into tears. She cried aloud in a dry cracked voice that suggested the rattle of fodder on dead stalks. She cried aloud like a child, for she had never learned to suppress a genuine sob. Her slight old frame shook heavily and seemed hardly able to sustain such violent grief.

"What's the matter, baby?" Jeff asked awkwardly. "Why you cryin' like all that?"

"I's jes thinkin'," she said.

"So you the one what's scairt now, hunh?"

"I ain't scairt, Jeff. I's jes thinkin' 'bout leavin' eve'thing like this— eve'thing we been used to. It's right sad-like."

Jeff did not answer, and presently Jennie buried her face again and cried.

The sun was almost overhead. It beat down furiously on the dusty wagon-path road, on the parched roadside grass and the tiny battered car. Jeff's hands, gripping the wheel, became wet with perspiration; his forehead sparkled. Jeff's lips parted. His mouth shaped a hideous grimace. His face suggested the face of a man being burned. But the torture passed and his expression softened again.

"You mustn't cry, baby," he said to his wife. "We gotta be strong. We can't break down."

Jennie waited a few seconds, then said, "You reckon we oughta do it, Jeff? You reckon we oughta go 'head an' do it, really?"

Jeff's voice choked; his eyes blurred. He was terrified to hear Jennie say the thing that had been in his mind all morning. She had egged him on when he had wanted more than anything in the world to wait, to re-consider, to think things over a little longer. Now she was getting cold feet. Actually there was no need of thinking the question through again. It would only end in making the same painful decision once more. Jeff knew that. There was no need of fooling around longer.

"We jes as well to do like we planned," he said. "They ain't nothin' else for us now—it's the bes' thing."

Jeff thought of the handicaps, the near impossibility, of making another crop with his leg bothering him more and more each week. Then there was always the chance that he would have another stroke, like the one that had made him lame. Another one might kill him. The least it could do would be to leave him helpless. Jeff gasped—Lord, Jesus! He could not bear to think of being helpless, like a baby, on Jennie's hands. Frail, blind Jennie.

The little pounding motor of the car worked harder and harder. The puff of steam from the cracked radiator became larger. Jeff realized that they were climbing a little rise. A moment later the road turned abruptly and he looked down upon the face of the river.

"Jeff."

"Hunh?"

"Is that the water I hear?"

"Hm. Tha's it."

"Well, which way you goin' now?"

"Down this-a way," he said. "The road runs 'long 'side o' the water a lil piece."

She waited a while calmly. Then she said, "Drive faster."

"A'right, baby," Jeff said.

The water roared in the bed of the river. It was fifty or sixty feet below the level of the road. Between the road and the water there was a long smooth slope, sharply inclined. The slope was dry, the clay hardened by prolonged summer heat. The water below, roaring in a narrow channel, was noisy and wild.

"Jeff."

"Hunh?"

"How far you goin'?"

"Jes a lil piece down the road."

"You ain't scairt, is you, Jeff?"

"Nah, baby," he said trembling. "I ain't scairt."

"Remember how we planned it, Jeff. We gotta do it like we said. Brave-like."

"Hm."

Jeff's brain darkened. Things suddenly seemed unreal, like figures in a dream. Thoughts swam in his mind foolishly, hysterically, like little blind fish in a pool within a dense cave. They rushed, crossed one another, jostled, collided, retreated and rushed again. Jeff soon became dizzy. He shuddered violently and turned to his wife.

"Jennie, I can't do it. I can't." His voice broke pitifully.

She did not appear to be listening. All the grief had gone from her face. She sat erect, her unseeing eyes wide open, strained and frightful. Her glossy black skin had become dull. She seemed as thin, as sharp and bony, as a starved bird. Now, having suffered and endured the sadness of tearing herself away from beloved things, she showed no anguish. She was absorbed with her own thoughts, and she didn't even hear Jeff's voice shouting in her ear.

Jeff said nothing more. For an instant there was light in his cavernous brain. The great chamber was, for less than a second, peopled by characters he knew and loved. They were simple, healthy creatures, and they behaved in a manner that he could understand. They had quality. But since he had already taken leave of them long ago, the remembrance did not break his heart again. Young Jeff Patton was among them, the Jeff Patton of fifty years ago who went down to New Orleans with a crowd of country boys to the Mardi Gras doings. The gay young crowd, boys with candy-striped shirts and rouged-brown girls in noisy silks, was like a picture in his head. Yet it did not make him sad. On that very trip Slim Burns had killed Joe Beasley—the crowd had been broken up. Since then Jeff Patton's world had been the Greenbriar Plantation. If there had been other Mardi Gras carnivals, he had not heard of them. Since then there had been no time; the years had fallen on him like waves. Now he was old, worn out. Another paralytic stroke (like the one he had already suffered) would put him on his back for keeps. In that condition, with a frail blind woman to look after him, he would be worse off than if he were dead.

Suddenly Jeff's hands became steady. He actually felt brave. He slowed down the motor of the car and carefully pulled off the road. Below, the water of the stream boomed, a soft thunder in the deep channel. Jeff ran the car onto the clay slope, pointed it directly toward the stream and put his foot heavily on the accelerator. The little car leaped furiously down the steep incline toward the water. The movement was nearly as swift and direct as a fall. The two old black folks, sitting quietly side by side, showed no excitement. In another instant the car hit the water and dropped immediately out of sight.

A little later it lodged in the mud of a shallow place. One wheel of the crushed and upturned little Ford became visible above the rushing water.

# Nursing Home Patient
## An Old Lady Dies

When the old, old, old lady
   Finally, finally died;
I was the only one,
   The only one who cried.
"Why do you weep," said someone?
   "It is a good thing that she died."
   But oh, the lonesome, lonesome way—
   That is the reason I cried.

# David H. Pryor
## Where We Put the Aged

Almost one million Americans, a large silent minority, are in 20,000 nursing homes. They've been sent there to die, in a halfway house somewhere between society and the cemetery. We've had the idea that if we could funnel more money into the nursing home industry, the quality of care would rise. We've been wrong: the patient has taken the backseat to profits. This is where government erred: it treated nursing home care as a housing, not a health program.

A few months ago, an *Associated Press* series of articles on the nursing home industry disclosed that:
• Physician care for the nursing home patient is so scarce that it is a national scandal; 10
• One-seventh of drug prescriptions to nursing patients are administered wrong, and drugs are commonly used to make patients "easier to handle";
• The average food-cost per patient in many nursing homes today is less than $1 per day;
• In a Topeka, Kansas home three-fourths of the patients checked had not been seen by a doctor in six months, and in Minnesota, the average amount of physician care per patient in 100 nursing homes was 2-1/2 minutes per week;
• The National Fire Prevention Association shows nursing homes at the 20 top of unsafe places to live.

A *New York Daily News* reporter, hired as a nurse's aide, found the food in several New York homes abominable, filthy rooms, roaches in glasses, dirt in water pitchers and indescribable conditions in bathrooms.

From other news reports we learn that a nursing home administrator may well have as his only qualifications that he was a junk dealer; that

355

tough federal regulations have been much slower reaching the nursing homes than federal dollars; that 87 nursing homes that failed to meet federal standards were paid $380,000 in the last half of 1968; that in Wisconsin, a 317-bed home went without regular state inspections for almost three years, although a 1967 check resulted in a four-page list of violations.

It will be recalled that 32 persons recently died at Marietta, Ohio in a "good" nursing home which had been allowed to operate with "deficiencies."

A maze of pyramiding new government programs such as Medicare and Medicaid, new methods of financing nursing homes, new formulas adopted by Social Security and welfare agencies to reimburse the proprietors of nursing homes, together with a lack of interest in both the enactment and enforcement of tough regulations which protect the patient—all this adds up to booming profits for the owners, and explosive and rising costs for the patient, their relatives and the American taxpayer. A Wall Street executive states that "in the nursing home business—there is no way to lose." Some 70 nursing home chains have been established in recent months which now sell their stock to the public. Mutual fund companies own approximately six million shares of these stocks. Nursing home securities are referred to as "the hottest stock on Wall Street." *Business Week* entitles an article, "Nursing Homes Offer an Investment Lure." The same publication elsewhere explains a novel financing plan whereby several nursing home chains induced doctors to find patients for them by selling a major interest in each home to a group of local physicians.

Only 10 percent of our nursing homes are non-profit institutions, and these as a general rule are operated by communities, locally supported hospitals, churches, religious organizations, or fraternal groups. Those who are entering the nursing-home-for-profit business, according to many of the prospectuses now on file with the Securities and Exchange Commission, are generally builders, contractors, restaurant operators, fast buck entrepreneurs.

The price per bed in these homes is zooming upwards at an alarming rate—$700 a month is not uncommon. In addition to the basic room and board fee, there are often "extras," which are not known until the first statement arrives.

I became interested in this scandal several years back while serving as a freshman legislator in the Arkansas House of Representatives. At each legislative session we found ourselves voting additional welfare payments for the local nursing home industry. We were told that the additional money would be spent for additional care. We never discovered what additional care or services would be improved or how the patient would benefit.

Coming to Washington, I spent four weekends as a volunteer worker at nursing homes in the area. I saw loneliness, despair, anxiety,—and boredom—total, absolute boredom. The only relief comes when the attendant brings a meal into the room. In one room of 14 beds, the proprietor woke an elderly lady, asked her how she was feeling and then told me that this particular patient had had a "slight heart attack" early in the day, but that they did not make a practice of calling the doctor on Sunday. In another home, as I was clipping the toenails of an 80-year-old veteran, he told me not to let the attendant see me do this as they charged $7 when they did it. I saw toothless patients served big slabs of cold meat, which they were incapable of cutting into bite-size portions. In a home of 80 patients, there was only one attendant on duty. In the hall I saw four helpless people in wheelchairs, three of whom were sitting in their own excretion. The attendant told me, "We just don't have enough help and the owners don't pay us enough to live on."

"Who shaves your older men?" I asked one proprietor. "About every three days, when they catch up with their other work, that is the job for the maintenance crew," was his reply. "How much does it cost to have a patient here?" I asked an attendant in a Maryland home. "It depends on their income," she said.

A friend of mine in Connecticut recently visited four nursing homes in his area with the idea of placing his father in an extended care facility. He saw "attendants ignore one old woman's call for help; I saw one owner talk in an insultingly derogatory way about a patient, in front of that very patient; I saw incredible filth and signs of neglect; and I heard things that seemed to me to evidence a callousness and crudity that I certainly would not want any parents of mine exposed to. The owner of the home said to me, 'Look, your father is getting old and he is hard to handle, right? You bring him right here, maybe in a few weeks you can take him home on a Sunday afternoon, but the first thing you've got to show these old people is who's boss.' The brochure the owner handed me refers to 'pleasant home atmosphere.' "

Several myths have been successfully sold to the American public. One of them is that all nursing homes or homes for the aged are strictly licensed, duly inspected, and that a "health team" is physically present at all times, or at least nearby to serve the patients. It's not true. Another myth is that if an institution states that it is "approved for Medicaid and Medicare," then it is a home which provides good service to the patient. That's also untrue. There is no control over the nursing home industry, though two out of three patients in nursing homes and homes for the aged in our country are kept there through some federal or federally assisted program. One chain nursing home owner said in a recent newspaper article that 85 cents of each dollar that flowed into his business came from government sources.

The taxpayers are paying $2 billion a year to the nursing home industry. All controls over where this money goes and what it buys are fragmented, self-frustrating and ineffectual. Both the Medicaid and Medicare agencies in the Department of Health, Education and Welfare issue standards for nursing homes participating in their respective programs; neither agency enforces its standards. In the case of Medicaid, which is a state-administered program, nursing homes are certified for participation by state agencies. Certification is often on the basis of surveys and reports by county agencies. The federal administrative agency, the Social and Rehabilitative Service, has virtually no control over the quality or frequency of these surveys and does not even receive information on the number of homes certified by the states. If a patient or his family writes to his representative in Congress to complain of conditions in a Medicaid nursing home, the complaint is usually referred to HEW for investigation. HEW in turn refers it to the state agency and from there to the county agency, which probably is responsible for permitting the condition to exist in the first place. The patient has nowhere to turn. No one is in charge.

The Social Security Administration must approve nursing homes for participation in Medicare as extended care facilities. Here too, the standards, which in many respects are vague, are actually applied by state and county agencies. Reports are sent to the regional offices of the Social Security Administration where the certifications are signed, with little or no knowledge of actual conditions in the homes. Social Security officials have no information on the qualifications of surveyors doing Medicare inspections.

The tremendous sum which federal programs are pouring into nursing home care is profoundly affecting the development and growth of the industry. The infusion of dollars has stimulated a building boom in nursing homes which is completely out of hand. Congress has appropriated funds to assist state and regional planning agencies in their efforts to rationalize the numbers, types and distribution of new health facilities; to curtail waste and duplication; and to provide our communities with a balanced complex of facilities which can deliver modern medical care in an effective and economical way. At the same time, Congress has frustrated those aims by enticing investment capital into the industry on a huge scale, with a virtual guarantee of business and profits.

The Securities and Exchange Commission is charged with serving the investor public. Let me then put to the SEC some questions the public needs to have answered: Are the nursing homes listed as properties of a particular company good or bad, are they properly staffed, do they give good care? Are some of these newly formed public companies simply devices for paper transfer of ownership and inflating the capitalization of the properties? Are the SEC and HEW working together to assess the burgeoning growth of public investment in nursing home chains? They are not. No one is protecting the public, no one is protecting the tax dollars, and no one is protecting the patients.

# Mae Smart
## An Old Woman's Story

Well, weather is a little cooler here today, as we had a nice rain and
electric storm last night. We needed the rain—it's been 90 and 91 the past
week. Said I'd write my life story. Well, I was born in Medicine Lodge,
Kansas, on April the 15th, 1886. My given name Myrtle Mae High. Was
raised on farm at Cicero, Kansas, and was one of family of eight children—
five boys and three girls. Cicero was very small. The Santa Fe tracks ran
through, it had the depot, post office, mill, the grocery store, and about
five houses. It was just a place between Wellington, Kansas, and Belle
Plaine, Kansas. We had a country school about a half mile from our farm.
I never attended any other school. Went only through the eighth grade, 10
though my brothers attended high school in Wellington.

When I was growing up, I never heard of movie shows, radios, or
TV. Our only source of entertainment was a box supper at the school
house or a spelling bee. We had a kerosene lamp to go out to the toilet at
night. We young people went to dances, usually at one of our friends'
houses, as we young people ran in a group, and we seemed to have fun.
Sometimes in the winter we took sleigh rides in the country. We were
raised very strict and my father wouldn't let us girls stand out on the
porch after dark and talk to boy friends, or even stand at the front gate
when we came home from a date. 20

I only went with two other boys besides my husband. My husband and
I knew each other since I was eight years old. He lived on a farm three
miles from our place and it was rather funny how we started dating. I
was going with his cousin, Jesse, and Jesse and I had a date for a Sunday
night to go to church, but he never came. I sure felt bad over that, so I
wrote him a letter. But he never answered. Jesse and I were supposed to

be going to a dance the next Friday night, at the farm of Mr. and Mrs. Smart. Harvey Smart was the boy I married. I thought I'd have to stay home, but my brother and his girl friend took me with them. At the dance, when I was dancing with Harvey Smart, he asked me if I had a date for that Sunday night, and I told him no. He asked me to go to church with him and I said yes. I thought of Jesse, and was pretty blue. I wondered how he could have treated me that way. The second time we went out, Harvey Smart asked me to marry him. Harvey was living on an eight-acre farm of his own and he was a bachelor. He had three hired help and was looking for a cook. I told him that was the reason he proposed to me.    *10* He then kissed me and I slapped him, as I wasn't used to that. And I told him I couldn't answer until the next Sunday night. I thought about it all week, as I was only nineteen, and he was four years older. I finally told my mother about Harvey and asked her if I could, and she said if you think you love him. She said it was O.K. with her. And I thought I loved him, and I told Harvey yes.

That was the last of January, 1906, and we were married in my folks' home on Sunday, July the 15th, 1906, at 4 P.M. Well, we had a nice wedding, but it started raining that day around 9 A.M. and it really rained all day and all night. The morning of the day we were married, Harvey's    *20* brother, Jewell, hitched up a team of horses to an old-fashion surrey and drove to Belle Plaine, nine miles away in the rain, to get the preacher and then took him home afterwards in the dark.

We spent the first night at home in my room, and then the next day was a nice sunshiny day and we drove over to Harvey's folks for our wedding dinner, and the third day we moved into the four-room house two miles away where Harvey lived, and we sure were happy. Harvey had his wheat cut and thrashing all done and he was ready to start fall plowing. We lived there for two years, and then we sold the farm and moved into Belle Plaine, where Harvey took up house painting. Then in 1910 we moved    *30* here to Cedar Rapids, Iowa, where I live still.

Well, our first baby, a boy, was born on December the 7th, 1908, and he weighed ten and three-quarters pounds. We named him Ira Lee Smart, but we always called him Lee. Lee was born during an election year, and my two daughters were also born during election years. Geneva Irene was born September the 28th, 1912, and she weighed nine and a half pounds. Velda Alveda was born September the 26th, 1916, and she weighed nine pounds.

Geneva Irene died November the 3rd, 1913, at Boise, Idaho, where we were visiting for a little time. One year, one month, and six days old.    *40* Velda Alveda died June the 25th, 1943, at Mercy Hospital in Cedar Rapids. She had double pneumonia. She died at the age of twenty-six years, and left a baby of thirteen months. Seemed so sad to go so young, and so much to live for. When Velda died, I could hardly take my grief.

That was a lot of sorrow for me in those days, as two years before, in 1941, my husband had dropped dead with a heart attack. It happened about five minutes after we came into the house on a Sunday evening from church. I was all alone when Harvey died, and a flower shop about a half block from our house was all lit up. Before, I was wondering what they were all lit up for, and Harvey he'd said it was probably because they were making flowers for a funeral. So a neighbor came over to stay with Harvey, as he had fallen on the floor and we had no phone, and I went down the street to use the flower shop's phone. The man in the flower shop said, "Who is your doctor?" and he said for me to go back home and he would call the doctor, but he said Harvey must be dead. When the flower man came to my house, he had the doctor and an undertaker friend with him, and I didn't think he needed to do this until he came first just with the doctor. As it happened, the undertaker would not touch Harvey till I got his Social Security card. As Harvey wasn't working, he didn't have it in his billfold, so I had to look for it, and this took me about a half an hour and I was so nervous that when I found it I just passed it into the undertaker's hand without saying anything. So the undertaker and the flower man picked up Harvey's body and put it in a black bag and carried it out. Velda's husband ran a confectionery store down by the Iowa Theater, and after the undertaker was gone I went down there. My son, Lee, was living at Olin, Iowa, and I had quite a time getting in touch with him. Well, that was February the 22nd, 1941, and Velda died two years later, and the day Velda died Lee was at Anamosa, Iowa, getting in the Army. He left for the Army three weeks later, and I'm telling you that with all the worry and sorrow my hair turned white.

Lee was gone for three and a half years, but he was lucky and his life was spared. He returned to his wife, who he had married on June the 25th, 1935 — the same day that Velda died eight years later — and he was the only child I had left. Lee was married for thirty-four years this summer, but no children. Still, I have one dear grandchild, Velda's son, George, and he was twenty-seven on May the 31st, 1969, and he is the only grandchild I have and the one I raised after his mother died. George is married, but no children, and they are married four years.

I forgot to mention, when I was a girl on the farm at Cicero we raised chickens, ducks, and geese. In the summer there were so many cyclones. The farmers' telephones had eight to ten families on one line, and all the houses had kerosene lamps. When Harvey and I moved to town off the farm, electric lights soon came and everyone was so happy.

Nowadays, I baby-sit five days a week, and I got TV. I'm a TV fan and I sure enjoy the stories. Celebrated my sixty-third wedding anniversary last July the 15th, and not many make it that long, but you see I've been alone twenty-eight years. Still, I have the one son, Lee, and he is over sixty now and has been retired from the Post Office four years. They live a block from me, Lee and his wife, and I live alone.

Well, it is P.M. now and has rained again most all A.M. Another flood at Waterloo, as a special news report came over TV several times today and said probably some people would have to be moving out of their homes. Sure is tough. I'm glad I don't live there.

This is not a very good story of my life, but it is all true, and my family have all passed on except my son and he is dear and precious to me. I don't know what I would do without him and his wife.

# Joe Glazer
## The Mill was Made of Marble

1. I dreamed that I had died
   And gone to my reward——
   A job in Heaven's textile plant
   On a golden boulevard

CHORUS: The mill was made of marble,
          The machines were made out of gold,
          And nobody ever got tired,
          And nobody ever grew old.

2. This mill was built in a garden——
   No dust or lint could be found.         10
   The air was so fresh and so fragrant
   With flowers and trees all around.

3. It was quiet and peaceful in heaven——
   There was no clatter or boom.
   You could hear the most beautiful music
   As you worked at the spindle and loom.

4. There was no unemployment in heaven;
   We worked steady all through the year;
   We always had food for the children;
   We never were haunted by fear.       20

5. When I woke from this dream about heaven
   I wondered if some day there'd be
   A mill like that one down below here on
       on earth
   For workers like you and like me.

# Joe Glazer
## Too Old to Work

1. You work in the factory all of your life,
   Try to provide for your kids and your wife.
   When you get too old to produce any more,
   They hand you your hat and they show you to the
   door.

CHORUS:

   Too old to work, too old to work,
   When you're too old to work and you're too young
   to die,
   Who will take care of you, how'll you get by,
   When you're too old to work and you're too young   10
   to die?

2. You don't ask for favors when your life is through;
   You've got a right to what's coming to you.
   Your boss gets a pension when he is too old;
   You helped him retire——you're out in the cold.

3. They put horses to pasture, they feed them on hay;
   Even machines get retired some day.
   The bosses get pensions when their days are through;
   Fat pensions for them, brother; nothing for you.

4. There's no easy answer, there's no easy cure;      20
   Dreaming won't change it, that's one thing for sure;
   But fighting together we'll get there some day,
   And when we have won we will no longer say:

# Joe Glazer
## Automation

1. I went down, down, down to the factory
   Early on a Monday morn.
   When I got down to the factory
   It was lonely, it was forlorn.
   I couldn't find Joe, Jack, John or Jim;
   Nobody could I see;
   Nothing but buttons and bells and lights
   All over the factory.

2. I walked, walked, walked into the foreman's office
   To find out what was what.                                    10
   I looked him in the eye and said, "What goes?"
   And this is the answer I got:
   His eyes turned red, then green, then blue
   And it suddenly dawned on me——
   There was a robot sitting in the seat
   Where the foreman used to be.

3. I walked all around, all around, up and down
   And across that factory.
   I watched all the buttons and the bells and the lights—
   It was a mystery to me.                                       20
   I hollered "Frank, Hank, Ike, Mike, Roy, Ray, Don, Dan,
   Bill, Phil, Ed, Fred, Pete!"
   And a great big mechanical voice boomed out:
   "All your buddies are obsolete."

4. I was scared, scared, scared, I was worried, I was sick

As I left that factory.
I decided that I had to see the president
Of the whole darn company.
When I got up to his office he was rushing out the door
With a scowl upon his face,
'Cause there was a great big mechanical executive
Sitting in the president's place.

5. I went home, home, home to my ever-loving wife
   And told her 'bout the factory.
   She hugged me and she kissed me and she                    10
   cried a little bit
   As she sat on my knee.
   I don't understand all the buttons and the lights
   But one thing I will say— —
   I thank the Lord that love's still made
   In the good old-fashioned way.

# Robert Coles
## The Lives of Migrant Farmers

Living in America today are many hundreds of thousands of people whose lives are characterized by continual movement by crop season from town to town, state to state and region to region. They are people whose hands harvest the fruit and vegetables we eat.

There are three large-scale pathways they follow (called "streams" by the farmers, public health doctors or government officials who are involved in one way or another with their lives). One is along the Pacific coast, drawing upon native white and Negro workers or Mexican workers, and moving from southern California up along to Washington and back as the harvesting season itself moves northward, then southward. There is a middle stream—heavily Mexican, but with a good number of whites and Negroes—which starts in the south central region of Texas, Louisiana or Oklahoma and moves northward in a wide arc, terminating in states like Minnesota, Michigan or Wisconsin. The third stream follows the Atlantic seaboard. It is made up mainly of Negroes, but has some whites too. Starting in Florida in late May and June its workers move steadily northward, up through Georgia, settling into the Carolinas and Virginia for some weeks, then into Delaware, New Jersey and New York—a few into New England. They stay north for the rest of the summer and early fall. Then by the thousands they return to Florida for a winter and spring of gathering the crops there, sometimes in one general area (from farm to farm) or sometimes moving from county to county in that state.

The history of migratory farm labor goes back well into the 19th century, when roving bands of men moved about reaping and bundling our wheat crops. However, much of American agriculture slowly became heavily mechanized, so that by the 1920's there was a serious crisis

10

20

367

developing in the lives of millions of farm workers whose labor was simply no longer needed. To the cities many of them went, even from the South,
whose farms and cotton plantations yielded more slowly to machines than
the giant wheat and corn fields of the Midwest. Many, however, stayed—
eking out what existence they could.

With the onset of the depression years of the 1930's, dispossessed
sharecroppers, or small farmers whose income was near nothing because
of the depression, or additional thousands driven from their dried, choked
land by a series of droughts, combined to offer a frightful spectacle to
their countrymen as they moved, by new thousands, hungry, fearful and    10
confused, across the continent in search of a decent chance of work. Their
fate—on their sharecropper farms or in migration—has been movingly
described by Agee, Steinbeck, and Carey McWilliams.

While many of these people also moved into the city, many others
remained loyal to their competence in farming by taking jobs as fruit
pickers and vegetable harvesters in the expanding farms dedicated to
those crops in California, in the Midwest and in Florida. With rapid
transportation by train and truck and refined methods of refrigerating
these once perishable commodities, there had developed in the period
after the first World War a large-scale industry of growing fruit and veg-   20
etable produce—once, of course, grown locally by farmers near the cities
they supplied. As these new farms—and the packing houses attached to
them—came into being they required workers to plant and gather their
crops, then pack them and load them on waiting boxcars and trucks.
The farms themselves were scattered over great distances, and in keeping
with the changing seasons, over entire regions of the nation. To work on
them men and their families would have to be willing to move regularly
and sometimes frequently, too.

Nor do these people have the most comfortable lives, in comparison to
the way most of us live. In large measure they live in houses whose ade-   30
quacy—let alone comfort—leaves much to be desired. Often they are
flimsy, rat-infested, one-room hovels with improper sanitation. In them
live large families, sleeping at close quarters on cots or on the floors, often
eating without utensils on the same floor. If some of these people live
more comfortable lives, many live under conditions which a paper like
this cannot hope to describe fairly. However, in general what most migrants share is more than occasional exposure to poor housing, bad sanitation, a diet poor in vitamins and protein, inadequate medical care,
continual movement—and consequent lack of firm association with any
particular community—a very limited income, and a lack of eligibility for   40
a number of privileges many of us either take for granted or consider
"rights"—the vote, a telephone, a library card, unemployment or welfare
benefits, minimum wage protection.

Such political, economic, social and cultural facts affect the lives of
these people, influencing the way they act, their view of themselves in
relationship to others around them, the assumptions they make about

the world. Such facts also become psychological forces as they bear down and help shape the thinking of children, the behavior of parents, the experiences of both. We cannot dwell on them here, but neither can we dismiss them with a sentence or two as part of a vaguely subordinate "background" to the psychological processes at work. In many respects these "environmental" forces significantly determine the way migrants touch and feed their children, toilet train them, bring them up to get along with one another and themselves as they grow and develop.

As much as anything our task was to see how these "external" facts became translated into internal ones, of fantasy, dream, action and per- 10 sonality development. Any introduction, therefore, to such psychiatric research must somehow make proper mention of its necessary and affirming kinship to sociological and anthropological observation as well as historical knowledge. It is not simply a matter of seeing the impact of a social system on people. It is one of seeing how, out of historical events in a given political and economic system, a social system has developed, with its own culture and frame of mind. Migrants, then, have a subculture even within that of the poor, including their own nonmigrant relatives.

## ORIGINS OF THIS STUDY 20

Our interest in these people was aroused in the course of a study of the adjustment of Negro and white school children to school desegregation in the South. Several of the Negro children and one white child had been born in sharecropper cabins in Mississippi, Alabama or South Carolina. Their early years had been spent on farms, and their parents had only recently moved into New Orleans or Atlanta, where they came upon the crisis of a serious social struggle that affected them and the education of their children. In the course of taking family histories we learned that in five families (four Negro and one white) there were uncles, aunts and cousins who had left those same fixed if no longer sustaining 30 farms to join the migrant labor force rather than the tide going steadily toward cities of the North or, in our cases, the South.

We initially wondered what made for such different choices, and what happened as a result of them to such differently lived lives. Through one Negro family in New Orleans we established preliminary contact with their relatives and other Negro families who harvest winter crops in Florida and move up the Atlantic states in summer and autumn doing likewise. We were unable to trace down the migrant relatives of our white family, but in the attempt met with other white migrant families in Florida and established effective communication with them. In preliminary visits we 40 interviewed at length public health doctors and nurses who have long been concerned with the severe medical problems which afflict the bodies of these people and the related sanitary problems which arise from their living and working conditions (contaminated drinking water, inadequate drainage and sewage facilities). We worked as a general physician in the mobile public health clinics which attempt to reach migrants (known to be suspicious and isolated) by seeking them out directly. We accompanied nurses on their "postnatal rounds." We did likewise with dietitians whose job it is — often against stubborn emotional resistance — to try to educate people whose diet is woefully unhealthy about ways of improving health through modification of food habits. (The irony of people surrounded by fresh fruit and vegetables, yet shunning them for themselves and their children in the face of medical advice to the contrary, was one of the first reminders we encountered that more than simply "material deprivation" was at work in these families.)

We also talked at considerable length with the farmers who employ —     10
and often provide living quarters for — migrants and have had considerable experience and difficulty with them and their habits of living. We spent a good deal of time talking with county agricultural agents in Florida and some northern states, learning the history of agriculture (and hence migrations of people to support it) in the various counties and states. We talked with some school teachers who must try to educate migrant children and visited schools where they are taught. We also talked with certain social workers who come into significant contact with these people and with those from church groups who, again, have come to know and tried to help these people while others of us have scarcely heard of them and     20
their kind of existence.

Eventually we selected ten families for more intensive study. Six of them were Negro and four white, all part of the eastern seaboard migration. We interviewed these mothers, fathers and children over a period of two years. Some months we visited them weekly at home. On later occasions we followed them in their migration northward, traveling in buses and trucks with them or in two instances in family cars. We lived with two Negro families and one white family for two weeks each. We tape-recorded our interviews and with young children both played games and placed heavy emphasis on drawing and painting pictures. We photo-     30
graphed homes and their interiors, fields and the way bodies and hands must posture themselves in them to harvest their crops, or buses and trucks with their dense "loads," so that we might document such conditions of existence and study their meaning to the people who live under them, work under them and move about under them.

## MIGRANCY: A STYLE OF LIFE

Our primary interest has been with the relationship between the "outside world" and the growth and development of the migrant child's mind. Migrant farmers live a kind of life that asserts itself upon their infants     40
and children and emerges once again in adults able to live with its demands. Just as we noted in our work with Negro children under the severe and threatening stresses of school desegregation, we must emphasize that the extreme poverty, the cultural deprivation and social fragmentation, in sum the uprootedness which characterized their lives falls not suddenly upon them (as it does upon the observer who tries to comprehend their

manner of survival) but as a constant fact of life from birth to death, summoning therefore a whole style of life, a full range of adaptive maneuvers. Perhaps if we take a migrant child at birth and follow his life along we will best combine the telling of the migrant's life with the psychodynamic developments in it of primary concern to us as psychiatrists.

### Infancy

In only two of the ten families we studied were the children delivered by doctors. The rest of the mothers relied upon midwives or simply relatives and friends. Frequently a pregnant mother returns "home" (where  10 relatives—parents, brothers and sisters, even cousins—maintain a permanent residence) to deliver a baby. In many instances this is not possible and children are delivered wherever the mother happens to be, often enough "on the road," that is, in the course of traveling for working purposes. We were struck by the casual attitude toward childbirth displayed by these mothers and their common knowledge of how to deliver children, remove the placenta, tie and sever the cord.

Many of them are quite afraid to deliver their babies in a hospital, fearful that the child in some way will be "hurt." For example, one of our mothers remarked that, "They say it's cleaner there and safer, but  20 I tried it once and I got scared to death and my baby didn't behave good. He cried more and didn't take my milk so easy." While many also complain that they simply have not sufficient money to pay for good medical and obstetrical care, it seems clear that even were such facilities free to them, their substantial fear, suspicions and superstitions would have to be overcome—and perhaps some accommodation on the part of the doctors and hospitals be made in keeping with the migrants' cultural attitudes towards childbearing and rearing.

Thus, migrants seem much less self-conscious about pregnancy and childbirth than not only middle-class families, but many of the urban  30 poor we have met in the South, both Negro and white. Though we observed some discrepancy between white and Negro families in this regard —the Negroes less shy or embarrassed—we also observed some discrepancy between poor whites we knew in Atlanta and New Orleans, or indeed on small farms in Georgia and South Carolina, and the white migrants we studied.

During the prenatal period the mothers constantly refer to their pregnancy even well before it is obvious. Other children are told about the fact as soon as menstruation stops. We heard one mother tell her four children, "We is getting a baby again, 'cause I don't bleed no more." As  40 her abdominal wall swelled in later months the children would often come up to touch and fondle it, even to talk to the baby inside. We saw similar behavior in the other families we came to know. Moreover, likely as not, the mother would wear little or no clothing in the early morning and evening hours. The mothers frequently wear heavy clothes during their work in the fields—pants, rubber boots and rubber guards on their knees to protect them during stoop labor—and are sometimes relieved to be rid of all clothing at home. Thus, the unborn child is publicly "seen," felt and followed along as he grows in the womb.

Many Negro migrant women—we did not notice this in whites—at this time become more religious, going with special frequency to the various churches that flourish among them. Names such as "The One and Only Church of God" and "God's True House of Faith" describe the more evangelical and customarily passionate among them. In addition more conventional denominations send ministries to migrants, and these ministries come perhaps into closer and more directly helpful contact    10 with them than any other segment of "our" population with the exception of certain public health service doctors, nurses, social workers and dietitians.

The increase in church attendance was attributed by several mothers to a desire to ensure a baby who would survive pregnancy, be born without complication *and live*. The loss of children due to miscarriages, the mishaps of difficult deliveries or the various untreated diseases of the first days and weeks of infancy are very much on the minds of these women.

Likely as not the child is born at home, in the presence of his brothers and sisters, or if a first child, his "father." (Many Negro migrants do not    20 formally marry, or may do so after several children have been born.) Of course, there may be several "fathers" to a given family of children, though the current husband is almost always called "father" by all children and his name is assumed. Since residences and schools alike constantly shift, this is an easier practice to follow than in the cities or rural areas where some of these same customs hold for nonmigrants, but with less formal cooperation from the society. White migrant families are much more likely to have a common father.

From the first day of birth the new child eats and sleeps with the rest of the family. Migrants quite often live in one-room houses, small shacks    30 which are built to cover people with a roof rather than help them divide their activities and time with one another in certain ways. The children are breast-fed, and so fed for a year or more without any other food, except perhaps soft drinks which are introduced in the first months. There is little of the modesty one sees in our predominant culture, and again even in the poorer sections of it. Children of five and six may fondle both baby and breast during the feeding period. There is no concept of a schedule of feeding. Infants are often brought to work, watched over by their brothers and sisters or grandmothers; their mother is summoned when the child cries, there to be fed with little interest in covering the breast    40 from anyone nearby.

The infant sleeps with his mother for the first few months, then is entrusted to the considerably older children, if there are any, rather than any siblings one or two years older. In such cases girls of five and six become quite occupied with introducing food to the child, playing with him, clothing him. If there are only very young children, the infant still will likely go to the oldest of these almost as a gift or birthright. We have seen families within families, younger children "belonging" to various older ones.

The young child sleeps with the older children—if he is a first or even second child he or she may sleep with his or her parents until enough children come to warrant a *second* bed or cot or sleeping bag. The infant thus grows and becomes a child in the midst of the constant physical presence of others—their noises, smells, actions and habits. He is constantly touched, held and seen by them and thus receives that sensory— especially tactile—stimulation, or we might say, metaphorically and literally both, that kind of nourishment.

The growing child of one or two responds to such an environment by talking and moving about with ease. He is often naked, allowed to be so and encouraged to be so. Since his parents follow the sun in pursuit of work made possible by the sun, he is usually quite comfortable without clothes. He is not toilet trained until he is well able to walk outside his house—usually in the second year, though sometimes well into the third year. The outside world is often his toilet, the nearby land of trees, thickets and grass. Many of these children have never been in a house that has a bathroom, never seen a bathtub or sink. The mothers tend to be fairly firm once they have decided to train the child. They or one of their other children quickly carry him outside, where he can continue, or if he is finished he may be left there a bit alone, told not to come in and prevented from doing so. That is a harsh fate, a cruel exile for children so constantly close to others. From what we can see, they rapidly seem to get the point. On the whole, then, toilet training seems to be accomplished quickly, without great self-consciousness on the part of anyone, indeed rather smoothly and effectively.

## Childhood

The children are allowed great freedom in moving about—their very inheritance—as they leave the infant and baby years to become walking, talking boys and girls. They are extraordinarily responsible for one another. They feed one another, clothe one another, sleep together and often work together, following their parents at picking in the fields as they become seven, eight or nine and thus old enough to do so.

These homes have practically no printed matter. Many migrants are illiterate. They do not read newspapers. They do not even receive mail. Their children fast pick up their parents' words, but they come to school with little preparation for books, maps or pictures. The walls of their homes are barren. Some of them, however, have seen a good deal of television. On the road they often cannot have it, because they are in homes unequipped for electricity. In Florida the same may hold; but it may not if they live in certain camps or housing compounds. The first thing purchased is a television set; and the children become utterly taken up with it for a while. After a while the enthusiasm seems to subside and then

stop altogether, enough so that the set is ignored for long spells. We
wondered how the children — and for that matter their parents — responded
to the comfortable world of America as it entered *their* world. We soon
learned that they seemed to respond to it as "our" children do to adventure stories, science fiction or plain comic strip stimulation of dream
and fantasy.

For example, one child of six told me he would some day board a rocket
to the moon, and on the way "get off to see the cities up there." Questioned earnestly by us about the existence of cities on the moon, he explained to us that he meant the cities and the life in them he saw on      10
television and passed by—at small but significant distances—in his
travels with his parents.

Particularly revealing are the drawings these children do at five and six
or eight and ten. They compare markedly with drawings we have seen
from Negro and white children in middle-class child guidance clinics or
poorer homes in the South. When asked to draw pictures of themselves
they consistently sketch their brothers and sisters *with* themselves. When
asked to limit themselves to a drawing of themselves, they hesitate, seemingly confused or paralyzed, or use the crayons in helter-skelter fashion
that results in no picture at all. They seem very much afraid of being      20
alone, of asserting on paper or in the games we played the kind of individuality rather commonly sought by children from different backgrounds.

For example, a seven-year-old boy was asked what would happen to a
soldier we isolated from other soldiers in a game we played together.
He said he would die of starvation. ("He'd better get back fast or he won't
eat and that'll end him.") All such games showed the children anxious to
have groups of soldiers close together. There were no isolated leaders,
and when we tried to establish their presence the children wanted them
back with the others, or feared for their lives. They seemed unable to
command their imaginative resources for situations that found people      30
on their own.

The games and drawings also gave us some indication of how these
children felt about themselves in relation to nonmigrant children. They
are, of course, well traveled; though they do not move on the main highways or the planes and trains the rest of us use. Still, with their parents
they see the land and its people, and from their parents they get a series
of notions about others. "I tells my children we feeds the rest of the children," one mother told us. Another mother constantly told her children that
the alternative to their kind of life was "trouble" or "no food and going to
jail." Several parents frequently remarked upon the good fortune of being      40
able to get what work they did as harvesters. The children were reminded
that they had cousins whose parents didn't work at all, and "they takes
to drinking and fighting all day long."

The children thus sense that they and their parents do something important for others, that those others have a better but distantly unobtain-
able life, that the alternative to the migrant life is not that better life but

one even worse than the one they know, full of danger and pain, and that their present life (whatever its trials) serves to keep them and their families from not only external hardship but internal disintegration.

How do the children tell us such ideas? They are obtained, of course, over time from their parents and from their own developing sensibilities. After knowing us for several months one child was finally able to formulate (and confide that formulation of) her impression of the life of city children. She drew a house so large as to cover almost the entire paper, then filled it with furniture. There was only one small window. The furniture seemed so abundant as to be a logjam. I had a sheaf of her drawings showing her *own* house; it had many windows and walls so drawn as to leave spaces that ranged from crevices to gaping holes. She invariably filled "her" houses with six, seven or nine people, but never any furniture. (She was one of six, her mother was pregnant, and of course with her father there were nine in the family.) We noted that the walls on the city home were scrupulously and thickly crayoned—and in red, instead of brown and black. The girl was telling us that she knew that other children lived in more solid, perhaps brick houses, less exposed and open to the wind or rain, filled with tables, chairs and beds she knew she did not have in her own. When we asked about the people who lived in the urban home, they slowly took on shape at her hands; parents and two children, all bigger and stockier than her own family. She had to draw them, incidentally, on another piece of paper, there being no room for them on the first piece. The house and furniture had monopolized all the space.

We have consistently similar drawings from other children, and as they become nine and ten, they can speak their observations more readily. One little white boy of seven emphasized his own kind of living (its rootlessness) by spending considerable time on the kind of foundation (including an elaborate cellar) he gave to the houses he imagined nonmigrants to have. A migrant child of nine explained the differences between his family and many others as follows: "We has to keep moving or we don't eat except from relief, if they give it to us . . . They have the work near their houses, and they has it all the time . . . They takes the pictures on TV in their homes, because most people can recall them and there aren't but a few of us, so we aren't there on the picture."

As migrant children become four and five they learn their mothers' wishes and develop the controls necessary for their later life. The power of police, traffic lights and other rules of the road are recited by their parents to them as they move along. Children are physically punished— hard and mean at times—for taking food not theirs, for squabbling with one another or failing to execute assigned tasks promptly—fetching water from a pump, holding the baby, feeding the dog. (Stray dogs abound in migrant camps, and are by no means ignored. One public health doctor said to us, "They may symbolize what they think of themselves, because they sure take care of them and feed them whatever they have to eat.") Older children are trained to follow after their parents, harvesting in the fields. They must learn how to pick tomatoes or pluck beans, and if they become slow or careless they are hit and shouted down. We have noticed that when punished in the fields they are very often hit by hand on their legs. It is leg work and hand work that makes for harvesters.

By the time a migrant child goes to school he has been taught his do's and don'ts, to fear certain others, to get along with people in certain ways. Impulsiveness, self-assertion, rivalrous expressions and envious feelings tend to be strongly discouraged at home, but allowed children as groups, that is, in conjunction with brothers and sisters. Thus, groups of children can fight other groups, or envy one another openly so long as it is done 10 collectively. Mothers show great warmth and open affection, kissing and fondling their children, rubbing the skin on their arms, but also quick anger toward them and severe punishment, most often slapping accompanied by shouting. Rarely is one child punished alone; often the mother will remind the others that they, too, have done similar wrongs in the past—and will in the future.

Very significant, we thought, was the absence of grudges in parents. A punished child will likely as not be embraced seconds or minutes after being punished, almost we sometimes thought as *part* of it. The result seems to be a sharply defined sense of limitation or restriction, one that 20 does not spread into general shyness or inhibition. This may explain what many observers of migrants notice, their capacity to change moods and behavior so rapidly: they can be fearfully, grimly silent (especially before the "strangers" of our world) and then quickly joyful and talkative with one another. "Their moods don't last," a nurse told us. We suspect that their early training sets the stage for what they will later need, a highly developed sense of flexibility in their personalities, an ability to manage the constant restrictions of the external world, but still not succumb to the apathy and despair that would fatigue and immobilize them. In a sense, then, there is a "bounce" to the way these children are 30 punished that teaches them fast recovery from a slap as well as specific, responsive obedience to it.

Much of the hardest punishment goes into confirming the child's sense of submission to the nonmigrant world, or passivity before it. There is a striking difference in the relationship between the child and his family "at home" or in travel, and the child at school, in the fields, even on the streets. At home the children play together easily and warmly. They are very free with their parents, and their parents with them. Open expression of love and demonstrations of it are seen. In children of eight and nine when one might expect otherwise, we hear boys talk openly of wishing 40 to marry their mothers, girls of wishing to marry their fathers. There is, later on, a substantial incidence of stepfather-stepdaughter sexual liaison, and those between fathers and daughters have been noted by social workers who observe both white and Negro migrants. Two mothers told us that such happenings were not rare, but were frowned upon and reported about as the "events" they apparently are: "It goes on sometimes, I think 'on the road' if the mother is getting ready to have a baby, or something like that . . . I don't think it goes on a lot. No, it shouldn't, but it does sometimes; maybe on account of drink, and you kind of get frustrated."

In point of fact the rigid incest barriers that hold for middle-class families seem less sturdy with these families, often fathered by several men, in constant movement, living and sleeping practically on top of one another despite their invariably large size. Their children are much less secretive, resort to much less furtive and symbolic maneuvers to express their attachment and direct love for their parents, and also their anger. Yet, in contrast to such physical intimacy and propinquity, openness of feeling and of anger, closeness of relationship between children, when migrant children meet many people on the "outside" (as their parents are apt to refer to anyone from a teacher to a farm manager) they often appear isolated, guarded, withdrawn, suspicious and apathetic or dull.

Thus, in many respects migrant children are brought up to have two rather explicit ways of responding to the two worlds of their family and "others." Though of course all children learn a version of that kind of distinction, there is a *contrast* to the twofold behavior in migrant children, a sharpness to that differentiation, that is quite special. It is at times uncannily as if they had two sets of attitudes, two personalities, one for their family, one for the rest of the world.

### From Childhood Straight into Adulthood

Migrant children become migrant adults with no ceremony, or time to be not quite either, so as to consolidate the one before taking up the other. If ever we as psychiatrists need to realize how much "youth" is a social and cultural concept as much as a matter of strict chronology, our acquaintance with migrant children is to be recommended. There are two elements that mark the beginning of adulthood in the migrant, and when both are fulfilled, he or she is an adult, and so treated by parents, brothers and sisters and neighbors. These are experience in working the fields and the onset of puberty.

By ten many migrant children—all of those we came to know—have put in considerable time at harvesting whatever crops their parents have worked at. In some southern states school times used to be adjusted so that children could help with cotton or other crops, and by no means has that practice yet vanished for many sharecropping regions. With migrants there is an even greater possibility for school schedules to yield to the needs of work: though states may insist that children within their territorial limits attend school, migrants tend to shuffle in and out of towns, counties and states, making it hard indeed for any regulatory agency to keep track of them. The children may spend most of the winter and spring in one Florida school, or they may move about from one school to another, or not attend any school for very long. Dropouts among even the more "stable" migrant population—those who do less moving about—tend to be high in the junior high years.

At 10 to 12 the children start becoming adults physiologically; many of them have already been working for several seasons. It is not long before they marry and have children. Brides of 14 and 15 are common, and their husbands are likely to be the same age or not very much older.

Before actual marriage the young men and women may live with their families and travel with them, but clearly at 12 to 14 they are "on their own time," as several mothers described the fact that their sons and daughters were going out at night, and often staying out. They were also earning money and keeping it rather than turning it in to their mothers. We noted that sexual maturation seemed to trigger the social and economic independence of the child with great speed. We wondered about the "defensive" nature of this fast departure, whether the highly crowded living conditions made a sexually aroused young man or woman "too much" for his parents to bear. The parents told us that they felt that migrants tended to "marry earlier" than sharecroppers, and certainly *part* of the explanation is the ease with which older migrant children can often make at least *some* money, and the fact that migrant farmers need their children rather less than do sharecroppers, whose children must help their parents work the land even when married, often for no money at all.

## Young Adulthood

Married couples and parents, workers and housekeepers, young migrant men and women (at 16 or 18, for example) *do* have their "platter parties" when they can join record machines with a source of electricity. On their way to work at six in the morning they can be seen literally dancing in the streets or pathways, often with a beer or two before they get on the buses which take them to the fields. Often their first child is given to the maternal grandmother as a kind of "present," though slowly the mother accepts responsibility for the baby, and with it for adulthood itself.

Many of the younger migrants try very hard to break out of the migrant stream to venture into cities for jobs, or at the least buy a car on time, which means they can travel by themselves rather than in the crowded trucks and buses that many of their parents may have to use—tired as they may be of depositing money for used cars that soon break hopelessly down. In large numbers they seem headed for disappointment. In our observations, it is not only their lack of education and the unemployment which afflicts their segment of the economy—serious problems indeed. They themselves are at once afraid when they approach the city, many of them unaware of just how to obtain work there. Moreover, we have talked with many earnest young migrant workers who are repelled by the prospect of sitting week after week waiting for jobs that do not in any case seem forthcoming. They are made anxious by the sight of relatives, friends or simply fellow human beings drawing relief (as migrants they are ineligible for it until they establish criteria for residence). Part of the explanation for their common anxious reluctance to join the ranks of the urban unemployed is perhaps based on fear of the city and its pervasive "authorities," and a developmental reliance upon the movement of travel, and farming done during it, for a sense of their own identity and self-respect.

One migrant (aged 17, with two children) told us his feelings as follows: "I tried the city for a job, and I moved in with a cousin, and no go. . . They was all on relief and I was supposed to get on when I could, after applying; but we got tired of waiting, and we just left one day . . . I'd rather keep 'on the season' and feel right than sit all day as they do and *do nothing.*" There were several psychological themes in this and other interviews with him: his awe and confusion before the complexities of bureaucratic procedure; his fear of the city, its people, will and customs; his restive inability to accommodate himself to a passive, idle, "taking" posture in contrast to the one he grew up to know—the energetic, kinetic, changeable and active one of migrants.

Young migrants, like their parents, show few inhibitions over sexuality. They have grown up with it, heard and seen it from their first days. Their parents have never seen fit to restrict their love-making to private or relatively secluded places. (They are generally not to be had, anyway.) In the evening hours as the children play noisily with one another, their parents have sexual relations. We noticed, however, that many young childless couples preferred privacy from their parents for such times—not always available while in transit. The woods are then often used.

Finally, we noticed a gradual change in mood or spirit in youthful migrants. At 20, at 22, they are full-fledged adults—we would call them "older" migrants. They have lost much of their interest in the possibilities of another kind of life; they often move about by themselves, no longer attached to their families and little interested in seeing and visiting them even when near them or migrating with them; they are caring for their own children. They have settled into the curious combination of industry and initiative (needed to keep moving over such distances, to keep working at such back-breaking work), lethargy and despair (reflected in their faces, their gestures, their way of slow movement, flattened speech, infrequent merrymaking). "We keeps going," said the father of one of our ten families, "but it ain't a good time like we once thought."

## THE PSYCHOPATHOLOGY OF MIGRANT LIFE

Having discussed some of the more significant features of growth and development as it takes place in migrant farm families, we might now mention—in the limited fashion allowed us at this time—some of the medical and psychiatric problems particularly evident in these people.

We have already noted the high infant mortality rate. From infancy through childhood a host of illnesses, uncorrected deformities and congential abnormalities or developmental disorders face the children; any psychiatric study cannot exclude such facts from a discussion of the sources of migrant psychopathology.

Striking to us is the evidence in our ten families, and in our work as a "general practice" physician beside the public health doctors, of tooth decay in children; of uncorrected disturbances of vision; of repeated ear infections that have resulted in faulty hearing; of valvular heart disease, congenital and rheumatic, associated with impaired circulation of blood; of continual parasitic diseases that produce diminished appetite, weakness and anemia; of vitamin deficiencies based on faulty eating habits, many of them from aversions as well as poverty or lack of availability; of chronic diarrheas, chronic fungal diseases of the skin, chronic tuberculosis; of untreated or poorly treated chronic and recurrent venereal    10 diseases; of chronic kidney and bladder infections; of muscle pains and bruises, or bone injuries or back diseases brought on by working conditions; of nerve palsies.

We find it difficult to see how such illnesses can help but affect the minds of people regularly suffering from not one but in all likelihood many of them. Fatigue, insomnia, loss of appetite, trouble in breathing or walking, pain, itching, bleeding, blurred or double vision, hardness of hearing are some of the symptoms of these diseases, and their psychological effects upon people will be appreciated.

To view the more formally psychiatric disorders seen in migrants, we    20 must see much of their behavior—as with all of us—as an attempt to adapt to (cope with) the particular kind of life which is theirs. We see little sense in taking middle-class social and cultural standards and transposing them to migrant families as measurements of their "normal" or "abnormal" behavior. While it is true that many migrants share an American citizenship with us all, their living conditions and habits have a quality all their own.

This said, we can, however, take notice of the breakdown of adjustment in these people, and try to indicate when it seems to happen and why. Migrant children generally start life with strong support from mothers    30 who predominantly breast-feed them for long, unanxious periods over many months, and offer constant affection and tenderness to them. Their toilet training is largely casual, basically unconcerned with time, frequency or specific place, though gradually firm on the distinction between house (or vehicle) and the "outside." Children learn to get along closely with brothers and sisters but scrap easily with other children; they are punished quickly but without prolonged residual hostility and allowed both to be openly affectionate and angry toward their parents. They are in contrast taught rigid controls before nonmigrants, and fear of them also.

What we see in migrant children, to some extent as a result of this, is    40 a preservation over the generations of a certain soundness of mind, self-confidence and self-esteem in one set of circumstances, in company with a rigid, anxious, fearful way of engaging with another set of circumstances. Thus, we have seen little to no childhood schizophrenia in migrant children, very few of the temper tantrums and bed-wetting complaints commonly seen in middle-class child guidance clinics. We have seen no specific "learning problems"—again so frequently seen in those clinics—because the entire culture of the migrants has a "learning problem" built into its whole way of life—work taking precedence over residence, let alone schooling, and parents basically tired and illiterate having no capacity to stimulate a taste for education in their young.

On the whole these children, at five or six, seem cheerful, spontaneous, affectionate to one another and relaxed, in spite of their frequently poor physical health and the comparatively hard life they and their parents must live. We feel, therefore, that there are positive forces at work in their family life that give them initial psychological strength to face the world.

However, bit by bit over time this initial stamina faces challenges and threats. Physical health deteriorates—the first sight of some of the teeth, squinting eyes, infected skin and bent backs of "young" migrants in their 20's confirms that fact—but of course further diagnostic examination and tests are required to establish the extent of the deterioration. The tight-knit, isolated protection that migrant living offers children yields to the demand that the child, in his early teens, establish his own livelihood, marriage and capacity to "keep going" (literally as well as metaphorically).

At this point migrants often develop a variety of "symptoms" or ways of thinking and feeling which indicate their response to the cumulative stresses of their kind of existence. They may drink heavily before or after work, using the cheap wine and beer they can afford to dull their senses in the face of, or in the wake of, their long hours of harvesting. They may become nasty and violent with one another, just as when children they were allowed to be toward neighbors. They often become careless and hurtful toward the homes furnished them by the farmers, destroying screen doors, stopping up the central plumbing facilities of a camp. Some may call such behavior "accidental;" but many farmers, in our opinion, are correct in sensing the barely submerged hostility and resentment at work in these people. Our interviews indicate that the migrants don't specifically "intend" to damage property, but are aware of feeling overworked and underpaid and carry those feelings around with them fairly constantly. When, after many months, we hesitantly "interpreted" for several of them a connection between those feelings and their ways of *not* caring for property, we met surprise and denials, followed several days later by admissions from two of the five migrants that they did in fact consciously kick doors or walls at times—and thus might well do other similar deeds without even knowing why.

Apathy, gloom and severe depressions are seen in many migrants. We have seen a number of depressions severe and crippling enough to be considered psychotic. In fact we have seen seven cases of psychotic behavior recognized as such by migrants and reported to us by members of the ten families we studied. They are people who are called "different," yet they work and are generally tolerated. Incidents of wildly dangerous behavior, suicidal and homicidal, have been reported to us, but never witnessed. Rarely, except for criminal reasons, do these people see psychiatrists or even mental hospitals, even when grossly schizophrenic. We thought two of our 17 adult informants (three of the homes were fatherless and without a continuing husband) psychotic, that is — in comparison to the others — guarded, depressed, hard to follow in thinking and inappropriate in mood. The hazards in such determinations, however, still puzzle us.

Migrants are particularly likely to use such psychological mechanisms as denial, projection and suppression. They favor conversion reactions (we saw paralyses and seizures which made no neurological sense) and tend to express a good deal of their anxiety or despair in somatic form (and language, too). "My blood is weak," or "my stomach is weary" may express depression and tension but also tell of episodes of bloody stools and gastritis. It is hard to separate the various causes and effects in such cases; but we have seen chronic complaints revive, summon a new interest in people whose reserve of energy had been depleted by a hard day or a disappointment — loss of a baby, breakdown of a car.

Of practical interest in a discussion of migrant psychopathology is their common refusal to eat oranges, grapefruit, tomatoes, cherries — the healthy foods they so desperately need. Even when they hear earnest and effective dietitians correlate in simple, stark language the relationship between their eating preferences and habits and their own and their children's ailments, many stubbornly refuse to make changes in their diets. Ignorance is surely one part of the explanation, but our interviews suggest that another part is a strong aversion to eating what they must live by and work upon. In several cases we saw real revulsion at the mention of eating or serving a tomato or orange — a real kind of fear, as if in some way all the anger they felt at having to harvest those foods for a living would eventually come to haunt them and live in them if they were consumed.

It is our impression that many migrants seem to have constructed a split in their personalities which results in two distinct personality styles. With their children and husbands or wives they will often be warm, open and smiling. At work, with strangers and often with one another while traveling or even walking the streets, they are guarded, suspicious, shrewdly silent or sullenly calculating in what they do have to say; and sometimes clearly apathetic, humorless or even bitter, resentful and touchy. Such alterations in mood and attitude appeared to us as grim and striking examples of the capacity of the human mind to respond to its environment and keep itself intact by developing a high order of ability to divide itself severely and categorically. Nowhere in our years with these people did we hear this put better than by the mother of one of our ten families: "We switches back and forth, from being in a good mood to a bad one because you learns how to travel and you just make your head travel with you, so you gives yourself and the kids a break from the field."

The problem of *differential behavior in white and Negro migrants* had to be considered by us. There were definite differences between the six

Negro and four white families studied along such variables as promis-
cuity (higher in Negroes), duration of breast-feeding (longer in Negroes),
tendency toward open expression of anger toward one another, by word
or deed (higher in whites), distance covered in yearly migrations (higher
in Negroes), number of children (slightly higher in Negroes).

We felt that in the important respects of viewing the infant as a rare
and thus specially valuable possession (to be nourished well indeed in
the early months), of generally having a "permissive" attitude toward
toilet training, of attitude toward education, toward the time their children
became adults and toward themselves in contrast to the world, the two
sets of families largely resembled one another. Other observers have told
us that in some cases white mothers are not as warm with their infants,
stricter with their children later and prone to more pervasive depression
—including more overt antisocial violence—when so disposed. (Of course
whites in the South can behave more aggressively "in public" than Negroes,
regardless of class or occupation.)

Our observations, however, tend to indicate that migrants, including
white migrants, have developed certain characteristic attitudes *on the basis
of their work and travel habits.* The constant movement, the threat of social
chaos, the cramped living and traveling, make for common problems
and remarkably similar responses to them which separate to some extent
migrant behavior from that of the rest of the *poor.* Indeed, we are in general
perhaps ill-advised to lump millions of poor people together—at least
psychologically—on the basis of their common relative lack of income.

In our work with southern families caught up in the various crises of
desegregation we have had occasion for a number of years to work with
poor Negroes and poor whites, in both rural and urban situations. We
certainly have spent a good number of months observing sharecroppers
and small farmers, again of both races. Migrant farmers once were mostly
poor farmers. They still are poor and they are still farmers, but they are
also migrants. As such there is a specific social and cultural condition
to their lives, and a specific psychological stress and challenge, too. If
poor people have their own culture grounded in the life and laws of the
slum or the rural village, migrants do not share in it—though they may of
course carry some of it with them in what they do possess, a life of mobility
that calls forth its own variation of habits and practices, surely resembling
the way poor people live more than middle-class people, but also different
from both.

## CONCLUSIONS

On the basis of our observation we draw the following conclusions:

1. Migrant farm workers comprise—by the hundreds of thousands—a
vastly ignored subculture whose work is essential to our well-stocked
tables, but whose lives are often simply not known to most of us. There
has, for example, been no psychiatric study of how these people manage
such strains as constant movement with its social and cultural disorgani-

zation, economic hardship, political disenfranchisement and the personal
and familial conditions of uprootedness in general.

2. This psychiatric investigation finds that in order to adapt to such
unusual facts of environment, migrants turn their isolated, mobile life
inward, becoming guarded and suspicious toward outsiders but,
in compensation for a rootless life, exceptionally close-knit with their
young children. They tend to be unusually warm and stimulating with
their infants and rather lax about disciplining them. They so treat them
that there appears to be significantly less hostility between the children,    *10*
much of it channeled toward other families as well as the world in general,
which is seen as unfriendly and punitive. Families thus become separated
from families, even within the migrant culture, so that the price of cohesion
within the family is isolation and alienation from others.

3. Migrant children progressively learn a sense of their own weakness
and inadequacy in comparison to the rest of the population, whose existence they comprehend and see from the distance of the traveler or television viewer. Their drawings and their play in games as well as their
words indicate that they see themselves as smaller, less able to make      *20*
decisions affecting their own lives and for some reason not clearly understood by them, stained, crippled or paralyzed.

4. Migrant children do not have the cultural accompaniment to physiological adolescence that we call "youth." They go directly into adulthood,
with its work, marriage and parenthood, in their early teens.

5. Migrants tend to be not only distrustful of others, but even hostile
toward many attempts to help them—with medicine, shelter or advice.
They tend to avoid the very food they harvest, often in a phobic manner.    *30*
Such behavior urges study of *why* it occurs and in what context of social
and economic facts.

6. Migrants develop a variety of psychiatric illnesses. Especially are
they susceptible to mood swings, violence toward one another, heavy
drinking and a severe kind of apathy, with loss of appetite, aimlessness
and indifference which may or may not go on to a more severe clinical
depression, with suicidal preoccupations or paranoid thinking.

7. The physical health of these people is generally quite poor, with a    *40*
host of diseases plaguing their skin, muscles, blood, vital organs and
nervous system from birth to death. These diseases also affect the minds
of those so afflicted, causing anxiety, fear, irritability and excitability,
withdrawal and moodiness.

8. There is an urgent need for closer study of the lives of migrant
farmers, and the problems in such a study are to some extent indicated.
We can only conclude this study by remarking upon the extraordinary

resilience shown by many of these people. The exertion of will they can muster — under the conditions of life they have as their very own — calls for further psychiatric study into how people manage stress and preserve, as well as lose, some of their psychological stability and human dignity.

# U.S. Constitution

ARTICLE XIX (1920)

The right of citizens of the United States to vote shall not be denied or abridged by the United States or by any States on account of sex.

The Congress shall have power to appropriate legislation to enforce the provisions of this article.

# Eleanor Flexner
## Early Steps Toward Equal Education

The movement to improve and widen education in the young democracy assumed many forms. It included the extension of free education to ever wider sections of the population, the professional training of teachers, provisions for financial endowment, and the development of institutions for advanced education and higher learning and research.

Within this broad framework of endeavor, women faced some particular handicaps. It was almost universally believed that a woman's brain was smaller in capacity and therefore inferior in quality to that of a man. Some of the earliest women to demand greater educational advantages did not desire greater opportunities for women; they merely believed that more knowledge would make them better mothers and more efficient housewives. Some of them opposed the nascent woman's rights movement when it began to emerge; it was, in the main, a younger generation of women, their imaginations nourished and their wits sharpened by the pioneers, who took the leadership in advancing the legal and economic position of their sex.

Perhaps it was just as well that the earliest women educators saw only so far and no further; there were enough obstacles ahead to daunt even the strongest. By 1812, despite the dissemination of a few fertilizing ideas, education for women had made little progress. It was still limited to the well-to-do few, and consisted largely of such pursuits as embroidery, painting, French, singing, and playing the harpsichord. Its foundation on woman's proper sphere had been clearly stated by the French philosopher Rousseau: "The whole education of women ought to be relative to men. To please them, to be useful to them, to make themselves loved and honored by them, to educate them when young, to care for

387

them when grown, to counsel them, to console them, and to make life sweet and agreeable to them—these are the duties of women at all times, and what should be taught them from their infancy."

But vast changes were in the making which would effectively challenge such a philosophy. In 1814 the first power-driven loom was set up at Waltham, Massachusetts, operated by one Deborah Skinner; in 1817 three looms were in operation in Fall River operated by Sallie Winters, Hannah Borden, and Mary Healy. They proved that the nimbleness and skill previously employed in spinning and weaving at home could be put to profitable use in factories in what was to be the first large-scale in-    10 dustry in the United States.

Following the Louisiana Purchase and the opening of most of the north-western continent to exploration and settlement, the Jacksonian era saw great strides in westward expansion and industrial development. Women were not only entering the new textile mills, they were also in increasing demand as teachers for a rapidly growing population. The need to equip them for the new duties being laid upon them was becoming harder to deny.

Among the earliest voices raised against outworn shibboleths was that of Hannah Mather Crocker, whose little tract, *Observations on the Real*    20 *Rights of Women,* published in 1818, shows the conflict between old and new. She admitted a heavy debt to the writings of Mary Wollstonecraft, but hedged on "the total independence of the female sex. We must be allowed to say, her theory is unfit for practice, even though some of her sentiments and distinctions would do honor to the pen, even of a man." She had further reservations about women studying subjects too abstruse for their physical makeup, such as metaphysics, or about entering public affairs:

> Females may console themselves and feel happy, that by the moral    30 distinction of the sexes they are called to move in a sphere of life re-mote from those masculine contentions, although they hold equal right with them of studying every branch of science, even jurisprudence. But it would be morally wrong, and physically imprudent, for any woman to attempt pleading at the bar of justice, as no law can give her the right of deviating from the strictest rules of rectitude and decorum.

Nevertheless Hannah Crocker unequivocally rejected the creed that woman must forever occupy an inferior position because of her inherent    40 frailties, as demonstrated for all time by the fall of Eve:

> We shall consider woman restored to her original right and dignity at the commencement of the Christian dispensation; although there must be allowed some moral and physical distinction of the sexes agreeably to the order of nature, still the sentiment must predominate that the

powers of the mind are equal in the sexes. . . . There can be no doubt
but there is as much difference in the powers of each individual of the
male sex as there is of the female; and if they received the same mode
of education, their improvement would be fully equal.

In 1819, one year after Mrs. Crocker's pamphlet had appeared, Governor DeWitt Clinton of New York (of Erie Canal fame) received *An Address
to the Public; Particularly to the Members of the Legislature of New York,
Proposing a Plan for Improving Female Education;* it was the work of
Mrs. Emma Willard, who had been quietly carrying out some novel peda- 10
gogical ideas which were to prove a turning point in women's education.

Born in Berlin, Connecticut, Emma Hart had been fortunate in her
father; he wanted the best possible education for a lively-minded daughter
who enjoyed grappling with mathematical problems for the sheer delight
of mastering them. But her pleasure was spoiled when she discovered
that most women were deprived of the study of higher mathematics because their brains were not considered equal to the strain. Slowly she
came to the realization that women would not be able to overcome such
prejudices without the knowledge and the discipline afforded by a systematized course of study. 20

Mrs. Willard, by then married to the head of an academy for boys in
Middlebury, Vermont, and herself teaching girls, requested the privilege
of attending the men's examinations at the University of Middlebury, in
order to familiarize herself not only with the subject matter but also with
teaching methods and standards in the fields barred to herself and her
pupils. Her request being denied, Mrs. Willard set herself to evolving
her own teaching methods, and training her own teachers. As a prerequisite she had to study each new subject by herself. "I spent from ten
to twelve hours a day in teaching and, on extraordinary occasions such
as preparing for examination, fifteen; besides having always under in- 30
vestigation some one new subject which, as I studied, I simultaneously
taught a class of my ablest pupils."

She did not stop with algebra and geometry, but went on to solid geometry (which, lacking textbooks, she taught with the aid of pyramids and
cones carved out of turnips and potatoes), trigonometry, and conic sections. She taught geography, not by having her pupils memorize the
distance between Peking and London, but by drawing maps; history was
presented as a living process rather than a list of names and dates.

Since her pupils not only survived such rigorous fare, but responded
with gusto, she was encouraged to present her *Address* to Governor 40
Clinton. Her goal was a seminary whose curriculum would also include
natural philosophy (science) and domestic science; she sought not only
a charter but financial endowment. Mrs. Willard spent much time in
Albany, pressing her ideas on members of the legislature. Decorum did
not permit her to appear publicly, but she did read the *Address* to several
individuals and to at least one larger group. Her biographer, Miss Alma

Lutz, has suggested that she was probably the first woman lobbyist.

Although Governor Clinton gave her his support, and the legislature voted her a charter for a seminary in Waterford, it balked at the idea of a subsidy. Mrs. Willard then turned to the prosperous town of Troy, just across the Hudson River from Albany, where she aroused the interest of some substantial citizens. The Town Council voted to raise $4000 for a building by a special tax, and additional funds for maintenance and staff by private subscription; in 1821, the Troy Female Seminary, the first endowed institution for the education of girls, opened its doors.

Here Emma Willard continued to introduce innovations into her course    10
of study, the most daring being the subject of physiology, at a time when any mention of the human body by ladies was considered the height of indelicacy.

> Mothers visiting a class at the Seminary in the early thirties were so shocked at the sight of a pupil drawing a heart, arteries and veins on a blackboard to explain the circulation of the blood, that they left the room in shame and dismay. To preserve the modesty of the girls, and spare them too frequent agitation, heavy paper was pasted over the pages in their textbooks which depicted the human body.    20

In 1828-1829 women's education received a lively impetus from the teachings of Frances Wright. Born in Scotland in 1795, well-schooled and widely-traveled, the friend of Lafayette and of many freethinkers, Miss Wright edited a newspaper in Robert Owen's Utopian colony of New Harmony in the Indiana frontier country, and later her own paper, the *Free Enquirer,* in New York. She achieved further notoriety by pioneering as a woman lecturer and by her radical philosophy, of which her advocacy of equal education for women was an integral part. Like Mary Wollstonecraft, she argued that men were themselves degraded by the    30
inferiority imposed on women; every relationship to which woman was a party—friendship, marriage or parenthood—suffered as long as she was regarded and treated as a lesser human being.

> Until women assume the place in society which good sense and good feeling alike assign to them, human improvement must advance but feebly. It is in vain that we would circumscribe the power of one half of our race, and that half by far the most important and influential. If they exert it not for good, they will for evil; if they advance not knowledge, they will perpetuate ignorance. Let women stand where they may in the scale of improvement, their position decides that of the race.    40

Since Miss Wright cut a wide swath in her lectures, her ideas on education were linked, in many minds, with such other incendiary views as her support of political action by workingmen, her challenge of all forms of religious obscurantism, and her insistence on the rational basis of all knowledge and the importance of free enquiry:

I am not going to question your opinions. I am not going to meddle with your beliefs. I am not going to dictate to your mind. All I say is, examine; enquire. Look into the nature of things. Search out the ground of your opinions, the *for* and the *against*. Know *why* you believe, understand *what* you believe, and possess a reason for the faith that is in you.

This was strong meat, and the easiest way to dispose of it as well as of Miss Wright's ideas on education for women was to fall back on accusations of atheism and free love; her reputation became such that later *10* woman's rights advocates were tagged "Fanny Wrightists" as the worst kind of abuse.

Yet her influence was enduring. No woman in the first half of the nineteenth century who challenged tradition escaped the effect of Frances Wright's leavening thought; nor was its impact limited to women alone. The lectures which she delivered in New York, Philadelphia, Baltimore, Boston, Cincinnati, Louisville, St. Louis, and elsewhere were largely before audiences of workingmen, who also read accounts of her addresses in the active labor press of the day; they helped to feed the rising popular demand for free education. *20*

As the electorate slowly broadened state by state to include all white males over twenty-one regardless of property qualifications, the demand that education likewise be made available to all, irrespective of income levels, became one of the important issues of the Jacksonian era; every voter needed to be responsible and intelligent, and therefore had a basic right to education. Yet it took the better part of the nineteenth century to achieve a nation-wide system of free education for males, from primary school through college. In the period before the Civil War, the states were largely concerned with establishing publicly-supported elementary schools. By 1860 there were still only some forty-odd high schools worthy *30* of the name in the entire country. Many which called themselves such were in reality little better than elementary schools.

Lacking the argument afforded by suffrage, education for girls who could not attend private schools advanced even more slowly. While they were permitted to go to elementary schools, however financed, from the earliest days, their admission into secondary and high schools took much longer. The opening of free high schools for girls in such cities as Boston and Philadelphia was a veritable milestone which occurred only after the Civil War.

Since convincing taxpayers and civic authorities that women were en- *40* titled to the same educational opportunities as men was to be a long and laborious task, private institutions continued for some time to be the principal recourse of young women seeking broader schooling. But here too a problem existed. The fees were necessarily high, and thus limited the student body to those with parents able to meet them. When the heads of such seminaries sought to broaden their student body, they were confronted with the need for outside supplementary financing. From her earliest teaching days Emma Willard had sought to take education out of the realm of a privilege for the well-to-do. Her method was to make grants, in the form of loans, which were repaid by her pupils after they had found teaching posts; it is estimated that she loaned more than $75,000 over the years for this purpose. But she knew it was no real solution to the problem, and it was not the least of Mrs. Willard's contributions to women's education that she first raised the question of private endowment for women's educational institutions.

Mrs. Willard also played a pioneer role in demanding, and providing    10
for, the training of teachers. Teaching was the first of the "professions" open to women, but since they had no training and only the most rudimentary schooling, their prestige was low and they could not command salaries anything like those of men who were often college or university graduates. The Willard Association for the Mutual Improvement of Female Teachers, founded by Mrs. Willard in 1837 as a sort of alumnae association, was the first organization to bring this matter to public attention. It was typical of Mrs. Willard's "modern" methods and also of her national reputation that she secured as Honorary Vice-Presidents of the Association such distinguished women as Sarah Josepha Hale, editor of    20
the famous *Godey's Lady's Book* magazine, and the poet and novelist, Lydia Sigourney.

The subjects Mrs. Willard taught her girls might appear as higher education to contemporaries, but they could not compare with what was offered to young men at Harvard and other colleges. The first institution which offered women a curriculum even remotely comparable to that available to men on the college level was Oberlin, which began as a "seminary" and developed into a rudimentary college. As such it held a special and deserved place in the affections of the early woman's rights leaders; Lucy Stone referred to the opening of Oberlin as "the gray dawn    30
of our morning."

Founded in 1833 in the 30-year-old state of Ohio, it was the first such institution to open its doors to all comers, regardless of race, color— or sex. The founders stated among its prominent objectives: "the elevation of the female character, bringing within the reach of the misjudged and neglected sex all the instructive privileges which hitherto have unreasonably distinguished the leading sex from theirs."

The earliest women students at Oberlin took a shortened "literary" course in deference to the prevailing creed that their minds could not assimilate the same fare as men's. The first woman graduated the "full    40
course" in 1841; close on her heels came Lucy Stone and Antoinette Brown, the former to become one of the outstanding orators of her day, the latter the first women to be ordained as a minister. It is noteworthy that both had stormy careers at Oberlin because of their feminist views, which brought them into constant conflict with the authorities:

Oberlin's attitude was that women's high calling was to be the mothers of the race, and that they should stay within that special sphere in order that future generations should not suffer from the want of devoted and undistracted mother care. If women became lawyers, ministers, physicians, lecturers, politicians or any sort of "public character" the home would suffer from neglect. . . . Washing the men's clothes, caring for their rooms, serving them at table, listening to their orations, but themselves remaining respectfully silent in public assemblages, the Oberlin "co-eds" were being prepared for intelligent motherhood and a properly subservient wifehood.        10

Among the women educators who accepted the status quo for women—with a difference—was Catharine Beecher, who conducted a successful seminary for girls in Hartford, Connecticut, from 1823 to 1827. Forced to give it up by the inroads made on her health by the familiar dual job of teaching and money-raising, she turned her attention to other facets of the problem of female improvement. She was concerned that the "surplus" females in the East, forced to earn their own livelihood by the large-scale westward migration of eligible males, were going into factories where they worked long hours at low wages under insanitary conditions.        20 Her remedy was twofold: either women should teach—and the enormous demand for properly trained teachers would go far to absorbing such a "surplus"—or they should address themselves to some form of domestic work:

When all the mothers, teachers, nurses and domestics are taken from our sex, which the best interests of society demand, and when all these employments are deemed respectable and are filled by well-educated women, there will be no supernumeraries found to put into shops and mills or to draw into the arena of public and political life.        30

Miss Beecher's concept of woman's highest calling was quickened by something new: her insistence that, in order to discharge her housewifely obligations properly, a woman needed not only a rounded education, but a training as technical as that of a lawyer or a doctor. She developed her ideas in a series of books on domestic science, physical culture, and even what we would call "marriage problems." Her crowning work in this field, *The American Woman's Home,* contains a mass of information ranging from recipes and sewing instructions to suggestions on proper ventilation, planning a house suited to easy housekeeping, and maintaining the niceties of harmonious family living!        40

But it was in her approach to the training of teachers, a concern that she shared with Emma Willard, that Miss Beecher made her greatest contribution. She believed that teaching, like homemaking, must be dignified by adequate training. She developed a scheme for what we would call normal schools in a chain of middle-western cities, of which only two or three materialized, and only one, Milwaukee-Downer College, survives today. To rouse public interest in the question she established organizations, the National Board of Popular Education in 1847 and the American Women's Educational Association in 1852. Although she remained decorously in the background, working through interested gentlemen who even read her speeches for her at public gatherings, Catharine Beecher was one of the founders of modern teacher training.

Looking back from our present vantage point, we can see that the single most significant step away from the concept that women needed an improved education only to carry out their housewifely or teaching duties  10 better came with the founding of Mount Holyoke in 1837. Generally regarded now as the oldest woman's college in the United States, it made no such claim at the time. It opened as a seminary, and there were other such institutions then in existence. Mount Holyoke did not achieve collegiate status until 1893, after Vassar, Wellesley, Smith, and Bryn Mawr; yet it opened the way for them all.

Its founder, Mary Lyon, followed the path charted by Emma Willard, but went much further; in the fifteen years between the first steps toward founding her school and her premature death at fifty-two, Miss Lyon established certain fundamental principles which succeeding institutions  20 accepted as axiomatic; the schools must have adequate financial endowment; they must try in some degree to make education available to girls of all economic groups; they must offer a curriculum more advanced than that envisaged even by Mrs. Willard; and they must prepare their students for more than homemaking or teaching.

Miss Lyon succeeded in her ambitious undertaking because, in addition to an indomitable will and a mind which left its fiery imprint on all whom she encountered, her purpose was perfectly suited to both time and place. Hers was a New England in which wider horizons for women were becoming a household controversy: where women were already more than  30 homemakers and pedagogues. They were working by the thousands in the red brick mill buildings springing up beside every creek and river. The year Mount Holyoke opened its doors, anti-slavery women were holding their first national convention in New York, and the Grimké sisters were touring Massachusetts, speaking publicly against slavery; the storm unleashed by their unladylike behavior was convulsing the churches. There was a ferment abroad which stirred even women in obscure villages to ideas and efforts undreamed of a few years earlier. To a person of Mary Lyon's gifts and determination, here were the soil and climate that she needed.  40

She was born on a marginal hill farm in western Massachusetts in 1797, and as a child already showed astonishing mental capacities; like Emma Willard, she soon reached the outposts of knowledge then accessible to women. Like Mrs. Willard, she began to teach, and in the process, to continue her own education, to extend the existing curriculum, and to reshape teaching methods. With Miss Zilpah Grant she ran a successful academy, first at Derry, New Hampshire, and then at Ipswich, Massachusetts, but she was not satisfied. She saw the price paid in poor health by Miss Grant and by her friend, Catharine Beecher, for their staggering labors. She saw good schools arise, and then vanish, if a wealthy supporter died or lost interest. Like Miss Beecher she was obsessed with the need for good teachers. Most of all, she brooded over the young women who, like herself, wanted an education they could not afford: "During the past year my heart has so yearned over the adult female youth in the common walks of life, that it has sometimes seemed as if there was a fire shut up in my bones. I would esteem it a greater favor to labor in this field than in any other on which I have fastened my attention." To her mother she wrote in the same vein: "I have for a great while been thinking about those young ladies who find it necessary to make such an effort for their education, as I made when I was obtaining mine. . . . I have looked out from my quiet scene of labor on the wide world, and my heart has longed to see many enjoying the privileges, who cannot for want of means. . . . Sometimes my heart has burned within me; and again I have bid it be quiet."

In 1834 she laid her plan for a new kind of educational institution for women before a number of businessmen and ministers, who finally assumed the responsibility of raising the $27,000 estimated as necessary to build and open the school.

Here lay one of the major obstacles to success. Miss Lyon was herself the heart of the enterprise; yet the proprieties required that she keep in the background. It was not even considered seemly that she be present at the trustees' meeting which voted to locate the school in South Hadley, Massachusetts. She wrote to Zilpah Grant: "It is desirable that the plans relating to the subject should not seem to originate with *us* but with benevolent *gentlemen*. If the object should excite attention there is danger that many good men will fear the effect on society of so much female influence, and what they will call female greatness."

But when it became apparent that the men hired as "agents" were unable to raise the needed funds in the face of not only public apathy but a gradually worsening economic situation which culminated in the panic and depression of 1837, Mary Lyon herself entered the field, carrying the green velvet bag which became famous all over New England. When her staunchest friends objected to her incessant traveling and appearances at public meetings to ask for money, as unladylike, she refused to compromise her dream for the sake of propriety:

"What do I do that is wrong?" she asked in a letter. "I ride in the stagecoach or cars without an escort. Other ladies do the same. I visit a family where I have been previously invited, and the minister's wife or some leading woman calls the ladies together to see me, and I lay our object before them. Is that wrong? I go with Mr. Hawks and call on a gentleman of known liberality at his own house, and converse with him about our enterprise. What harm is there in that? If there is no harm in doing these things once, what harm is there in doing them twice, thrice or a dozen times? My heart is sick, my soul is pained with this empty gentility, this genteel nothingness. I am doing a great work, I cannot come down."

Miss Lyon herself raised the first $1,000 with which to launch the campaign, primarily from her former Ipswich students and teachers. Next she won support from men of means whom she visited under the escort of one or more of her trustees: there were two donations of $1,000   10 each, one of $640, one of $500. But in the last analysis the greater part of the money was raised because Mary Lyon, sometimes accompanied by a gentleman but very often alone, went to as large a cross-section of the population of New England as she could reach.

The greater portion of the total sum was raised from farmers and small townsfolk—men whose livelihood did not come easily, and women without any source of income except their handiwork, or what husbands or fathers might give them. In the old ledgers there are eloquent entries of five dollars, ones and threes, fifty cents, and one gift of six cents. Much of this money was raised at church meetings, small parlor gatherings, and   20 sewing circles. There was a young girl in a sewing circle at West Brookfield, who was making a shirt to help a young man through theological seminary, and whose thoughts as she listened to Miss Lyon have come down to us: "How absurd it was for her to be working to help educate a student who could earn more money toward his own education in a week, by teaching, than she could earn in a month; and she left the shirt unfinished and hoped that no one would ever complete it." Her name was Lucy Stone.

It took four long years to raise the money, put up the building, and open Mount Holyoke. Often the outcome seemed in doubt, even to the trustees.   30 The building had been started long before all the funds were in hand, and it was still not quite finished on the day in November 1837 when students began arriving. Many of them spent their first night with the best families in South Hadley, whose womenfolk rallied to loan furnishings for the rooms still lacking necessary equipment.

To the first group of girls and the parents who brought them, Miss Lyon communicated her own sense of urgency and triumph; no freshman on the threshold of her college life would ever feel quite the exhilaration and significance which fused that group, under Miss Lyon's influence:

Girls, stiff with riding almost continuously since before dawn, on the   40 last afternoon of grace were swung down from chaises by fathers and friends' fathers, to stumble through a side door into a five-storied brick building that rose, stark and blindless, out of a waste of sand. Deacon Porter was helping lay the front threshold, paint pots and work benches furnished the parlors, and Miss Lyon met them in the diningroom. There stood tables spread for the hungry; near by, a merry group of

young women were hemming linen and finishing off quilts and counter-
panes. Hammer strokes resounded through the house. Coatless, on his
knees in "seminary hall," Deacon Safford tacked matting, looking up
with a smiling word to newcomers: "We are in glorious confusion now,
but we hope for better order soon." . . . Trustees' wives washed dishes
in the kitchen . . . A girl's journal remarks: "Helped to get the first
breakfast at Holyoke. Miss Lyon and I were the first to appear in the
kitchen." . . . Examinations began to go forward amid the clamor of
alien activities. Singly, in twos, in groups, the girls took them, teachers
and students seated together on the stairs, or side by side on a pile of          10
mattresses in a hall-way, little oases of scholarly seclusion . . . And
then at four o'clock, when the last tack had been driven in "seminary
hall," a pause fell on the fleet occupations. With examinations far from
finished, and many loads of furniture still on the road, a bell rang, and
Mount Holyoke opened.

Behind this adventurous group of students was an admission policy as
startling as anything else in Miss Lyon's scheme: an age limit (no girl less
than sixteen years old was accepted), an embryonic system of examinations, and the conscious *selection* of girls on the basis of their maturity          20
and promise of intellectual growth. The requirements for entering the
first year were roughly those in effect at the best seminaries of the day,
but the substitution of a systematic three-year course instead of the usual
two years, and its content, as stated in the sober prose of the 1837-1838
catalogue, marked a new era.

Prospective students were examined in the general principles of English grammar, modern geography, history of the United States, Watts'
*On the Mind,* Colburn's *First Lessons,* and 'the *whole* of Adams' New
Arithmetic or what should be the equivalent in written arithmetic." Those
fulfilling these requirements, faced the following prospectus of courses          30
in the new seminary:

> Junior (first year): English Grammar, Ancient Geography, Ancient
> and Modern History, Sullivan's Political Class Book, Botany, New-
> man's Rhetoric, Euclid, Human Physiology.
> Second (or middle) Year: English Grammar continued, Algebra,
> Botany continued, Natural Philosophy, Smellie's Philosophy of
> Natural History, Intellectual Philosophy.
> Studies of the Senior Class: Chemistry, Astronomy, Geology, Eccle-
> siastical History, Evidences of Christianity, Whately's Logic, Whately's          40
> Rhetoric, Moral Philosophy, Natural Theology, Butler's Analogy.

Students were also required to take part in calisthenics, music, and
French, as well as domestic duties, an item which aroused much controversy. (Miss Lyon claimed it cut costs and thus helped the school to sur-

vive; it probably also reassured some parents and supporters who might have been fearful that the students were moving too far out of their natural sphere!)

This curriculum had much the same impact on the educational world of the 1830's as did the "Harvard Annex" and Bryn Mawr entrance examinations some fifty years later. However dry the enumeration of texts, however rigid and now outworn the course of study, its significance can hardly be overstated. The long struggle first envisaged by Judith Sargent Murray and launched by Emma Willard, taking women beyond the pudding and the nursery, had passed a decisive stage. Mary Lyon had put into their hands the means by which they could carry on that struggle in many different directions. What a few had dreamed and dared was now being proved in life and practice: that women's minds were constituted, in bulk and cell structure and endowment, the same as those of their masculine counterparts: that, given opportunity, discipline, and direction, they could encompass the same subject matter as a man; and that such an education was worth a sizable financial investment on the part of the parent, the philanthropist, and the community. The way had been cleared for the opening of Vassar in 1865, of Smith and Wellesley in 1875, of the "Harvard Annex" in 1879, of Bryn Mawr in 1885. It was becoming clear, to the dismay and regret of some, that there was no telling where it would all end.

As long as the institution of slavery existed, an educated Negro was not only an anachronism but a threat. To educate him was to disprove the premise of racial inferiority on which slavery was founded, and also to arm him for the struggle for freedom. It was illegal in southern states to teach a slave how to read. Although there are reports of schools conducted by Negro women in Louisiana, South Carolina, and Georgia, they were for the children of the freed Negroes, and they were rare. When Sarah Grimké tried to teach her slave maid to read, she did so behind a locked bedroom door and by the light of blazing pine knots. They were soon discovered, and the lessons stopped.

"At the North," in the phrase of the day, where slavery was abolished state by state over a period of fifty years beginning in 1790, colored children were nevertheless barred from the common schools in many places down to the Civil War. Laura Haviland, devoted crusader for freedom, testified that even in the Northwest Territory, where slavery had been abolished in 1787, there was not a school in the whole state of Michigan in 1837 that a colored child or adult could attend. Negroes were taxed in Ohio in the 1840's to support "public schools," but their children could not enter them.

Inevitably, the Negro girl suffered more deprivation than her brothers. If a white woman was supposed to be mentally incapable of receiving the same education as a man, and Negroes were inferior to whites, it followed that the Negro girl had the least possible potential for mental growth.

And yet, it had already been proved that a colored woman could be not only educated but capable of creative work. The honor and tragedy of such proof had fallen to Phillis Wheatley, who as a child of six had been captured in West African Senegal by slave traders, had survived the Middle Passage, and had been sold in the Boston slave market in 1759. She was extraordinarily fortunate; her owners were both educated and kind. They gave her the best possible schooling, and when she demonstrated her abilities as a poet and Latinist, they freed her but kept her in their home. Writing verse in the classical style of the day, Phillis wrote among others an "Ode to General Washington," which he gracefully acknowledged. After the Revolutionary War she journeyed to England, where she was feted by literary society.

Then her patrons died; the man she married proved worthless and left her destitute with three children. In 1784, when she was thirty-one years old, she died with a newborn child in her arms in an unheated Boston rooming-house, of cold and starvation.

There was no place in the world for a Phillis Wheatley yet. As the movement for the abolition of slavery began to pick up headway, it might have been expected that the education of Negro girls would become a matter of wider concern. That it did so even briefly was due to the heroism of one woman, and it is significant that none followed her example for some twenty years. The hazards encountered by Prudence Crandall in 1833-1834 in her effort to teach Negro pupils in a small Connecticut village are a measure of the obstacles that lay across the path of Negro girls looking for an education in the "free North" at that time.

Miss Crandall was a Quaker who conducted a successful school for young ladies in Canterbury, some forty miles southeast of Hartford. Her servant was a free Negro woman, engaged to marry the local "agent" of the *Liberator,* the fiery Abolitionist paper conducted by William Lloyd Garrison. She influenced Miss Crandall to accept a Negro girl, Sarah Harris, into her school of select and sheltered young misses. A storm of protest blew up; faced with the demand that she oust her new pupil, Miss Crandall closed her school instead.

Canterbury was taken aback, but found the episode was a mere prelude. Miss Crandall embarked on a series of journeys to Boston, Providence, and New York, where she took counsel with abolitionist leaders. Advertisements appeared in the *Liberator,* asking Negro parents to send their daughters to her for instruction. In April, just two months after she had closed one school, she opened another with seventeen Negro pupils.

Canterbury had never considered itself pro-slavery in sentiment. But such of its citizens as concerned themselves with the issue at all favored its solution by colonization: the return of the country's Negro population to Africa. They certainly never bargained for a school for Negro girls, backed—of all things—by abolitionist firebrands.

When the pillars of the community failed to close the school by threats, they resorted to other means of persuasion. Miss Crandall was jailed on a vagrancy charge—presumably laid against her pupils rather than herself—

and when that failed to stand up in court, a special law was rushed through the Connecticut legislature making it illegal for a Connecticut citizen to teach a pupil from another state!

While this measure dragged through the courts (where it was ultimately reversed), other time-honored methods were applied: the school's windows were broken; pupils and teachers (Miss Crandall was aided by her sister Almira) were stoned as they went for walks; manure was dropped in the well; local storekeepers refused to sell food, and doctors denied their services.

For one year and a half, Miss Crandall and her pupils held fast. She and her school became a symbol. Supporters from nearby communities brought food; her father carted water from his well two miles away. Abolitionists sent funds, and when they came to visit, the students gave recitations, dressed in their best. The girls themselves appeared as witnesses on Miss Crandall's behalf in court and wrote letters to abolitionist newspapers. In the end it was her concern for their lives that caused Prudence Crandall to retreat. One night, shortly after an attempt at arson had gutted the cellar, masked men brought battering rams into position and swung them against the walls of the house and the front door. Students and teachers spent a sleepless night upstairs while the rooms below were virtually demolished. The next day Miss Crandall announced that the school had closed.

Canterbury had won. But Miss Crandall's defeat marks the beginning of a long struggle in which she is honored as a pioneer. Today a woman's dormitory in Howard University in Washington, the first institution for the higher education of Negroes of both sexes founded after the Civil War, bears the name of Crandall Hall.

Prudence Crandall's struggle is all the more memorable when viewed in the context of her day. In 1833, Mount Holyoke was still a dream in Mary Lyon's mind. The voices of the first women to speak against slavery in public had not yet been raised. The first diffident women's anti-slavery societies would not be organized for another year. Yet Prudence Crandall traveled widely ("unladylike," Miss Lyon's friends called *her* fund-raising travels!) disregarded not only threats but flying stones, and carried on her school in a virtual state of seige for eighteen months. Here was a struggle to give many a woman not only food for thought but heart as well. Prudence Crandall belongs not only to the anti-slavery movement, but also to that for woman's rights.

# Nancy L. Ross
## Homosexual Revolution

In October of last year, 65 professional people gathered in San Francisco for a symposium sponsored by the Council on Religion and the Homosexual. For three days, teachers, clergymen, psychiatrists, lawyers and anyone else interested listened to homosexuals describe not only their personal and social problems, but also their lifestyles.

Each evening after the sessions, the homosexuals took the group out on the town to restaurants, bars and cinemas where they had a chance to see gay life in action; couples of the same sex dancing together, male go-go dancers and strippers, female impersonators, and films showing nude homosexual lovers.

"You don't just show somebody a homosexual in a gray flannel suit and say this is it; we wanted the straights (heterosexuals) to see everything," declared an organizer. The symposium received such favorable reaction from participants that it was repeated and will be held for the third time next month.

In September of this year, the Gay Liberation Front picketed the *Village Voice* in New York to protest the use of what they considered derogatory terms referring to them in editorial copy and the refusal (temporary, it turned out) of the newspaper to use the words "gay" or "homosexual" in classified ads.

The demonstration followed by less than two months a riot by 500 homophiles (homosexuals and sympathizers) protesting a police raid on a gay bar in Greenwich Village, and present sodomy laws. Crying "Gay Power to Gay People" and singing "We Shall Overcome," they threw firebombs and bricks at police. There were no wholesale arrests or reprisals. The militants vow to continue.

401

Though few Americans heard of these incidents and fewer still participated, their significance should not be overlooked. Together they illustrate, on the one hand, the new openness, and, on the other, the new militancy on the part of homosexuals, who call themselves America's second largest minority group, estimated at anywhere between eight and 15 million men and women. (Of course the great majority, as in any other group, continue to lead their own private, and often in this case secret, lives without getting involved in causes.)

Taking their cue from the black revolution, militant leaders are using the same tactics to obtain justice, equality and power for homosexuals. *10* Others, taking advantage of our permissive society, seek to bring out into the open a subject formerly as taboo as abortion and birth control. (The codeword "gay," first used in the '20s, is a reminder of days when "homosexual" was scarcely mentionable in public.)

As among black leaders, controversy has developed within the ranks of homosexuals as to the best method of achieving their ends. San Francisco's Leo Laurence, an avowed militant, revolutionary homosexual, has allied himself with organizations like the Black Panthers. Jack Nichols, managing editor of New York's *Screw* magazine, suggests, instead, peaceful protests such as a subway kiss-in and a dance-in to integrate straight *20* night clubs. The latter technique was tried successfully this fall at the Electric Circus in Greenwich Village.

*Come Out!,* "a newspaper by and for the gay community," in its first issue, dated Nov. 14, 1969, castigates *Gay Power,* a New York paper run largely by nonhomosexuals, for trying to "cash in on the new interest in homosexuality via the new freedom of the press." *Come Out* charged that on one issue *Gay Power* had attacked well-known homosexuals by name in print, endorsed Mafia-run bars in New York and included "borderline" pornography.

*The Advocate,* a Los Angeles homophile paper, condemns brashness *30* as well as violence and even cautions against "the implications of alliance with nonhomosexuals whose already poor image can do more harm than the temporary gain of a few people on a picket line."

While it is true public protests by homosexuals orginated in Washington in 1965 with picketing the White House, the Pentagon, the State Department and the Civil Service Commission, there is as yet no militancy here of the New York or Los Angeles ilk. The gay community has better relations with the police than in those cities. Washington retains a large measure of conservatism inimical to homosexuality. And, just as important, homosexuals employed by the government fear to declare themselves *40* lest they lose their jobs.

Homosexuality in the nation's capitol remains largely underground, but an increasing number of cracks have appeared in the earth's surface.

Society's awareness, though not necessarily its tolerance, of homosexuality has grown, due in part to the spate of movies and plays on the subject in the past two years. Homosexuals complain that plays like the off-Broadway hit, "The Boys in the Band," do more harm than good by presenting stereotype gays—limp-wristed, mincing, effeminate types out to destroy themselves and everyone else. The reaction gap between gays and straights to these plays is further illustrated by a new one entitled "And Puppy Dog Tails." This is the first play to depict *happy* homosexuals, showing affection to one another. It received raves from gay reviewers, but was panned by *New York Times* drama critic Clive Barnes as having an unbelievable plot as well as poor writing, construction and characterization.

The release this week of the National Institute of Mental Health's report recommending the repeal of laws against homosexual acts between consenting adults in private and reassessment of bans by employers against hiring homosexuals comes at a time when, despite the new permissiveness and concern for minorities, two out of three Americans, according to a CBS poll, still regard homosexuals with "disgust, discomfort or fear."

Were these reforms to be effected, "it would be the millenium," commented a homosexual.

Until now, nearly all of his new freedoms—and there have been many in the past two or three years—have been extra-legal. An admitted homosexual still cannot get U.S. government security clearance, serve in the army or, with one exception, the civil service. In a precedent-setting move, New York City abolished this last prohibition in May of this year.

This past spring, a Los Angeles homophile group put up its own candidate for City Council (he lost). And, for several years, politicians have accepted invitations by homosexual groups to address them and, in some instances, accept their active support.

The Bay Area's Film Festival this month featured the first gay all-male nude film made by Pat Rocco, a pioneer in that genre. Los Angeles ran its second annual Groovy Guy beauty contest this summer with males parading in tight blue jeans and briefs. The Metropolitan Community Church in Los Angeles, founded last fall by a gay preacher for gays, now has a congregation of several hundred.

Activites of this nature remain unthinkable in Washington, at least for the present, in the opinion of many people. For instance, the gay community, in the metropolitan area, which is said by members to range from 100,000 to 250,000 (including married persons whose primary sexual preference runs toward homosexual relations), has no newspaper like the *Advocate* or *Come Out*. The only publications are the homophile Mattachine Society's conservative newsletter, devoted mainly to legal matters, and a nascent mimeographed sheet of somewhat the same genre called *Gay Blade.*

There are no movie houses specializing in homosexual films. The Andy Warhol gay "skin-flick" entitled "Flesh" was screened for the first time by a local theater just a week ago.

Thus it is evident Washington does not yet compare with New York or California. Local openness is best measured against the situation 20 years

ago. At that time two or three gay bars existed under strict police super-
vision. Pay-offs, though not limited to homosexual hang-outs, were
common. Entrapment of homosexuals and arrests were frequent.

Today the *International Guild Guide* — available at certain downtown
bookstores — lists approximately 20 bars, nightclubs and restaurants
catering exclusively to homosexuals and that number again which welcome them along with straight patrons. By comparison, San Francisco
with a smaller population has 100. Washington homosexuals still prefer
the privacy of their own homes. And there are those who disdain bars
and even gay parties completely.                                          10

The establishments, located primarily in Georgetown, the Capitol
Hill area and along 14th street, are rated — up to "utterly fantastic" — and
coded so the visitor knows what to expect: lesbians, hustlers, military,
leather-jacket toughs, primarily Negroes, elegant atmosphere, drag show,
dancing, at your own risk, etc.

It is just within the past year or two that unisexual dancing has become
commonplace in gay clubs; male go-go dancers perform wearing only
little pieces of netting, and moderate displays of affection (light kissing
and touching) are permitted.

In general the police now leave homosexuals alone in private and in     20
clubs except upon receiving complaints of soliciting or lewd conduct.
Decorum is usually maintained in places frequented by upper-middle-
class homosexuals. Inspector Walter Bishop, head of the morals squad,
says the last club raid took place two years ago at a club where patrons were
found "on the floor." Pay-offs have almost entirely stopped, say bar owners.
Similarly arrests have stopped. Male homosexual arrests in 1960 totaled
496; in 1968, 69. Today, sodomy is becoming as rare a charge as heresy;
a lesser charge like disorderly conduct or loitering is customarily sub-
stituted.

But laws against homosexuality remain on the books. Just last week,    30
the Alcoholic Beverage Commission suspended a gay club's license on
11 counts, one of which was indecent language and acts. In 1969 this
means using four-letter words in sexually suggestive statements over the
microphone and a male customer touching another male's groin and
making provocative remarks.

Just as gay night spots have proliferated in recent years, so have bookstores, because of liberalization of pornography laws. Washington now
numbers 24 shops selling erotic material, some of it slanted toward homosexuals. Whereas 10 years ago complete nudity was prohibited in
magazines, nowadays beefcake — the masculine equivalent of cheesecake —  40
can show anything with the exception of sexual acts, evidence or intent
thereof. (No comparable magazines exist for lesbians because women,
say pornographers, are not aroused by nude pictures.)

A clothing store, founded three years ago, specializes in gay apparel
as well as more conventional attire. It does not carry leather-and-chain
sado-masochistic clothing popular on the West Coast and also worn by

some Washington homosexuals.

Buttons and bumper stickers with "Gay is Good" have been circulated since last summer. And the steam bath, which a homosexual reporter described in the *Los Angeles Advocate* as "sex on the assembly line," has also made its appearance here within this period.

These innovations, which affect only a minute percentage of the population, do not, per se, constitute a homosexual revolution. Rather, they should be regarded in the light of the total social upheaval currently taking place in this country.

What is more important than the changes themselves is the attitude 10 toward them, both on the part of homosexuals and the world at large. Therein lies the revolution, of which the new militancy and openness are merely the methods.

# Haynes Johnson
## Kent's Fifth Victim

When Mary Vecchio came home from Kent State last spring in her flowered miniskirt and sandals held together by tape, she broke down and cried. "I'm so glad to be home," she said, as she embraced her father. It was "the most wonderful thing."

The scene of that tearful airport reunion—Mary, the gangling big-eyed girl with the long dark hair, angular face, and high cheek bones, surrounded by her emotional family, brothers, sisters, mother, father—was recorded by an army of newspaper photographers and television cameramen. The happy ending to an American tragedy.

Mary Vecchio, the "mystery coed" whose look of horror as she knelt 10 over a slain student had been captured by a photographer to become a symbol of national protest, was home.

She wasn't even a coed, it turned out. Just a 14-year-old who had run away from home and turned up, by chance, on the campus the day the Guardsmen fired into the crowd of students, killing four of them. Her parents had seen that picture and identified her. Now, at the airport, it was over.

A week ago last Thursday, Mary Vecchio, now 15, was committed for a six-month period to a juvenile home south of Miami. She had run away again. The Kent State aftermath, her lawyer says, "has ruined her. You 20 can't put that kind of load on a 14-year-old girl and expect her to take it. And if you want to be sociological about it, the family unit for all practical purposes has been destroyed."

He was referring to the climate at home to which Mary returned: the parents who refused to let their children see Mary; the insults in the community; the attitude of the high-school principal who initially suspended

406

her ("The youngsters didn't want to have anything to do with her—and I was proud of them," he says); the policeman who, her parents and lawyer contend, harassed Mary, picking her up four times on charges ranging from loitering to sniffing transmission fluid (none of the charges stood up in court: Mary has never been convicted of a crime); the restrictions imposed by the youth curfew ordinance of Opa Locka coupled with the restrictions of her own parents; the exploiters who manufactured and sold T-shirts and 6-foot posters showing Mary kneeling over the dead student's body, all without the Vecchios' permission; the monthly proceedings before the juvenile judge because Mary had been placed on probation after she ran away; the transfer to a new school, where she encountered new problems because of her notoriety; the testimony she had to give before the Kent State grand jury—and the FBI—and the state's attorney; the charges by the governor of Florida, Claude Kirk, made over state-wide television, implying that Mary was part of a Communist plot; and the torrent of mail—obscene, abusive, vicious hate mail—that poured into the Vecchio household from throughout America.

Perhaps above all, it was the attitude of people that made Mary Vecchio a symbol of "American problems of wayward youth," student protests, violence, "anti-Americanism."

In a sense, she has become the fifth victim of Kent State.

The letters alone were enough to leave lasting scars. Mary's mother, Claire, a heavy-set woman with coal black hair and dark eyes, keeps them in a box in her bedroom.

"I still get shocked," she said, opening the box and taking out the letters, "because I don't believe in bad language myself."

"Look at that," she said, pulling out a newspaper clipping.

It showed the pictures of the four slain students, along with one of Mary. Her face had been X-ed out in red ink. Across the top was written: It's too bad you weren't shot." Mrs. Vecchio shook her head and said: "Can you imagine her looking at that?"

Others, opened at random, read:

"We are wondering why you still worry about your daughter, being she slept with all those hippies that are all diseased. We have no doubt she'll wind up being one of the biggest whores and prostitutes."

"The pictures in all the magazines in this country and abroad of you receiving with welcome arms your daughter is really a *farce*. If you wanted to find her, you could have. There are ways."

"We believe she should be placed in a juvenile home where she would not cause any trouble on campuses across the country. . . "

"Some young people here know what she is—a dirty, foul, syphillitic whore.

"If she is ever seen in Ohio again she will be shot."

It was signed: "A taxpayer of Ohio."

"Keep your hoodlum daughter in Florida where she belongs. What you need is a good beating with a strap, beating until you bleed good red blood. Your parents should have left you where you were. You don't deserve to be associated with decent people."

"I am a veteran, I done my hitch. . . the soldiers hang your picture up and spit on it. See how you stand with the Army??? You should do the world a favor and kill yourself."

One from Pleasantville, N.Y., began "Dear Mary Ann" the way she was identified in the press, although her parents call her "Mary," and said:

"You hippie Communist bitch!

"Did you enjoy sleeping with all those Dope Fiends and Negroes when you were in Ohio? The deaths of the Kent State four are on the conscience    10
of yourself and other rabble rousers like you.

"Congratulations."

The Vecchios themselves received threatening letters. "Even I got letters saying they were going to get me for raising such a radical into the world," Mrs. Vecchio says. "There was one letter that said they were going to come here and abolish the whole family, like the Sharon Tate thing. The FBI still has that one."

Mary, she says, has now changed completely.

"She was the happiest child, the friendliest person you ever saw," her mother said. "When she smiled she made you happy. They said in her    20
school it was like the sunshine coming in. And that laugh! When you heard that laugh, you had to laugh.

"But Mary is so different now. She is so nervous. She can't even talk about it. And they're still calling her a Communist. Even her relatives say they're ashamed of her."

Others who know Mary well see different aspects of change. Her father, Frank, a 49-year-old maintenance man for the Dade County Port Authority, says: "Mary don't care for nothing in the world. Nothing. Years ago, she had love for life, love for her family, love for the baby, but now she doesn't have anything to live for. She's not the same girl. Nowhere the same."    30

Phillip Vitello, a Coral Gables lawyer who represents Mary, describes Mary in different terms. "The story's even worse than it seems," he says. "It's affected her mind to a tremendous degree. She's become more withdrawn. She refuses to relate to anybody. Now, she won't even talk to me or to her parents or to the judge."

None of this is to suggest that Mary Vecchio was a problem-free child, a carefree Shirley Temple of the 1970s who merely liked to wander. Like many other youths, Mary was confused and rebelling. She thought her parents too strict, school too confining, the community unappealing. The Vecchios had moved here from Worcester, Mass., nearly 25 years ago,    40
a young couple of Italian extraction who proceeded to have six children in 24 years: a girl, 22; a boy, 21; a girl, 18; a boy, 17. Mary is the fifth child. She has a baby sister, aged 3.

The Vecchios believed in exercising a firm hand. They were not permis - sive parents.

Indeed, while the Vecchios give the impression to a stranger that theirs was a normal family atmosphere, the record paints a different portrait. The older children had a history of running away, also, and there have been difficulties involving their parents. Vecchio, who has a reputation for hot-headedness, had been jailed in the past for breach of the peace. His wife several times has sworn out warrants "for disputes between themselves," one policeman said.

Home for Mary apparently was hardly a happy place.

In school Mary was not a gifted student. She liked sports. The only thing her parents can recall her wanting to become was an athletics instructor. Besides, she was extremely tall for her age and sex. Mary stands 6 feet. No wonder she was mistaken for a coed, instead of a 14-year-old junior high student.

Mrs. Vecchio thinks her daughter's problems began to take serious form during the antiwar Vietnam moratorium demonstrations in the fall of 1969. Mary became involved, but it wasn't just the war. She chafed at various restrictions—at home and in school. On Valentine's Day, 1970, Mary ran away. She hitch-hiked up the Sunshine State Parkway, and made it as far as Atlanta.

There, she met a group of young people. Her parents call them "hippies," but the word has lost its original meaning. After staying in Atlanta for some time, a group said they were going up to Kent State University, in Ohio. Mary went along. She was there that day when the Guardsmen fired from the hill into the students standing along the parking lot. As Mary was to discover, the Kent State tragedy did not end with the sudden volley fired from "blanket hill." It followed her all the way home.

Opa Locka, north of Miami, may not be a typical town—what is?—but it has never been one of those American datelines of trouble. Its only claim to national note came 10 years ago. The CIA used to transport Cuban refugees from there to Guatemala in preparation for the Bay of Pigs invasion.

The town itself is small and sleepy, a place of modest homes inhabited by hard-working citizens. The only thing that seems unusual about it are the names of the streets: Opa Locka's city planners gave them exotic names out of the Arabian nights. The Vecchios live on Salih Drive next to Caliph Street. Alibaba Avenue is a main thoroughfare two blocks away.

Frank Vecchio calls himself one of Opa Locka's pioneers. "This was the most wonderful town you could live in," he says. But as for now: "I don't even want to walk in this town."

Vecchio is bitter. "No matter where Mary went, in a restaurant or anywhere, she was harassed," he says. "She was told she was not welcome."

One night after Mary came home, he and Mary and the Vecchios' youngest child, the 3-year-old girl, went to the Chicken and Sub Restaurant in Opa Locka. As soon as they walked in, the manager recognized them.

"He said that she wasn't a decent person, nothing but a Communist," Vecchio says. "He said, 'you and your whole family are Communists, and I don't have to serve any Communists.'"

An argument developed. The manager called the police. Vecchio was arrested on charges of public profanity (he denies cursing) and paid $61 in court costs when the case came up.

Vecchio also claims that Mary was harassed by the police and by the school principal. After Opa Locka police picked up Mary four times, the Vecchios filed a million-dollar suit against the department, charging Mary's civil rights were being violated. That suit is still pending.                    10

Police Chief Herb Chastian will not talk about the Vecchio case. "Truthfully, I'd rather not make any statement about it," he says. "I'd rather not discuss the case."

Mary's former principal, at Westview Junior High, denies that he treated the girl any differently from any other student. He describes what happened this way:

"When she came back, the youngsters did not accept her. She was a truant. She was a disciplinary problem. She used profanity. She was a disturbing influence within the classroom, so we suspended her. She tried to get attention in the manner of her conduct.                    20

"I disciplined her every time she did something wrong. I tried to make her a better girl. She kept misbehaving and I punished her—and I would do it again. The influence she could have on the other students wasn't good. All I can judge her on is the conduct that she exhibited in the classroom."

He also said:

"To be frank with you, I never wanted her back in my school, but I had to take her."

While the reasons are unclear, there is no question that parents told their children to stay away from Mary Vecchio after she came back to     30 Opa Locka. "The word was out that Mary was a bad influence," her father says.

Mary's final act of rebellion a few weeks ago grew out of an inconsequential incident. She wanted to go to a rock concert on a Saturday night, and her parents said no. Mary went anyway. She did not return home.

"We waited Sunday and we waited Monday. So Tuesday we reported her missing to the police," her mother says. A few days later Mary was picked up in a girl friend's apartment. She was taken before a juvenile court proceeding because she had violated her probation.                    40

"When Judge Weaver asked her why she had run away, Mary simply said, 'to go to a rock concert,'" Philip Vitello, her lawyer, says.

Mary was committed to the Kendall Youth Home, south of Miami. There, the judge, her parents, and her lawyer hope, she will receive counseling and training.

"I would define Mary as confused," the lawyer says. "She's in a situation where she's not cognizant of the consequences of what she's done. She's lost the ability to relate to normal things.

"One of the most tragic aspects of it is the attitude so many people have about communism."

Vitello says he himself received threatening letters because he represented her. "People would say if I had any sense I wouldn't represent a Communist."

As for Mary, he said, she was caught between two extremes: those who reviled her because of what they thought she represented, and those who made her a hero of the revolution. Her mail broke down that way. The lawyer added:

"It was interesting to me how many of those letters were of the religious nut variety. I got things like that myself. Frankly, it frightened me, and I'm not a 14-year-old girl."

He recalled the time Mary gave testimony before the Kent State grand jury in Miami. "She was asked what a Communist was, and she couldn't define it." Then he said:

"They kept asking her why she was there at Kent State and she said she didn't want America to be involved in a war, and they said, 'You're only 14 years old. What difference does it make to you?' and Mary said: 'If you'll explain to me why America has to be involved in a war I'll explain to you what happened at Kent State.'"

Looking back on the experience, her lawyer says, "I'll tell you. This shook my faith in an awful lot of things."

But there he was speaking only for himself. Mary Vecchio's problem is more extreme.

"Only time will tell," he says, "if the next 10 years can undo the last 10 months."

FRANKLIN   *The Two Worlds of Race: A Historical View*  □  RASPBERRY   *Do Blacks Now Seek Separatism*   □   U.S. SUPREME COURT   *Brown v. Board of Education, 1954*  □   ROOSEVELT   *Assimilation*  □   JOHNSON   *The Repeal of Racism*  □  PUCINSKI   *Ethnic Heritage Studies Act, 1971*  □   BATES   *America, the Beautiful*  □

# The American Ideal:
## documents, assessments

# Introduction

When we think of the words, "law" and "justice," we don't usually think of them as warring against each other. Instead we take it more or less for granted that they operate side by side. John Hope Franklin, in "The Two Worlds of Race," points out that often they do conflict. Some laws were passed for no other reason than to keep familiar injustices going. There were various excuses: People were more "comfortable" this way. Some of us soothed ourselves with the thought that this was done in just a few Southern states. But Franklin, a black historian, tells us that in 1913 the federal government segregated its *own* restrooms, offices, and eating places. And the Ku Klux Klan didn't terrorize just Southern blacks. It spread into the North, striking out at Jews and Catholics along the way.

More and more, these abuses, some legal and others not, have been called to our attention. In light of them the Declaration of Independence seems ironic. Many minority groups could use the same arguments against America that its founding fathers used to announce its birth! The Declaration of Independence has, in fact, been effectively parodied by blacks, Indians, and others. Very few words need to be changed to make the point.

The writings in this section are tied together by

the admission that we've been wrong. You may find Theodore Roosevelt's views a bit outdated—you may find, too, that his ideas run counter to other articles in this book. For example, the "tangle of squabbling nationalities," which Roosevelt fears, would impress the author of "The Ethnic Bag" as a very healthy awareness of one's roots. What's important here is that Roosevelt is writing to counteract a wave of prejudice against Americans who had recently come from other shores. In the same vein, Lyndon Johnson, in "The Repeal of Racism," makes no bones about saying that America's immigration policy was unfair. Nor does the 1954 Supreme Court decision attempt to hide our mistakes.

This book may seem to some a catalog of the sins of the past and present. We don't mean it to be just that. We want, instead, to speak out as the men in this section do, to admit our mistakes and try to mend our ways. No "Love it or Leave it" stickers, please. There's no leaving it. We *are* America: "America the Beautiful" and the ideal it expresses is neither fanciful nor too far away to be realized.

# John Hope Franklin
## The Two Worlds of Race:
## A Historical View

Measured by universal standards the history of the United States is indeed brief. But during the brief span of three and one-half centuries of colonial and national history Americans developed traditions and prejudices which created the two worlds of race in modern America. From the time that Africans were brought as indentured servants to the mainland of English America in 1619, the enormous task of rationalizing and justifying the forced labor of peoples on the basis of racial differences was begun; and even after legal slavery was ended, the notion of racial differences persisted as a basis for maintaining segregation and discrimination. At the same time, the effort to establish a more healthy basis for the   *10* new world social order was begun, thus launching the continuing battle between the two worlds of race, on the one hand, and the world of equality and complete human fellowship, on the other.

For a century before the American Revolution the status of Negroes in the English colonies had become fixed at a low point that distinguished them from all other persons who had been held in temporary bondage. By the middle of the eighteenth century, laws governing Negroes denied to them certain basic rights that were conceded to others. They were permitted no independence of thought, no opportunity to improve their minds or their talents or to worship freely, no right to marry and enjoy   *20* the conventional family relationships, no right to own or dispose of property, and no protection against miscarriages of justice or cruel and unreasonable punishments. They were outside the pale of the laws that protected ordinary humans. In most places they were to be governed, as the South Carolina code of 1712 expressed it, by special laws "as may restrain the disorders, rapines, and inhumanity to which they are naturally prone

417

and inclined. . . . " A separate world for them had been established by law and custom. Its dimensions and the conduct of its inhabitants were determined by those living in a quite different world.

By the time that colonists took up arms against their mother country in order to secure their independence, the world of Negro slavery had become deeply entrenched and the idea of Negro inferiority well established. But the dilemmas inherent in such a situation were a source of constant embarrassment. "It always appeared a most iniquitous scheme to me," Mrs. John Adams wrote her husband in 1774, "to fight ourselves for what we are daily robbing and plundering from those who have as good a right 10 to freedom as we have." There were others who shared her views, but they were unable to wield much influence. When the fighting began General George Washington issued an order to recruiting officers that they were not to enlist "any deserter from the ministerial army, nor any stroller, negro, or vagabond, or person suspected of being an enemy to the liberty of America nor any under eighteen years of age." In classifying Negroes with the dregs of society, traitors, and children, Washington made it clear that Negroes, slave or free, were not to enjoy the high privilege of fighting for political independence. He would change that order later, but only after it became clear that Negroes were enlisting with the "minis-   20 terial army" in droves in order to secure their own freedom. In changing his policy if not his views, Washington availed himself of the services of more than 5,000 Negroes who took up arms against England.

Many Americans besides Mrs. Adams were struck by the inconsistency of their stand during the War for Independence, and they were not averse to making moves to emancipate the slaves. Quakers and other religious groups organized antislavery societies, while numerous individuals manumitted their slaves. In the years following the close of the war most of the states of the East made provisions for the gradual emancipation of slaves. In the South, meanwhile, the anti-slavery societies were unable to effect   30 programs of state-wide emancipation. When the Southerners came to the Constitutional Convention in 1787 they succeeded in winning some representation on the basis of slavery, in securing federal support of the capture and rendition of fugitive slaves, and in preventing the closing of the slave trade before 1808.

Even where the sentiment-favoring emancipation was pronounced, it was seldom accompanied by a view that Negroes were the equals of whites and should become a part of one family of Americans. Jefferson, for example, was opposed to slavery, and if he could have had his way, he would have condemned it in the Declaration of Independence. It did   40 not follow, however, that he believed Negroes to be the equals of whites. He did not want to "degrade a whole race of men from the work in the scale of beings which their Creator may *perhaps* have given them. . . . I advance it therefore, as a suspicion only, that the blacks, whether originally a distinct race, or made distinct by time and circumstance, are inferior to the whites in the endowment both of body and mind." It is entirely possible that Jefferson's later association with the extraordinarily able Negro astronomer and mathematician, Benjamin Banneker, resulted in some modification of his views. After reading a copy of Banneker's almanac, Jefferson told him that it was "a document to which your whole race had a right for its justifications against the doubts which have been entertained of them."

In communities such as Philadelphia and New York, where the climate was more favorably disposed to the idea of Negro equality than in Jefferson's Virginia, few concessions were made, except by a limited number of Quakers and their associates. Indeed, the white citizens in the City of Brotherly Love contributed substantially to the perpetuation of two distinct worlds of race. In the 1870's, the white Methodists permitted Negroes to worship with them, provided the Negroes sat in a designated place in the balcony. On one occasion, when the Negro worshippers occupied the front rows of the balcony, from which they had been excluded, the officials pulled them from their knees during prayer and evicted them from the church. Thus, in the early days of the Republic and in the place where the Republic was founded, Negroes had a definite "place" in which they were expected at all times to remain. The white Methodists of New York had much the same attitude toward their Negro fellows. Soon, there were separate Negro churches in these and other communities. Baptists were very much the same. In 1809 thirteen Negro members of a white Baptist church in Philadelphia were dismissed, and they formed a church of their own. Thus, the earliest Negro religious institutions emerged as the result of the rejection by white communicants of their darker fellow worshippers. Soon there would be other institutions — schools, newspapers, benevolent societies — to serve those who lived in a world apart.

Those Americans who conceded the importance of education for Negroes tended to favor some particular type of education that would be in keeping with their lowly station in life. In 1794, for example, the American Convention of Abolition Societies recommended that Negroes be instructed in "those mechanic arts which will keep them most constantly employed and, of course, which will less subject them to idleness and debauchery, and thus prepare them for becoming good citizens of the United States." When Anthony Benezet, a dedicated Pennsylvania abolitionist, died in 1784 his will provided that on the death of his wife the proceeds of his estate should be used to assist in the establishment of a school for Negroes. In 1787 the school of which Benezet had dreamed was opened in Philadelphia, where the pupils studied reading, writing, arithmetic, plain accounts, and sewing.

Americans who were at all interested in the education of Negroes regarded it as both natural and normal that Negroes should receive their training in separate schools. As early as 1773 Newport, Rhode Island, had a colored school, maintained by a society of benevolent clergymen of the Anglican Church. In 1798 a separate private school for Negro children was established in Boston; and two decades later the city opened its first public primary school for the education of Negro children. Meanwhile, New York had established separate schools, the first one opening its doors in 1790. By 1814 there were several such institutions that were generally designated as the New York African Free Schools.

Thus, in the most liberal section of the country, the general view was that Negroes should be kept out of the main stream of American life. They were forced to establish and maintain their own religious institutions, which were frequently followed by the establishment of separate benevolent societies. Likewise, if Negroes were to receive any education, it should be special education provided in separate educational institutions. This principle prevailed in most places in the North throughout the period before the Civil War. In some Massachusetts towns, however, Negroes gained admission to schools that had been maintained for whites. But the School Committee of Boston refused to admit Negroes, arguing that the natural distinction of the races, which "no legislature, no social customs, can efface renders a promiscuous intermingling in the public schools disadvantageous both to them and to the whites." Separate schools remained in Boston until the Massachusetts legislature in 1855 enacted a law providing that in determining the qualifications of students to be admitted to any public school no distinction should be made on account of the race, color, or religious opinion of the applicant.

Meanwhile, in the Southern states, where the vast majority of the Negroes lived, there were no concessions suggesting equal treatment, even among the most liberal elements. One group that would doubtless have regarded itself as liberal on the race question advocated the deportation of Negroes to Africa, especially those who had become free. Since free Negroes "neither enjoyed the immunities of freemen, nor were they subject to the incapacities of slaves," their condition and "unconquerable prejudices" prevented amalgamation with whites, one colonization leader argued. There was, therefore, a "peculiar moral fitness" in restoring them to "the land of their fathers." Men like Henry Clay, Judge Bushrod Washington, and President James Monroe thought that separation—expatriation—was the best thing for Negroes who were or who would become free.

While the colonization scheme was primarily for Negroes who were already free, it won, for a time, a considerable number of sincere enemies of slavery. From the beginning Negroes were bitterly opposed to it, and only infrequently did certain Negro leaders, such as Dr. Martin Delany and the Reverend Henry M. Turner, support the idea. Colonization, however, retained considerable support in the most responsible quarters. As late as the Civil War, President Lincoln urged Congress to adopt a plan to colonize Negroes, as the only workable solution to the race problem in the United States. Whether the advocates of colonization wanted merely to prevent the contamination of slavery by free Negroes or whether they actually regarded it as the just and honorable thing to do, they represented an important element in the population that rejected the idea of the Negro's assimilation into the main stream of American life.

Thus, within fifty years after the Declaration of Independence was written, the institution of slavery, which received only a temporary reversal during the Revolutionary era, contributed greatly to the emergence of the two worlds of race in the United States. The natural rights philosophy appeared to have little effect on those who became committed, more and more, to seeking a rationalization for slavery. The search was apparently so successful that even in areas where slavery was declining, the support for maintaining two worlds of race was strong. Since the Negro church and school emerged in Northern communities where slavery was dying, it may be said that the free society believed almost as strongly in racial separation as it did in racial freedom.

The generation preceding the outbreak of the Civil War witnessed the development of a set of defenses of slavery that became the basis for much of the racist doctrine to which some Americans have subscribed from then to the present time. The idea of the inferiority of the Negro enjoyed wide acceptance among Southerners of all classes and among many Northerners. It was an important ingredient in the theory of society promulgated by Southern thinkers and leaders. It was organized into a body of systematic thought by the scientists and social scientists of the South, out of which emerged a doctrine of racial superiority that justified any kind of control over the slave. In 1826 Dr. Thomas Cooper said that he had not the slightest doubt that Negroes were an "inferior variety of the human species; and not capable of the same improvement as the whites." Dr. S. C. Cartwright of the University of Louisiana insisted that the capacities of the Negro adult for learning were equal to those of a white infant; and the Negro could properly perform certain physiological functions only when under the control of white men. Because of the Negro's inferiority, liberty and republican institutions were not only unsuited to his temperament, but actually inimical to his well-being and happiness.

Like racists in other parts of the world, Southerners sought support for their ideology by developing a common bond with the less privileged. The obvious basis was race; and outside the white race there was to be found no favor from God, no honor or respect from man. By the time that Europeans were reading Gobineau's *Inequality of Races,* Southerners were reading Cartwright's *Slavery in the Light of Ethnology.* In admitting all whites into the pseudo-nobility of race, Cartwright won their enthusiastic support in the struggle to preserve the integrity and honor of *the* race. Professor Thomas R. Dew of the College of William and Mary comforted the lower-class whites by indicating that they could identify with the most privileged and affluent of the community. In the South, he said, "no white man feels such inferiority of rank as to be unworthy of association with those around him. Color alone is here the badge of distinction, the true mark of aristocracy, and all who are white are equal in spite of the variety of occupation."

Many Northerners were not without their own racist views and policies in the turbulent decades before the Civil War. Some, as Professor Louis Filler has observed, displayed a hatred of Negroes that gave them a sense of superiority and an outlet for their frustrations. Others cared nothing one way or the other about Negroes and demanded only that they be kept separate. Even some of the abolitionists themselves were ambivalent on the question of Negro equality. More than one antislavery society was agitated by the suggestion that Negroes be invited to join. Some members thought it reasonable for them to attend, but not to be put on an "equality with ourselves." The New York abolitionist, Lewis Tappan, admitted "that when the subject of acting out our profound principles in treating     10 men irrespective of color is discussed heat is always produced."

In the final years before the beginning of the Civil War, the view that the Negro was different, even inferior, was widely held in the United States. Leaders in both major parties subscribed to the view, while the more extreme racists deplored any suggestion that the Negro could ever prosper as a free man. At Peoria, Illinois, in October 1854, Abraham Lincoln asked what stand the opponents of slavery should take regarding Negroes. "Free them, and make them politically and socially, our equals? My own feelings will not admit of this; and if mine would, we well know that those of the great mass of white people will not. Whether this feeling     20 accords with justice and sound judgment, is not the sole question, if indeed, it is any part of it. A universal feeling, whether well or ill founded, cannot be safely disregarded. We cannot, then, make them equals."

The Lincoln statement was forthright, and it doubtless represented the views of most Americans in the 1850's. Most of those who heard him or read his speech were of the same opinion as he. In later years, the Peoria pronouncement would be used by those who sought to detract from Lincoln's reputation as a champion of the rights of the Negro. In 1964, the White Citizens' Councils reprinted portions of the speech in large advertisements in the daily press and insisted that Lincoln shared their     30 views on the desirability of maintaining two distinct worlds of race.

Lincoln could not have overcome the nation's strong predisposition toward racial separation if he had tried. And he did not try very hard. When he called for the enlistment of Negro troops, after issuing the Emancipation Proclamation, he was content not only to set Negroes apart in a unit called "U. S. Colored Troops," but also to have Negro privates receive $10 per month including clothing, while whites of the same rank received $13 per month plus clothing. Only the stubborn refusal of many Negro troops to accept discriminatory pay finally forced Congress to equalize compensation for white and Negro soldiers. The fight for union that     40 became also a fight for freedom never became a fight for equality or for the creation of one racial world.

The Lincoln and Johnson plans for settling the problems of peace and freedom never seriously touched on the concomitant problem of equality. To be sure, in 1864 President Lincoln privately raised with the governor of Louisiana the question of the franchise for a limited number of

Negroes, but when the governor ignored the question the President let the matter drop. Johnson raised a similar question in 1866, but he admitted that it was merely to frustrate the design of radical reformers who sought a wider franchise for Negroes. During the two years following Appomattox Southern leaders gave not the slightest consideration to permitting any Negroes, regardless of their service to the Union or their education or their property, to share in the political life of their communities. Not only did every Southern state refuse to permit Negroes to vote, but they also refused to provide Negroes with any of the educational opportunities that they were providing for the whites.          10

The early practice of political disfranchisement and of exclusion from public educational facilities helped to determine subsequent policies that the South adopted regarding Negroes. While a few leaders raised their voices against these policies and practices, it was Negroes themselves who made the most eloquent attacks on such discriminations. As early as May 1865, a group of North Carolina Negroes told President Johnson that some of them had been soldiers and were doing everything possible to learn how to discharge the higher duties of citizenship. "It seems to us that men who are willing on the field of battle to carry the muskets of the Republic, in the days of peace ought to be permitted to carry the bal-          20
lots; and certainly we cannot understand the justice of denying the elective franchise to men who have been fighting *for* the country, while it is freely given to men who have just returned from *four* years fighting against it." Such pleas fell on deaf ears, however; and it was not until 1867, when Congress was sufficiently outraged by the inhuman black codes, widespread discriminations in the South, and unspeakable forms of violence against Negroes, that new federal legislation sought to correct the evils of the first period of Reconstruction.

The period that we know as Radical Reconstruction had no significant or permanent effect on the status of the Negro in American life. For a          30
period of time, varying from one year to fifteen or twenty years, some Negroes enjoyed the privileges of voting. They gained political ascendancy in a very few communities only temporarily, and they never even began to achieve the status of a ruling class. They made no meaningful steps toward economic independence or even stability; and in no time at all, because of the pressures of the local community and the neglect of the federal government, they were brought under the complete economic subservience of the old ruling class. Organizations such as the Ku Klux Klan were committed to violent action to keep Negroes "in their place" and, having gained respectability through sponsorship by Confederate          40
generals and the like, they proceeded to wreak havoc in the name of white supremacy and protection of white womanhood.

Meanwhile, various forms of segregation and discrimination, developed in the years before the Civil War in order to degrade the half million free Negroes in the United States, were now applied to the four million Negroes who had become free in 1865. Already the churches and the military were completely segregated. For the most part the schools, even in the North, were separate. In the South segregated schools persisted, even in the places where the radicals made a halfhearted attempt to desegregate them. In 1875 Congress enacted a Civil Rights Act to guarantee the enjoyment of equal rights in carriers and all places of public accommodation and amusement. Even before it became law Northern philanthropists succeeded in forcing the deletion of the provision calling for desegregated schools. Soon, because of the massive resistance in the North as well as in the South and the indifferent manner in which the federal government enforced the law, it soon became a dead letter everywhere. When it was declared unconstitutional by the Supreme Court in 1883, there was universal rejoicing, except among the Negroes, one of whom declared that they had been "baptized in ice water."

Neither the Civil War nor the era of Reconstruction made any significant step toward the permanent elimination of racial barriers. The radicals of the post-Civil War years came no closer to the creation of one racial world than the patriots of the Revolutionary years. When Negroes were, for the first time, enrolled in the standing army of the United States, they were placed in separate Negro units. Most of the liberals of the Reconstruction era called for and worked for separate schools for Negroes. Nowhere was there any extensive effort to involve Negroes in the churches and other social institutions of the dominant group. Whatever remained of the old abolitionist fervor, which can hardly be described as unequivocal on the question of true racial equality, was rapidly disappearing. In its place were the sentiments of the business men who wanted peace at any price. Those having common railroad interests or crop-marketing interests or investment interests could and did extend their hands across sectional lines and joined in the task of working together for the common good. In such an atmosphere the practice was to accept the realities of two separate worlds of race. Some even subscribed to the view that there were significant economic advantages in maintaining the two worlds of race.

The post-Reconstruction years witnessed a steady deterioration in the status of Negro Americans. These were the years that Professor Rayford Logan has called the "nadir" of the Negro in American life and thought. They were the years when Americans, weary of the crusade that had, for the most part, ended with the outbreak of the Civil War, displayed almost no interest in helping the Negro to achieve equality. The social Darwinists decried the very notion of equality for Negroes, arguing that the lowly place they occupied was natural and normal. The leading literary journals vied with each other in describing Negroes as lazy, idle, improvident, immoral, and criminal. Thomas Dixon's novels, *The Klansman* and *The Leopard's Spots,* and D. W. Griffith's motion picture, "The Birth of A Nation," helped to give Americans a view of the Negro's role in American history that "proved" that he was unfit for citizenship, to say nothing of equality. The dictum of William Graham Sumner and his followers that "stateways cannot change folkways" convinced many Americans that legislating equality and creating one great society where race was irrelevant was out of the question.

But many Americans believed that they *could* legislate inequality; and they proceeded to do precisely that. Beginning in 1890, one Southern state after another revised the suffrage provisions of its constitution in a manner that made it virtually impossible for Negroes to qualify to vote. The new literacy and "understanding" provisions permitted local registrars to disqualify Negroes while permitting white citizens to qualify. Several states, including Louisiana, North Carolina, and Oklahoma, inserted "grandfather clauses" in their constitutions in order to permit 10 persons, who could not otherwise qualify, to vote if their fathers or grandfathers could vote in 1866. (This was such a flagrant discrimination against Negroes, whose ancestors could not vote in 1866, that the United States Supreme Court in 1915 declared the "grandfather clause" unconstitutional.) Then came the Democratic white primary in 1900 that made it impossible for Negroes to participate in local elections in the South, where, by this time, only the Democratic party had any appreciable strength. (After more than a generation of assaults on it, the white primary was finally declared unconstitutional in 1944.)

Inequality was legislated in still another way. Beginning in the 1880's, 20 many states, especially but not exclusively in the South, enacted statutes designed to separate the races. After the Civil Rights Act was declared unconstitutional in 1883 state legislatures were emboldened to enact numerous segregation statutes. When the United States Supreme Court, in the case of Plessy *v.* Ferguson, set forth the "separate but equal" doctrine in 1896, the decision provided a new stimulus for laws to separate the races and, of course, to discriminate against Negroes. In time, Negroes and whites were separated in the use of schools, churches, cemeteries, drinking fountains, restaurants, and all places of public accommodation and amusement. One state enacted a law providing for the separate 30 warehousing of books used by white and Negro children. Another required the telephone company to provide separate telephone booths for white and Negro customers. In most communities housing was racially separated by law or practice.

Where there was no legislation requiring segregation, local practices filled the void. Contradictions and inconsistencies seemed not to disturb those who sought to maintain racial distinctions at all costs. It mattered not that one drive-in snack bar served Negroes only on the inside, while its competitor across the street served Negroes only on the outside. Both were committed to making racial distinctions; and in communities 40 where practices and mores had the force of law, the distinction was everything. Such practices were greatly strengthened when, in 1913, the federal government adopted policies that segregated the races in its offices as well as in its eating and rest-room facilities.

By the time of World War I, Negroes and whites in the South and in parts of the North lived in separate worlds, and the apparatus for keeping the worlds separate was elaborate and complex. Negroes were segregated by law in the public schools of the Southern states, while those in the Northern ghettos were sent to predominantly Negro schools, except where their numbers were insufficient. Scores of Negro newspapers sprang up to provide news of Negroes that the white press consistently ignored. Negroes were as unwanted in the white churches as they had been in the late eighteenth century; and Negro churches of virtually every denomination were the answer for a people who had accepted the white man's religion even as the white man rejected his religious fellowship.

Taking note of the fact that they had been omitted from any serious    10
consideration by the white historians, Negroes began in earnest to write the history of their own experiences as Americans. There had been Negro historians before the Civil War, but none of them had challenged the white historians' efforts to relegate Negroes to a separate, degraded world. In 1882, however, George Washington Williams published his *History of the Negro Race in America* in order to "give the world more correct ideas about the colored people." He wrote, he said, not "as a partisan apologist, but from a love for the truth of history." Soon there were other historical works by Negroes describing their progress and their contributions and arguing that they deserved to be received into the full fellowship of Ameri-    20
can citizens.

It was in these post-Reconstruction years that some of the most vigorous efforts were made to destroy the two worlds of race. The desperate pleas of Negro historians were merely the more articulate attempts of Negroes to gain complete acceptance in American life. Scores of Negro organizations joined in the struggle to gain protection and recognition of their rights and to eliminate the more sordid practices that characterized the treatment of the Negro world by the white world. Unhappily, the small number of whites who were committed to racial equality dwindled in the post-Reconstruction years, while government at every level showed no interest    30
in eliminating racial separatism. It seemed that Negro voices were indeed crying in the wilderness, but they carried on their attempts to be heard. In 1890 Negroes from twenty-one states and the District of Columbia met in Chicago and organized the Afro-American League of the United States. They called for more equitable distribution of school funds, fair and impartial trial for accused Negroes, resistance "by all legal and reasonable means" to mob and lynch law, and enjoyment of the franchise by all qualified voters. When a group of young Negro intellectuals, led by W. E. B. Du Bois, met at Niagara Falls, Ontario, in 1905, they made a similar call as they launched their Niagara Movement.    40

However eloquent their pleas, Negroes alone could make no successful assault on the two worlds of race. They needed help—a great deal of help. It was the bloody race riots in the early years of the twentieth century that shocked civic minded and socially conscious whites into answering the Negro's pleas for support. Some whites began to take the view that the existence of two societies whose distinction was based solely on race was inimical to the best interests of the entire nation. Soon, they were taking the initiative and in 1909 organized the National Association for the Advancement of Colored People. They assisted the following year in establishing the National Urban League. White attorneys began to stand with Negroes before the United States Supreme Court to challenge the "grandfather clause," local segregation ordinances, and flagrant miscarriages of justice in which Negroes were the victims. The patterns of attack developed during these years were to become invaluable later. Legal action was soon supplemented by picketing, demonstrating, and boycotting, with telling effect particularly in selected Northern communities.                                10

The two world wars had a profound effect on the status of Negroes in the United States and did much to mount the attack on the two worlds of race. The decade of World War I witnessed a very significant migration of Negroes. They went in large numbers—perhaps a half million—from the rural areas of the South to the towns and cities of the South and North. They were especially attracted to the industrial centers of the North. By the thousands they poured into Pittsburgh, Cleveland, and Chicago. Although many were unable to secure employment, others were successful and achieved a standard of living they could not have imagined only a few years earlier. Northern communities were not altogether friendly and      20 hospitable to the newcomers, but the opportunities for education and the enjoyment of political self-respect were the greatest they had ever seen. Many of them felt that they were entirely justified in their renewed hope that the war would bring about a complete merger of the two worlds of race.

Those who held such high hopes, however, were naive in the extreme. Already the Ku Klux Klan was being revived—this time in the North as well as in the South. Its leaders were determined to develop a broad program to unite "native-born white Christians for concerted action in the preservation of American institutions and the supremacy of the white race." By the time the war was over, the Klan was in a position to make      30 capital of the racial animosities that had developed during the conflict itself. Racial conflicts had broken out in many places during the war; and before the conference at Versailles was over race riots in the United States had brought about what can accurately be described as the "long, hot summer" of 1919.

If anything, the military operations which aimed to save the world for democracy merely fixed more permanently the racial separation in the United States. Negro soldiers not only consituted entirely separate fighting units in the United States Army, but, once overseas, were assigned to fighting units with the French Army. Negroes who sought service with the      40 United States Marines or the Air Force were rejected, while the Navy relegated them to menial duties. The reaction of many Negroes was bitter, but most of the leaders, including Du Bois, counseled patience and loyalty. They continued to hope that their show of patriotism would win for them a secure place of acceptance as Americans.

Few Negro Americans could have anticipated the wholesale rejection they experienced at the conclusion of World War I. Returning Negro soldiers were lynched by hanging and burning, even while still in their military uniforms. The Klan warned Negroes that they must respect the rights of the white race "in whose country they are permitted to reside." Racial conflicts swept the country, and neither federal nor state governments seemed interested in effective intervention. The worlds of race were growing further apart in the postwar decade. Nothing indicated this more clearly than the growth of the Universal Negro Improvement Association, led by Marcus Garvey. From a mere handful of members at the end of the war, the Garvey movement rapidly became the largest secular Negro group ever organized in the United States. Although few Negroes were interested in settling in Africa—the expressed aim of Garvey—they joined the movement by the hundreds of thousands to indicate their resentment of the racial duality that seemed to them to be the central feature of the American social order.

More realistic and hardheaded were the Negroes who were more determined than ever to engage in the most desperate fight of their lives to destroy racism in the United States. As the editor of the *Crisis* said in 1919, "We return from fighting. We return fighting. Make way for Democracy! We saved it in France, and by the Great Jehovah, we will save it in the U.S.A., or know of the reason why." This was the spirit of what Alain Locke called "The New Negro." He fought the Democratic white primary, made war on the whites who consigned him to the ghetto, attacked racial discrimination in employment, and pressed for legislation to protect his rights. If he was seldom successful during the postwar decade and the depression, he made it quite clear that he was unalterably opposed to the un-American character of the two worlds of race.

Hope for a new assault on racism was kindled by some of the New Deal policies of Franklin D. Roosevelt. As members of the economically disadvantaged group, Negroes benefited from relief and recovery legislation. Most of it, however, recognized the existence of the two worlds of race and accommodated itself to it. Frequently bread lines and soup kitchens were separated on the basis of race. There was segregation in the employment services, while many new agencies recognized and bowed to Jim Crow. Whenever agencies, such as the Farm Security Administration, fought segregation and sought to deal with people on the basis of their needs rather than race they came under the withering fire of the racist critics and seldom escaped alive. Winds of change, however slight, were discernible, and nowhere was this in greater evidence than in the new labor unions. Groups like the Congress of Industrial Organizations, encouraged by the support of the Wagner Labor Relations Act, began to look at manpower resources as a whole and to attack the old racial policies that viewed labor in terms of race.

As World War II approached, Negroes schooled in the experiences of the nineteen-twenties and thirties were unwilling to see the fight against Nazism carried on in the context of an American racist ideology. Some white Americans were likewise uncomfortable in the role of freeing Europe of a racism which still permeated the United States; but it was the Negroes who dramatized American inconsistency by demanding an end to discrimination in employment in defense industries. By threatening to march on Washington in 1941 they forced the President to issue an order forbidding such discrimination. The opposition was loud and strong. Some state governors denounced the order, and some manufacturers skillfully evaded it. But it was a significant step toward the elimination of the two worlds.

During World War II the assault on racism continued. Negroes, more  10 than a million of whom were enlisted in the armed services, bitterly fought discrimination and segregation. The armed services were, for the most part, two quite distinct racial worlds. Some Negro units had white officers, and much of the officer training was desegregated. But it was not until the final months of the war that a deliberate experiment was undertaken to involve Negro and white enlisted men in the same fighting unit. With the success of the experiment and with the warm glow of victory over Nazism as a backdrop, there was greater inclination to recognize the absurdity of maintaining a racially separate military force to protect the freedoms of the country.                                                                                    20

During the war there began the greatest migration in the history of Negro Americans. Hundreds of thousands left the South for the industrial centers of the North and West. In those places they met hostility, but they also secured employment in aviation plants, automobile factories, steel mills, and numerous other industries. Their difficulties persisted as they faced problems of housing and adjustment. But they continued to move out of the South in such large numbers that by 1965 one third of the twenty million Negroes in the United States lived in twelve metropolitan centers of the North and West. The ramifications of such large-scale migration were numerous. The concentration of Negroes in communities  30 where they suffered no political disabilities placed in their hands an enormous amount of political power. Consequently some of them went to the legislatures, to Congress, and to positions on the judiciary. In turn, this won for them political respect as well as legislation that greatly strengthened their position as citizens.

Following World War II there was a marked acceleration in the war against the two worlds of race in the United States. In 1944 the Supreme Court ruled against segregation in interstate transportation, and three years later it wrote the final chapter in the war against the Democratic white primary. In 1947 the President's Committee on Civil Rights called  40 for the "elimination of segregation, based on race, color, creed, or national origin, from American life." In the following year President Truman asked Congress to establish a permanent Fair Employment Practices Commission. At the same time he took steps to eliminate segregation in the armed services. These moves on the part of the judicial and executive branches of the federal government by no means destroyed the two worlds of race, but they created a more healthy climate in which the government and others could launch an attack on racial separatism.

The attack was greatly strengthened by the new position of world leadership that the United States assumed at the close of the war. Critics of the United States were quick to point to the inconsistencies of an American position that spoke against racism abroad and countenanced it at home. New nations, brown and black, seemed reluctant to follow the lead of a country that adhered to its policy of maintaining two worlds of race—the one identified with the old colonial ruling powers and the other with the colonies now emerging as independent nations. Responsible      10
leaders in the United States saw the weakness of their position, and some of them made new moves to repair it.

Civic and religious groups, some labor organizations, and many individuals from the white community began to join in the effort to destroy segregation and discrimination in American life. There was no danger, after World War II, that Negroes would ever again stand alone in their fight. The older interracial organizations continued, but they were joined by new ones. In addition to the numerous groups that included racial equality in their over-all programs, there were others that made the creation of one racial world their principle objective. Among them were the Congress      20
of Racial Equality, the Southern Christian Leadership Conference, and the Student Non-Violent Coordinating Committee. Those in existence in the 1950's supported the court action that brought about the decision against segregated schools. The more recent ones have taken the lead in pressing for new legislation and in developing new techniques to be used in the war on segregation.

The most powerful direct force in the maintenance of the two worlds of race has been the state and its political subdivisions. In states and communities where racial segregation and discrimination are basic to the way of life, the elected officials invariably pledge themselves to the      30
perpetuation of the duality. Indeed, candidates frequently vie with one another in their effort to occupy the most extreme segregationist position possible on the race question. Appointed officials, including the constabulary and, not infrequently, the teachers and school administrators, become auxiliary guardians of the system of racial separation. In such communities Negroes occupy no policy-making positions, exercise no influence over the determination of policy, and are seldom even on the police force. State and local resources, including tax funds, are at the disposal of those who guard the system of segregation and discrimination; and such funds are used to enforce customs as well as laws and to disseminate information      40
in support of the system.

The white community itself acts as a guardian of the segregated system. Schooled in the specious arguments that assert the supremacy of the white race and fearful that a destruction of the system would be harmful to their own position, they not only "go along" with it but, in many cases, enthusiastically support it. Community sanctions are so powerful, moreover, that the independent citizen who would defy the established order would find himself not only ostracized but, worse, the target of economic and political reprisals.

Within the community many self-appointed guardians of white supremacy have emerged at various times. After the Civil War and after World War I it was the Ku Klux Klan, which has shown surprising strength in recent years. After the desegregation decision of the Supreme Court in 1954 it was the White Citizens' Council, which one Southern editor has called the "uptown Ku Klux Klan." From time to time since 1865, it has been the political demagogue, who has not only made capital by urging his election as a sure way to maintain the system but has also encouraged the less responsible elements of the community to take the law into their own hands.

Violence, so much a part of American history and particularly of Southern history, has been an important factor in maintaining the two worlds of race. Intimidation, terror, lynchings, and riots have, in succession, been the handmaiden of political entities whose officials have been unwilling or unable to put an end to it. Violence drove Negroes from the polls in the 1870's and has kept them away in droves since that time. Lynchings, the spectacular rope and faggot kind or the quiet kind of merely "doing away" with some insubordinate Negro, have served their special purpose in terrorizing whole communities of Negroes. Riots, confined to no section of the country, have demonstrated how explosive the racial situation can be in urban communities burdened with the strain of racial strife.

The heavy hand of history has been a powerful force in the maintenance of a segregated society and, conversely, in the resistance to change. Americans, especially Southerners whose devotion to the past is unmatched by that of any others, have summoned history to support their arguments that age-old practices and institutions cannot be changed overnight, that social practices cannot be changed by legislation. Southerners have argued that desegregation would break down long-established customs and bring instability to a social order that, if left alone, would have no serious racial or social disorders. After all, Southern whites "know" Negroes; and their knowledge has come from many generations of intimate association and observation, they insist.

White Southerners have also summoned history to support them in their resistance to federal legislation designed to secure the civil rights of Negroes. At every level—in local groups, state governements, and in Congress—white Southerners have asserted that federal civil rights legislation is an attempt to turn back the clock to the Reconstruction era, when federal intervention, they claim, imposed a harsh and unjust peace. To make effective their argument, they use such emotion-laden phrases as "military occupation," "Negro rule," and "black-out of honest government." Americans other than Southerners have been frightened by the Southerners' claim that civil rights for Negroes would cause a return to the "evils" of Reconstruction. Insecure in their own knowledge of history, they have accepted the erroneous assertions about the "disaster" of radical rule after the Civil War and the vengeful punishment meted out to the South by the Negro and his white allies. Regardless of the merits of these arguments that seem specious on the face of them—to say nothing of their historical inaccuracy—they have served as effective brakes on the drive to destroy the two worlds of race.

One suspects, however, that racial bigotry has become more expensive in recent years. It is not so easy now as it once was to make political capital out of the race problem, even in the deep South. Local citizens— farmers, laborers, manufacturers—have become a bit weary of the promises of the demagogue that he will preserve the integrity of the races if he is, at the same time, unable to persuade investors to build factories and bring capital to their communities. Some Southerners, dependent on tourists, are not certain that their vaunted racial pride is so dear, if it keeps visitors away and brings depression to their economy. The cities that see themselves bypassed by a prospective manufacturer because of their reputation in the field of race relations might have some sober second thoughts about the importance of maintaining their two worlds. In a word, the economics of segregation and discrimination is forcing, in some quarters, a reconsideration of the problem.

It must be added that the existence of the two worlds of race has created forces that cause some Negroes to seek its perpetuation. Some Negro institutions, the product of a dual society, have vested interests in the perpetuation of that society. And Negroes who fear the destruction of their own institutions by desegregation are encouraged by white racists to fight for their maintenance. Even where Negroes have a desire to main-tain their institutions because of their honest commitment to the merits of cultural pluralism, the desire becomes a strident struggle for survival in the context of racist forces that seek with a vengeance to destroy such institutions. The firing of a few hundred Negro school teachers by a zealous, racially-oriented school board forces some second thoughts on the part of the Negroes regarding the merits of desegregation.

The drive to destroy the two worlds of race has reached a new, dramatic, and somewhat explosive stage in recent years. The forces arrayed in behalf of maintaining these two worlds have been subjected to ceaseless and powerful attacks by the increasing numbers committed to the elimination of racism in American life. Through techniques of demonstrating, picketing, sitting in, and boycotting they have not only harrassed their foes but marshaled their forces. Realizing that another ingredient was needed, they have pressed for new and better laws and the active support of govern-ment. At the local and state levels they began to secure legislation in the 1940's to guarantee the civil rights of all, eliminate discrimination in employment, and achieve decent public and private housing for all.

While it is not possible to measure the influence of public opinion in the drive for equality, it can hardly be denied that over the past five or six years public opinion has shown a marked shift toward vigorous support of the civil rights movement. This can be seen in the manner in which the mass-circulation magazines as well as influential newspapers, even in the South, have stepped up their support of specific measures that have as their objective the elimination of at least the worst features of racism. The discussion of the problem of race over radio and television and the use of these media in reporting newsworthy and dramatic events in the world of race undoubtedly have had some impact. If such activities have not brought about the enactment of civil rights legislation, they have doubtless stimulated the public discussion that culminated in such legislation. 10

The models of city ordinances and state laws and the increased political influence of civil rights advocates stimulated new action on the federal level. Civil rights acts were passed in 1957, 1960, and 1964—after almost complete federal inactivity in this sphere for more than three quarters of a century. Strong leadership on the part of the executive and favorable judicial interpretations of old as well as new laws have made it clear that the war against the two worlds of race now enjoys the sanction of the law and its interpreters. In many respects this constitutes the most significant development in the struggle against racism in the present century.

The reading of American history over the past two centuries impresses 20 one with the fact that ambivalence on the crucial question of equality has persisted almost from the beginning. If the term "equal rights for all" has not always meant what it appeared to mean, the inconsistencies and the paradoxes have become increasingly apparent. This is not to say that the view that "equal rights for some" has disappeared or has even ceased to be a threat to the concept of real equality. It is to say, however, that the voices supporting inequality, while no less strident, have been significantly weakened by the very force of the numbers and elements now seeking to eliminate the two worlds of race.

# William Raspberry
## Do Blacks Now
## Seek Separatism?

White liberals must be very perplexed these days.

They used to be partners with blacks in the drive for racial integration. Now, it increasingly appears, they are the only integrationists left on the face of the earth.

What has happened? Don't black people believe in racial integration any more? Were the segregationists right all along when they said that people were happier with their own kind? Is black separatism the wave of the future?

The consternation stems from the fact that for the first time the integration/segregation issue is being debated in black terms, not white, 10 which means to a large degree that it is no longer considered a very important issue at all.

This is not to say that the relationship between the races doesn't matter to most black people. It is to say that an awful lot of black folk — militant, moderate and otherwise — are coming to realize just what many white people mean by integration, and they don't like it.

The white person who professes to favor integration as the means for solving the country's racial dilemma almost certainly means the absorption of black people into white institutions.

What this means is that formerly white institutions (whether schools, 20 churches or neighborhoods) remain essentially white while the formerly black institutions simply disappear.

Suppose physicians or dentists or lawyers decide it silly to maintain separate professional associations, one predominantly white, the other predominantly black. Which group do you expect will survive the merger?

The whole business appears to be based on the assumption that there is something basically wrong with being black—an assumption which too many blacks have shared. Integration, at least as the term is commonly used, is an attempt to solve the "problem" of being black by diluting the blackness as much as possible.

A good many avid egalitarians spent much of their time trying to demonstrate that there is essentially no difference between people. But their demonstrations almost always seem to say: Except for the color of our skin.

And while it was true that black people couldn't look white, they could at least act white. The reward for their successful imitation of white people would be admittance into white schools, clubs and neighborhoods.

Interestingly enough, although it was white people who devised this formula for acceptance, blacks were the only ones who believed it. They don't anymore, and as a result many white people feel threatened.

It seems fair to conclude that white people (speaking generally, of course) are never so happy as when black folk are seeking to be integrated into the white mainstream and failing at it.

That may sound bitter, but think about it. White America could have had integration at any time it wanted to—and still could have it now, for that matter.

White America doesn't want integration, but it doesn't want black people to stop trying for it, either. If you want to alarm white people, let a group of blacks withdraw and organize independently.

The unwholesome reputations of Black Muslims and various Black Power advocates, all over the country stem largely from the fact that blacks who separate because they want to separate are viewed as a threat to white people.

Some of the black disinterest in integration is a deliberate attempt to make white people feel threatened; some of it results from the reluctance of some black people to compete with whites.

But an awful lot of it, I think, has come about because blacks have decided that the question of integration is and always has been a question white people will have to answer.

Not many black people are holding their breath.

# The Declaration of Independence
## July 4, 1776

When in the course of human events, it becomes necessary for one people to dissolve the political bands which have connected them with another, and to assume among the powers of the earth, the separate and equal station to which the Laws of Nature and of Nature's God entitle them, a decent respect to the opinions of mankind requires that they should declare the causes which impel them to the separation.

We hold these truths to be self-evident, that all men are created equal, that they are endowed by their Creator with certain unalienable rights, that among these are life, liberty and the pursuit of happiness. That to secure these rights, governments are instituted among men, deriving their 10 just powers from the consent of the governed. That whenever any form of government becomes destructive of these ends, it is the right of the people to alter or to abolish it, and to institute new government, laying its foundation on such principles and organizing its powers in such form, as to them shall seem most likely to effect their safety and happiness. Prudence, indeed, will dictate that governments long established should not be changed for light and transient causes; and accordingly all experience hath shown, that mankind are more disposed to suffer, while evils are sufferable, than to right themselves by abolishing the forms to which they are accustomed. But when a long train of abuses and usurpations, 20 pursuing invariably the same object evinces a design to reduce them under absolute despotism, it is their right, it is their duty, to throw off such government, and to provide new guards for their future security. Such has been the patient sufferance of these Colonies; and such is now the necessity which constrains them to alter their former systems of government. The history of the present King of Great Britain is a history of repeated injuries and usurpations, all having in direct object the establishment of an absolute tyranny over these States. To prove this, let facts be submitted to a candid world.

He has refused his assent to laws, the most wholesome and necessary for the public good.

He has forbidden his Governors to pass laws of immediate and pressing importance, unless suspended in their operation till his assent should be obtained; and when so suspended, he has utterly neglected to attend to them.

He has refused to pass other laws for the accommodation of large 10 districts of people, unless those people would relinquish the right of representation in the Legislature, a right inestimable to them and formidable to tyrants only.

He has called together legislative bodies at places unusual, uncomfortable, and distant from the depository of their public records, for the sole purpose of fatiguing them into compliance with his measures.

He has dissolved representative houses repeatedly, for opposing with manly firmness his invasions on the rights of the people.

He has refused for a long time, after such dissolutions, to cause others to be elected; whereby the legislative powers, incapable of annihilation, 20 have returned to the people at large for their exercise; the State remaining in the meantime exposed to all the dangers of invasion from without and convulsions within.

He has endeavoured to prevent the population of these States; for that purpose obstructing the laws of naturalization of foreigners; refusing to pass others to encourage their migration hither, and raising the conditions of new appropriations of lands.

He has obstructed the administration of justice, by refusing his assent to laws for establishing judiciary powers.

He has made judges dependent on his will alone, for the tenure of their 30 offices, and the amount and payment of their salaries.

He has erected a multitude of new offices, and sent hither swarms of officers to harass our people, and eat out their substance.

He has kept among us, in times of peace, standing armies without the consent of our legislatures.

He has affected to render the military independent of and superior to the civil power.

He has combined with others to subject us to a jurisdiction foreign to our constitution, and unacknowledged by our laws; giving his assent to their acts of pretended legislation: 40

For quartering large bodies of armed troops among us:

For protecting them, by a mock trial, from punishment for any murders which they should commit on the inhabitants of these States:

For cutting off our trade with all parts of the world:

For imposing taxes on us without our consent:

For depriving us, in many cases, of the benefits of trial by jury:

For transporting us beyond seas to be tried for pretended offences:

For abolishing the free system of English laws in a neighbouring Province, establishing therein an arbitrary government, and enlarging its boundaries so as to render it at once an example and fit instrument for introducing the same absolute rule into these Colonies:

For taking away our Charters, abolishing our most valuable laws, and altering fundamentally the forms of our governments:

For suspending our own Legislatures, and declaring themselves invested with power to legislate for us in all cases whatsoever.

He has abdicated government here, by declaring us out of his protec-    10
tion and waging war against us.

He has plundered our seas, ravaged our coasts, burnt our towns, and destroyed the lives of our people.

He is at this time transporting large armies of foreign mercenaries to complete the works of death, desolation and tyranny, already begun with circumstances of cruelty and perfidy scarcely paralleled in the most barbarous ages, and totally unworthy the head of a civilized nation.

He has constrained our fellow citizens taken captive on the high seas to bear arms against their country, to become the executioners of their friends and brethren, or to fall themselves by their hands.    20

He has excited domestic insurrections amongst us, and has endeavoured to bring on the inhabitants of our frontiers, the merciless Indian savages, whose known rule of warfare, is an undistinguished destruction of all ages, sexes, and conditions.

In every stage of these oppressions we have petitioned for redress in the most humble terms: our repeated petitions have been answered only by repeated injury. A prince whose character is thus marked by every act which may define a tyrant is unfit to be the ruler of a free people.

Nor have we been wanting in attention to our British brethren. We have warned them from time to time of attempts by their legislature to extend    30
an unwarrantable jurisdiction over us. We have reminded them of the circumstances of our emigration and settlement here. We have appealed to their native justice and magnanimity, and we have conjured them by the ties of our common kindred to disavow these usurpations, which would inevitably interrupt our connections and correspondence. They too have been deaf to the voice of justice and of consanguinity. We must, therefore, acquiesce in the necessity, which denounces our separation, and hold them, as we hold the rest of mankind, enemies in war, in peace friends.

We, therefore, the Representatives of the United States of America, in General Congress assembled, appealing to the Supreme Judge of the    40
world for the rectitude of our intentions, do, in the name, and by authority of the good people of these Colonies, solemnly publish and declare, That these United Colonies are, and of right ought to be Free and Independent States; that they are absolved from all allegiance to the British Crown, and that all political connection between them and the State of Great Britain, is and ought to be totally dissolved; and that as Free and Inde-

pendent States, they have full power to levy war, conclude peace, contract alliances, establish commerce, and to do all other acts and things which Independent States may of right do. And for the support of this declaration, with a firm reliance on the protection of Divine Providence, we mutually pledge to each other our lives, our fortunes, and our sacred honor.

John Hancock, *President*
[other signatures follow]

# Brown v. Board of Education
## U.S. Supreme Court, 1954

MR. CHIEF JUSTICE WARREN delivered the opinion of the court.

These cases come to us from the States of Kansas, South Carolina, Virginia, and Delaware. They are premised on different facts and different local conditions, but a common legal question justifies their consideration together in this consolidated opinion.

In each of the cases, minors of the Negro race, through their legal representatives, seek the aid of the courts in obtaining admission to the public schools of their community on a nonsegregated basis. In each instance, they had been denied admission to schools attended by white children under laws requiring or permitting segregation according to race. 10

This segregation was alleged to deprive the plaintiffs of the equal protection of the laws under the Fourteenth Amendment. In each of the cases other than the Delaware case, a three-judge Federal District Court denied relief to the plaintiffs on the so-called "separate but equal" doctrine announced by this court in *Plessy v. Ferguson* [1896].

Under that doctrine, equality of treatment is accorded when the races are provided substantially equal facilities, even though these facilities be separate. In the Delaware case, the Supreme Court of Delaware adhered to that doctrine, but ordered that the plaintiffs be admitted to the white schools because of their superiority to the Negro schools. 20

The plaintiffs contend that segregated public schools are not "equal" and cannot be made "equal," and that, hence, they are deprived of the equal protection of the laws. Because of the obvious importance of the question presented, the Court took jurisdiction. Argument was heard in the 1952 term, and reargument was heard this term on certain questions propounded by the Court.

Reargument was largely devoted to the circumstances surrounding the adoption of the Fourteenth Amendment in 1868. It covered, exhaustively, consideration of the Amendment in Congress, ratification by the States, then existing practices in racial segregation, and the views of proponents and opponents of the Amendment.

This discussion and our own investigation convince us that, although these sources cast some light, it is not enough to resolve the problem with which we are faced.

At best, they are inconclusive. The most avid proponents of the post-war Amendments undoubtedly intended them to remove all legal distinc-  10 tions among "all persons born or naturalized in the United States."

Their opponents, just as certainly, were antagonistic to both the letter and the spirit of the Amendments and wished them to have the most limited effect. What others in Congress and the state legislature had in mind cannot be determined with any degree of certainty.

An additional reason for the illusive nature of the Amendment's history, with respect to segregated schools, is the status of public education at that time. In the South, the movement toward free common schools, supported by general taxation, had not yet taken hold. Education of white children was largely in the hands of private groups. Education of Negroes  20 was almost nonexistent, and practically all of the race was illiterate. In fact, any education of Negroes was forbidden by law in some States.

Today, in contrast, many Negroes have achieved outstanding success in the arts and sciences as well as in the business and professional world. It is true that public school education at the time of the Amendment had advanced further in the North, but the effect of the Amendment on Northern States was generally ignored in the congressional debates.

Even in the North, the conditions of public education did not approximate those existing today. The curriculum was usually rudimentary; ungraded schools were common in rural areas; the school term was but  30 three months a year in many States; and compulsory school attendance was virtually unknown.

As a consequence, it is not surprising that there should be so little in the history of the Fourteenth Amendment relating to its intended effect on public education.

In the first cases in this court construing the Fourteenth Amendment, decided shortly after its adoption, the Court interpreted it as proscribing all State-imposed discriminations against the Negro race.

The doctrine of "separate but equal" did not make its appearance in this court until 1896 in the case of *Plessy v. Ferguson* . . . involving not  40 education but transportation. . . .

American courts have since labored with the doctrine for over half a century. In this court, there have been six cases involving the "separate but equal" doctrine in the field of public education. . . .

In none of these cases was it necessary to reexamine the doctrine to grant relief to the Negro plaintiff. And in *Sweatt v. Painter* [1950] . . .

the Court expressly reserved decision on the question whether *Plessy v. Ferguson* should be held inapplicable to public education.

In the instant cases, that question is directly presented. Here, unlike schools involved have been equalized, or are being equalized, with respect to buildings, curricula, qualifications and salaries of teachers, and other "tangible" factors.

Our decision, therefore, cannot turn on merely a comparison of these tangible factors in the Negro and white schools involved in each of the cases. We must look instead to the effect of segregation itself on public education.                                                                                          10

In approaching this problem, we cannot turn the clock back to 1868, when the Amendment was adopted, or even to 1896, when *Plessy v. Ferguson* was written. We must consider public education in the light of its full development and its present place in American life throughout the nation. Only in this way can it be determined if segregation in public schools deprives these plaintiffs of the equal protection of the laws.

Today, education is perhaps the most important function of State and local governments. Compulsory school attendance laws and the great expenditures for education both demonstrate our recognition of the importance of education to our democratic society. It is required in the per-   20
formance of our most basic public responsibilities, even service in the armed forces. It is the very foundation of good citizenship.

Today, it is a principal instrument in awakening the child to cultural values, in preparing him for later professional training, and in helping him to adjust normally to his environment.

In these days, it is doubtful that any child may reasonably be expected to succeed in life if he is denied the opportunity of an education. Such an opportunity, where the State has undertaken to prove it, is a right which must be made available to all on equal terms.

We come then to the question presented: Does segregation of children   30
in public schools solely on the basis of race, even though the physical facilities and other "tangible" factors may be equal, deprive the children of the minority group of equal education opportunities? We believe that it does.

In *Sweatt v. Painter* . . . in finding that a segregated law school for Negroes could not provide them equal educational opportunities, this court relied in large part on "those qualities which are incapable of objective measurement but which make for greatness in a law school."

In *McLaurin v. Oklahoma State Regents* [1950] . . . the Court, in requiring that a Negro admitted to a white graduate school be treated like   40
all other students, again resorted to intangible considerations: ". . . his ability to study, engage in discussions and exchange views with other students, and, in general, to learn his profession."

Such considerations apply with added force to children in grade and high school. To separate them from others of similar age and qualifications solely because of their race generates a feeling of inferiority as to their status in the community that may affect their hearts and minds in a way unlikely ever to be undone.

The effect of this separation on their educational opportunities was well stated by a finding in the Kansas case by a court which nevertheless felt compelled to rule against the Negro plaintiffs:

> Segregation of white and colored children in public schools has a detrimental effect upon the colored children. The impact is greater when it has the sanction of the law; for the policy of separating the races is usually interpreted as denoting the inferiority of the Negro group. 10
>
> A sense of inferiority affects the motivation of a child to learn. Segregation with the sanction of law, therefore, has a tendency to retard the educational and mental development of Negro children and to deprive them of some of the benefits they would receive in a racially integrated school system. Whatever may have been the extent of psychological knowledge at the time of *Plessy v. Ferguson,* this finding is amply supported by modern authority.

. . . Any language in *Plessy v. Ferguson* contrary to this finding is rejected. 20

We conclude that in the field of public education the doctrine of "separate but equal" has no place. Separate educational facilities are inherently unequal. Therefore, we hold that the plaintiffs and others similarly situated for whom the actions have been brought are, by reason of the segregation complained of, deprived of the equal protection of the laws guaranteed by the Fourteenth Amendment. This disposition makes unnecessary any discussion whether such segregation also violates the Due Process clause of the Fourteenth Amendment.

Because these are class actions, because of the wide applicability 30 of this decision, and because of the great variety of local conditions, the formulation of decrees in these cases presents problems of considerable complexity. On reargument, the consideration of appropriate relief was necessarily subordinated to the primary question—the constitutionality of segregation in public education.

We have now announced that such segregation is a denial of the equal protection of the laws. In order that we may have the full assistance of the parties in formulating decrees the cases will be restored to the docket, and the parties are requested to present further argument on Questions 4 and 5 previously propounded by the Court for the re- 40 argument this term.

The Attorney General of the United States is again invited to participate. The Attorneys General of the States requiring or permitting segregation in public education will also be permitted to appear as *amici curiae* upon request to do so by September 15, 1954, and submission of briefs by October 1, 1954.

*It is so ordered.*

# Theodore Roosevelt
## Assimilation

There is no room in this country for hyphenated Americanism. When I refer to hyphenated Americans, I do not refer to naturalized Americans. Some of the very best Americans I have ever known were naturalized Americans, Americans born abroad. But a hyphenated American is not an American at all. This is just as true of the man who puts "native" before the hyphen as of the man who puts German or Irish or English or French before the hyphen. Americanism is a matter of the spirit and of the soul. Our allegiance must be purely to the United States. We must unsparingly condemn any man who holds any other allegiance. But if he is heartily and singly loyal to this republic, then no matter where he was 10 born, he is just as good an American as any one else.

## AN AMERICAN IS AN AMERICAN AND NOTHING ELSE

The one absolutely certain way of bringing this nation to ruin, of preventing all possibility of its continuing to be a nation at all, would be to permit it to become a tangle of squabbling nationalities, an intricate knot of German-Americans, Irish-Americans, English-Americans, French-Americans, Scandinavian-Americans or Italian-Americans, each preserving its separate nationality, each at heart feeling more sympathy with Europeans of that nationality, than with the other citizens of the Ameri- 20 can republic. . . . The man who calls himself an American citizen, . . . [yet who] shows by his actions that he is primarily the citizen of a foreign land, plays a thoroughly mischievous part in the life of our body politic. He has no place here; and the sooner he returns to the land to which he feels his real heart-allegiance, the better it will be for every good American. . . .

444

### THE MEN WHO HAVE FOUGHT OUR WARS

I appeal to history. Among the generals of Washington in the Revolutionary War were Greene, Putnam, and Lee, who were of English descent; Wayne and Sullivan, who were of Irish descent; Marion, who was of French descent; Schuyler, who was of Dutch descent; and Muhlenberg and Herkimer, who were of German descent. But they were all of them Americans and nothing else, just as much as Washington. Carroll of Carrollton was a Catholic; Hancock a Protestant; Jefferson was heterodox from the standpoint of any orthodox creed; but these and all the other    10
signers of the Declaration of Independence stood on an equality of duty and right and liberty, as Americans and nothing else.

So it was in the Civil War. Farragut's father was born in Spain and Sheridan's father in Ireland; Sherman and Thomas were of English and Custer of German descent; and Grant came of a long line of American ancestors whose original home had been Scotland. But the Admiral was not a Spanish-American; and the Generals were not Scotch-Americans or Irish-Americans or English-Americans or German-Americans. They were all Americans and nothing else. This was just as true of Lee and of Stonewall Jackson and of Beauregard. . . .    20

### THE MEN IN ROOSEVELT'S ADMINISTRATION

To take charge of the most important work under my administration, the building of the Panama Canal, I chose General Goethals. Both of his parents were born in Holland. But he was just plain United States. He wasn't Dutch-American; if he had been I wouldn't have appointed him. So it was with such men, among those who served under me, as Admiral Osterhaus and General Barry. The father of one was born in Germany, the father of the other in Ireland. But they were both Americans, pure and simple, and first-rate fighting men in addition.    30

In my Cabinet at the time there were men of English and French, German, Irish, and Dutch blood, men born on this side and men born in Germany and Scotland; but they were all Americans and nothing else; and every one of them was incapable of thinking of himself or of his fellow-countrymen, excepting in terms of American citizenship. If any of them had anything in the nature of a dual or divided allegiance in his soul, he never would have been appointed to serve under me, and he would have been instantly removed when the discovery was made. There wasn't one of them who was capable of desiring that the policy of the United States should be shaped with reference to the interests of any    40
foreign country or with consideration for anything, outside of the general welfare of humanity, save the honor and interest of the United States, and each was incapable of making any discrimination whatsoever among the citizens of the country he served, of our common country, save discrimination based on conduct and on conduct alone.

## TRAITOROUS TO VOTE AS A "HYPENATED AMERICAN"

For an American citizen to vote as a German-American, an Irish-American, or an English-American, is to be a traitor to American institutions; and those hyphenated Americans who terrorize American politicians by threats of the foreign vote are engaged in treason to the American republic.

# Lyndon B. Johnson
## The Repeal of Racism

. . . This bill that we sign today is not a revolutionary bill. It does not effect the lives of millions. It will not reshape the structure of our daily lives, or really add importantly to either our wealth or our power.

Yet it is still one of the most important acts of this Congress and of this administration.

For it does repair a very deep and painful flaw in the fabric of American justice. It corrects a cruel and enduring wrong in the conduct of the American nation. . . .

### THE QUOTA SYSTEM ABOLISHED 10

This bill says simply that from this day forth those wishing to immigrate to America shall be admitted on the basis of their skills and their close relationship to those already here.

This is a simple test, and it is a fair test. Those who can contribute most to this country—to its growth, to its strength, to its spirit—will be the first that are admitted to this land.

The fairness of this standard is so self-evident that we may well wonder that it has not always been applied. Yet the fact is that for over four decades the immigration policy of the United States has been twisted and has been distorted by the harsh injustice of the national origins quota 20 system.

Under that system the ability of new immigrants to come to America depended upon the country of their birth. Only three countries were allowed to supply 70 per cent of all the immigrants.

Families were kept apart because a husband or a wife or a child had been born in the wrong place.

447

Men of needed skill and talent were denied entrance because they came from southern or eastern Europe or from one of the developing continents.

This system violated the basic principle of American democracy—the principle that values and rewards each man on the basis of his merit as a man.

It has been un-American in the highest sense because it has been untrue to the faith that brought thousands to these shores even before we were a country.

Today, with my signature, this system is abolished.                                    10

We can now believe that it will never again shadow the gate to the American nation with the twin barriers of prejudice and privilege.

## AMERICA BUILT BY STRANGERS

Our beautiful American was built by a nation of strangers. From a hundred different places or more, they have poured forth into an empty land, joining and blending in one mighty and irresistible tide.

The land flourished because it was fed from so many sources—because it was nourished by so many cultures and traditions and peoples.

And from this experience, almost unique in the history of nations, has come America's attitude toward the rest of the world. We, because of what   20
we are, feel safer and stronger in a world as varied as the people who make it up—a world where no country rules another and all countries can deal with the basic problems of human dignity and deal with those problems in their own way.

Now, under the monument which has welcomed so many to our shores, the American nation returns to the finest of its traditions today.

The days of unlimited immigration are past.

But those who do come will come because of what they are, and not because of the land from which they sprang.

When the earliest settlers poured into a wild continent, there was   30
no one to ask them where they came from. The only question was: Were they sturdy enough to make the journey, were they strong enough to clear the land, were they enduring enough to make a home for freedom, and were they brave enough to die for liberty if it became necessary to do so?

And so it has been through all the great testing moments of American history. This year we see in Viet-Nam men dying—men named Fernandez and Zajac and Zelinko and Mariano and McCormick.

Neither the enemy who killed them nor the people whose independence they have fought to save ever asked them where they or their parents came from. They were all Americans. . . .                                   40

By eliminating that same question as a test for immigration the Congress proves ourselves worthy of those men and worthy of our own traditions as a nation. . . .

## ELLIS ISLAND AND THE STATUE OF LIBERTY:
## AMERICAN SYMBOLS

Over my shoulder here you can see Ellis Island, whose vacant corridors echo today the joyous sounds of long-ago voices.

And today we can all believe that the lamp of this grand old lady is brighter today, and the golden door that she guards gleams more brilliantly in the light of an increased liberty for the people from all the countries of the globe.

# Roger Pucinski
## Ethnic Heritage Studies
## Act, 1971

To provide a program to improve the opportunity of students in elementary and secondary schools to study cultural heritages of the various ethnic groups in the Nation.

*Be it enacted by the Senate and House of Representatives of the United States of America in Congress assembled,* That this Act may be cited as the "Ethnic Heritage Studies Act of 1971".

Sec. 2. The Elementary and Secondary Education Act of 1965 is amended by adding at the end thereof the following new title:

### TITLE IX—ETHNIC HERITAGE STUDIES                     10

*Statement of Policy*

Sec. 901. This title is enacted in recognition of the heterogeneous composition of the Nation and of the fact that in a multi-ethnic society a greater understanding of the contributions of one's own heritage and those of one's fellow citizens can contribute to a more harmonious, patriotic, and committed populace. It is further enacted in recognition of the principle of all students in the elementary and secondary schools of the Nation should have an opportunity to learn about the differing and unique contributions to the national heritage made by each ethnic     20 group. Therefore, it is the purpose of this title to assist schools and school systems in affording each of their students an opportunity to learn about the nature of his own cultural heritage and to study the contributions to the Nation made by other cultural heritages.

*Ethnic Heritage Studies Projects*

Sec. 902. The Commissioner is authorized to arrange through

grants to public and private nonprofit educational agencies and organizations for the establishment and operation of a number of ethnic heritage studies projects. Each such project shall carry on activities related to a single culture or regional group of cultures.

## Authorized Activities

Sec. 903. Each provided for under this title shall—

(1) develop curriculum materials for use in elementary and secondary schools which deal with the history, geography, society, economy, literature, art, music, drama, language, and general culture of the ethnic heritage or regional group of heritages with which the project is concerned, and the contributions of that ethnic heritage or regional group of heritages to the American heritage,

(2) disseminate curriculum materials to permit their use in elementary and secondary schools throughout the Nation, and

(3) provide training for persons utilizing or preparing to utilize the curriculum materials developed under this title.

## Administrative Provisions

Sec. 904. (a) In carrying out this title, the Commissioner shall make arrangements which will utilize (1) the research facilities and personnel of museums and of colleges and universities, (2) the special knowledge of ethnic groups in local communities, and (3) the expertise of elementary and secondary school teachers.

(b) Funds appropriated to carry out this title may be used to cover all or part of the cost of establishing and operating the projects, including the cost of research materials and resources, academic consultants and the cost of training of staff for the purpose of carrying out the purposes of this title.

## Authorization of Appropriations

Sec. 905. There is authorized to be appropriated to carry out this title for the fiscal year ending June 30, 1972, the sum of $20,000,000, and for the fiscal year ending June 30, 1973, the sum of $30,000,000.

# Katherine Lee Bates
## America, The Beautiful

1.  O beautiful for spacious skies,
      For amber waves of grain,
    For purple mountain majesties
      Above the fruited plain.
    America! America! God shed His grace on thee;
    And crown thy good with brotherhood
      From sea to shining sea.

2.  O beautiful for pilgrim feet
      Whose stern impassion'd stress                    10
    A thoroughfare for freedom beat
      Across the wilderness.
    America! America! God mend thine every flaw,
    Confirm thy soul in self-control,
      Thy liberty in law.

3.  O beautiful for heroes prov'd
      In liberating strife,
    Who more than self their country loved,
      And mercy more than life.                         20
    America! America! May God thy gold refine
    Till all success be nobleness,
      And every gain divine.

4. O beautiful for patriot dream
   That sees beyond the years
Thine alabaster cities gleam
   Undimmed by human tears.
America! America! God shed His grace on thee,
And crown thy good with brotherhood
   From sea to shining sea.